Matters of Life and Death

Matters of Life and Death

NEW INTRODUCTORY ESSAYS IN MORAL PHILOSOPHY

TOM L. BEAUCHAMP
HUGO ADAM BEDAU
WILLIAM T. BLACKSTONE
JOEL FEINBERG
JAN NARVESON
ONORA O'NEILL
JAMES RACHELS
PETER SINGER

Edited by Tom Regan

North Carolina State University at Raleigh

RANDOM HOUSE 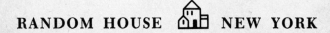 NEW YORK

First Edition
987654321
Copyright © 1980 by Random House, Inc.

Library of Congress Cataloging in Publication Data

Matters of life and death.

Includes bibliographies and index.
1. Ethics—Addresses, essays, lectures. 2. Social
ethics—Addresses, essays, lectures.   I. Beauchamp,
Tom L.   II. Regan, Tom.
BJ1012.M37   170   79-21562
ISBN 0–394–32114–6

Text design by Shaun Johnston
Cover design by Charles Goslin

Manufactured in the United States of America

The following page constitutes an extension of the copyright page.

ACKNOWLEDGMENTS

Grateful acknowledgment is made to the following authors and publishers for permission to reprint selections from copyrighted material:

From Stewart Alsop, "The Right to Die with Dignity." Copyright © 1974 by Stewart Alsop. Reprinted from *Good Housekeeping Magazine*.

From Joseph V. Sullivan, "The Immorality of Euthanasia." © 1975 by Prometheus Books, Buffalo, New York.

From Philippa Foot, "Euthanasia," *Philosophy and Public Affairs* 6, no. 2 (Winter 1977). Copyright © 1977 by Philippa Foot. Excerpts reprinted by permission of the author and Princeton University Press.

From "The Definition of Suicide." © 1968 by The New York Times Company. Reprinted by permission.

From Tom L. Beauchamp, William T. Blackstone, and Joel Feinberg, ed., *Philosophy and the Human Condition* (forthcoming). Reprinted by permission of Prentice-Hall, Inc.

From Judith Jarvis Thomson, "A Defense of Abortion," *Philosophy and Public Affairs* 1, no. 1 (Fall 1971). Copyright © 1971 by Princeton University Press. Excerpts reprinted by permission.

From *The Teaching of Reverence for Life* by Albert Schweitzer. Translated by Richard and Clara Winston. Copyright © 1965 by Holt, Rinehart and Winston. Reprinted by permission of Holt, Rinehart and Winston, Publishers.

From *A Sand County Almanac with Other Essays on Conservation from Round River* by Aldo Leopold. Copyright © 1949, 1953, 1966; renewed 1977 by Oxford University Press, Inc. Reprinted by permission.

From Eugene Odum, "Environmental Ethic and the Attitude Revolution." Reprinted from *Philosophy and Environmental Crisis* by permission of The University of Georgia Press. © 1974 by The University of Georgia Press.

To the Memory of
William T. (Bill) Blackstone

PREFACE

This book consists of original essays that illustrate the application of moral theory to topics of vital practical concern—to matters of life and death. It is intended primarily for persons taking their first course in moral philosophy or philosophy generally.

There is no single order in which the essays should be read. The present arrangement has been selected for the following reason: The force of a moral question is perhaps clearest when the individual is told to refrain from doing something that does not cause anyone else any obvious harm. Why should an individual's liberty be limited in this way? The essays on euthanasia and suicide raise this question in especially clear terms and so have been placed first.

The point of a moral question is also clear when someone has been mistreated or harmed. It is natural to ask what morality will allow us to do to the person causing the harm, including what forms of punishment are justifiable. What morality allows us to do if people are violently assaulted is the central question considered in the essay "Violence and War." The morality of one form of punishment—capital punishment—is considered in the essay that follows.

Morality, however, arguably requires that we widen our horizons and think about the harm that may be done to beings who are not clearly human, either potentially or actually. The essays "Abortion" and "Animals and the Value of Life" are especially relevant in this regard. Both contain extended examinations of the concept of a person, and both challenge the views that all and only human beings are persons and that all and only human beings can be harmed.

The essay on famine also extends our moral horizons. It asks us to think about the moral perplexities of famine relief. The victims of famine normally are not only geographically distant from us; psychologically, they may be distant as well. But although this distance may make the essay less than the best one with which to begin exploring moral philosophy, it does not diminish the moral importance of the issues examined.

Similar considerations underlie the positioning of the essay on environmental ethics. If, as some have speculated, it is difficult for human beings to be unselfish and to consider the interests of other people, how much more difficult is it for us to act on behalf of the environment. To ask us to extend our moral horizons so far that we include the environment is an idea we might perhaps better work toward than begin with.

The Introduction has two principal aims. First, it attempts to explain some assumptions that are common to the several essays—for example, some assumptions concerning how *not* to answer moral questions. Second, it attempts to place the issues treated in the essays within the broader context of moral theory. By no means a complete examination of moral theory, the Introduction is a place to get acquainted with some new ideas that can be applied to the essays that follow.

It is a pleasure to thank the contributors for their cooperation; Jane Cullen, of Random House, for her support and encouragement; John Sturman, also of Random House, for his help; Ruth Boone and Callie Clarke for their much needed and appreciated typing assistance; Randolph Carter, Dale Jamieson, David Marsland, and Richard I. Nagel for their helpful comments on earlier drafts of the Introduction; and my wife, Nancy, and my children, Karen and Bryan, for coping with my seclusion and preoccupation while seeing this project through to its completion.

Tom Regan

Raleigh, North Carolina
August 1, 1978

CONTENTS

5. *Capital Punishment*

Matters of Life and Death

I

Introduction

TOM REGAN

The essays in this volume deal with questions about the value of life and the morality of killing and letting die. It is difficult to imagine more important questions. We live amid a sea of death-by-killing, something we are reminded of every day by stories in the news. A husband decapitates his wife and children, then leaps to his own death. A convicted murderer is executed by a firing squad. Wars between nations break out and the death toll of combatants and civilians mounts daily. In antiseptic modern hospitals, in squalid ghetto tenements, human fetuses are aborted. Elsewhere, a fatally ill woman, wracked by unrelenting, untreatable pain, is given an overdose of sleeping pills by her son and dies quietly in her sleep. Familiar stories all. We know them well, at least at a distance. They are what people talk about, a lot.

How ought we to think about all these cases of killing? In the case of suicide, for example, ought we to think that all suicides are wrong and should be prevented? Or is it more reasonable to think that no one has a right to stop a person from doing what he or she wants, including taking one's own life? Or imagine: A close friend has been in an automobile accident. His face is permanently disfigured. He has lost both arms. He will never walk again, never even leave his bed. He is in almost constant pain. He pleads with us to kill him. Ought we to do so? Since he is not going to die soon as a result of his injuries, wouldn't we be guilty of murder if we killed him? And isn't murder always wrong? The questions come easily. Answers, and the means of defending them, may not.

The issues we must face go beyond just those that involve killing, however. Imagine that a baby is lying face down in a shallow pond. We can save the child if we but lift her from the water. Suppose we don't do anything, and the child dies. Here there is no question of our *killing* the baby. But we *have* let the baby die. And sometimes letting someone die seems to be a terribly immoral thing to do. Yet, an estimated 10,000 human beings die every day from lack of food. If we are doing nothing to prevent this, are we then just as guilty as someone who would let a small baby drown when he or she could prevent it? Like the questions about the morality of suicide and euthanasia, this question cannot be omitted from an examination of the morality of killing and letting die.

But not just human beings are killed; it is not just human beings who are allowed to die. In all large cities, vast numbers of animals are killed every day to supply us with the meat we are accustomed to eating. An estimated 3 billion chickens, for example, are killed every year in the United States alone. In these same cities, moreover, scientists are daily at work testing the safety of new products, such as deodorants and eye shadow, by using laboratory animals. One standard test is the LD_{50}. 'LD' stands for "lethal dose"; '50' stands for the fact that the animals must be force-fed the product in question until at least 50 percent of them die. This establishes the product's lethal dose. The animals who survive the LD_{50} test normally are killed also. Millions upon millions of animals are killed in the name of such research. Can this use of animals be justified? Or is their routine use as research subjects morally objectionable? Ought it to be stopped? If we are seriously to think about the morality of killing and letting die, the killing and letting die of animals cannot escape our notice.

But there is more. Virgin forests and wilderness areas are destroyed to make room for roads, pipelines, resort complexes. Rivers become clogged avenues of waste and pollution, and myriad forms of complex vegetative and animal life are destroyed. There is even talk of the ocean "dying." Are we doing anything wrong when nature is treated in this way, and if so, why? Is it possible to develop an environmental ethic in which trees and fields, the creatures of the sea and sagebrush have a *right* to life? Or is the idea of a right necessarily restricted to human beings?

The essays in this volume explore these and related questions. The authors of these essays are moral philosophers. Moral philosophers are persons who take a special interest in thinking carefully about questions that concern moral right and wrong, good and bad, duty and obligation. Their objectives include understanding questions like those posed in the preceding paragraphs and in giving what they think are the most reasonable answers to them. No one of the questions examined in the essays will be considered in detail in this Introduction. Instead, ideas of a general scope will be explained, and these ideas will be used to formulate a series of questions that can be taken to the essays themselves. In this way we can view the essays in a broader perspective and recognize their many common assumptions and ideas.

I. META-ETHICS

§1 CONCEPTUAL ANALYSIS

The first idea that requires attention is that of conceptual analysis. Philosophers frequently use the words 'conceptual analysis' to refer to the activity of clarifying our concepts or ideas. Since we use words to express our concepts, conceptual analysis aims at reaching a clearer understanding of the meanings of words. Achieving such clarity is absolutely vital. If we do not have a clear understanding of the meanings of words, we will not have a clear understanding of our questions. And if we do not understand our questions, we will not understand what count as answers to them. This is especially true in the case of questions that ask whether something is morally right or wrong—for example, whether the use of violence is wrong. If we do not understand what violence is, how can we even begin to consider the question of its morality?

One way to think about conceptual analysis is in terms of necessary and sufficient conditions. If x is a necessary condition of y, then y cannot be the case if x is not the case; in other words, if not x, then not y. Being a plane closed figure or having interior angles, for example, is a necessary condition of something's being a triangle. A sufficient condition is different. If a is a sufficient condition of b, then b will be the case if a is the case; that is, if a, then b. Being a plane closed figure with three sides or three interior angles, for example, is a sufficient condition of something's being a triangle.

A necessary condition may not also be sufficient, and *vice versa*. For example, while being a plane closed figure is a necessary condition of something's being a triangle, it is not sufficient: There are many plane closed figures that are not triangles—e.g., rectangles. Again, that something is a Cadillac Seville is a sufficient condition of its being a car, but being a Cadillac Seville is not a necessary condition of being a car: There are many cars that are not Cadillac Sevilles.

The ideas of necessary and sufficient conditions relate to the activity of conceptual analysis in the following way. Conceptual analysis can be understood as the attempt to state the necessary and sufficient conditions of the correct use of a given concept. The aims of conceptual analysis are thus (1) to state, so far as it is possible, those conditions which, if they are *not* satisfied, prevent the concept in question from being correctly applied—the necessary conditions of correct use—and (2) to state those conditions which, if they *are* satisfied, permit the concept to be correctly applied—the sufficient conditions of correct use. In this view of conceptual analysis, an analysis is itself correct to the extent that it states the necessary and sufficient conditions of correct use.

Now, sometimes it is not possible to give a complete set of necessary and sufficient conditions, and sometimes the conditions given cannot be very precise. For example, though a triangle must have no more nor less than three interior angles, how many hairs a person must be missing to be bald is far less precise. We should not expect all concepts to be analyzable in the way concepts in mathematics, say, are. Some "defy analysis" in the sense that it is not possible to give a complete set of quite precise necessary and sufficient conditions. However, even in the case of these concepts, one ought to strive to reach the highest degree of completeness and precision possible. The more complete and exact we can make our understanding of a given concept, the more likely we will understand those questions in which the concept figures.

If we think of the concepts that play central roles in the essays in this volume—suicide, euthanasia, and violence, for example—we can anticipate some difficulties for conceptual analysis. Unlike 'triangle', these concepts are not very precise. Take suicide. Many people think that a necessary and sufficient condition of a man's act being a suicide is that he killed himself intentionally. But both these ideas—'intentional' and 'self-killing'—are not as precise as 'three interior angles', which makes it necessary to think hard about them to see just what they do and do not mean. In his essay on this topic, Tom L. Beauchamp discusses this analysis of suicide and considers cases that call its correctness into question—for example, a case where a terminally ill man refuses medical treatment that would prolong his life and dies as a result. Here there seems to be no reason to say that the man killed himself—the disease killed him. And yet, might it not be true to say that he committed suicide?

The reasons that can be given for or against competing analyses of the concept of suicide must await a reading of Beauchamp's essay. And similar remarks apply to alternative analyses of the other important concepts that dot the landscape in each of the essays. In the essays by Joel Feinberg and Peter Singer, for example, the concept of a person is examined at length, and the view that being a human being is a necessary and sufficient condition of being a person is subjected to a critical review. As these examples suggest, philosophers do not always agree on what the correct analysis of a given concept is, even when they agree that conceptual analysis is important. The merits of alternative analyses will have to be considered in the essays that lie ahead.

§2 IS THERE A CORRECT METHOD FOR ANSWERING MORAL QUESTIONS?

The conceptual analysis of key moral concepts is one part of what is called meta-ethics. The other major component of meta-ethics is the inquiry into the correct method for answering moral questions.

Whether there even exists such a method is a very controversial question. Some philosophers think there is; others think not. And among those who think there is, some think it is one thing, while others think it is something different.

It will not be possible to examine this controversy in all the detail it deserves. Instead, a rough sketch will be given of some of the central issues. Two ideas in particular are important. First, there is the matter of how *not* to answer moral questions; this idea is explored in §3. Second, there is the idea of an ideal moral judgment; this is discussed in §4. The relevance of these ideas to the essays will be explained as we proceed.

§3 SOME WAYS NOT TO ANSWER MORAL QUESTIONS

Moral Judgments and Personal Preferences   Some people like classical music; others do not. Some people think bourbon is just great; others detest its taste. Some people will go to a lot of trouble to spend an afternoon in the hot sun at the beach; others can think of nothing worse. In all these cases disagreement in preference exists. Someone likes something; someone else does not. Are moral disagreements, disagreements over whether something is morally right or wrong, the same as disagreements in preference?

It does not appear so. For one thing, when a person (say, John) says he likes something, he is not denying what another person (Jane) says, if she says she does not like it. Suppose John says "I [John] like bourbon," and Jane says "I [Jane] do not like bourbon." Then clearly Jane does not deny what John says. To deny what John says, Jane would have to say "You [John] do not like bourbon," which is not what she says. So, in general, when two persons express conflicting personal preferences, the one does not deny what the other affirms. It is perfectly possible for two conflicting expressions of personal preference to be true at the same time.

When two people express conflicting judgments about the morality of something, however, the disagreement is importantly different. Suppose John says "Abortion is always wrong," while Jane says "Abortion is never wrong." Then Jane *is* denying what John affirms; she is *denying* that abortion is always wrong, so that, if what she said were true, what John said would have to be false. Some philosophers have denied this. They have maintained that moral judgments should be understood as expressions of personal preferences. Though this view deserves to be mentioned with respect, it is doubtful that it is correct. When people say that something is morally right or wrong, it is always appropriate to ask them to give reasons to support their judgment, reasons for accepting their judgment as correct. In the case of personal preferences, however, such requests are inappropriate. If John says he likes to go to the beach, it hardly seems apt to press him to give reasons to support his judgment; indeed, it hardly seems that he has made a *judgment* at all. If he says abortion is always wrong, however, a judgment has been expressed, and it is highly relevant to press John for his reasons for thinking what he does. If he were to reply that he had no reasons, that he just did not like abortions, it would not be out of place to complain that he speaks in a misleading way. By saying that abortion is wrong, John leads his listeners to believe that he is making a judgment about abortion, not merely expressing some fact about himself. If all that he means is that he personally does not like abortions, that is what he should say, not that abortion is wrong.

This difference between conflicting expressions of personal preference and conflicting moral judgments points to one way not to answer moral questions. Given that moral judgments are not just expressions of personal preference, it follows that moral right and wrong cannot be determined by finding out about the personal preferences of some particular person—say, John. This is true even in the case of our own preferences. Our personal preferences are important certainly, but we do not answer moral questions by saying what we like or dislike.

Moral Judgments and Feelings   Closely connected with personal preferences are a person's feelings, and some philosophers have maintained that words like 'right' and 'wrong' are devices we use to express how we feel about something. On this view, when Jane says that abortion is never wrong, what she conveys is that she has certain positive feelings (or at least that she does not have any feelings of disapproval) toward abortion, whereas when John says abortion is always wrong, what he conveys is that he does have feelings of disapproval. This position encounters problems of the same kind as those raised in the previous section. It is always appropriate to ask that support be given for a moral judgment. It is not appropriate to ask for support in the case of mere expressions of feeling. True, if John is sincere, one can infer that he has strong negative feelings about abortion. But his saying that abortion is always wrong does not appear to be simply a way of venting his feelings. As in the case of a person's preferences, so also in the case of a person's feelings: neither by itself provides answers to moral questions.

Why Thinking It Is So Does Not Make It So   The same is true about what someone thinks. Quite aside from his feelings, John, if he is sincere, does think that abortion is always wrong. Nevertheless, if his judgment ("Abortion is always wrong") is a moral judgment about the wrongness of abortion, what he means cannot be "I [John] think that abortion is wrong." If it were, then he would not be affirming something that Jane denies, when she says "Abortion is never wrong." Each would merely be stating that each thinks something, and it is certainly possible for it *both* to be true that *John* thinks that abortion is always wrong *and,* at the same time, that *Jane* thinks that abortion is never wrong. So if John is denying what Jane affirms, then he cannot merely be stating that he thinks that abortion is always wrong. Thus, the fact that John thinks abortion is wrong is just as irrelevant to establishing its wrongness as the fact that he feels a certain way about it. And the same is true concerning the fact that we think what we think. Our thinking something right or wrong does not make it so.

The Irrelevance of Statistics Someone might think that though what one person thinks or feels about moral issues does not settle matters, what all or most people think or feel does. A single individual is only one voice; what most or all people think or feel is a great deal more. There is strength in numbers. Thus, the correct method for answering questions about right and wrong is to find out what most or all people think or feel; opinion polls should be conducted, statistics compiled. That will reveal the truth.

This approach to moral questions is deficient. All that opinion polls can reveal is what all or most people think or feel about some moral question—for example, "Is capital punishment morally right or wrong?" What such polls cannot determine is whether what all or most people think about such an issue is true or that what all or most people feel is appropriate. There may be strength in numbers, but not truth, at least not necessarily. This does not mean that "what we all think (or feel)" is irrelevant to answering moral questions. Later on, in fact (§§6–8), we will see how, given that certain conditions have been met, "what we all think" might provide us with a place from which to begin our search for what is right and wrong, and why. Nevertheless, *merely* to establish that all (or most) people think that, say, capital punishment is morally justified is not to establish that it *is* morally justified. In times past, most (possibly even all) people thought the world is flat. And possibly most (or all) people felt pleased or relieved to think of the world as having this shape. But what they thought and felt did not make it true that the world is flat. The question of its shape had to be answered without relying on what most people think or feel. There is no reason to believe moral questions differ in this respect. Questions of right and wrong cannot be answered just by counting heads.

The Appeal to a Moral Authority Suppose it is conceded that we cannot answer moral questions by finding out what someone (say, John) thinks or feels; or by finding out what all or most people think or feel. After all, a single individual like John, or most or all people like him, might think or feel one way when he or they should think or feel differently. But suppose there is a being who never is mistaken when it comes to moral questions: if this being judges that something is morally right, it *is* morally right; if it is judged wrong, it *is* wrong. No mistakes are made. Let us call such a being a "moral authority." Might appealing to a moral authority be a satisfactory way to answer moral questions?

Most people who think there is a moral authority think that this being is not an ordinary person but a god. This causes problems immediately. Whether there is a god (or gods) is a very controversial question, and to rest questions of right and wrong on what a god says (or the gods say) is already to base morality on an intellectually unsettled foundation. The difficulties go deeper than this, however, since even if there is a god who is a moral authority, very serious questions must arise concerning whether people have understood (or can understand) what this authority says about right and wrong. The difficulties that exist when Jews and Christians consult the Bible ("God's revelation to man") can be taken as illustrative. Problems of interpretation abound. Some who think that drinking is wrong think they find evidence in the Bible that God thinks so too; others think they find evidence that He does not. Some who think that homosexuality is declared wrong by God cite what they think are supporting chapters and verses; others cite other chapters and verses that they think show God does not think homosexuality is wrong, or they cite the same passages and argue that they should be interpreted differently. The gravity of these and kindred problems of interpretation should not be underestimated. Even if there is a moral authority, and even if the god whom Jews and Christians worship should happen to be this authority, that would not make it a simple matter to find out what is right and wrong. The problem of finding out what God thinks on these matters would still remain. In view of the fundamental and long-standing disagreements concerning the correct interpretation of the Bible, this would be no easy matter.

Problems of interpretation aside, it is clear that the correct method for answering moral questions does not consist in discovering what a moral authority says. Even if there is a moral authority, those who are not moral authorities can have no reason for thinking that there is one unless the judgments of this supposed authority can be checked for their truth or reasonableness, and it is not possible to check for this unless what is true or reasonable can be known independently of any reliance on what the supposed authority says. If, however, there must be some independent way of knowing what moral judgments are true or reasonable, the introduction of a moral authority will not succeed in providing a method for answering moral questions. That method will have to illuminate how what is morally right and wrong can be known independently of the supposed moral authority, not how this can be known by relying on such an authority.

§4 THE IDEAL MORAL JUDGMENT

The ideas discussed in §3 are relevant to the essays in this volume because the authors never argue that something is right or wrong on the grounds of their personal preferences, or because they personally feel one way or the other, or because they think it right or wrong, or because all or most people feel or think a certain way, or because some alleged moral authority has said or revealed that something is right or wrong. It is important to realize the ways that these philosophers do not argue; and it is also important to understand some of the arguments that can be given against arguing in these ways. This is what has been briefly explained in §3. What now needs to be described is an approach to moral questions that is not open to the objections raised against the methods considered so far.

The approach described in what follows turns on how the following question is answered: "What requirements would someone have to meet to make an ideal moral judgment?" Considered ideally, that is, what are the conditions that anyone would have to satisfy to reach a moral judgment as free from fault and error as possible? Now, by its very nature, an *ideal* moral judgment is just that—an ideal. Perhaps no one ever has or ever will completely meet all the requirements set forth in the ideal. But that does not make it irrational to strive to come as close as possible to fulfilling it. If we can never quite get to the finish, we can still move some distance from the starting line.

There are at least six different ideas that must find a place in our description of the ideal moral judgment. A brief discussion of each follows.

a. Conceptual Clarity   This is an idea mentioned earlier. Its importance is obvious. If someone tells us that euthanasia is always wrong, we cannot determine whether that statement is true before we understand what euthanasia is. Similar remarks apply to other controversies. In the case of abortion, for example, many think the question turns on whether the fetus is a person; and that will depend on what a person is—that is, on how the concept 'person' should be analyzed. Clarity by itself may not be enough, but thought cannot get far without it.

b. Information   We cannot answer moral questions in our closets. Moral questions come up in the real world, and a knowledge of the real-world setting in which they arise is essential if we are seriously to seek rational answers to them. For example, in the debate over the morality of capital punishment, some people argue that convicted murderers ought to be executed because, if they are not, they may be (and often are) paroled; and if they are paroled, they are more likely to kill again than are other released prisoners. Is this true? Is this a fact? We have to come out of our closets to answer this (or to find the answer others have reached on the basis of their research); and answer it we must if we are to reach an informed judgment about the morality of capital punishment. It and related questions are surveyed in Hugo Bedau's essay on that topic. The importance of getting the facts, of being informed, is not restricted just to the case of capital punishment by any means. It applies all across the broad sweep of moral inquiry.

c. Rationality   Rationality is a difficult concept to analyze. Fundamentally, however, it involves the ability to recognize the connection between different ideas, to understand that if some statements are true, then some other statements must be true while others must be false. Now, it is in logic that rules are set forth that tell us when statements do follow from others, and it is because of this that a person who is rational often is said to be logical. When we speak of the need to be rational, then, we are saying that we need to observe the rules of logic. To reach an ideal moral judgment, therefore, we must not only strive to make our judgment against a background of information and conceptual clarity; we must also take care to explore how our beliefs are logically related to other things that we do or do not believe. For example, imagine that John thinks all abortions are morally wrong; and suppose that his wife, Mary, recently has had an abortion. Then John is not being rational or logical if he *also* believes that there was nothing immoral about Mary's abortion. Rationally he *cannot* believe this while believing the other things we assume he believes. Logically, it is *impossible* for both of the following statements to be true: (1) All abortions are morally wrong, and (2) Mary's abortion was not morally wrong. Whenever someone is committed to a belief or group of beliefs that cannot possibly all be true at the same time, that person is said to be committed to a *contradiction*. John, then, is committed to a contradiction. And so, too, perhaps, are some of those who argue about the morality of the issues discussed in the anthology. Jan Narveson, for example, in his essay on violence and war, argues that anyone who says violence is wrong and will not approve the use of a little violence to prevent greater violence is committed to a contradiction, thereby rendering his or her position (to use Narveson's term) "incoherent." To fall short of the ideal moral judgment by committing oneself to a contradiction is to fall as far short as one possibly can.

d. Impartiality   Partiality involves favoring someone or something above others. For example, if a father is partial to one of his children, then he will be inclined to give the favored child more than he gives his other children. In some cases, perhaps, partiality is a fine thing; but a partiality that excludes even thinking about or taking notice of the needs, interests, and desires of others seems far from what is needed in an ideal moral judgment. The fact that someone has been harmed, for example, always seems to be a relevant consideration, whether this someone is favored by us or not. In striving to reach the correct answer to moral questions, therefore, we must strive to guard against extreme, unquestioned partiality; otherwise we shall run the risk of having our judgment clouded by bigotry and prejudice.

This theme of the removal of partiality looms very large in a number of the essays. In Singer's essay, for example, arguments are presented against the view that we should be partial only to the interests of human beings; the interests of animals, too, should be considered, he argues. William Blackstone considers the view that we should go even further and extend the range of our moral concern to the environment generally, for its own sake. And Onora O'Neill's essay on famine makes it clear that, even if we restrict our moral concern only to human beings, we cannot exclude some human beings just because they live in distant lands and are unknown to us personally.

e. Coolness   All of us know what it is like to do something in the heat of anger that we later regret. No doubt we have also had the experience of getting so excited that we do something that later on we wish we had not done. Emotions are powerful forces, and though life would be a dull wasteland without them, we need to appreciate that the more volatile among them can mislead us; strong emotion is not a reliable guide to doing (or judging) what is best. This brings us to the need to be "cool." 'Being cool' here means "not being in an emotionally excited state, being in an emotionally calm state of mind." The idea is that the hotter (the more emotionally charged) we are, the more likely we are to reach a mistaken moral conclusion, while the cooler (the calmer) we are, the greater the chances that we will avoid making mistakes.

The position is borne out by common experience. People who are in a terribly excited state may not be able to retain their rationality. Because of their deep emotional involvement, they may not be able to attain impartiality; and because they are in an excited emotional state, they may not even care about learning what happened or why. Like the proverb about shooting first and asking questions later, a lack of coolness can easily lead people to judge first and ask about the facts afterwards. The need to be "cool," then, seems to merit a place on our list.

f. Correct Moral Principles   The concept of a moral principle has been analyzed in different ways. At least this much seems clear, however: For a principle to be a *moral* principle (as distinct from, say, a scientific or legal principle), it must declare how all rational, free beings ought to act. The explanation of why a moral principle can apply only to free beings (those having free will) is as follows. Beings who lack free will cannot control how they behave; the only way they *can* behave is as they *do* behave, which makes it pointless to say how they *ought* to behave. Beings who have free will, however, *can* control how they behave; it is up to them whether they choose to act in one way rather than another; and thus it is meaningful to say that they ought or ought not to act in certain ways.

The explanation of why moral principles are restricted to rational beings is similar. The whole point of a moral principle is to provide rational guidance to beings faced with choices among various alternatives. It would therefore be senseless to think that moral principles apply to things (for example, sticks and stones) incapable of being guided by what is rational. Only rational beings can be guided by rational principles. Thus, it is only to rational beings that moral principles can apply.

Now, it is commonly thought that human beings have free will and are rational beings. At least this is commonly thought to be true of most humans. Small babies and severely mentally deficient humans, for example, are unable to make free choices based on reason. Thus, they cannot be guided by moral principles, and moral principles cannot apply to their conduct. Most humans, however, do have the capacity to reason. Whether they also have free will is far less certain. The existence of free will is one of the oldest and most controversial of philosophy's problems, one that is well beyond the scope of this anthology. For present purposes, it is enough to realize that moral principles can apply only to rational, free beings *and* that the contributors all assume that their readers are likely to be amongst those beings to whom these principles do apply.

How does the idea of a correct moral principle relate to the concept of an ideal moral judgment? In an ideal moral judgment, it is not enough that the judgment be based on complete information, complete impartiality, complete conceptual clarity, etc. It is also essential that the judgment be based on *the correct* or *the most reasonable* moral principle(s). Ideally, one wants not only to make the correct judgment, but to make it for the correct reasons. The idea of correct moral principles will be discussed further (in Part II, especially §§6–8).

§5 NO DOUBLE STANDARDS ALLOWED

This portrait of the ideal moral judgment, or something very like it, forms the background of the several essays in this anthology. Their authors do not always explicitly say that, for example, impartiality or rationality are ideals worth striving for; but the manner in which they argue makes it clear that these ideals play an important role in their examinations of the views of others. Accordingly, these philosophers imply that it would be fair to apply these same ideals to their own thinking. In the case of each essay, therefore, we can ask:

1. Have important concepts been analyzed, and, if so, have they been analyzed correctly?
2. Does the author argue from a basis of knowledge of the real-life setting(s) in which the moral question arises?
3. Is the author rational? (Do the arguments presented observe the rules of logic?)
4. Is there a lack of impartiality? (Is someone, or some group, arbitrarily favored over others?)
5. Are things argued for in a state of strong emotion? (Are deep feelings rhetorically vented in the place of hard thinking?)
6. Are the moral principles used correct ones? (Is any effort expended to show that they are?)

These six questions, then, though they do not exhaust all possibilities, at least provide a place to begin. It is pertinent to ask how our authors pose these questions of the persons whose views they examine. But fairness requires that these same questions be asked of each author's views too. No double standards are allowed.

II. NORMATIVE ETHICS

Earlier, meta-ethics was characterized as the inquiry into the meaning of key concepts (for example, euthanasia and suicide) as well as the inquiry into whether there is a correct method for answering moral questions. Meta-ethical questions, however, by no means exhaust the philosophical interest in ethics. A second main area of inquiry commonly is referred to as *normative ethics.* Philosophers engaged in normative ethics attempt to go beyond the questions concerning meaning and method that arise in meta-ethics; the goal they set themselves is nothing short of determining what are the correct moral principles—those principles, that is, by which all free, rational beings ought morally to be guided. Thus, there is an important connection between the goal of normative ethics and the concept of an ideal moral judgment. An ideal moral judgment, we have said, must be based on correct moral principles, and it is just the question 'What principles are the correct ones?' that is at the heart of normative ethics. Unless the normative ethical philosopher succeeds in stating what are the correct moral principles, therefore, there can be no hope of even approaching the ideal moral judgment.

What then are the correct moral principles? Not surprisingly, a variety of answers has been offered. Not all of them can be considered here, and no one can be considered in much detail. But enough can be said to make some important ideas intelligible.

§6 CONSEQUENTIALIST THEORIES

One way to begin the search for the correct moral principle(s) is to think about cases where we all believe that something wrong has been done. However, it is important to understand that the class of persons referred to by the expression 'we all believe' is not necessarily as universal as it might at first appear. For suppose that Henry's belief or judgment is based on very sketchy information, or was formed in the heat of anger, or is a product of unquestioned prejudice. Then Henry's belief does not compute, so to speak; that is, because Henry's judgment falls so far short of the ideal moral judgment, we are justified in (that is, we have good reasons for) excluding it. Thus, the persons referred to by 'we all believe' are not just anybody and everybody; they are only those persons who most fully satisfy the first five conditions of the ideal moral judgment explained previously—those who are conceptually clear, informed, rational, impartial, and cool. It is the beliefs of these persons, not the beliefs of those who are prejudiced, say, that provide us with a place to begin the search for the final element in the ideal moral judgment—namely, the correct moral principle(s). So, by saying that a place to begin this search is with "what we all believe," we do not contradict what was said earlier (§3) about the irrelevance of statistics. What was said there *still* remains true: *Merely* to establish what all (or most) people think or believe about moral questions is not to establish what is right or wrong, let alone why it is.

So let us begin with a case where those who most fully approach the requirements of impartiality, conceptual clarity, etc. would all agree that something wrong has been done. For example, imagine that Beth has a favorite record. She enjoys listening to it and likes to share it with her friends. Sue likes the record too, and could afford to buy it, only then she could not afford to buy something else she wants but does not need. So, Sue steals the record. As a result, Beth experiences some unhappiness. When she thinks about the missing record, she is distraught and frustrated, and the enjoyment she would have had, if Sue had not stolen the record, is canceled. Beth, then, is worse off, both in terms of the unhappiness she experiences and in terms of lost enjoyment. Thinking along these lines has led some philosophers to theorize that what makes stealing wrong is that it is the cause of bad results—for example, it causes such experiences as the frustration and disappointment Beth feels.

Next imagine this case. Suppose there is a certain country that forbids black people from being in public after six o'clock. Bill, who is black, could get a job and support his family if the law did not prevent his free movement. As it is, he is chronically unemployed, and he and his family suffer accordingly. Thus, like the case of stealing, here we again have something that is the cause of bad results, and some philosophers have theorized that it is this fact that makes the law in question unjust.

Many philosophers have not stopped with the cases of stealing and injustice. Roughly speaking, the one common and peculiar characteristic of every wrong action, they have theorized, is that it leads to bad results, whereas the one common and peculiar characteristic of every right action, again roughly speaking, is that it leads to good results. Philosophers who accept this type of view commonly are referred to as *consequentialists,* an appropriate name, given their strong emphasis on the results or consequences of actions. Theories of this type also are called *teleological theories,* from the Greek *telos,* meaning "end" or "purpose," another fitting name, since, according to these thinkers, actions are not right or wrong in themselves; they are right or wrong, according to these theories, if they promote or frustrate the purpose of morality—namely, to bring about the greatest possible balance of good over evil.

Now, in normative ethics, when someone advances a principle that states what makes all right actions right and all wrong actions wrong, they do so in the course of advancing a *normative ethical theory.*

Theoretically, there are at least three different types of teleological, normative ethical theories.

1. *Ethical egoism:* According to this theory, roughly speaking, whether any person (A) has done what is morally right or wrong depends solely on how good or bad the consequences of A's action are *for A.* How *others* are affected is irrelevant, unless how they are affected in turn alters the consequences for A.
2. *Ethical altruism:* According to this theory, roughly speaking, whether any person (B) has done what is morally right or wrong depends solely on how good or bad the consequences of B's action are *for everyone except B.* How *B* is affected is irrelevant, unless how *B* is affected in turn alters the consequences for anyone else.
3. *Utilitarianism:* According to this theory, roughly speaking, whether any person (C) has done what is morally right or wrong depends solely on how good or bad the consequences of C's action are *for everyone affected.* Thus, how *C* is affected is relevant; but so is how *others* are affected. How *everyone* concerned is affected by the good or bad consequences is relevant.

These are not very exact statements of these three types of teleological, normative ethical theories, but enough has been said about two of them—namely, ethical egoism and ethical altruism—to enable us to understand why most philosophers find them unsatisfactory. Both seem to fall far short of the ideal of impartiality, ethical egoism because it seems to place arbitrary and exclusive importance on the good or welfare of the individual agent, and ethical altruism because it seems to place arbitrary and exclusive importance on the good or welfare of everyone else. Moreover, both theories arguably lead to consequences that clash with undoubted cases of wrong action. This is perhaps clearest in the case of ethical egoism. Provided only that, all considered, stealing the record did not lead to less than the best results *for Sue,* what she did was not morally wrong, according to ethical egoism. But that is something we would most likely deny. Faced with the choice between accepting ethical egoism or giving up the conviction that what Sue did was wrong, most philosophers choose to reject the theory and retain the conviction.

It is utilitarianism, then, that seems to represent the strongest possible type of teleological theory. Certainly it is the one that has attracted the most adherents; not unexpectedly, therefore, it is the one that figures most prominently in the essays in this volume. It will be worth our while, therefore, to examine it at slightly greater length.

§7 UTILITARIANISM

'The Principle of Utility' is the name given to the fundamental principle advocated by those who are called utilitarians. This principle has been formulated in different ways. Here is a common formulation:

> Everyone ought to act so as to bring about the greatest possible balance of intrinsic good over intrinsic evil for everyone concerned.

Already it must be emphasized that utilitarians do not agree on everything. In particular, they do not all agree on what is intrinsically good and evil. Some philosophers (called *ethical hedonists*) think that pleasure and pleasure alone is intrinsically good (or good in itself), whereas pain, or the absence of pleasure, and this alone, is intrinsically evil (or evil in itself). Other philosophers have advanced different theories of intrinsic good and evil. These troubled waters can be bypassed, however, since the ideas of special importance for our purposes can be discussed independently of whether ethical hedonism, for example, is true.

Act- and Rule-Utilitarianism   One idea of special importance is the difference between act-utilitarianism and rule-utilitarianism. *Act-utilitarianism* is the view that the Principle of Utility should be applied to individual actions; *rule-utilitarianism* states that the Principle of Utility should be applied mainly to rules of action. The act-utilitarian says that whenever people have to decide what to do, they ought to perform that act which will bring about the greatest possible balance of intrinsic good over intrinsic evil. The rule-utilitarian says something different: People ought to do what is required by justified moral rules. These are rules that would lead to the best possible consequences, all considered, if everyone were to abide by them. If a justified rule unambiguously applies to a situation, and if no other justified moral rule applies, then the person in that situation ought to choose to do what the rule requires, even if, in that particular situation, performing this act will not lead to the best consequences. Thus, act-utilitarians and rule-utilitarians, despite the fact that both profess to be utilitarians, can reach opposing moral judgments. An act that is wrong according to the rule-utilitarian, because it is contrary to a justified moral rule, might not be wrong according to the act-utilitarian's position.

Some Problems for Act-Utilitarianism   Is act-utilitarianism correct? Many philosophers answer no. Among the reasons given against this theory is that act-utilitarianism appears to imply that some acts that are most certainly wrong might be right. Recall the example of Sue's stealing. According to act-utilitarianism, whether Sue's theft was morally right or not depends on this and this alone: Were the net consequences of her act at least as good as the consequences that would have resulted if she had done anything else? Suppose they were. Then act-utilitarianism would imply that what she did was right. Yet her theft seems clearly wrong. Thus, we again seem to be faced with a choice between either (a) retaining the conviction that Sue's theft was wrong, or (b) accepting the theory of act-utilitarianism. We cannot choose to have both. In the face of such a choice, reason seems to be on the side of retaining the conviction and rejecting the theory.

Act-utilitarians actively defend their position against this line of criticism. The debate is among the liveliest and most important in normative ethics. The point that bears emphasis here is that *rule*-utilitarians do not believe that *their* version of utilitarianism can be refuted by the preceding argument. This is because they maintain that Sue's theft is wrong because it violates a justified moral rule—the rule against stealing. Thus, the rule-utilitarian holds that his position not only does not lead to a conclusion that clashes with the conviction that Sue's theft is wrong; this position actually illuminates *why* the theft is wrong—namely, because it violates a rule whose adoption by everyone can be defended by an appeal to the Principle of Utility.

Some Problems for Rule-Utilitarianism One success does not guarantee that all goes well, and many philosophers think that rule-utilitarianism, too, is inadequate. The most important objection turns on considerations about justice. The point of the objection is that rule-utilitarianism apparently could justify rules that would be grossly unjust. To make this clearer suppose there were a rule that discriminated against persons because of the color of their skin. Imagine this rule (*R*): "No one with black skin will be permitted in public after six o'clock." If we think about *R*, its unfairness jumps out at us. It is unjust to discriminate against people simply on the basis of skin color. However, although it is clear that *R* would be unjust, might not *R* conceivably be justified by appealing to the Principle of Utility? Certainly it seems possible that everyone's acting according to *R* might bring about the greatest possible balance of intrinsic good over intrinsic evil. True, black people are not likely to benefit from everyone's acting according to *R*. Nevertheless, on balance, their loss might be more than outweighed by nonblacks' gains, especially if blacks are a small minority. Thus, if rule-utilitarianism could be used to justify flagrantly unjust rules, it is not a satisfactory theory.

Can the rule-utilitarian meet this challenge? Philosophers are not unanimous in their answer. As was the case with the debate over the correctness of act-utilitarianism, this debate is too extensive to be examined further here. Nevertheless, enough has been said to suggest the importance of utilitarianism and to anticipate some of the ways it surfaces in the essays.

To begin with, some of the philosophers in this anthology are utilitarians—for example, Singer holds this theory. Moreover, even those who are not utilitarians (or are not clearly so) often use utilitarian arguments to support their position. Beauchamp, for example, argues that a rule permitting suicide under certain conditions can be defended on a rule-utilitarian basis. Moreover, even those philosophers who are most clearly not utilitarians—for example, O'Neill—discuss this theory. In a word, there is not a single essay in which utilitarianism does not put in an appearance, so that the following questions can be asked of each.

1. Is the philosopher being read a utilitarian?
2. If so, of what kind—act or rule?
3. If the philosopher is a utilitarian, are persuasive arguments adduced in support of the utilitarian answers given?
4. Is the possible clash between justice and utility examined?
5. If the philosopher being read is not a utilitarian, then what arguments, if any, are given against the correctness of the principle of utility and how rationally compelling are these arguments?
6. Moreover, if the philosopher is not a utilitarian, what other principle (or principles), if any, is subscribed to?
7. How rationally compelling are the arguments, if any, that are given in support of the principle(s)?

§8 NONCONSEQUENTIALISM

'Nonconsequentialism' is a name frequently given to normative ethical theories that are not forms of consequentialism. In other words, any theory that states that moral right and wrong are *not* determined solely by the relative balance of intrinsic good over intrinsic evil commonly is called a nonconsequentialist theory. Theories of this type are also called *deontological* theories, from the Greek *deon,* meaning "duty." Such theories might be either (a) extreme or (b) moderate. An extreme deontological theory holds that the intrinsic good and evil of consequences are totally irrelevant to determining what is morally right or wrong. A moderate nonconsequentialist theory holds that the intrinsic good and evil of consequences are relevant to determining what is morally right and wrong but that they are not the only things that are relevant and may not be of greatest importance in some cases. A great variety of nonconsequentialist theories, both extreme and moderate, have been advanced. Why have some philosophers been attracted to such theories?

The Problem of Injustice   A central argument advanced against all forms of consequentialism by many nonconsequentialists is that no consequentialist theory (no form of ethical egoism, ethical altruism, or utilitarianism) can account for basic convictions about justice and injustice—for example, that it is unjust to deny Bill his liberty just because he is black. The point these deontologists make is that to treat Bill unjustly not only is wrong; to treat him unjustly is to wrong or harm *him.* Fundamentally, according to these thinkers, it is because people are wronged or harmed when treated unjustly, quite apart from the value of the consequences this may have for everyone else involved, that all consequentialist theories ultimately prove to be deficient.

Suppose these deontologists are correct. Some deontological theory would then be called for. A number of such theories have been advanced. Some theorists, following the lead of the German philosopher Immanuel Kant (1724–1804), have argued that injustice is wrong because it fails to show proper respect for free, rational beings; in particular, it involves treating such beings as mere means to someone else's end. Precisely what it means to treat someone without "proper respect" or as a "mere means" is not transparent, but this conception of injustice is an important one and is discussed in a number of the essays, in particular the essays by Bedau and O'Neill. It is related at certain points to the deontological position that injustice involves the violation of basic moral rights. To understand this position requires understanding the idea of basic moral rights.

Basic Moral Rights Versus *Correlative Moral Rights* *Basic* moral rights are rights that *do not follow from* any more basic moral principle. In particular, these rights do not follow from the Principle of Utility. It is difficult to overemphasize this point. A utilitarian might be able consistently to maintain that people have moral rights in a certain sense; possibly he or she could allow that moral rights are *correlated* with duties—for example, correlated with Sue's duty not to steal Beth's record is Beth's moral right not to have Sue (or anyone else) steal from her. However, for a utilitarian, moral rights cannot be *basic;* at the very most they can be correlated with those duties that, given the Principle of Utility, we are supposed to have. Those who believe in basic moral rights are of another mind. For example, if the right to life is a basic moral right, then this *right, not* the Principle of Utility or any other moral principle, is the ground or basis of the duty not to take the life of another person. In a word, basic moral rights, if there are any, are themselves the grounds of moral duties, not *vice versa*.

Both those who believe in basic moral rights and those who believe that moral rights are correlated with moral duties can agree on certain points about moral rights. In particular, both can agree that the concept of a moral right differs from the concept of a legal right. An explanation of some principal differences follows.

§9 LEGAL RIGHTS AND MORAL RIGHTS

First, moral rights, if there are any, are *universal,* while legal rights need not be. Legal rights depend upon the law of this or that country, and what is a matter of legal right in one country may not be so in another. For example, in the United States any citizen eighteen years old or older has the legal right to vote in federal elections; but not everyone in every nation has this same legal right. If, however, persons living in the United States have a moral right to, say, life, then *every* person in every nation has this same moral right, whether or not it is also recognized as a legal right.

Second, moral rights are *equal* rights. If all persons have a moral right to life, then all have this right equally; it is not a right that some (for example, males) can possess to a greater extent than others (for example, females). Neither, then, could this moral right be possessed to a greater extent by the inhabitants of one country (for example, one's own) than by the inhabitants of some other country (for example, a country with which one's own country is waging war). This last consideration proves to be of some importance in Narveson's discussion of war.

Third, moral rights are *inalienable,* meaning they cannot be transferred to another—for example, they cannot be lent or sold. If Bill has a moral right to life, then it is his and it cannot become anyone else's. Bill may give his life for his country, sacrifice it in the name of science, or destroy it himself in a fit of rage or despair. But he cannot give, sacrifice, or destroy his right to life. Whether he can do anything that, so to speak, cancels his right (the more common terminology is 'forfeit his right') is an important, difficult question, one that is especially relevant to the question of the morality of capital punishment, as Bedau makes clear in his essay on that topic.

§10 LEGAL JUSTICE AND MORAL JUSTICE

Moral and legal rights are connected in important ways with moral and legal justice. Legal justice requires that one respect the legal rights of everyone, while moral justice demands that everyone's moral rights be honored. The two—legal justice and moral justice—do not necessarily coincide. Laws themselves may be morally unjust. For example, a country might have a law that unfairly discriminates against some of its inhabitants because of their sex; imagine that it denies that women have a legal right to life but guarantees this legal right to all males. Then legal justice is done in this country if this law is enforced. But it does not follow that moral justice is done. That depends not on whether there is a law in this country, but on whether the law recognizes and protects the moral rights of the country's inhabitants. If it does, then the law is both legally and morally just; if it does not, then, though the law may be legally just, it lacks moral justice. Thus, this law in particular and "the law" in general are appropriate objects of moral assessment, a theme that emerges in the essays on euthanasia, abortion, suicide, the environment, and capital punishment.

§11 WHAT ARE RIGHTS?

Whether rights are moral or legal, basic or correlative, the question remains: What are rights? How is the concept of a right to be analyzed? Various answers have been given, ranging from the view that rights are an individual's entitlements to be treated in certain ways to the view that they are valid claims that an individual can make, or have made on his or her behalf, to have one's interests or welfare taken into account. What is common to these answers is that a right involves the idea of a *justified constraint upon how others may act*. If Beth has a right to *x*, then others are constrained not to interfere with her pursuit or possession of *x*, at least so long as her pursuit or possession of *x* does not come into conflict with the rights of others. If it does, Beth may be exceeding her rights, and a serious moral question would arise. But aside from cases of exceeding one's rights and, as may sometimes be the case, of forfeiting them, the possession of a right by one individual places a justified limit on how other individuals may treat the person possessing the right. Whether rights are entitlements or valid claims, and whether they are basic or correlative, rights involve a justified constraint or limitation on how others may act.

§12 THE CRITERIA OF RIGHT-POSSESSION

Suppose the concept of a moral right is clear and that some beings have moral rights. Many questions would still remain to be explored. One in particular stands out: What are the criteria of right-possession? Or, in terms explained earlier (§1), What are the necessary and sufficient conditions of right-possession? Again, many different answers have been proposed. Here are some examples: (a) All and only free, rational beings have moral rights; (b) All and only conscious beings have them; (c) All and only beings who are able to use a language have these rights; (d) All and only beings who have a concept of themselves as an enduring entity (as a self) have moral rights.

How might one rationally choose among these alternatives? This methodological question is hotly disputed, but one way to proceed here is as follows. Suppose that not only "normal" adult human beings, but also infants, the senile, and the mentally enfeebled of all ages have moral rights. If this much were granted, there would be powerful grounds for denying the correctness of some of the proposed criteria of right-possession listed above. Infants, for example, have no concept of themselves as an enduring entity, so that, if they have moral rights, this proposed criterion cannot be correct; having a concept of oneself as an enduring entity cannot be a *necessary* condition of having rights, granting the assumption about infants, etc., having rights. Neither could being free and rational be correct, since many mentally enfeebled humans lack these capacities. And the same is true of the ability to use a language, since it sets as a necessary condition of right-possession a capacity that many human beings (some of the mentally enfeebled, again) fail to satisfy. In this way, then, an argument could be developed against the correctness of various proposed criteria of right-possession. To argue in favor of the correctness of a proposed criterion would consist, at least in part, in asking whether any given criterion sets forth conditions that those humans assumed to have rights (infants, the enfeebled, etc.) can satisfy. If there is such a criterion, then its claim to correctness is to that degree a strong one, given our assumptions. The criterion of being conscious, for example, arguably passes this test, and thus, given our assumptions, must be considered to be a strong candidate for the correct criterion of right-possession.

§13 WHAT BEINGS POSSESS WHAT MORAL RIGHTS?

Suppose that the criterion of being conscious is the correct criterion of right-possession; then *only* those beings who are conscious, and *all* those beings who are conscious, have moral rights. Now, if this is true, a position would have been reached that is fraught with enormous practical implications, many of which are explored in the essays. To begin with, there are many nonhumans who are conscious—namely, many nonhuman animals. If all conscious beings have moral rights, then these animals have moral rights; and if these animals have moral rights, we must seriously stop to inquire whether we are doing anything that violates their rights when we eat or experiment upon them. This is a question that is pursued in considerable depth by Singer in his essay. Moreover, there are some *human* beings who lack consciousness—namely, those who are comatose. If a being must be conscious to have moral rights, then has the comatose individual lost all rights? This is an issue discussed in James Rachels's essay on euthanasia.

Still, *is* consciousness a necessary condition of right-possession? Recall that the reason underlying the introduction of the idea of basic moral rights was that it seems possible to act in ways that harm or wrong people. But why must the ideas of harming or wronging be limited to people or to conscious beings? Might it not be possible to harm or wrong nonconscious entities? If a tree is killed or the sagebrush is destroyed, have they not been harmed? And if they have, might not the idea that nonconscious entities have moral rights demand serious consideration? These questions figure prominently in Blackstone's essay, "The Search for an Environmental Ethic." They are closely connected with questions about the value of life, some of which will be discussed below (§16).

Short of extending moral rights to trees or sagebrush, there may be grounds for rejecting the view that consciousness is a necessary condition of right-possession. Possibly the *potential* for consciousness must be added, an addition that at once *excludes* trees and sagebrush, and *includes* many more beings than are included if just consciousness is accepted. In particular, adding the potential for consciousness would necessitate including many human *fetuses* in the class of beings having moral rights. And if these beings are included, how can one avoid the conclusion that abortion violates the fetus' right to life? The debate revolving around this idea is a central theme in the essay on abortion by Joel Feinberg. Clearly, to ask about the criteria of right-possession is not an idle, merely theoretical question like asking how many angels can dance on the head of a pin.

To establish what beings can and do have moral rights, however, may not necessarily establish all the moral rights they have. Consider the three rights enshrined in the American Declaration of Independence: the rights to life, liberty, and the pursuit of happiness. Someone who argues that a given being, A, has a right to life, does not necessarily have to believe that A also has the right to liberty. If, for example, sense can be made of the idea of extending a right to life to trees and plants, it would not follow that a right to liberty must also be attributed. This would be meaningless, since plants lack the power to exercise choice. Or consider the status of animals. Perhaps it is possible to argue in support of the view that they have a moral right not to be made to suffer unnecessary pain. Still, does it follow necessarily that they have *other* moral rights—for example, a right to life? Singer, for one, answers no. Thus, the question of *what* moral rights a being has must be examined separately from the question of what beings satisfy the criteria for the possession of moral rights.

§14 WHEN RIGHTS CONFLICT

One final question relating to the topic of rights deserves our attention. It sometimes happens that one person's rights conflict with another's. The case of abortion illustrates this well. Suppose that both the fetus and the pregnant woman have a right to life. And suppose that, as sometimes happens, the medical situation is such that if the fetus is permitted to be born, the woman will die, whereas if steps are taken to enable the woman to live, the fetus will die. Since both rights cannot prevail, whose, the fetus' or the woman's, ought to? Just two ways of thinking about conflicting rights will be described here.

The Idea of Innocence   Innocence is an important moral idea. In the case of punishment, for example, it is morally wrong to punish someone who is known to be innocent. Innocence might be extremely important in some cases where rights conflict. Suppose the right to life of two beings, A and B, conflict; and suppose, further, that A is innocent of any wrongdoing whereas B is in this situation because B has not acted responsibly—for example, perhaps B has been negligent. Then ought not A's right to life prevail over B's? Ought not such cases of conflict be settled by appealing to the following rule: "Whenever the right to life of two beings conflict, the right to life of the innocent party must always take precedence over the right to life of the party who is not innocent"?

Unfortunately, the situation is not so simple. For though innocence always is a relevant moral consideration, it is not clear that it should always be given a place of preeminence. To make this clearer, let us apply the previous argument to the case of abortion. The fetus, it is agreed, is innocent. Let us assume, however, that the woman and the prospective father have acted irresponsibly: they have not taken due precautions to avoid pregnancy. Thus, it hardly seems fair to abort the fetus. But suppose we know that the fetus, if it is permitted to develop, will become a grossly deformed child—no arms or legs, blind, and acutely mentally defective. Is the fact that the fetus is innocent, while the potential parents are not, a sufficiently weighty reason to insist that, morally speaking, the fetus ought not to be aborted? Are there not other, possibly weightier, reasons in addition to the comparative innocence of the parties in question? Many philosophers think so. Feinberg explores some of their arguments in his essay on abortion. But the kind of problem just described, where rights conflict, is to be met with in many of the essays.

One Role of the Principle of Utility   All but the most extreme non-consequentialist can allow that an appeal to the Principle of Utility is always relevant even if not always decisive. Possibly utility has a role to play when the rights of innocent persons conflict. To illustrate this possibility, suppose a hijacker has attached to an innocent hostage a time bomb that, if it goes off, will kill ten other innocent persons; and suppose that the only possible way to prevent the bomb from going off is to kill the hostage. What ought to be done? If we kill the hostage, we kill an innocent person; but if we do not kill the hostage, ten innocent persons will be killed. The innocence of the persons involved may not be enough to give us moral direction. Possibly an appeal to the Principle of Utility would. The point is, even if there are *basic* moral rights, and even if the utilitarian cannot account for them, one could *both* believe in basic moral rights *and* allow that the Principle of Utility should play some role in our thinking about what is right and wrong—for example, in cases where the basic moral rights of innocent people conflict.

§15 ANOTHER SET OF QUESTIONS

As before, the preceding discussion of rights provides a set of questions rather than a set of answers. Here are some of the questions that apply to the essays.

1. Does the author affirm or deny that there are basic moral rights?
2. In either case, how is the concept of a right understood?
3. If an author does believe that there are basic moral rights, what arguments are given to support this position and how strong are these arguments?
4. What criteria of right-possession are advanced and how well are they defended?
5. If moral rights are appealed to, what beings are supposed to have them, what rights are various beings supposed to have,

and how compelling are the arguments given in support of the positions taken on these questions?
6. If cases where rights conflict are considered, then what principle(s) are appealed to to resolve these conflicts, and how compelling are the arguments given in support of accepting said principle(s)?

Like the other questions listed in the preceding discussion, the ones just asked go to the center of the essays. Though not all are examined in every essay, some are examined in each.

§16 THE VALUE OF LIFE

One idea mentioned earlier (§13) is that of the value of life. There are many questions that must be asked about this idea. Is life itself valuable, or is it rather that life is a necessary condition of other kinds of value? If life itself is valuable, why is it, and what kind of value does it have? If it is life itself that is valuable, are the lives of all living beings equally valuable? If it is said that only the lives of certain beings (say, human beings) are valuable, then what are the grounds for restricting the value of life in this way? These questions demand close scrutiny and are examined in many of the essays.

The idea of life's value is connected with most of the ideas discussed in this Introduction. Its relevance to the question of moral rights will have to serve as illustrative. Suppose that the life of any human being (Bill) has a kind of value that does not depend on anyone else happening to find Bill useful or fun to be with; in other words, suppose Bill's life, and the life of any other person, is *inherently* valuable. Then it might be possible to argue that Bill and other persons have a moral right to life *because* their lives are inherently valuable. And this, if it were true, could have direct implications for debates over the morality of capital punishment, euthanasia, suicide, etc. If it is morally wrong to destroy an inherently valuable life, why are not all cases of capital punishment, euthanasia, and suicide morally wrong? As we might expect, just this question is considered in the essays on these respective topics. But the idea of life's value finds a place in each essay. To ask about the role that this idea plays in the several essays, therefore, is to formulate a final question that can be asked of each.

2
Euthanasia

JAMES RACHELS

In this essay we shall discuss the major moral and legal questions concerning euthanasia. Is euthanasia morally permissible, or is it morally wrong? Should it be against the law, or should it be legal?

It would be useful if we could define at the outset exactly what we mean by the word 'euthanasia'. But that is not an easy task. The word derives from two Greek words that mean, literally, "a good death," but we mean much more by it than that. The nearest English synonym for 'euthanasia' is 'mercy killing', which is close. Beyond that, it is hard to give a precise definition because the word is used in connection with a wide variety of cases.

I. INTRODUCTION

§1 THE CENTRAL CASE

Let's begin by looking at a case that illustrates perfectly what euthanasia is. (Incidentally, all the examples of euthanasia that I use throughout this essay are taken from real life.)

> Albert A., a hospital patient, was dying of cancer, which had spread throughout his body. The intense pain could no longer be controlled. Every four hours he would be given a painkiller, but over many months of treatment he had built up a tolerance for the drug, until now it would relieve the pain for only a few minutes each time. Albert knew that he was going to die anyway, for the cancer could not be cured. He did not want to linger in agony, so he asked his doctor to give him a lethal injection to end his life without further suffering. His family supported this request.

It would have been illegal for the doctor to grant this request—in fact, it would have been first degree murder—so Albert was not given the injection.

If the doctor had killed Albert, it would have been a perfect example of euthanasia. The case would have had these five important features:

1. The patient would have been deliberately killed.
2. The patient was going to die soon anyway.
3. The patient was suffering terrible pain.
4. The patient asked to be killed.
5. The killing would have been an act of mercy; that is, the *reason* for the killing would have been to prevent further needless suffering and to provide the patient with a "good death," or at least as good as it could be under the circumstances.

When all these features are present, we have the clearest possible case of euthanasia.

It is easy to find other examples of the same kind. Here is one in which the patient's request *was* granted:

> Barbara B. was a multiple amputee and diabetic in constant pain, who was told that she could live for only a few more months. She begged her husband to kill her, and he did, by electrocution. The husband was charged with murder and was convicted. On sentencing day the judge wept. Mr. B., who could have spent decades in prison, was sentenced to a year and a day. He never wavered in his opinion that he had done the right thing, and he said that his act was an act of love.

§2 RELATED CASES

There are many other cases in which the above five features are *not* all present to which the word 'euthanasia' is also commonly applied. For example:

> Charles C. begged to be killed after being paralyzed from the neck down in an automobile accident. The doctors ignored the request, but his brother did not. The brother brought a sawed-off shotgun into the hospital and fatally wounded him.

This case is different from the previous ones because Charles C. was not going to die soon anyway, and he wanted to be killed, not because he was in pain, but because he did not want to live as a hopeless invalid. Other people, of course, might have had a different preference. Others might prefer to live paralyzed, rather than not to live at all. But not Charles C; he preferred to die.

> Donald D. had been a jet pilot and a rodeo performer and was in the prime of life when he was severely burned over 67 percent of his body by an exploding gas line. He was grotesquely disfigured, blinded, lost the use of both his arms and legs, and was in constant

horrible pain for many months as all the most sophisticated techniques of modern medicine were used to keep him alive. When
rational, he would ask to be killed—specifically, he wanted an overdose of heroin. He refused to give permission for treatment, and so
a psychiatrist was called in to declare him "incompetent" to withhold
consent. After interviewing Donald, the psychiatrist decided that he
was in fact competent. But, having won his point, Donald suddenly
changed his mind and consented to further treatment. He eventually
regained partial use of his limbs and went to law school.

In all the cases I have mentioned so far, the patient is conscious,
at least arguably rational, and requests death. In the following case,
however, the patient is not rational and makes no such request:

> Edward E., eighty-nine years old, had suffered three heart attacks,
> had bad kidneys, suffered various other ailments, and was hopelessly
> senile. He was hospitalized for his heart condition, and most of the
> time was only semiconscious. He was unable even to recognize mem-
> bers of his own family. There was no expectation of significant im-
> provement in his condition. The attending physician instructed the
> hospital staff that if he should suffer another attack, nothing should
> be done to save him. Shortly afterwards, Edward's heart failed, no
> action was taken, and he died.

This is a very common sort of case, in which doctors have to decide
how much is to be done to prolong lives that have become meaningless
even to the patients themselves. In addition to the fact that the patient
is not rational and that death is not requested, there are two other
important features of this case that should be noted. First, the patient
is not killed, but is merely allowed to die. And second, the reason for
allowing the patient to die is not as a kindness to him. The patient is
not allowed to die for his own good, since he is not suffering. Rather,
he is allowed to die because it is felt that there is simply no longer any
point in keeping him alive. The case of Edward E. is similar in these
ways to the following case:

> Frances F. was in a permanent coma, being kept alive by machines
> and fed intravenously. She had suffered such severe brain damage
> that she could never wake up. She could be keep alive indefinitely
> by the use of artificial life-support systems, but if these machines were
> turned off she would die. The machines were turned off, and she died.

Like Edward, Frances did not ask to die, and like him, she was really
unable to express an opinion in the matter. The attending physician
judged that there was no point in keeping her alive—death would be
neither kind nor cruel for her, since it would make no difference at
all as far as *she* was concerned—so she was allowed to die.

§3 SOME DISTINCTIONS

At this point I want to introduce a bit of terminology. The phrase
'*active* euthanasia' is used to refer to cases in which the patient is
killed, for example by being given a lethal injection. The phrase

'*passive* euthanasia' refers to cases in which the patient is not killed but merely allowed to die. In passive euthanasia we simply refrain from doing anything to keep the patient alive—for example, we may refuse to perform surgery, administer medication, give a heart massage, or use a respirator—and let the person die of whatever ills are already present. It is important to note this distinction, because many people believe that, although active euthanasia is immoral, passive euthanasia is morally all right. They believe that, while we should never actually kill patients, it is sometimes all right to let them die.

In addition to the distinction between active and passive euthanasia, it is important to bear in mind the difference between voluntary, nonvoluntary, and involuntary euthanasia. *Voluntary* euthanasia occurs whenever the patient requests death. The cases of Barbara B. and Charles C. are both examples of voluntary euthanasia, since both patients asked to be killed. *Nonvoluntary* euthanasia occurs when the patient is unable to form a judgment or voice a wish in the matter and, therefore, expresses no desire whatever. The cases of Edward E. and Frances F. are both instances of nonvoluntary euthanasia; Edward was senile and only semiconscious, while Frances was permanently comatose, so neither could form a preference.

Finally, *involuntary* euthanasia occurs when the patient says that he or she does not want to die, but is nevertheless killed or allowed to die. In this essay I will not be concerned with involuntary euthanasia. My view is that it is simply murder, and that it is not justified. If a person *wants* to live on, even in great pain, and even with the certainty of a horrible end, that is the individual's right. I believe that most people would agree with this judgment, but at any rate, I will not discuss this sort of case any further. Rather, attention will be focused primarily on voluntary euthanasia, and, to a somewhat lesser extent, on nonvoluntary euthanasia.

§4 THE MAIN ISSUES

We have now looked at a number of cases and noted some of the important similarities and differences among them. Now let us return to our original question: What are we to understand by the word 'euthanasia'? Primarily it means killing someone—or letting someone die—who is going to die soon anyway, at the person's own request, as an act of kindness. This is the central case. The other cases I have described are called "euthanasia" because of their similarities to it.

In what follows we will be concerned mainly with the morality of euthanasia in the central case. The two main issues are: first, is it morally permissible to kill or let die someone who is going to die soon anyway, at the person's own request, as an act of kindness? And second, should such killing or letting die be against the law?

Along the way I will also discuss the morality of killing, or letting die, in the other cases I have described, since many of the same problems are involved. However, it is primarily the central case that will concern us.

Let me add one word of caution: We must be careful not to confuse the question of whether euthanasia *is* against the law with the very different question of whether it *ought to be* against the law. As a matter of fact, in the United States, active euthanasia is against the law. But it does not follow from this fact that active euthanasia ought to be against the law, for it *could be* that this is an unwise law that ought to be stricken from the books. The law itself can be the object of moral criticism. Once, for example, it was against the law in the southern United States for black people and white people to eat together in restaurants. But this legal rule was clearly a bad one, and it was changed after moral objections were raised forcefully against it. In the same spirit, we will ask whether the law prohibiting active euthanasia is a good one or a bad one, and whether it ought to be changed.

II. AN HISTORICAL PERSPECTIVE

We cannot conclude that any practice is morally right simply because people believe that it is right, or because historically the practice has been accepted. What we believe, or what our culture accepts, may be wrong. Nevertheless, in order to place our convictions in context, it is useful to reflect on the history of those beliefs and to compare them with the beliefs of people who live, or who have lived, in societies different from our own.

§5 ATTITUDES FROM THE ANCIENT WORLD

The people of ancient Greece took an attitude toward human life that is very different from our own. They did not believe that all human life is precious, or that it must be preserved at all costs. In Sparta, for example, it was required by law that deformed infants be put to death —this was considered better than an unhappy life for them and their parents. The approval of infanticide was not limited to Sparta; in Athens, which we consider to have been a more enlightened community, the destruction of deformed or unhealthy babies was also approved. The Athenians did not *require* that they be killed, but on the other hand there was no condemnation of the practice, either. It is worth remembering that we are not talking about a crude, backward society, but about one of the world's great civilizations, which produced some of our finest literature, art, and philosophy, as well as virtually inventing science and mathematics.

The fact that the Greeks approved infanticide is not a sign that they placed little value on human life. They were not a murderous people, and they took a stern view of some other types of killing. In general, they did not approve of suicide: Pythagoras, Plato, and Aristotle all rejected it as a cowardly way of avoiding life's hardships and one's duties to self and state. However, all three of these philosophers thought it foolish to prohibit suicide in *every* situation, and they allowed that in cases of incurable disease accompanied by great pain, a person has the right to choose an earlier death. Unfortunately, the Greek whose views are most often remembered on this subject was not really representative. Hippocrates, sometimes counted as the "father of medicine," was the author of an oath that is still taken by new doctors; in it, the doctors pledge that "If any shall ask of me a drug to produce death I will not give it, nor will I suggest such counsel." This part of the Hippocratic Oath would not have been endorsed, without qualification, by the majority of Greek thinkers.

The Romans adopted many of the Greeks' attitudes. The Stoic philosopher Seneca, for example, wrote without apology that "We destroy monstrous births, and drown our children if they are born weakly and unnaturally formed."[1] If anything, the Romans regarded killing—in special circumstances—even more indifferently than the Greeks. The Stoic and Epicurean philosophers thought suicide an acceptable option *whenever* one no longer cared for life. The most famous statement of this attitude is by Epictetus: "If the room is smoky, if only moderately, I will stay; if there is too much smoke I will go. Remember this, keep a firm hold on it, the door is always open."[2] To those with such a frame of mind, it seemed obvious that euthanasia was preferable to a miserable, lingering death. Seneca, again, wrote:

> I will not relinquish old age if it leaves my better part intact. But if it begins to shake my mind, if it destroys my faculties one by one, if it leaves me not life but breath, I will depart from the putrid or the tottering edifice. If I know that I must suffer without hope of relief I will depart not through fear of the pain itself but because it prevents all for which I would live.[3]

§6 THE EARLY CHRISTIAN VIEW

The coming of Christianity caused vast changes in these attitudes. The early Church was resolutely pacifist and opposed the killing of humans in *every* context. Infanticide was prohibited, for it was thought that all who are born of woman, no matter how monstrous or miserable, have immortal souls. Suicide was forbidden because one's life was viewed as a trust from God, and only God has the right to take it. Considering the nonpacifist views of most modern Christians, the reader may be surprised to learn that participation in warfare was also condemned by the early Church. The Church fathers—Lactantius, Tertullian, Origen—were in agreement on all of this. Of war, Tertullian wrote: "Can it be lawful to handle the sword, when the Lord himself has declared that he who uses the sword shall perish by it?"[4]

The Church continued to denounce infanticide and suicide, but it soon modified its position on war. A sympathetic interpretation of this change might be that Christians came to recognize a valid moral difference between killing in a just war and other forms of killing. A less sympathetic view is taken by the sociologist-philosopher Edward Westermarck, who remarked in his classic work *Christianity and Morals*:

> A divine law which prohibited all resistance to enemies could certainly not be accepted by the State, especially at a time when the Empire was seriously threatened by foreign invaders. Christianity could therefore never become a State religion unless it gave up its attitude towards war. And it gave it up.[5]

The early Church had also condemned capital punishment, which was not surprising considering the number of Church figures, including Jesus himself and St. Peter, who had been executed. But this position, too, was soon modified, bringing the Church's stance more into line with political requirements. The imposition of death by the State was said to be all right, so long as priests took no part in the proceedings.

But the Church's opposition to euthanasia continued, and under its influence, what for the Greek and Roman philosophers had been a compassionate solution to the problem of lingering, degrading death became a mortal sin. Suffering, no matter how horrible or seemingly pointless, came to be viewed as a burden imposed by God himself, for purposes known to Him, which men and women must bear until the "natural" end. This attitude prevailed throughout the Middle Ages, and was not seriously challenged until the sixteenth century.

§7 OTHER RELIGIONS AND CULTURES

But I do not want to give the impression that the prohibition of euthanasia is exclusively a Christian doctrine. Jewish law also forbids it. In fact, we find a rare consensus among rabbinic authorities on this subject. The medieval Jewish theologians were no less emphatic than their Christian counterparts: The great Maimonides, for example, wrote in the twelfth century that "One who is in a dying condition is regarded as a living person in all respects . . . He who touches him (thereby causing him to expire) is guilty of shedding blood."[6] The Islamic tradition is also uncompromising, for the Koran explicitly states that the suicide "shall be excluded from heaven forever," and voluntary euthanasia is regarded as simply a form of assisted suicide.[7] So not only Christianity but all these religious traditions conspire to withhold a merciful death to those who suffer—or, to look at things from an opposite point of view, conspire to affirm the preciousness of life even when life is most wretched.

If we turn for a moment to the experience of other cultures, we find a striking contrast. While these developing Western traditions were opposing euthanasia, most Eastern peoples were comfortably accepting it. In China, Confucian ethics had always allowed voluntary death in the case of hopeless disease, and the great Eastern religions, including Shintoism and Buddhism, took a similar attitude. In *The Dialogues of Buddha* there are described two holy men who commit suicide to escape incurable illness, and this is said to be no obstacle to their attaining "nirvana," the spiritual goal of all Buddhist endeavor. Among so-called primitive societies, there is a wide range of attitudes toward euthanasia, but it is easy to compile long lists of cultures in which the suicide or killing of those with intolerable illness is approved; one historian mentions eighteen such societies in the space of two pages.[8]

§8 DISSENTERS

But now let us return to our historical sketch of Western attitudes. As I said, after Christianity became a state religion, opposition to euthanasia, as well as to suicide, infanticide, and abortion, took a firm hold on the minds of almost everyone who bothered to think seriously about it. Throughout the Middle Ages, the prohibition on these practices was virtually unchallengeable. Not until 1516 do we find an important defense of mercy killing. In that year Sir Thomas More, later to be made a saint of the Church, wrote in his *Utopia* that in the imaginary perfect community:

> When any is taken with a torturing and lingering pain, so that there is no hope either of cure or ease, the priests and magistrates come and exhort them, that, since they are now unable to go on with the business of life, are become a burden to themselves and all about them, and they have really outlived themselves, they should no longer nourish such a rooted distemper, but choose rather to die since they cannot live but in such misery.[9]

Remarkably, More advocates in this passage not only that euthanasia be permitted, but that it be *urged* on the desperately ill, even when they are reluctant to accept it. This certainly seems to be going too far; I do not know of any other advocate of euthanasia who would agree with More about *that*. Nevertheless, More adds that a person who refuses euthanasia is to be cared for as well as possible.

Gradually, more and more thinkers came to believe that the prohibition on euthanasia ought to be relaxed. It was, however, a very slow movement, and those who favored the relaxation remained in a distinct minority. After Thomas More, the next notable proponent of euthanasia was Francis Bacon, credited as one of the founders of modern philosophy. A hundred years after More's *Utopia,* Bacon defined the role of the physician as "not only to restore the health, but to mitigate pain and dolours; and not only when such mitigation may conduce to recovery, but when it may serve to make a fair and easy passage."[10]

§9 MODERN SECULAR THOUGHT

Seventeenth- and Eighteenth-Century Thought   During the seventeenth and eighteenth centuries, philosophers began to move away from the idea that morality requires a religious foundation. Although most were still theists, and God still held a prominent place in their understanding of the universe, they did not think that right and wrong consisted in following God's commandments, and they did not look to the Church as a primary source of moral guidance. Instead, human reason and the individual conscience were regarded as the sources of moral insight. This did not mean, however, that these thinkers abandoned all traditional moral views. Although they were revolutionary in their ideas concerning the *sources* of morality, often they were not so radical in their particular moral opinions. The most famous German philosophers, Kant (1724–1804) and Hegel (1770–1831), held that moral truths are known through the use of reason alone; but when they exercised their reason on such matters as suicide and euthanasia, they discovered that the Church had been right all along. A notable exception to this way of thinking was the greatest British philosopher, David Hume (1711–1776), who argued vigorously that one has the right to end one's life when he or she pleases. Hume, who was a sceptic about religion, particularly tried to refute theological arguments to the contrary.

It is one thing for a philosopher to argue that morality is separate from religion, or that the basis of morality is not necessarily religious, but it is quite a different matter for those ideas to affect popular thinking. In spite of the growing secularization of philosophical thought in the seventeenth and eighteenth centuries, in the popular mind, ethics was still very much tied to religion. The Protestant Reformation had created many churches where before there had been the one Church; and for Protestants the authority of the Church had been replaced by the individual believer's direct relationship with God. But still, people's moral duties were conceived as the outgrowth of their religious beliefs, and the purpose of the moral life was still thought to be the service of God. Then in the nineteenth century a remarkable thing happened: a philosophical movement, utilitarianism, not only captured the imaginations of philosophers but revolutionized popular thinking as well.

Utilitarianism   Jeremy Bentham (1748–1832) argued that the purpose of morality is not the service of God or obedience to abstract moral rules, but the promotion of the greatest possible happiness for creatures on earth. What we ought to do is calculate how our actions, laws, and social policies will actually affect people (and other animals, too). Will they result in people being made happier, in people having better lives? Or will they result in people being made more miserable? According to Bentham, our decisions should be made on that basis, and *only* on that basis.

But Bentham did not stop when he had articulated this as a theoretical idea. He was concerned with bringing about social change and not merely with voicing a philosophy. Bentham became the leader of a group of philosophers, economists, and politicians who sought to reform the laws and institutions of England along utilitarian lines, and the social and intellectual life of people in the English-speaking countries has not been the same since. Bentham argued, for example, that in order to maximize happiness, the law should not seek to enforce abstract moral rules or meddle in the private affairs of citizens. What consenting adults do in private is strictly their own business, and the law has no right to interfere. The law should concern itself with people's behavior only when they may do harm to others. This idea, now so familiar a part of liberal ideology, was radically new when the Benthamites first urged it on their fellow Englishmen.

The implications for euthanasia were obvious. For the utilitarians, the question was simply this: Does it increase or decrease human happiness to provide a quick, painless death for those who are dying in agony? Clearly, they reasoned, the only consequences of such actions will be to decrease the amount of misery in the world; therefore, euthanasia must be morally right. Moreover, as Bentham's famous follower John Stuart Mill (1806–1873) put it, the individual is sovereign over his own body and mind; where one's own interests are concerned, there is no other authority. Therefore, if one wants to die quickly rather than linger in pain, that is strictly a personal affair, and the government has no business intruding. Indeed, Bentham himself requested euthanasia in his last moments.

§10 RECENT DEVELOPMENTS

The utilitarian movement changed the way people think. Today, the calculation of benefits and harms is routinely accepted as a primary way of determining what is right and what is wrong. (The fact that contemporary philosophers spend so much time criticizing and arguing about utilitarianism only attests to its tremendous influence.) As a result, more and more people have come to favor euthanasia. In 1936, there was organized in England the Voluntary Euthanasia Society, with an eminent surgeon as its first president and many physicians among its sponsors. This was followed in the United States by the organization of such groups as the Euthanasia Society of America, the Euthanasia Educational Council, and the Society for the Right to Die. Advocacy of active euthanasia is no longer confined to a few figures on the fringes of academic thought. It is publicly supported by thousands of doctors, lawyers, scientists, and clergymen (including many Catholics), as well as philosophers; and although active euthanasia is still illegal, bills are being introduced in various legislative bodies every year in an attempt to legalize it.

§11 THE POSITION OF THE AMERICAN MEDICAL ASSOCIATION

The preceding historical sketch must be qualified in an important way. Throughout the history of our subject, most people have thought that the distinction between active euthanasia and passive euthanasia is morally important; and many of those who condemned active euthanasia raised no objection against passive euthanasia. Even when killing was thought to be wrong, allowing people to die by not treating them was thought in some circumstances to be all right. Four centuries before Christ, we find Socrates saying of a physician, with approval, ". . . bodies which disease had penetrated through and through he would not have attempted to cure . . . he did not want to lengthen out good-for-nothing lives."[11] Neither the Christians nor the Jews, in the centuries following, significantly altered this basic idea; both viewed *allowing to die,* in circumstances of hopeless suffering, as morally permissible. It was killing that was zealously opposed.

The morality of allowing people to die by not treating them has become critically important in recent years because of advances in medical technology. By using such devices as respirators, heart-lung machines, and intravenous feeding, we can now keep almost anybody alive indefinitely, even after he or she has become nothing more than a "human vegetable," without thought or feeling or hope of recovery. The maintenance of life by such artificial means is, in these cases, sadly pointless. Virtually everyone who has thought seriously about the matter agrees that it is morally all right, at some point, to cease treatment and allow such people to die. No less a figure than the Pope has concurred: as recently as 1958, Pius XII reaffirmed that we may "allow the patient who is virtually already dead to pass away in peace."[12]

In December 1973, the American Medical Association issued a statement, "The Physician and the Dying Patient," in which it announced its official policy on euthanasia. That statement reaffirmed the traditional ban on mercy killing but also accepted the traditional view of letting die as (in some circumstances) all right. It said, in its entirety:

> The intentional termination of the life of one human being by another—mercy killing—is contrary to that for which the medical profession stands and is contrary to the policy of the American Medical Association.
>
> The cessation of the employment of extraordinary means to prolong the life of the body when there is irrefutable evidence that biological death is imminent is the decision of the patient and/or his immediate family. The advice and judgment of the physician should be freely available to the patient and/or his immediate family.

Since passive euthanasia is relatively uncontroversial, most of our attention in what follows will be given to active euthanasia.

III. ARGUMENTS SUPPORTING THE MORALITY OF ACTIVE EUTHANASIA

§12 THE IMPORTANCE OF ARGUMENT

We come now to the most important part of our investigation. So far we have seen that there is widespread agreement that passive euthanasia is morally all right, in at least some cases, but that active euthanasia is much more controversial. We have seen that in the course of Western history, some thinkers have approved of active euthanasia, but most have condemned it. We have seen that in some other cultures, a more tolerant attitude is taken toward active euthanasia. And finally, we have examined the position of the medical establishment in our own country, according to which active euthanasia is always "contrary to that for which the medical profession stands," even though passive euthanasia is said to be in some circumstances all right. But, while all of this is valuable as background information, none of it directly touches the most important issue. We want to know, most of all, whether euthanasia—active or passive—*really is moral,* or whether in fact it is immoral.

How are we to go about answering this question? We cannot discover whether euthanasia is immoral simply by consulting our feelings. Our feelings may be nothing more than irrational prejudice; they may have nothing to do with the truth. At one time most people "felt" that people of other races are inferior, and that slavery is God's own plan. Our feelings about euthanasia may also be mistaken, so we cannot rely on them.

If we want to discover the truth about euthanasia, there is only one way this can be done, namely, by examining and analyzing the *arguments,* or reasons, that can be given for and against it. If cogent, logical arguments can be given in favor of euthanasia, and if at the same time the arguments against it can be refuted, then it is morally acceptable, no matter what emotions or preconceptions one might have. And likewise, if upon analyzing the arguments, we find that the strongest case is against euthanasia, we shall have to conclude that it is immoral, no matter what our feelings were previously.

This is true not only of euthanasia but of any moral matter whatever. A moral judgment—*any* moral judgment—is true only if there are good reasons in its support. If someone tells you that you ought to do something, or that a certain action would be wrong, you may ask *why* you ought to do it, or why that action would be wrong, and if no answer can be given, you may reject that advice as arbitrary and unfounded. In this way moral judgments are very different from mere expressions of preference. If someone says "I like coffee," there does not have to be a *reason;* this is merely a statement about individual tastes. And if someone else says "I don't like coffee," this is merely a statement about *different* personal tastes. There is nothing for these two to argue about, and there is no question of who is right and who is wrong (they are both right). There is no such thing as "rationally supporting" one's like or dislike of coffee. However, when *moral* claims are being made, rational support is in order; and the truth is simply the position that has the best reasons on its side. The attempt to determine what is true in morals, then, is always a matter of analyzing and weighing up reasons. Otherwise, morality degenerates into nothing more than prejudice, propaganda, and crass self-interest, without claim on any rational person.

§13 THE ARGUMENT FROM MERCY

Preliminary Statement of the Argument   The single most powerful argument in support of euthanasia is the argument from mercy. It is also an exceptionally simple argument, at least in its main idea, which makes one uncomplicated point. Terminal patients sometimes suffer pain so horrible that it is beyond the comprehension of those who have not actually experienced it. Their suffering can be so terrible that we do not like even to read about it or think about it; we recoil even from the descriptions of such agony. The argument from mercy says: Euthanasia is justified because it provides an end to *that.*

The great Irish satirist Jonathan Swift took eight years to die, while, in the words of Joseph Fletcher, "His mind crumbled to pieces."[13] At times the pain in his blinded eyes was so intense he had to be restrained from tearing them out with his own hands. Knives and other potential instruments of suicide had to be kept from him. For the last three years of his life, he could do nothing but sit and drool; and when he finally died it was only after convulsions that lasted thirty-six hours.

Swift died in 1745. Since then, doctors have learned how to eliminate much of the pain that accompanies terminal illness, but the victory has been far from complete. So, here is a more modern example.

Stewart Alsop was a respected journalist who died in 1975 of a rare form of cancer. Before he died, he wrote movingly of his experiences as a terminal patient. Although he had not thought much about euthanasia before, he came to approve of it after rooming briefly with someone he called Jack:

> The third night that I roomed with Jack in our tiny double room in the solid-tumor ward of the cancer clinic of the National Institutes of Health in Bethesda, Md., a terrible thought occurred to me.
> Jack had a melanoma in his belly, a malignant solid tumor that the doctors guessed was about the size of a softball. The cancer had started a few months before with a small tumor in his left shoulder, and there had been several operations since. The doctors planned to remove the softball-sized tumor, but they knew Jack would soon die. The cancer had metastasized—it had spread beyond control.
> Jack was good-looking, about 28, and brave. He was in constant

pain, and his doctor had prescribed an intravenous shot of a synthetic opiate—a pain-killer, or analgesic—every four hours. His wife spent many of the daylight hours with him, and she would sit or lie on his bed and pat him all over, as one pats a child, only more methodically, and this seemed to help control the pain. But at night, when his pretty wife had left (wives cannot stay overnight at the NIH clinic) and darkness fell, the pain would attack without pity.

At the prescribed hour, a nurse would give Jack a shot of the synthetic analgesic, and this would control the pain for perhaps two hours or a bit more. Then he would begin to moan, or whimper, very low, as though he didn't want to wake me. Then he would begin to howl, like a dog.

When this happened, either he or I would ring for a nurse, and ask for a pain-killer. She would give him some codeine or the like by mouth, but it never did any real good—it affected him no more than half an aspirin might affect a man who had just broken his arm. Always the nurse would explain as encouragingly as she could that there was not long to go before the next intravenous shot—"Only about 50 minutes now." And always poor Jack's whimpers and howls would become more loud and frequent until at last the blessed relief came.

The third night of this routine, the terrible thought occurred to me. "If Jack were a dog," I thought, "what would be done with him?" The answer was obvious: the pound, and chloroform. No human being with a spark of pity could let a living thing suffer so, to no good end.[14]

The NIH clinic is, of course, one of the most modern and best-equipped hospitals we have. Jack's suffering was not the result of poor treatment in some backward rural facility; it was the inevitable product of his disease, which medical science was powerless to prevent.

I have quoted Alsop at length not for the sake of indulging in gory details but to give a clear idea of the kind of suffering we are talking about. We should not gloss over these facts with euphemistic language, or squeamishly avert our eyes from them. For only by keeping them firmly and vividly in mind can we appreciate the full force of the argument from mercy: If a person prefers—and even begs for—death as the only alternative to lingering on *in this kind of torment,* only to die anyway after a while, then surely it is not immoral to help this person die sooner. As Alsop put it, "No human being with a spark of pity could let a living thing suffer so, to no good end."

The Utilitarian Version of the Argument In connection with this argument, the utilitarians should be mentioned again. They argued that actions and social policies should be judged right or wrong *exclusively* according to whether they cause happiness or misery; and they argued that when judged by this standard, euthanasia turns out to be morally acceptable. The utilitarian argument may be elaborated as follows:

1. Any action or social policy is morally right if it serves to increase the amount of happiness in the world or to decrease the

amount of misery. Conversely, an action or social policy is morally wrong if it serves to decrease happiness or to increase misery.

2. The policy of killing, at their own request, hopelessly ill patients who are suffering great pain, would decrease the amount of misery in the world. (An example could be Alsop's friend Jack.)

3. Therefore, such a policy would be morally right.

The first premise of this argument, (1), states the Principle of Utility, which is the basic utilitarian assumption. Today most philosophers think that this principle is wrong, because they think that the promotion of happiness and the avoidance of misery are not the *only* morally important things. Happiness, they say, is only one among many values that should be promoted: freedom, justice, and a respect for people's rights are also important. To take one example: People *might* be happier if there were no freedom of religion; for, if everyone adhered to the same religious beliefs, there would be greater harmony among people. There would be no unhappiness caused within families by Jewish girls marrying Catholic boys, and so forth. Moreover, if people were brainwashed well enough, no one would mind not having freedom of choice. Thus happiness would be increased. But, the argument continues, even if happiness *could* be increased this way, it would not be right to deny people freedom of religion, because people have a right to make their own choices. Therefore, the first premise of the utilitarian argument is unacceptable.

There is a related difficulty for utilitarianism, which connects more directly with the topic of euthanasia. Suppose a person is leading a miserable life—full of more unhappiness than happiness—but does *not* want to die. This person thinks that a miserable life is better than none at all. Now I assume that we would all agree that the person should not be killed; that would be plain, unjustifiable murder. Yet it *would* decrease the amount of misery in the world if we killed this person—it would lead to an increase in the balance of happiness over unhappiness—and so it is hard to see how, on strictly utilitarian grounds, it could be wrong. Again, the Principle of Utility seems to be an inadequate guide for determining right and wrong. So we are on shaky ground if we rely on *this* version of the argument from mercy for a defense of euthanasia.

Doing What Is in Everyone's Best Interests   Although the foregoing utilitarian argument is faulty, it is nevertheless based on a sound idea. For even if the promotion of happiness and avoidance of misery are not the *only* morally important things, they are still very important. So, when an action or a social policy would decrease misery, that is *a* very strong reason in its favor. In the cases of voluntary euthanasia we are now considering, great suffering is eliminated, and since the patient requests it, there is no question of violating individual rights.

That is why, regardless of the difficulties of the Principle of Utility, the utilitarian version of the argument still retains considerable force.

I want now to present a somewhat different version of the argument from mercy, which is inspired by utilitarianism but which avoids the difficulties of the foregoing version by not making the Principle of Utility a premise of the argument. I believe that the following argument is sound and proves that active euthanasia *can* be justified:

1. If an action promotes the best interests of *everyone* concerned, and violates *no one's* rights, then that action is morally acceptable.
2. In at least some cases, active euthanasia promotes the best interests of everyone concerned and violates no one's rights.
3. Therefore, in at least some cases active euthanasia is morally acceptable.

It would have been in everyone's best interests if active euthanasia had been employed in the case of Stewart Alsop's friend Jack. First, and most important, it would have been in Jack's own interests, since it would have provided him with an easier, better death, without pain. (Who among us would choose Jack's death, if we had a choice, rather than a quick painless death?) Second, it would have been in the best interests of Jack's wife. Her misery, helplessly watching him suffer, must have been almost equal to his. Third, the hospital staff's best interests would have been served, since if Jack's dying had not been prolonged, they could have turned their attention to other patients whom they could have helped. Fourth, other patients would have benefited since medical resources would no longer have been used in the sad, pointless maintenance of Jack's physical existence. Finally, if Jack himself requested to be killed, the act would not have violated his rights. Considering all this, how can active euthanasia in this case be wrong? How can it be wrong to do an action that is merciful, that benefits everyone concerned, and that violates no one's rights?

§14 THE ARGUMENT FROM THE GOLDEN RULE

"Do unto others as you would have them do unto you" is one of the oldest and most familiar moral maxims. Stated in just that way, it is not a very good maxim: Suppose a sexual pervert started treating others as he would like to be treated himself; we might not be happy with the results. Nevertheless, the basic idea behind the Golden Rule is a good one. The basic idea is that moral rules apply impartially to everyone alike; therefore, you cannot say that you are justified in treating someone else in a certain way unless you are willing to admit that that person would also be justified in treating *you* in that way if your positions were reversed.

Kant and the Golden Rule   The great German philosopher Immanuel Kant (1724–1804) incorporated the basic idea of the Golden Rule into his system of ethics. Kant argued that we should act only on rules that we are willing to have applied universally; that is, we should behave as we would be willing to have *everyone* behave. He held that there is one supreme principle of morality, which he called "the Categorical Imperative." The Categorical Imperative says;

> Act only according to that maxim by which you can at the same time will that it should become a universal law.[15]

Let us discuss what this means. When we are trying to decide whether we ought to do a certain action, we must first ask what general rule or principle we would be following if we did it. Then, we ask whether we would be willing for everyone to follow that rule, in similar circumstances. (This determines whether "the maxim of the act"—the rule we would be following—can be "willed" to be "a universal law.") If we would not be willing for the rule to be followed universally, then we should not follow it ourselves. Thus, if we are not willing for others to apply the rule to *us*, we ought not apply it to *them*.

In the eighteenth chapter of St. Matthew's gospel there is a story that perfectly illustrates this point. A man is owed money by another, who cannot pay, and so he has the debtor thrown into prison. But he himself owes money to the king and begs that *his* debt be forgiven. At first the king forgives the debt. However, when the king hears how this man has treated the one who owed him, he changes his mind and "delivers him unto the tormentors" until he can pay. The moral is clear: If you do not think that others should apply the rule "Don't forgive debts!" to *you*, then you should not apply it to others.

The application of all this to the question of euthanasia is fairly obvious. Each of us is going to die someday, although most of us do not know when or how. But suppose you were told that you would die in one of two ways, and you were asked to choose between them. First, you could die quietly, and without pain, from a fatal injection. Or second, you could choose to die of an affliction so painful that for several days before death you would be reduced to howling like a dog, with your family standing by helplessly, trying to comfort you, but going through its own psychological hell. It is hard to believe that any sane person, when confronted by these possibilities, would choose to have a rule applied that would force upon him or her the second option. And if we would not want such a rule, which excludes euthanasia, applied to us, then we should not apply such a rule to others.

Implications for Christians   There is a considerable irony here. Kant, as we have already noted, was personally opposed to active euthanasia, yet his own Categorical Imperative seems to sanction it. The larger irony, however, is for those in the Christian Church who have for centuries opposed active euthanasia. According to the New Testament accounts, Jesus himself promulgated the Golden Rule as the supreme moral principle—"This is the Law and the Prophets," he said. But if this is the supreme principle of morality, then how can active euthanasia be always wrong? If I would have it done to me, how can it be wrong for me to do likewise to others?

R. M. Hare has made this point with great force. A Christian as well as a leading contemporary moral philosopher, Hare has long argued that "universalizability" is one of the central characteristics of moral judgment. ('Universalizability' is the name he gives to the basic idea embodied in both the Golden Rule and the Categorical Imperative. It means that a moral judgment must conform to universal principles, which apply to everyone alike, if it is to be acceptable.) In an article called "Euthanasia: A Christian View," Hare argues that Christians, if they took Christ's teachings about the Golden Rule seriously, would not think that euthanasia is always wrong. He gives this (true) example:

> The driver of a petrol lorry [i.e., a gas truck] was in an accident in which his tanker overturned and immediately caught fire. He himself was trapped in the cab and could not be freed. He therefore besought the bystanders to kill him by hitting him on the head, so that he would not roast to death. I think that somebody did this, but I do not know what happened in court afterwards.
>
> Now will you please all ask yourselves, as I have many times asked myself, what you wish that men should do to you if you were in the situation of that driver. I cannot believe that anybody who considered the matter seriously, as if he himself were going to be in that situation and had now to give instructions as to what rule the bystanders should follow, would say that the rule should be one ruling out euthanasia absolutely.[16]

We might note that *active* euthanasia is the only option here; the concept of passive euthanasia, in these circumstances, has no application.

We have looked at two arguments supporting the morality of active euthanasia. Now let us turn to some arguments that support the opposite view, that active euthanasia is immoral.

IV. ARGUMENTS OPPOSING THE MORALITY OF ACTIVE EUTHANASIA

§15 THE ARGUMENT FROM THE WRONGNESS OF KILLING

Almost everyone accepts the principle of the value of human life, in one form or another. Religious people speak of the "sanctity" of life, and although nonreligious people may not like the theological overtones of the word 'sanctity', they nevertheless agree that human life is precious and ought to be protected. They all agree that it is wrong to kill people. The simplest and most obvious objection to active euthanasia, then, is that it is a violation of the moral rule against killing.

But to this the advocate of euthanasia has an easy answer. The rule against killing is not absolute; it has exceptions. People may disagree about exactly which exceptions should be allowed, but there is general agreement that there *are* exceptions. Most people would agree that it is permissible to kill in self-defense, if that is the only way to prevent someone from murdering you. Others would add that it is permissible to kill in time of war, provided that the war is just and you are observing the rules of war. Some think that capital punishment is morally permissible, as a way of dealing with vicious murderers. Others believe that abortion is a justified exception to the rule. Thus, even though killing people is *usually* wrong, it is not *always* wrong. And once this much is admitted, defenders of euthanasia can simply claim that euthanasia is one of the justified exceptions to the rule.

There are two arguments that might be given to show that euthanasia is a justified exception to the rule. First, killing is objectionable only because, in normal cases, the person who is killed loses something of great value—life itself. In being deprived of life, a person is *harmed*. In euthanasia, however, this is not true. If a dying person, whose life holds nothing but torment, says that such a life no longer has value, that surely can be a reasonable judgment. We are not doing harm by putting an end to the person's misery. So, in the special case of euthanasia we do not have the same reasons for objecting to killing that we have in the normal cases. Second, killing a person is, usually, a violation of the individual's right to life. But if a person *asks* to be killed, the killing is not a violation of individual rights. (This is a general point that applies to other rights as well. If, for example, you steal something that belongs to me, you violate my property rights; but if I ask you to take it, and you do, then you do not violate my rights.) For these reasons, saying that euthanasia is a violation of the rule against killing is not enough to prove that it is wrong.

§16 RELIGIOUS ARGUMENTS

Religious people often oppose euthanasia and claim that it is immoral, but there is often nothing particularly religious about the *arguments* they use. The argument from the wrongness of killing, for example, does not require any theological assumptions. Therefore, when assessing that argument, we did not need to get into any matters of religion at all.

There are some other arguments, however, that are distinctively religious. Since these arguments do require theological assumptions, they have little appeal to nonreligious people or to religious people whose presuppositions are different. Here are three of the most popular such arguments:

a. What God Forbids   It is sometimes said that active euthanasia is not permissible simply because God forbids it, and we know that God forbids it by the authority of either Scripture or Church tradition.

Thus, one eighteenth-century religionist wrote that, in the case of aged and infirm animals,

> God, the Father of Mercies, hath ordained Beasts and Birds of Prey to do that distressed creature the kindness to relieve him his misery, by putting him to death. A kindness which *We* dare not show to our own species. If thy father, thy brother, or thy child should suffer the utmost pains of a long and agonizing sickness, though his groans should pierce through thy heart, and with strong crying and tears he should beg thy relief, yet thou must be deaf unto him; he must wait his appointed time till his charge cometh, till he sinks and is crushed with the weight of his own misery.[17]

When this argument is advanced, it is usually advanced with great confidence, as though it were *obvious* what God requires. Yet we may well wonder whether such confidence is justified. The Sixth Commandment does not say, literally, "Thou shalt not *kill*"—that is a bad translation. A better translation is "Thou shalt not *murder*," which is different, and which does not obviously prohibit euthanasia. Murder is by definition *wrongful* killing; so, if you do not think that a given kind of killing is wrong, you will not call it murder. That is why the Sixth Commandment is not normally taken to forbid killing in a just war; since such killing is (allegedly) justified, it is not called murder. Similarly, if euthanasia is justified, it is not murder, and so it is not prohibited by the commandment. At any rate, it is clear that we cannot infer that euthanasia is wrong *because* it is prohibited by the commandment.

If we look elsewhere in the Christian Bible for a condemnation of euthanasia, we cannot find it. These scriptures are silent on the question. We do find numerous affirmations of the sanctity of human life and of the Fatherhood of God, and some theologians have tried to infer a prohibition of euthanasia from these general precepts. But we also find exhortations to kindness and mercy, and the Golden Rule proclaimed as the sum of all morality; and these principles, as we have seen, support euthanasia rather than condemn it.

We *do* find a clear condemnation of euthanasia in Church traditions. Regardless of whether there is scriptural authority for it, the Church has historically opposed mercy killing. It should be emphasized, however, that this is a matter of history. Today, many religious leaders favor active euthanasia and think that the historical position of the Church has been mistaken. It was an Episcopal minister, Joseph Fletcher, who in his book *Morals and Medicine*[18] formulated the classic modern defense of euthanasia. Fletcher does not stand alone among his fellow churchmen. The Euthanasia Society of America, which he heads, includes many other religious leaders; and the recent "Plea for Beneficent Euthanasia," sponsored by the American Humanist Association, was signed by more religious leaders than persons in any other category.[19] So it certainly cannot be claimed that *contemporary* religious forces stand uniformly opposed to active euthanasia.

It is noteworthy that even Roman Catholic thinkers are today reassessing the Church's traditional ban on mercy killing. The Catholic philosopher Daniel Maguire, of Marquette University, has written one of the best books on the subject, *Death by Choice*.[20] Maguire maintains that "it may be moral and should be legal to accelerate the death process by taking direct action, such as overdosing with morphine or injecting potassium"; and moreover, he proposes to demonstrate that this view is *"compatible with historical Catholic ethical theory,"* contrary to what most opponents of mercy killing assume! Historical Catholic ethical theory, he says, grants individuals permission to act on views that are supported by "good and serious reasons," even when a different view is supported by a majority of authorities. Since the morality of active euthanasia *is* supported by "good and serious reasons," Maguire concludes that Catholics are permitted to accept that morality and act on it. At the very least, they do *not* have to assume that euthanasia is immoral because "God forbids it."

b. The Idea of God's Dominion   Our second theological argument starts from the principle that "The life of man is solely under the dominion of God." It is for God alone to decide when a person shall live and when he shall die; therefore, we have no right to "play God" and arrogate this decision unto ourselves. So euthanasia is forbidden.[21]

The most remarkable thing about this argument is that people still advance it today, even though it was decisively refuted over 200 years ago by the great British philosopher David Hume. Hume made the simple but devastating point that *if it is for God alone to decide when we shall live and when we shall die, then we "play God" just as much when we cure people as when we kill them.* Suppose a person is sick and we have the medicine to cure him or her. If we do cure the person, then we are interfering with God's right to decide whether a person will live or die! Hume put the point this way:

> Were the disposal of human life so much reserved as the peculiar providence of the Almighty that it were an encroachment on his right, for men to dispose of their own lives; it would be equally criminal to act for the preservation of life as for its destruction. If I turn aside a stone which is falling upon my head, I disturb this course of nature, and I invade the peculiar providence of the Almighty by lengthening out my life beyond the period which by the general laws of matter and motion he had assigned it.[22]

We alter the length of a person's life when we save it just as much as when we take it. Therefore, if the taking of life is to be forbidden on the grounds that only God has the right to determine how long a person shall live, then the saving of life should be prohibited on the same grounds. We would then have to abolish the practice of medicine. But everyone concedes that this would be absurd. Therefore, we may *not* prohibit active euthanasia on the grounds that only God has the right to determine how long a life shall last. This seems to be a complete refutation of this argument.

c. Suffering and God's Plan   The last religious argument we shall consider is the following. Suffering is a part of life; God has ordained that we must suffer as part of his Divine plan. Therefore, if we were to kill people to "put them out of their misery," we would be interfering with God's plan. Bishop Joseph Sullivan, a prominent Catholic opponent of euthanasia, expresses the argument in this passage from his essay "The Immorality of Euthanasia":

> If the suffering patient is of sound mind and capable of making an act of divine resignation, then his sufferings become a great means of merit whereby he can gain reward for himself and also win great favors for the souls in Purgatory, perhaps even release them from their suffering. Likewise the sufferer may give good example to his family and friends and teach them how to bear a heavy cross in a Christlike manner.
>
> As regard those that must live in the same house with the incurable sufferer, they have a great opportunity to practice Christian charity. They can learn to see Christ in the sufferer and win the reward promised in the Beatitudes. This opportunity for charity would hold true even when the incurable sufferer is deprived of the use of reason. It may well be that the incurable sufferer in a particular case may be of greater value to society than when he was of some material value to himself and his community.[23]

This argument may strike some people as simply grotesque. Can we imagine this being said, seriously, in the presence of suffering such as that experienced by Stewart Alsop's friend Jack? "We know it hurts, Jack, and that your wife is being torn apart just having to watch it, but think of what a good opportunity this is for you to set an example. You can give us a lesson in how to bear it." In addition, some might think that euthanasia is exactly what *is* required by the "charity" that bystanders have the opportunity to practice.

But, these reactions aside, there is a more fundamental difficulty with the argument. For if the argument were sound, it would lead not only to the condemnation of euthanasia but of *any* measures to reduce suffering. If God decrees that we suffer, why aren't we obstructing God's plan when we give drugs to relieve pain? A girl breaks her arm; if only God knows how much pain is right for her, who are we to mend it? The point is similar to Hume's refutation of the previous argument: This argument, like the previous one, cannot be right because it leads to consequences that no one, not even the most conservative religious thinker, is willing to accept.

Conclusion   Each of these three arguments depends on religious assumptions. I have tried to show that they are all bad arguments, but I have *not* criticized them simply by rejecting their religious presuppositions. Instead, I have criticized them on their own terms, showing that these arguments should not be accepted even by religious people. As Daniel Maguire emphasizes, the ethics of theists, like the ethics of all responsible people, should be determined by "good and serious reasons," and these arguments are not good no matter what world view one has.

§17 THE POSSIBILITY OF UNEXPECTED CURES

We have seen that euthanasia cannot be proved immoral by the argument that killing is always wrong, and that the most popular religious arguments against it are unsound. There is one additional argument we must now consider. Euthanasia may be opposed on the grounds that we cannot really tell when a patient's condition is hopeless. There are cases in which patients have recovered even after doctors had given up hope; if those patients had been killed, it would have been tragic, for they would have been deprived of many additional years of life. According to this argument, euthanasia is immoral because we never know for certain that the patient's situation is hopeless. *Any* so-called hopeless case might defy the odds and recover.

Those who advance this argument usually intend it as an argument against active euthanasia but not passive euthanasia. Nevertheless, we should notice that if this argument were sound it would rule out passive euthanasia as well. Suppose we allow someone to die by ceasing treatment; for example, we disconnect the artificial life-support systems that are necessary to maintain life. It *may* be that, if we had continued the treatment, the patient would eventually have recovered. Therefore, we cannot appeal to the possibility of unexpected recovery as an objection to active euthanasia without also objecting to passive euthanasia on the same grounds.

It must be admitted that doctors have sometimes made mistakes in labeling patients as "hopeless," and so we should be *very* cautious in any given case before saying that there is no chance of recovery. But it does *not* follow from the fact that doctors have *sometimes* been mistaken that they can *never* know for sure that any patient is hopeless. That would be like saying that since some people have sometimes confused a Rolls Royce with a Mercedes, no one can ever be certain which is which. In fact, doctors do sometimes know for sure that a patient cannot recover. There may be spontaneous remissions of cancer, for example, at a relatively early stage of the disease. But after the cancer has spread throughout the body and reached an advanced stage of development, there will be no hope whatever. Although there may be some doubt about some cases—and when there is doubt, perhaps euthanasia should not be considered—no one with the slightest medical knowledge could have had any doubt about Alsop's friend Jack. He was going to die of that cancer, and that is all there was to it. No one has *ever* recovered from such a dreadful condition, and doctors can explain exactly why this is so.

The same goes for patients in irreversible coma. Sometimes there is doubt about whether the patient can ever wake up. But in other cases there is no doubt, because of extensive brain damage that makes waking impossible. This is not merely a layman's judgment. Some of the best minds in the medical profession have argued that, in carefully defined cases, persons in irreversible coma should be regarded as *already dead!* In 1968, the *Journal of the American Medical Association* published the report of a committee of the Harvard Medical School, under the chairmanship of Dr. Henry K. Beecher, containing such a recommendation.[24] This report spells out, in precise terms, "the characteristics of a *permanently* nonfunctioning brain." There are four clinical signs of brain death. First, there is no response to stimuli that would be quite painful if felt; second, there is no movement or spontaneous breathing; third, there are no reflexes, such as swallowing or contraction of the pupils in response to bright light; and finally, there is an isoelectric (sometimes mistakenly called a "flat") electroencephalogram. It is noteworthy that all these signs may be present even while the heart still beats spontaneously, without the aid of machines. Yet the Harvard committee assures us that when these signs are present for a twenty-four-hour period, we may as well declare the patient dead.

What, then, are we to conclude from the fact that doctors have sometimes been mistaken in declaring patients hopeless? We may surely conclude that extreme care should be taken so as to avoid other such mistakes, and we may perhaps conclude that in any case where there is the slightest doubt, euthanasia should not be considered. However, we may *not* conclude that doctors *never* know when a case is hopeless. Sadly, we know that in some cases there simply is no hope, and so in those cases the possibility of an unexpected cure cannot be held out as an objection to euthanasia.

V. THE QUESTION OF LEGALIZATION

We turn now to the question of whether euthanasia ought to be illegal, which is different from the question of whether it is immoral. Some people believe that, even if euthanasia is immoral, it still should not be prohibited by law, since if a patient *wants* to die, that is strictly a personal affair, regardless of how foolish or immoral the desire might be. On this view, euthanasia is comparable to sexual promiscuity; both are matters for private, individual decision and not government coercion, regardless of what moral judgment one might make. Others take a very different view and argue that active euthanasia *must* remain illegal, even if some individual acts of euthanasia are morally good, because the *consequences* of legalizing active euthanasia would be so terrible. They argue that legalized euthanasia would lead to a break-down in respect for life that would eventually make all of our lives less secure. We shall consider the merits of these two arguments in §§ 20 and 21 below. But first, let us study something of the present legal situation respecting euthanasia.

§18 HOW MERCY KILLERS ARE TREATED IN COURT

In 1939, a poor immigrant named Repouille, living in California, killed his 13-year-old son with chloroform. The boy, one of five children in the family, had suffered a brain injury at birth that left him virtually mindless, blind, mute, deformed in all four limbs, and with no control over his bladder or bowels. His whole life was spent in a small crib.

Repouille was tried for manslaughter in the first degree—apparently the prosecutor was unwilling to try him for first-degree murder, even though technically that charge could have been brought—but the jury, obviously sympathetic with him, brought in a verdict of *second*-degree manslaughter. From a legal point of view their verdict made no sense, since second-degree manslaughter presupposes that the killing was not intentional. Obviously the jury was intent on convicting him on only the mildest possible offense, so they ignored this legal nicety. They further indicated their desire to forgive the defendant by accompanying the verdict with a recommendation for "utmost clemency." The judge agreed with them and complied by staying execution of the five-to-ten-year sentence and placing Repouille on probation.[25]

What Repouille did was clearly illegal, but the lenient treatment he received is typical of those tried for "mercy killing" in American courts. (The court regarded this as a case of euthanasia, even though it does not fit our strict definition.) Sometimes, as in the case of Robert Weskin, the jury will simply find the defendant not guilty. Weskin's mother was dying of leukemia in a Chicago hospital, in terrible pain, and Weskin took a gun into the hospital and shot her three times. He made no attempt to hide what he had done, saying, "She's out of her misery now. I shot her." He was indicted for murder, and legally it was an open-and-shut case. But the jury refused to convict him.[26]

From a strictly legal point of view, the juries' actions in both the Repouille case and the Weskin case were incorrect. In practice, however, juries have great discretion and can do practically anything they choose. (About the only thing they can't do is convict a defendant of a *more serious* charge than is made in the indictment.) What juries choose to do depends very much on the details of the particular case. For example, if the *manner* of the killing is especially gruesome, or if the killer tries to lie his way out, a jury might not be so sympathetic:

> In one case a lawyer killed his six-month-old mongoloid son by wrapping an uninsulated electrical cord around his wet diaper and putting the baby on a silver platter to insure good contact before plugging the cord into the wall. At the trial he claimed that the child's death

was an accident, and he was convicted of first-degree murder and sentenced to electrocution himself, although the sentence was later commuted to life.[27]

There have been only two occasions on which *doctors* have been tried for mercy killing in this country. In New Hampshire in 1950, Dr. Herman Sander gave a patient four intravenous injections of air and then noted on the patient's chart that he had done so. The patient, who had terminal cancer, had asked to be put out of her misery. At the trial, the defense claimed that the patient was already dead at the time of the injections—which was a bit strange, since if the woman was already dead why were the injections given? Anyway, the jury acquitted Dr. Sander. The next such trial of a physician, and the only other one in the United States to date, occurred twenty-four years later in New York. Dr. Vincent Montemareno was charged with giving a lethal injection of potassium chloride to a patient with terminal cancer. At first the prosecutor announced that the case would be tried as a case of mercy killing; Dr. Montemareno, he said, had killed the patient to put her out of misery. But by the time the trial opened, the prosecutor had changed his mind and claimed that the doctor had murdered the patient for his own convenience, so that he would not have to return to the hospital later in the evening. At the conclusion of the trial the jury promptly voted to acquit.

But whatever juries may or may not do, active euthanasia is clearly against the law. The legal status of passive euthanasia is more uncertain. In practice, doctors do allow hopeless patients to die, and as we have seen, the American Medical Association officially endorses this policy when the patient or his family requests it and when "extraordinary" means would be required to keep the patient alive. The legal status of such actions (or nonactions) is uncertain because, although there are laws against "negligent homicide" under which criminal charges could be brought, no such charges have been brought so far. Here district attorneys, and not juries, have exercised their discretion and have not pressed the issue.

It makes an important difference from a legal point of view whether a case of passive euthanasia is voluntary or nonvoluntary. Any patient—except one who has been declared legally "incompetent" to withhold consent—always has the right to refuse medical treatment. By refusing treatment, a patient can bring about his or her own death and the doctor cannot be convicted for "letting the person die." It is *nonvoluntary* passive euthanasia, in which the patient does not request to be allowed to die, that is legally uncertain.

§19 THE CASE OF KAREN ANN QUINLAN

There has been one famous case in which the question of nonvoluntary passive euthanasia was put before the courts. In April 1975, a 21-year-old woman named Karen Ann Quinlan, for reasons that were never made clear, ceased breathing for at least two fifteen-minute periods. As a result, she suffered severe brain damage, and, in the words of the attending physicians, was reduced to "a chronic persistent vegetative state" in which she "no longer had any cognitive function." Accepting the doctors' judgment that there was no hope of recovery, her parents sought permission from the courts to disconnect the respirator that was keeping her alive in the intensive-care unit of a New Jersey hospital. The Quinlans are Roman Catholics, and they made this request only after consulting with their priest, who assured them that there would be no moral or religious objection if Karen were allowed to die.

Various medical experts testified in support of the Quinlans's request. One doctor described what he called the concept of "judicious neglect," under which a physician will say: "Don't treat this patient anymore . . . It does not serve either the patient, the family, or society in any meaningful way to continue treatment with this patient." This witness also explained the use of the initials 'DNR'—"Do Not Resuscitate"—by which doctors instruct hospital staff to permit death. He said:

> No physician that I know personally is going to try and resuscitate a man riddled with cancer and in agony and he stops breathing. They are not going to put him on a respirator . . . I think that would be the height of misuse of technology.[28]

The trial court, and then the Supreme Court of New Jersey, agreed that the respirator could be removed and Karen Quinlan allowed to die in peace. The respirator was disconnected. However, the nuns in charge of her care in the Catholic hospital opposed this decision, and anticipating it, had begun to wean Karen from the respirator so that by the time it was disconnected she could remain alive without it. (Reviewing these events, one prominent Catholic scholar commented angrily, "Some nuns always were holier than the church."[29]) So Karen did not die; and at this writing she remains in her "persistent vegetative state," emaciated and with deformed limbs and with no hope of ever awakening, but still alive in the biological sense.

It is anticipated that the Quinlan decision will set a precedent for future cases, and that the legal right to terminate treatment in such circumstances will become established. If so, then the law will not have been particulary innovative; it will only have caught up, somewhat belatedly, with medical practice, public opinion, and the best thought of the day concerning passive euthanasia. The question that will then remain is: What about *active* euthanasia? Should *it* be legalized, too?

§20 AN ARGUMENT FOR LEGALIZING ACTIVE EUTHANASIA: THE RIGHT TO LIBERTY

Should active euthanasia be legalized? We have already reached a number of conclusions that bear on this issue. We have seen that there are powerful arguments supporting the view that active euthanasia is morally permissible, and that the arguments opposing it are weak. If active euthanasia is moral, as these arguments suggest, why should it not be made legal? We have noted that whenever charges have been brought against "mercy killers," prosecutors have had great difficulty securing convictions. Juries have not wanted to punish genuine mercy killers, and judges have not been willing to impose heavy sentences. So if active euthanasia were legalized, it would seem little more than an official acknowledgment of attitudes that already exist in the court-room.

However, none of this really proves that active euthanasia ought to be legalized. We need to turn now to arguments that are addressed more directly to the issue of legalization. One such argument is the "argument from the right to liberty." According to this argument, each dying patient should be free to choose euthanasia, or to reject it, simply as a matter of personal liberty. No one, including the government, has the right to tell another what choice to make. If a dying patient wants euthanasia, that is a private affair; after all, the life belongs to the individual, and so that individual should be the one to decide.

Mill's Principle   This argument starts from the principle that people should be free to live their own lives as they themselves think best. But of course the right to liberty is not completely unrestricted. We should not be free to murder or rape or steal. It is an interesting theoretical problem to explain why *those* restrictions should be placed on our freedom, while many other restrictions are unacceptable. The classical solution to this problem was provided by Bentham, who observed that in murder, rape, and theft, *we are doing harm to other people.* That, he reasoned, is what makes the difference. So he suggested this principle: People's freedom may be restricted only to prevent them from doing harm to others. Bentham's famous disciple, John Stuart Mill, gave this principle its most elegant expression when he wrote:

> ... the sole end for which mankind are warranted, individually or collectively, in interfering with the liberty of action of any of their number, is self-protection. The only purpose for which power can be rightfully exercised over any member of a civilized community, against his will, is to prevent harm to others. His own good, either physical or moral, is not a sufficient warrant ... Over himself, over his own body and mind, the individual is sovereign.[30]

With apologies to Bentham, I will call this "Mill's Principle." There are two general classes of interferences that Mill's Principle would prohibit. First, we cannot force a person to conform to our ideas of right and wrong so long as the person is not harming others. Take homosexuality, for example. Many people think that homosexual behavior is immoral. The implication of Mill's principle is that, even if it were immoral, we have no business trying to force people to stop being homosexuals; for so long as they harm no one else, it is no one else's business what they do in private. It is important to notice that this argument does *not* depend on the assumption that homosexuality is morally all right (although, indeed, it well might be). It simply does not matter, so far as this argument is concerned, whether it is moral or immoral. All that matters is whether homosexuals, as a result of their homosexuality, do any harm to other people. If they do not, then others have no right to force their moral views on them.

Second, if Mill's Principle is correct, then we may not interfere with a person's actions "for his own good." We may think people are behaving foolishly, for example, if they invest their money in a highly speculative stock. And suppose they are. The point is that, if it is *their* money and only they will be hurt by it, then it is their business and we have no right to interfere. Now we might have the right to *advise* them against the investment, and urge them not to make it, but in the end it is their decision and not ours. The same goes for other, similar cases. If someone is feeling poorly, we may advise or urge a visit to a doctor, but we have no right to force this on a person, even "for his own good." It is one's own health, and, as Mill put it, "Over himself, over his own mind and body, the individual is sovereign." (Mill excluded children and mental incompetents from the scope of this rule on the grounds that they are incapable of making rational choices concerning their own interests.)

Implications for Euthanasia   If Bentham and Mill are correct, a terminal patient who wishes to end his or her life rather than continue suffering certainly has the right to do so. The life belongs to the individual; no one else has the right to interfere; and that's that. But this only establishes a right to *suicide* in such cases. A further, additional step is required to reach the conclusion that we may kill the person. It is, however, easy to see how to provide the extra step in the argument. Mill's Principle covers not only the actions of individuals acting alone but of groups of individuals who voluntarily agree to act together. Homosexual alliances, for example, do not involve individuals acting alone but groups of two or more. The relevant question is: Does their conduct affect anyone other than themselves, the "consenting adults" who are involved in the affair? If not, then others have no right to interfere. An act of euthanasia, in which the patient requests a lethal drug and the doctor provides it, is a "private affair" in this sense; those participating are "consenting adults," and no one else's interests need be involved. Therefore, if we are to respect the right to liberty of dying patients, we must respect their right to enter into euthanasia agreements with their doctors, or with any other competent adults willing to help them.

This argument can also be made to apply to patients in irreversible coma, in the following way. Of course patients in irreversible coma are not able to request that they be killed or allowed to die. Nevertheless, they may leave instructions beforehand that if their condition becomes hopeless, they are to be killed or allowed to die. Some state medical societies have actually encouraged patients to leave such instructions and have designed forms for this purpose. Like the American Medical Association, these societies do not condone killing, but they do approve allowing patients to die by ceasing treatment. So in 1973, the Connecticut State Medical Society endorsed a "background statement" to be signed by patients, which includes this sentence: "I value life and the dignity of life, so that I am not asking that my life be directly taken, but that my life not be unreasonably prolonged or the dignity of life destroyed." Other state medical groups followed suit, and in 1976 the state of California enacted legislation that recognized the legal right of doctors to allow the deaths of patients who sign such statements. Following Mill's Principle, we could say that the right of patients to leave such instructions and to have them carried out is just one implication of their right to control their own affairs, regardless of whether other people think their decisions are right or wrong or wise or foolish.

§21 AN ARGUMENT AGAINST LEGALIZING ACTIVE EUTHANASIA: THE SLIPPERY SLOPE

Now we shall examine the most widely used argument *against* legalizing active euthanasia, the slippery-slope argument.

Statement of the Argument   The basic idea of the argument is that if euthanasia were legally permitted, it would lead to a general decline in respect for human life. In the beginning, we might kill people only to put them out of extreme agony. Our motives would be honorable, and the results might be good. However, once we had started cold-bloodedly killing people, where would it stop? Where would we draw the line? The point is that once we accept killing in some cases, we have stepped onto a "slippery slope," which we will inevitably slide down, and in the end life will be held cheap. Sometimes a different analogy—called the "wedge" argument—is used; then it is said that once we admit the thin edge of the wedge, we are on the way to abandoning our traditional view of the importance of human life.

Bishop Sullivan puts the argument this way:

> . . . to permit in a single instance the direct killing of an innocent person would be to admit a most dangerous wedge that might eventually put all life in a precarious condition. Once a man is permitted on his own authority to kill an innocent person directly, there is no way of stopping the advancement of that wedge. There exists no longer any rational grounds for saying that the wedge can advance so far and no further. Once the exception has been made it is too late; hence the grave reason why no exception may be allowed. That is why euthanasia under any circumstances must be condemned.

More specifically, Sullivan says:

> If voluntary euthanasia were legalized, there is good reason to be-
> lieve that at a later date another bill for compulsory euthanasia would
> be legalized. Once the respect for human life is so low that an inno-
> cent person may be killed directly even at his own request, compul-
> sory euthanasia will necessarily be very near. This could lead easily
> to killing all incurable charity patients, the aged who are a public
> care, wounded soldiers, all deformed children, the mentally afflicted,
> and so on. Before long the danger would be at the door of every
> citizen.[31]

Although Sullivan writes from a Catholic point of view, it is clear
that this argument is not a religious one. It requires no religious assumptions of any kind. And, in fact, non-Catholics have used this
argument, too. Philippa Foot is a leading British moral philosopher.
Unlike Sullivan, she thinks that in some individual cases, active euthanasia is *morally* all right. However, she thinks it should not be
legalized, because of "the really serious problem of abuse":

> Many people want, and want very badly, to be rid of their elderly
> relatives and even of their ailing husbands or wives. Would any safe-
> guards ever be able to stop them describing as euthanasia what was
> really for their own benefit? And would it be possible to prevent the
> occurrence of acts which were genuinely acts of euthanasia but mor-
> ally impermissible because infringing the rights of a patient who
> wished to live? . . . the possibility of active voluntary euthanasia might
> change the social scene in ways that would be very bad. As things are,
> people do, by and large, expect to be looked after if they are old or
> ill. This is one of the good things that we have, but we might lose it,
> and be much worse off without it. It might come to be expected that
> someone likely to need a lot of looking after should call for the doctor
> and demand his own death. Something comparable could be good in
> an extremely poverty-stricken community where the children genu-
> inely suffered from lack of food; but in rich societies such as ours it
> would surely be a spiritual disaster.[32]

The conclusion of the argument is that no matter what view you take
of individual instances of mercy killing, as a matter of social policy we
ought to enforce a rigorous rule against it. Otherwise, we are courting
disaster.

To assess this argument, we need to distinguish between two very
different forms it might take. We may call these the *logical* version
of the argument and the *psychological* version.

The Logical Interpretation of the Slippery Slope   The logical form of
the argument goes like this. Once a certain practice is accepted, from
a logical point of view we are committed to accepting certain other
practices as well, since there are no good reasons for not going on to
accept the additional practices once we have taken the all-important
first step. But, the argument continues, the additional practices

are plainly unacceptable; therefore, the first step had better not be taken.

Interpreted in this way, the slippery-slope argument makes a point about *what you are logically committed to* once certain practices are accepted. It says that once you allow euthanasia for the patient in terrible agony, *you are logically committed* to approving of euthanasia in other cases as well. Bishop Sullivan, in the passage previously quoted, apparently intends this, for he says that "Once a man is permitted on his own authority to kill an innocent person directly . . . *there exists no longer any rational grounds* for saying that the wedge can advance so far and no further." But this is clearly false. There *are* rational grounds for distinguishing between the man in agony who wants to die and other cases, such as that of an old infirm person who does not want to die. It is easy to say what the rational ground is. It is simply that in the first case the person requests death, whereas in the second case the person does not request it. Moreover, in the first case, the person is suffering terribly, and in the second case the person is not. These are morally relevant differences to which we can appeal in order to distinguish the cases; therefore, we are *not* logically committed to accepting "euthanasia" in the second case merely because we approve it in the first. Thus, the logical form of the slippery-slope argument does not work in the case of euthanasia. It does not prove that active euthanasia ought to be legally prohibited in every case.

The Psychological Interpretation of the Slippery Slope   This form of the argument is very different. It claims that once certain practices are accepted, *people shall in fact* go on to accept other, more questionable practices. This is simply a claim about what people will do and not a claim about what they are logically committed to. Thus, this form of the argument says that if we start off by killing people to put them out of extreme agony, we shall *in fact* end up killing them for other reasons, regardless of logic and nice distinctions. Therefore, if we want to avoid the latter, we had better avoid the former. This is the point that Mrs. Foot is making, and it is a much stronger argument than what I have called the "logical" version of the slippery slope.

How strong is the psychological version of the argument? Does it show that active euthanasia ought to be illegal? The crucial question is whether legalizing active euthanasia would in fact lead to terrible consequences. This is an empirical question—a question of fact— about which philosophers have no special inside information. But then, neither does anyone else; there is no definitive "scientific" answer to this question. Each of us is left to form his or her own best estimate concerning what would happen in our society if active euthanasia came to be accepted. For myself, I do *not* believe that it would lead to any sort of general breakdown in respect for life, for several reasons.

First, we have a good bit of historical and anthropological evidence that approval of killing in one context does not necessarily lead to killing in different circumstances. As has been previously mentioned, in ancient Greece, people killed defective infants without any feeling of shame or guilt—but this did *not* lead to the easy approval of other types of killing. Many instances of this kind could be cited. In Eskimo societies, the killing of infants and feeble old people was widely accepted as a measure to avoid starvation; but among the Eskimos murder was virtually unheard of. Such evidence suggests that people are able to distinguish between various types of cases, and keep them separated fairly well.

Second, in our own society killing has been, and still is, accepted in many circumstances. For example, we allow killing in self-defense. But what if it were argued that we should not allow this, on the grounds that acceptance of killing in self-defense would inevitably lead to a breakdown in respect for life? Of course, we know that this is not true, because we know that acceptance of killing in self-defense *has not* led to any such consequences. But why hasn't it? Because, first, it is rather unusual for anyone to have to kill in self-defense—most of us never face such a situation—and second, we are not so stupid that we are unable to distinguish this case, in which killing is justified, from other cases in which it is not justified. Exactly the same seems to be true of killing people who ask to be killed to put them out of misery. Such cases would be fairly rare—most of us know of such cases only by reading of them—and we can distinguish them from other, very different cases fairly easily.

Third, Mrs. Foot fears that "It might come to be expected that someone likely to need a lot of looking after should call for the doctor and demand his own death." But this situation would become possible *only if* it were legal for doctors to kill *anyone* who requests it. It would not be possible under a legal arrangement that authorized doctors to administer euthanasia only to terminal patients of special kinds.

Finally, it must be admitted that if active euthanasia were legalized, there would inevitably be *some* abuses, just as there are abuses of virtually every social practice. No one can deny that. The crucial issue is whether the abuses, or the bad consequences generally, would be *so* numerous as to outweigh the advantages of legalized euthanasia. We must remember that the choice is not between a present policy that is benign and an alternative that is potentially dangerous. The present policy has its evils too, and for patients like Stewart Alsop's friend Jack those evils are all too real. We must not forget that these evils have to be weighed against any feared disadvantages of the alternative. For these reasons, my own conclusion is that the psychological version of the slippery-slope argument does *not* provide a decisive reason why active euthanasia should be kept illegal. The possibility of bad consequences should perhaps make us proceed cautiously in this area; but it should not stop us from proceeding at all.

§22 HOW TO LEGALIZE ACTIVE EUTHANASIA: A MODEST PROPOSAL

Opposition to the legalization of active euthanasia comes from those who believe it is immoral, from those who fear the consequences of legalization, and from those who believe that, although it may be a fine idea in theory, in practice it is impossible to devise any workable laws to accommodate active euthanasia. This last point is important. If we wanted to legalize active euthanasia, exactly how could we go about doing it? Who should be granted the awesome power to decide when a person may be put to death? Should patients or doctors or the patient's family be allowed to decide on their own? Or should some sort of hospital committee be authorized to make the decision? And if so, exactly who should sit on such a committee? What if those who are given the power abuse it? Shall they then be liable to charges of murder? If so, then it would seem that they do not really have the power to decide; but if not, their power is unchecked and they have a license to do as they please. It is easy to think of objections to almost any proposed scheme, so it is no wonder that even those who approve active euthanasia in theory are often wary of actually legalizing it.

I want to make a modest proposal concerning how active euthanasia might be legalized so as to avoid all these problems. Before outlining this proposal, I need to make some elementary points about American law.

Individuals charged with a crime have no obligation to prove their innocence. The burden of proof is on the prosecution, and the defense may consist entirely in pointing out that the prosecution has not decisively proven guilt. If the prosecution has not discharged its obligation to prove guilt, the jury's duty is to acquit the defendant.

However, if the prosecution does establish a strong case against the defendant, a more active defense is required. Then there are two options available. The defendant may deny having done the criminal act in question. Or, while admitting to the act, the defendant may nevertheless argue that he or she should not be punished for it.

There are two legally accepted ways of arguing that a person should not be punished for an act even while admitting that the act is prohibited by law and that the person did it. First, an *excuse* may be offered, such as insanity, coercion, ignorance of fact, unavoidable accident, and so on. If it can be shown that the defendant was insane when the crime was committed or that he was coerced into doing it or that it was an unavoidable accident, then the defendant may be acquitted. Second, a *justification* may be offered. A plea of self-defense against a charge of murder is an example of a justification. The technical difference between excuses and justifications need not concern us here.

Here is an example to illustrate these points. Suppose you are charged with murdering a man, and the prosecution can make a strong case that you did in fact kill the victim. You might respond by trying to show that you did *not* kill him. Or you might admit that you killed him, and then have your lawyers argue that you were insane or that the killing was a tragic accident for which you are blameless or that you had to kill him in self-defense. If any of these defenses can be made out, then you will be acquitted of the crime even though you admittedly did kill the victim.

When such a defense is offered, the burden of proof is on the defense, and not the prosecution, to show that the facts alleged are true. The prosecution does not have to show that the defendant was sane; rather, the defendant (or the defendant's lawyers) must prove that he or she was insane. The prosecution does not have to prove that the killing was not done in self-defense; instead the defense must prove that is was. Thus it is not quite accurate to say that under American law the burden of proof is always on the prosecution. If the defendant concedes to having performed the act in question but claims an excuse or justification for the act, the burden of proof may shift so that the defense is required to show that the excuse or justification should be accepted.

Now, my proposal for legalizing active euthanasia is that a plea of mercy killing be acceptable as a defense against a charge of murder in much the same way that a plea of self-defense is acceptable as a defense. When people plead self-defense, it is up to them to show that their own lives were threatened and that the only way of fending off the threat was by killing the attacker first. Under my proposal, someone charged with murder could also plead mercy killing; and then, if it could be proven that the victim while competent requested death, and that the victim was suffering from a painful terminal illness, the person pleading mercy killing would also be acquitted.

Under this proposal no one would be "authorized" to decide when a patient should be killed any more than people are "authorized" to decide when someone may be killed in self-defense. There are no committees to be established within which people may cast private votes for which they are not really accountable; people who choose to mercy kill bear full legal responsibility, as individuals, for their actions. In practice, this would mean that anyone contemplating mercy killing would have to be very sure that there are independent witnesses to testify concerning the patient's condition and desire to die; for otherwise, one might not be able to make out a defense in a court of law —if it should come to that—and would be legally liable for murder. However, if this proposal were adopted, it would *not* mean that every time active euthanasia was performed a court trial would follow. In clear cases of self-defense, prosecutors simply do not bring charges, since it would be a pointless waste of time. Similarly, in clear cases of mercy killing, where there is no doubt about the patient's hopeless condition or desire to die, charges would not be brought for the same reason.

Thus, under this proposal, the need to write difficult legislation permitting euthanasia is bypassed. The problems of formulating a statute, which were mentioned at the beginning of this section, do not arise. We would rely on the good sense of judges and juries to separate the cases of justifiable euthanasia from the cases of unjustifiable murder, just as we already rely on them to separate the cases of self-defense and insanity and coercion. Some juries are already functioning in this way but without legal sanction: when faced with genuine mercy killers, they refuse to convict. The main consequence of my proposal would be to sanction officially what these juries already do.

VI. CONCLUSION

We have now examined the most important arguments for and against the morality of euthanasia, and we have considered arguments for and against legalizing it. It is time to summarize our conclusions. What do the arguments show?

First, in the central case of the terminal patient who wants to be killed rather than die slowly in agony, we are led inescapably to the conclusion that active euthanasia is morally acceptable and that it ought to be made legal. The morality of euthanasia in this case is supported by such diverse ethical precepts as the Principle of Utility, Kant's Categorical Imperative, and the Golden Rule. Euthanasia here serves the interests of everyone concerned: it is a mercy to the patient, it reduces the emotional strain of death on the patient's family and friends, and it conserves medical resources. Moreover, if doctors are legally forbidden to provide a painless death to such patients at their request, it is an unwarranted restriction on the freedom of the patients; for it is *their* life, and so it is their right to decide. The arguments opposing euthanasia, both morally and legally, are not nearly so strong.

Second, in the case of the patient in an irreversible coma, we are struck by the fact that as far as *the patient's own* interests are concerned, it does not really matter whether he or she lives or dies. Although this unfortunate patient is still alive in the biological sense, life was over when consciousness was lost for the final time. That is why it seems so pointless to continue maintaining life by artificial means, especially when doing so is emotionally destructive to those who love the patient, and when medical resources could be used better to help those who still can be helped. In this type of case, then, our conclusion must also be that euthanasia is justified. The only qualification, suggested by the argument from the possibility of unexpected cures, is that we must be certain that the coma really *is* irreversible.

These are our main conclusions. Some readers may find them hard to accept. This is understandable; for the idea of deliberately killing someone goes against very deep moral feelings. The principle of the value of life is an especially fundamental one, not to be taken lightly. Nonetheless, I believe that the arguments we have considered show that in these tragic cases, killing may be not only permissible but mandatory.

NOTES

1. *De. Ira.* i, 15.
2. *Dissertations,* I, IX, 16.
3. *De. Ira.* i, 15.
4. *De Corona,* 11.
5. E. Westermarck, *Christianity and Morals* (1939), 239.
6. *Mishneh Torah, Book of Judges,* "Laws of Mourning," 4:5.
7. Raanan Gillon, "Suicide and Voluntary Euthanasia: Historical Perspective," in A. B. Downing, ed., *Euthanasia and the Right to Die* (Los Angeles: Nash Publishing Co., 1969), 181.
8. Gillon, 182–183.
9. From Book II of More's *Utopia.*
10. *New Atlantis* (1626).
11. Plato, *Republic,* III, 407–e.
12. *The Pope Speaks,* IV, 4: "Address to the International Congress of Anesthesiologists."
13. *Morals and Medicine* (Boston: Beacon Press, 1960), 174.
14. "The Right to Die with Dignity," *Good Housekeeping,* August 1974, 69, 130.
15. *Foundations of the Metaphysics of Morals,* 422.
16. *Philosophic Exchange* (Brockport, New York), II:1 (Summer 1975), 45.
17. Humphrey Primatt, *A Dissertation on the Duty of Mercy and the Sin of Cruelty to Brute Animals* (London, 1776), 65.
18. See footnote 13 above.
19. *The Humanist,* July–August 1974, 5.
20. Garden City, New York: Doubleday, 1973. Also see Maguire's article "A Catholic View of Mercy Killing," in Marvin Kohl, ed., *Beneficent Euthanasia* (Buffalo, New York: Prometheus Books, 1975), 34–43, from which the following quotations are taken.
21. See Joseph V. Sullivan, "The Immorality of Euthanasia," in Kohl, ed., *Beneficent Euthanasia,* 14.
22. "Of Suicide" (1784).
23. Kohl, ed., *Beneficent Euthanasia,* 19.
24. "A Definition of Irreversible Coma," *Journal of the American Medical Association,* 205 (1968), 85–88.
25. *Repouille* v. *United States,* 165 F.2d 152 (1947).
26. *Miami News,* 3 July 1973, 3-A.
27. Yale Kamisar, "Some Non-Religious Views Against Proposed Mercy-Killing Legislation," *Minnesota Law Review,* 6, May 1958, 1022.
28. Supreme Court of New Jersey, 70 N.J. 10, 355 A.2d 647 (1976).
29. Andrew M. Greely, review of *Karen Ann: The Quinlans Tell Their Story* by Joseph and Julia Quinlan, in *The New York Times Book Review,* 9 October 1977, 10–11.
30. J. S. Mill, *On Liberty,* ch. 1.

31. Kohl, ed., *Beneficent Euthanasia*, 24.
32. "Euthanasia," *Philosophy and Public Affairs*, 6:2 (Winter 1977), 111–112.

SUGGESTIONS FOR FURTHER READING

Further readings are mentioned below in connection with the sections of the essay to which they are most pertinent.

§§5–9 For information on the history of attitudes toward euthanasia, see Edward Westermarck, *The Origin and Development of the Moral Ideas*, 2 vols. (London: 1906–1908), and W. E. H. Lecky, *History of European Morals*, 2 vols. (New York: 1919).

§11 In James Rachels, "Active and Passive Euthanasia," *New England Journal of Medicine*, vol. 292 (1975), pp. 78–80, it is argued that the distinction between killing and letting die has no moral importance; therefore, contrary to the traditional doctrine, active and passive euthanasia are morally equivalent. This article is reprinted in *Social Ethics*, edited by Thomas Mappes and Jane Zembaty (New York: McGraw-Hill, 1977). This anthology also contains a defense of the distinction by Tom L. Beauchamp, "A Reply to Rachels on Active and Passive Euthanasia."

§§13–14 For additional arguments in favor of euthanasia, see Joseph Fletcher, *Morals and Medicine* (Boston: Beacon Press, 1960); Daniel Maguire, *Death by Choice* (Garden City: Doubleday, 1973); and various essays in *Beneficent Euthanasia*, edited by Marvin Kohl (Buffalo: Prometheus Books, 1975), and in *Euthanasia and the Right to Die*, edited by A. B. Downing (Los Angeles: Nash Publishing Company, 1969).

On the argument from the Golden Rule, see especially R. M. Hare, "Euthanasia: A Christian View," *Philosophic Exchange* II:1 (Summer 1975).

§§15–17 For additional arguments opposing euthanasia, see various articles in the anthologies edited by Kohl and Downing. "The Immorality of Euthanasia," by Joseph V. Sullivan (in the Kohl volume) is especially interesting; Sullivan advances almost all the antieuthanasia arguments considered in this essay. Another article in the Kohl volume, "Jewish Views of Euthanasia," by Byron L. Sherwin, is a good source of information about Jewish attitudes, which are generally antieuthanasia.

§18 Daniel Maguire provides a good, readable account of the present state of the law, together with arguments for changing it, in *Death by Choice*.

§19 The parents of Karen Ann Quinlan have written their own account of the events leading up to the court's decision to allow disconnection of the life-support systems: *Karen Ann: The Quinlans Tell Their Story*, by Joseph and Julia Quinlan (New York: Doubleday, 1977). For negative reactions to the court's decision, see a special issue of *Christianity and Crisis*, January 19, 1976. The February 1976 issue of *Hastings Center Report* contains a number of articles on the case reacting more favorably to the decision.

§§20–22 In *The Sanctity of Life and the Criminal Law* (New York: Alfred Knopf, 1957), the British jurist Glanville Williams argues that euthanasia ought to be legalized. Yale Kamisar, a professor of law at the University of Michigan, criticizes Williams's proposals in an article, "Euthanasia Legislation:

Some Non-Religious Objections," which is included in *Euthanasia and the Right to Die,* edited by Downing. Downing's book also contains a rejoinder by Williams.

R. M. Hare, in the article previously mentioned, takes the view that although active euthanasia may be justified in some individual cases, still it probably should not be legalized because of possible abuses (the slippery-slope argument). On this point, also see Hare's article "Medical Ethics: Can the Moral Philosopher Help?" in *Philosophical Medical Ethics,* edited by Spicker and Engelhardt (Dordrecht: Reidel, 1977).

3
Suicide

TOM L. BEAUCHAMP

Families often conceal the fact that a death in the family was a suicide, and, generally speaking, we all tend to be puzzled and stunned when our friends take their own lives. Most of us in fact react to suicide with an instinctive revulsion. Such attitudes have led to a social situation in which motivations toward suicide are not well understood, and even the serious dimensions of the social problem are seldom confronted or discussed. But suicide is a fact of everyday life. It is the second-ranking cause of death among college students (behind accidents), and about 22,000 to 25,000 people kill themselves every year in the United States. According to the World Health Organization, it can be reasonably estimated that (in reporting nations) about 1,000 people commit suicide every day. Moreover, the persons most knowledgeable about problems of suicidal patients commit suicide more often than any other segment of the population: The physician suicide rate is variously estimated at two to three times the rate of the general population; and the rate for psychiatrists increases to two to three times that of the physician rate. These are only a few of the staggering statistics about suicide gathered in recent years.

Suicides present a number of unresolved moral problems about the value of life. Philosophers have talked about the moral permissibility or impermissibility of suicide at least since Plato (430–350 B.C.) and Aristotle (384–322 B.C.), and several major writings on suicide have been bequeathed to us from major figures in the history of philosophy. There are at least two reasons why interest in the morality of suicide has increased in recent years. First, biomedical technology has made it possible for ill and seriously injured persons to prolong their lives beyond a point at which, in former times, they would have died. Many of these patients are seriously ill and in considerable agony. The suicide rate is remarkably high in some of these populations, and numerous people have come to think not only that suicide is justified in such cases but even that those who are incapacitated should be assisted in their acts of suicide. Slogans such as "the right to die" and "death with dignity" have grown up around such cases. Second, although suicide laws have been repealed recently in many jurisdictions in the United States, repeal is a matter of present debate in others. It is clear that this debate turns more on moral considerations than on legal ones.

The major objective of this essay is to evaluate critically certain views about the morality of suicide. I shall proceed in the following way. First, in §§1–6, I shall characterize and assess proposed analyses of the concept of suicide. Then, after having chosen what appears to be the most adequate analysis, I shall identify four moral principles that are relevant to discussing the morality of suicide (§§7–10). These principles will then be applied to the thought of two of the most influential writers on suicide: in §11, the position of the philosophical theologian St. Thomas Aquinas (1224–1274) is discussed, while in §12, the utilitarian position of the eighteenth-century Scottish philosopher David Hume (1711–1776) is explored. In the concluding section (§13) to this part of the essay, Hume's position is defended. Only when we reach §14 do I raise the question of the morality of trying to prevent someone from committing suicide, and here again, a utilitarian answer is presented and defended. The morality of suicide intervention, therefore, lies far down the road.

I. THE DEFINITION OF SUICIDE

§1 SOME CONCEPTUAL DIFFICULTIES

Although debate about the legality, rationality, and morality of suicide has increased in recent years, only fragmentary attention has been devoted to the development of an adequate definition of suicide. Yet the development of an adequate definition will have important practical consequences. The way we classify actions is indicative of the way we think about them, and in the present case such classifications have immediate relevance for medicine, ethics, and law.

The following 1968 case illustrates some of the conceptual difficulties involved in correctly classifying a case as a suicide or as a non-suicide:

> *N.Y. Times,* February 7, 1968: Phoenix, Ariz., Feb. 6 (AP) -
> Linda Marie Ault killed herself, policemen said today, rather than make her dog Beauty pay for her night with a married man.
> " 'I killed her. I killed her. It's just like I killed her myself,' "
> a detective quoted her grief-stricken father as saying.

" 'I handed her the gun. I didn't think she would do anything like that.'"

The 21-year-old Arizona State University coed died in a hospital yesterday of a gunshot wound in the head.

The police quoted her parents, Mr. and Mrs. Joseph Ault, as giving this account:

" 'Linda failed to return home from a dance in Tempe Friday night. On Saturday she admitted she had spent the night with an Air Force lieutenant.'"

The Aults decided on a punishment that would "wake Linda up." They ordered her to shoot the dog she had owned about two years.

On Sunday, the Aults and Linda took the dog into the desert near their home. They had the girl dig a shallow grave. Then Mrs. Ault grasped the dog between her hands, and Mr. Ault gave his daughter a .22-caliber pistol and told her to shoot the dog.

Instead, the girl put the pistol to her right temple and shot herself.

The police said there were no charges that could be filed against the parents except possibly cruelty to animals.

Linda Marie Ault killed herself, as this story recounts, but is she a suicide? This question can be asked about a great many "suicides," and it is by no means an idle question or one of interest only to those who compile dictionaries. For example, the accuracy of statistics about suicide depends on knowledge that reported suicides are really suicides. Adequate statistics, then, depend not only on careful reporting but on our concept of suicide. This problem plagues those who plan programs for the prevention of suicide, insurance agents who must assess the legitimacy of certain claims, and lawyers and judges who must ascertain the extent of protections afforded by the law. Social scientists have registered similar difficulties:

> The following questions remain: how does the researcher identify his subjects (i.e. suicides) for study, if he does not know what 'suicide' means; how does one locate 'suicidal statements' or a 'suicidal action'? There seems to be the assumption that the individual understands himself better than any observer. This is not necessarily true. In defining the situation wholly in terms of the definitions offered by the patient, error can occur by accepting that definition as the *only* one. In doing so, the researcher may have become so personally involved in the relationship that he could no longer stand outside it. . . .[1]

There seem to be two general reasons for confusion over the precise nature of suicide. First, social attitudes and customs are commonly reflected in linguistic definitions adopted by a culture. If suicide is socially disapproved, then the definition may reflect this disapproval by eliminating all praiseworthy actions from being "suicides." That is, an act will not be *called* suicide unless it incurs disapproval. For example, if self-killing is generally disapproved in a society—while great value is placed on being buried with one's spouse—then an act of ending one's life in order to be buried with one's spouse may be called "sacrificial," not suicidal. Similarly, if some forms of self-killing are approved in a culture, then actions that are both risky and socially beneficial, and that may eventuate in death, might naturally be regarded as suicides. For example, a doctor who experimented on herself for the benefit of children in her care while knowing that she probably would die from the experiment, and who did die as a result of the experiment, might be considered a suicide.

A second and related reason for definitional confusion about suicide has to do with different assessments of the suicide's exact intentions. Sacrificial actions perhaps most trouble us: An act of self-killing is generally called "suicide" if performed to relieve oneself; it is generally called "sacrifice" if performed to relieve others. For example, when a spy takes a lethal poison in order not to reveal secrets, or when the driver of a runaway car rams into a hill in order to avoid killing others (knowing that he or she will die), or when a person stops using life-support equipment in order to relieve his or her family's anguish, we may be perplexed as to whether the action is a suicide, even if it is in a reasonable sense an *intentional* self-caused death.

These are some of the issues we will have to face in what follows. Before turning to them, brief mention should be made of the method I shall employ in attempting a conceptual analysis of "suicide." It is clear in the case of many actions that they are *correctly* classified as acts of suicide. Other actions, however, are less clearly instances of suicide; and still others are borderline cases between suicide and, for example, accidental death or heroic sacrifice. Any satisfactory definition of suicide must be able to account for the clear cases and to pinpoint why borderline cases are troublesome. I shall attempt to provide a definition of this order that captures our ordinary meaning of the term 'suicide'. On the other hand, there can be reasons for resisting the ordinary meaning of terms when they tend to prejudicial conclusions that might be drawn in moral philosophy, and the term 'suicide' presents problems of this sort. I shall return to this issue after developing the ordinary meaning.

§2 STANDARD DEFINITIONS

In recent years three kinds of definition have been popular as ways of understanding suicide. The first is simple and might be called the prevailing definition: suicide occurs if and only if there is an intentional termination of one's own life. Contemporary moral philosophers such as R. B. Brandt and Eike-Henner Kluge have employed similar definitions, and the definition also is located in *Gould's Medical Dictionary* and *The Encyclopedia of Bioethics*.[2] The second definition, by contrast, supposedly does not rely on the intent to terminate life and derives from the sociologist Emile Durkheim:

> The term suicide is applied to all cases of death resulting directly or indirectly from a positive or negative act of the victim himself, which he knows will produce this result.[3]

This second definition in effect broadens the scope of 'suicide', but the third definition is still broader than the other two and has fittingly been called the "omnibus definition." As contemporary sociologist Ronald Maris has stated it:

> Suicide occurs when an individual engages in a life-style that he knows might kill him (other than living another day)—and it does [kill him]. This is an omnibus definition of suicide, which includes various forms of self-destruction, such as risk-taking and many so-called "accidents."[4]

It is fairly easy both to see why these three definitions have been popular and to grasp the connection between them. The first seems consistent with ordinary linguistic usage, as is reflected in the way most dictionaries define suicide. The second definition is attractive to social scientists, insurance companies, coroners, and anyone else who must *verify* that a particular piece of behavior was a suicide. Durkheim accepted the second and rejected the first because the first appeals to the presence of an intention to die—something not easily verifiable. For example, in the case of many drownings, poisonings, and falls from tall buildings, we simply are not able to ascertain what the person's intention was, let alone that death was intended. Whether or not Durkheim's substitution of knowledge for intention is any improvement is debatable, because knowledge too is hard to verify; but at least we can understand his reasons for seeking a modification of intentional definitions.

The third definition has come into vogue for similar reasons to those just discussed. The word 'know' in Durkheim's definition seems objectionable to those who support the third definition, because the suicidal person rarely *knows* that his act will produce death. If "he knows will produce" is replaced by some weaker expression, such as "might produce," then Durkheim's definition has in effect been transformed into the third. Since a great many risk-taking behaviors may produce death (though this cannot be *known* in advance), the number of suicides will be greatly expanded by this definitional maneuver. And there are some plausible reasons for this shift. A contemporary psychiatrist, Erwin Stengel, has observed that the majority of "suicides" have ambivalent intentions about whether to take their lives and cannot correctly be said either to want to live or to want to die.[5] But their tendencies toward self-destruction lead them to take extreme risks and to inflict various types of severe damage on their own bodies. Since these persons are not clearly suicides according to either the first or the second definition, it is thought that neither definition should be accepted; and thus we get the third omnibus definition. In this case, the reason for the definition emerges more from psychiatric considerations than from the practical problems of social scientists and coroners.

§3 THE INADEQUACIES OF STANDARD DEFINITIONS

What, if anything, is wrong with these standard definitions? The third definition seems unacceptable because it would significantly warp the concept of suicide as we know it: Those who engage in waterfall rafting, hang gliding, police bomb-squad work, mountain diving (into oceans), and space explorations of an adventuresome sort—and who die as a result of these activities—would be suicides if this definition were accepted. Smokers, excessively fast drivers, and those who serve in a dangerous division of the armed services would similarly have to be declared suicidal. Moreover, the definition fails to preserve the distinction between accidental death and suicide in all cases where high risks are systematically taken (for example, risks taken by terrorists). This result seems to require too much of a sacrifice of our ordinary notion of suicide, and for insufficiently powerful reasons. Consequently, I shall lay aside this third definition and concentrate exclusively on the first two definitions.

The first problem to notice about each of the first two definitions is that they omit all mention of *the precise nature of the intention* (motivation) or knowledge involved in a suicide. Durkheim, of course, eliminated all mention of intentions because of the difficulty of ascertaining what someone's intentions are. Those who accept the first definition apparently accept it rather than Durkheim's because, to their way of thinking, the act of self-killing cannot be unintentional and remain a suicide, and it also cannot be a suicide if there is some other intended consequence besides self-caused death. (They do not, however, insist that it is the exclusively intended consequence.) But is the matter this simple? While I am willing to concede for our purposes that suicide must be an *intentional* self-killing (a matter that is far from obvious),[6] much more needs to be said about precisely what must be intended.

Consider, as an example of these problems, a captured soldier who, given the "choice" of being executed or of executing himself, chooses self-execution. Since coercion is heavily involved in this intentional self-killing, we do not classify it as a suicide, just as we do not think that Socrates committed suicide by intentionally drinking the hemlock, thereby causing his death. Now change the case slightly: Suppose that our imagined soldier is free of all coercion and intentionally terminates his life solely in order to avoid divulging critical information sure to be extracted by the enemy. The method chosen to terminate his life is a feigned escape attempt, when it is known for certain that he will be shot. It seems inappropriate to say without further explanation that because he intentionally terminated his own life, he therefore committed suicide. Surely, some will say, the nature of the intention—the agent's reasons for acting—as well as the circumstances under which the intention was formed, makes a difference; though neither definition takes account of such considerations.

The initial problems with both of these two attempts at the definition of suicide have been at least partially captured by the American philosopher Joseph Margolis:

> A man may knowingly, and willingly, go to his death, be rationally capable of avoiding death, deliberately not act to save his life, and yet not count as a suicide. In this sense, we usually exclude the man who sacrifices his life to save another's, the religious martyr who will not violate his faith, the patriot who intentionally lays down his life for a cause. Not that men in such circumstances may not be suiciding; only that they *cannot be said to be suiciding solely for those reasons.* Some seem to have thought otherwise [such as] Durkheim. . . .[7]

I shall assume the correctness of this insight for the moment in order to construct a more satisfactory definition of suicide than those found in the above three definitions. Here is a start in the direction of a more adequate definition: The death of person A is a suicide only if: (1) A's own death is intentionally caused[8] by A, and (2) A's action is noncoerced. Although these two conditions fit well with our judgments about common suicides—where, e.g., notes confessing depression are left, nonaccidental drug overdoses are taken, and revolvers are employed—the matter cannot be quite this simply resolved, as we shall now see.

§4 THE PROBLEM OF TREATMENT REFUSAL

There is a class of difficult cases, as yet undiscussed, for such a definition. These cases involve persons who suffer from a terminal illness or mortal injury, and who refuse some medical therapy without which they will die, but with which they could live longer. For example, refusal to allow a blood transfusion or an amputation, and refusal of further kidney dialysis are now familiar facts of hospital life. But are they suicides? Two facts about such cases are noteworthy. First, these acts certainly *can* be suicides, because *any* means productive of death can be used to the end of suicide. Pulling the plug on one's respirator is not relevantly different from plunging a knife into one's heart, if the reason for putting an end to life is identical in the two cases. Second, suicidal acts can also be sacrificial. For example, if a person were suffering from a costly terminal disease, then it would be an altruistic (even if perhaps misguided) action to take one's own life in order to spare one's family the inordinate cost of providing the care; but it would nonetheless be suicide.

Still, the seriously suffering person with end-stage renal disease who refuses to continue dialysis and dies a "natural" death does not strike most as a suicide. Why not? Three features of such situations need to be distinguished in order to answer this question:

1. whether the death is *intended* by the agent;
2. whether an *active* means to death is selected;

3. whether a *nonfatal condition* is present (no terminal disease or mortal injury exists).

To the extent that we have unmistakable cases of actions by an agent that involve an *intentionally caused death* using an *active* means where there is a *nonfatal* condition, the more inclined we are to classify such acts as suicides; whereas to the extent such conditions are absent, the less inclined we are to call the acts suicides. For example, if a seriously but not mortally wounded soldier turns his rifle on himself and intentionally brings about his death, it is a suicide. But what about the seriously ill patient of ambiguous intentions, suffering from a terminal illness, and refusing yet another blood transfusion?

Although considerations of terminal illness and of intention are important, the main source of our present definitional problem is the active/passive distinction. A passively allowed, "natural" death seems foreign to the notion of suicide, both because the death is at least in part not caused by the agent and because the 'cide' part of 'suicide' entails "killing," which is commonly contrasted with allowing to die. Here our concept of suicide begins to make linguistic contact with that to which suicide specifically stands in contrast, *viz.,* a naturally caused death. And clearly not all naturally caused deaths can be eliminated from consideration as suicides, precisely because of the relevance of the agent's intention. The person might be using such a "passive" means (e.g., failing to take requisite drugs) as a socially acceptable and convenient way of ending it all. People who so intend to end their lives cannot be excluded as suicides merely because they select a passive means to this end.

In the face of this complex mixture of elements, the following generalization may be offered about such cases: An act is *not* a suicide if the person who dies suffers from a terminal disease or from a mortal injury which, by refusal of treatment, he or she passively allows to cause his or her death—even if the person intends to die.[9] However, this analysis does not seem adequate for all cases. For example, think of a patient with a terminal condition who could easily avoid dying for a long time but who chooses to end his or her life immediately by not taking cheap and painless medication. This counterexample might incline us toward the view that a time restriction is also needed. But this restriction probably could not be reasonably formulated, and I am inclined to think that we have come as close to an understanding of suicide as the concept permits. If in the end the analysis offered has become slightly reforming (one that requires that we change the ordinary meaning of 'suicide' somewhat), perhaps the vagaries of the concept itself are responsible. I conclude, then, that the proper analysis of the notion of suicide must include the two conditions earlier mentioned (intended death and noncoercion), plus the qualification required by refusal-of-treatment cases. This conclusion will be more readily understandable after examination of a final set of cases.

§5 THE PROBLEM OF SACRIFICIAL DEATHS

There remains the problem of so-called "altruistically motivated (or other-regarding) suicide." Lifeboat situations have provided some famous examples. Suppose a lifeboat will not sustain the number of people who climb aboard, and for some to live some must die. Suppose that a person of advanced years and questionable health, without the ability to swim, voluntarily jumps overboard, drowning immediately. A life has been sacrificed for the welfare of others. Is this act a suicide? Many are inclined to say it is not. In order to see why, a distinction must be introduced between suicidal self-killing and merely self-caused death (where both involve intentional acts). Such a distinction is clearly at work in the coerced, self-inflicted, but nonsuicidal death of the soldier, for example, and so far the distinction may be accepted.

The key notion responsible for our not classifying some intentional self-killings as suicides seems to some to be that of *sacrifice*. Perhaps those who sacrifice their lives are not conceived as "suicides" for an interesting reason: Because we see such actions from the suicide's point of view as having plausible claim to being justified for *other-regarding*—not *self-regarding*—reasons, and hence we logically exclude these self-sacrificial acts from the realm of the suicidal. We may not ourselves think of them as being *actually* justified, but rather as being justified from the point of view of the agent who causes or perhaps fails to prevent his or her own death.[10] A similar proposal has been suggested by Joel Feinberg as an explanation of our intuitions about suicide and sacrifice (though Feinberg does not endorse a particular definition of suicide based on this approach):

> We tend to exclude self-sacrificial acts of heroism such as diving in front of a speeding truck to push a small child out of danger, or falling on a live hand grenade to save one's buddies. Traditionally such forms of self-destruction have not been considered suicide at all. Yet most traditional moralists would deny the right of a terminal patient to volunteer to be killed on the operating table so that his organs might be used to save the lives of injured children. That would not be called "suicide" only because a doctor would be the instrument of the patient's will, but if the patient himself injected the fatal fluid into his own arm it would probably be called "suicide" despite his altruistic motives. By and large, however, the term "suicide" has been reserved for self-killings done from self-serving motives, particularly from the desire to avoid suffering or humiliation for oneself. But usage has been inconsistent in respect to this requirement, generating considerable puzzlement.[11]

Sadly, exclusions based on self-sacrificial acts will not help much in structuring a definition of suicide unless further qualifications are introduced. The monk in Vietnam who pours gasoline over his body and burns himself to death as a protest against his government does not do so for his own sake but for the sake of his beloved countrymen, just as the father who kills himself in the midst of a famine so that his wife and children have enough to eat acts from self-sacrificial motives. Many cases of this general description of suicidal actions would have to be declared nonsuicides if the approach were taken that other-regarding, sacrificial acts fail to qualify as suicides.

In the face of this new complexity, a course paralleling the one for refusal-of-treatment cases may be taken: An act is *not* a suicide if one is caused to die by a life-threatening condition not intentionally brought about through one's own actions. Interestingly, this approach does not turn on the notion of sacrifice, the original problem compelling consideration of these cases. It makes no difference whether the action is sacrificial or nonsacrificial, so long as the condition causing death is not brought about *by the agent* for the purpose of ending his or her life. (Think of a disease contracted during the kind of dangerous medical experiments doctors may perform on themselves.) This conclusion is somewhat troublesome, because the agent does intend to die in those cases of sacrifice where a person has the option either to live or to act in protection of others' lives, and then specifically chooses a course of action that brings about his or her own death. Nonetheless, in such cases *it cannot be said that the person brings about the life-threatening condition causing death in order to cause death,* and that fact is the crucial matter.

There are further parallels between this kind of case and the refusal-of-treatment cases previously discussed. Three relevant ingredients can again be distinguished:

1. whether the death is *intended* by the agent;
2. whether the death is *caused by* the agent (or is caused to the agent);
3. whether the action is *self-regarding* (or is other-regarding).

Here the main source of confusion is not the "active/passive" distinction, but rather the parallel "caused by/caused to" distinction. To cause one's own death in order to die is to kill oneself, but to have death caused by some alien condition in the course of an action with multiple objectives may not be. (Think again of a dangerous medical experiment.) Here we might say that the killing/being killed distinction is involved, and that it functions rather like the killing/letting die distinction previously discussed.

A good test case for the above analysis is the now classic case of Captain Oates, who walked into the Antarctic snow to die because he was suffering from an illness that hindered the progress of a party attempting to make its way out of a severe blizzard.[12] According to the contemporary English philosopher R. F. Holland, Oates was not a suicide because: "in Oates's case I can say, 'No [he didn't kill himself]; the blizzard killed him.' Had Oates taken out a revolver and shot himself I should have agreed he was a suicide."[13] I cannot agree with Holland's estimate. On the analysis offered above, Oates's heroic sacrifice is a suicide because of the active steps that he took to bring about his death. Although the climatic conditions proximately caused his death, he *brought about* the relevant life-threatening condition causing his death (exposure to the weather) in order that he die. There is no relevant difference between death by revolver and death by exposure to freezing weather when both equally are life-threatening conditions used to cause one's own death. However, the Oates case is not an easy one to declare a suicide. It is a close call precisely because there is both multiple causation and multiple intent: the action is an heroic way of being *causally responsible* for placing oneself in *conditions that cause* death, and death was intended as a merciful release from an intolerable burden, not only because of Oates's suffering but also because of his knowledge that he was imperiling the lives of his colleagues. Moreover, his release from these burdens was apparently his major objective. No wonder the Oates case has become a classic in literature on the definition of suicide: it is hard to imagine a case sitting more astride the boundaries between suicide and nonsuicide.[14]

Although the analysis proposed above does not differ in its larger perspective from that of Joseph Margolis's, the point at which we part company is now evident, for Margolis argues as follows:

> The Buddhist monk who sets fire to himself in order to protest the war that he might have resisted in another way will not be said to have committed suicide if the *overriding* characterization of what he did fixes on the ulterior objective of influencing his countrymen. . . . [If there is] some further purpose that he serves instrumentally, then we normally refuse to say he has suicided . . .[15]

Margolis thinks there is a decisive difference between whether one's overriding reason is some sacrificial objective or the objective of ending one's life. In my view the matter is more complicated and has little to do with the notions of sacrifice, martyrdom, and patriotism. It has rather to do with whether death is caused by one's own arrangement[16] of the life-threatening conditions causing death for the purpose of bringing about death (whether this purpose be the overriding reason or not). Since the monk arranges the conditions, precisely for this purpose (though for others as well), he is a suicide.

§6 CONCLUSION

We have arrived, then, at an understanding of suicide that is fairly simple, even if somewhat more complicated than the definitions with which we began: An act is a suicide if a person intentionally brings about his or her own death in circumstances where others do not coerce him or her to the action, except in those cases where death is caused by conditions not specifically arranged by the agent for the purpose of bringing about his or her own death. There is, of course, more that we should like to know about this definition than can be pursued here. In particular, four features of the definition deserve further analysis:

1. What counts as *coercive*?
2. What counts as *intending one's own death*?
3. What counts as a *condition specifically arranged by an agent*?
4. What counts as a *relevant cause of death*?

Until these matters are further clarified, the kind of precision in a conceptual analysis that we would like to see is missing. For example, what are we to say of people who intentionally starve themselves in order that ill members of their families may have an increased food supply? Are such people in any sense coerced? What is the causally relevant factor in their deaths? Is the condition that ultimately kills them not a condition specifically arranged by an agent? Do these people intend their own deaths?

While I would agree that my analysis does not have the rigor we would like to see in sharpened conceptual analyses, I do think the essential lines of an adequate analysis of the ordinary language concept of suicide have now been set out with sufficient precision that we can move on to the main part of our business, which is a discussion of the morality of suicide.

II. PRINCIPLES RELEVANT TO DISCUSSING THE MORALITY OF SUICIDE

How are we to determine whether a particular act of suicide is or is not immoral? Understandably, this question is complex, and we shall not be able to answer it with confident finality. But this much, at least, seems reasonable to assume: If a particular act of suicide is wrong, then it will have certain similarities, certain shared features, with other wrong actions; conversely, if a particular act of suicide is not morally wrong, then it will share similar features with other actions that are not morally wrong. Those philosophers who have tried to develop a *general normative theory of right and wrong* have tried to discover what these shared features are, both in the case of all those actions that are morally right and in the case of all those actions that are morally wrong. Some moral philosophers have argued that the fundamental theory determining right action rests on the following claim:

> An action is morally right if and only if it produces at least as great a balance of value over disvalue as any available alternative action.

This principle is known as the *Principle of Utility*, and philosophers who subscribe to the view that this alone is the basic principle of morality are referred to as *utilitarians*. Though they frequently disagree concerning exactly what things are valuable and how value is to be determined, utilitarians are united by their belief that the Principle of Utility determines the rightness and wrongness of all moral actions.

Other moral philosophers have argued that there are one or more fundamental principles of ethics that differ from the Principle of Utility. For example, the following is offered as a nonutilitarian principle determining right action:

> An action is morally right if and only if it is the action required by a duty that is at least as strong as any other duty in the circumstances.

Philosophers who accept this nonutilitarian account of the principles of moral duty are referred to as *deontologists.* They are united by their conviction that the rightness of actions may be determined by features of the action other than the balance of value over disvalue produced by the action.

Theories of these two general sorts are used by moral philosophers to support a great many other derivative moral principles (and rules, such as that it is right to keep our promises and wrong to break them). Not all of these principles are needed for or even applicable to a discussion of the morality of suicide. But in order to take a reasoned approach to this otherwise emotionally charged subject, we need to have on hand those principles that permit us to take a consistent position on the issues. I want to suggest, without further argument, that four moral principles are directly relevant to discussions of suicide. Most types of ethical theory would recognize at least two of these principles as valid, although theories differ over their relative significance and rank them in different orders of priority. But let us see what these principles are before discussing the question of priority.

§7 THE PRINCIPLE OF UTILITY

The first of these principles is the Principle of Utility itself. For present purposes this principle need not be construed as the sole ethical principle, but rather as one moral consideration among others. As we have seen, utilitarians look to the consequences of actions, to the value and the disvalue produced, to see what the impact on the interest and welfare of all concerned will be if a particular action is performed. The interests of the person contemplating suicide, the interests of dependents, the interests of relatives, etc., must all be considered in the calculation of positive values and disvalues that would result from the action. The fact that people love the person contemplating suicide and that they value the person's contribution to the community are both to be considered in making an assessment of the contemplated action. So are the interests of those to whom the person owes debts, etc. In the majority of possible cases of suicide, a calculation would show that more disvalue in the form of grief, guilt, and deprivation would be produced than value gained were someone to commit suicide. Hence, the Principle of Utility would generally dictate that an act of suicide is not justified. However, there are cases where considerations about consequences would not automatically fall on the side of disvalue. For example, imagine someone who has neither dependents nor debts and is suffering from massive pain. Suppose further that this person's family has suffered extensively and that everyone in the family believes death would be a merciful release. An intentional overdose taken by the person could satisfy the utilitarian proposal that the greatest possible amount of value, or at least the smallest possible amount of disvalue, should be brought about by one's action.

Utilitarians claim that utilitarian considerations alone should determine the morality of an act of suicide. Their point is that even if there exists a firm rule in a society, such as "Do not kill another person except in self-defense," the reason for this rule is utilitarian—that is, the rule exists in that society because it functions to minimize the doing of evil while maximizing everyone's sense of security and well-being. A rule like "Do not kill yourself," a utilitarian might insist, also exists to maximize the value or at least to minimize the creation of disvalue. The utilitarian may of course not be correct in arguing that utility alone determines the rightness of such an action. However, most moral philosophers would recognize that utility is *a* principle deserving consideration in most moral decisions.

§8 THE PRINCIPLE OF AUTONOMY

The second principle deserving mention is one commonly thought to derive from a philosophy opposed to utilitarianism—e.g., Immanuel Kant's (1724–1804), or some similar deontological system. This principle is sometimes referred to as the Principle of Respect for Persons, by which is usually meant that individuals should be allowed to be self-determining agents making their own evaluations and choices when their own interests are at stake. However, in order to be more specific, I shall refer to this principle as the Principle of Autonomy. What, now, is required by this principle?

The autonomous individual is capable of deliberation and of actions based on such deliberations. To respect such self-determining agents is to recognize them as entitled to determine their own destiny, with due regard to their considered evaluations and view of the world, even if it is strongly believed that their evaluation or their outlook is wrong and even potentially harmful to them. To respect their autonomy, then, is at a minimum to respect their views and to accord to them the right to have their own opinions and to act upon them, so long as those actions produce no serious harms to other persons. To grant persons such a right is to say that they are entitled to autonomous expression without external restraint. It follows that to show a lack of respect for an autonomous agent is either to show disrespect for that person's deliberate choices or to deny the individual the freedom to act on those choices when such interference would affect in important ways that person's present and future interests. It would, therefore, be a showing of disrespect to deny such persons the right to commit suicide when, in their considered judgment, they ought to do so and there would likely be no serious adverse consequences for other persons. (Kant, however, did not hold this view about suicide.)

Some philosophers have believed that autonomy is a primary principle taking precedence over all other moral considerations. From this view, voluntary action must be allowed, even if many other persons would be rendered unhappy by a decision to commit suicide. However, this principle, like that of utility, will here be recognized as only *one* important moral principle governing the morality of suicide, and not as the sole or overriding consideration on all occasions.

§9 THE PRINCIPLE OF HUMAN WORTH

A third principle often appealed to in discussions of suicide may be called the Principle of Human Worth. According to this view, human life has value in itself. What makes suicide wrong is that it is an act of killing that destroys something of inherent value—that is, a life that is valuable not for any other value it brings into existence but simply because of its own inherent value. As this principle is usually construed, it may sometimes be permissible to *allow someone to die* instead of attempting heroic efforts to save the person. For example, if someone is terminally ill and is going to die in a short period of time, it is believed acceptable for such a person or the person's family to decide to allow a natural death. But it is not acceptable to *kill*, because one then becomes morally responsible for an active destruction of life. It is important to note that according to this view, the act of killing is wrong not because it produces social disutility, nor because it violates someone's autonomy. Rather, it is wrong simply because it is an intentional, active termination of human life. The Principle of Human Worth is thus entirely independent of the two principles previously discussed.

One could have a number of different reasons for holding this principle. It might be believed that life is a gift from God and therefore is only to be terminated at God's own appointed moment. Or one might think that, unlike the rest of the animal kingdom, human life is characterized by a dignity setting it apart from all other creatures. These and related issues are explored in several essays in this anthology. It is not important for our purposes, however, to canvass all the possible reasons for holding this view. All such views coalesce into a single belief: Human life is valuable in itself, and it is always a wrong-making characteristic of any action that it is an intentional termination of human life. Still, despite this coalescence into a single central belief, there are stronger and weaker ways of interpreting this

principle. Taking the strongest possible view, it is always wrong intentionally to terminate any human life, whatever the circumstances—
whether in capital-punishment cases or as an act of self-defense or by
abortion or by suicide or by any means whatever. A noticeably weak
version of the principle is that the inherent value of life itself is always
a consideration when one is contemplating the intentional termination of a life—but is only a consideration and not necessarily the most
important one.

Few would now defend either the strongest or the weakest version
of this principle. A middle position—the interpretation most who defend this principle would support—is that killing is permissible only
if it is necessary to save the life of at least one other innocent person
or if it is necessary to preserve the very existence of a (morally worthy)
society. Henceforth, when I speak of the Principle of Human Worth,
I shall be referring to versions of the principle closely connected to this
middle position.

§10 THE THEOLOGICAL PRINCIPLE

A fourth principle, often assumed in discussions of suicide, will here
be termed the Theological Principle. According to this view, suicide
and other acts are morally wrong because they violate a direct command of God against the taking of human life. Those who support this
principle commonly attempt to ground morality in theology (rather
than in philosophy, culture, or whatever). Several quite specific appeals have pervaded literature opposed to suicide. It has been argued,
for example, that human persons (or perhaps their souls) receive the
gift of life from God, and therefore suicides sin against their creator
by the act of destroying their lives. It is also contended that because
murder is specifically prohibited by God's direct command and because suicide is self-murder, suicide is therefore morally wrong—unless directly commanded by God. Many theologically based arguments
against suicide turn on an account of some special design of providence, e.g., that suicide violates an obligation to God by interfering
with the divinely ordained order of the universe. It is not always clear
in these theories what God's "order" is, but the notion of God's ap-
pointing a special purpose for each human life is especially prominent
in these arguments.

Some philosophers, and many theologians, have believed that the
Theological Principle is so fundamental to morality that theological
considerations alone determine the morality of an act of suicide. One
who espouses this view argues that suicide is always morally wrong
unless there exists a theological reason, probably based on a direct
command of God, that excuses the act of suicide. Philosophers opposed to the Theological Principle have pointed out that there are
grave difficulties in determining what God's purposes and commands
are, and that whether God's commands are morally right is something

that must be proved, not merely assumed. However, it is important to note that the Theological Principle rests squarely on *theological* grounds rather than philosophical ones. If theology gives reasons that are valid independently of philosophy, then philosophical objections will not refute these reasons. This reiterates the point that the Theological Principle is grounded in theology, not in autonomy, utility, or a philosophical view of inherent human worth.

We have now completed our survey of the four basic principles that play a major role in ethical thinking about suicide. These principles should not, of course, be construed as mutually exclusive. One could hold to some version of two or more of the principles, thereby giving moral force to a plurality of principles that must be weighed and balanced in different circumstances. However, as we shall now see, some major philosophers in the history of Western thought have tended to promote some one or two of these principles as having priority over the others.

III. TWO OPPOSED PHILOSOPHIES OF SUICIDE

In this section two very different and historically prominent philosophies of suicide will be considered: the philosophies of St. Thomas Aquinas and David Hume. These philosophers clearly illustrate the application of the ethical principles mentioned in the previous section to moral problems of suicide. For both philosophers, arguments about the permissibility and impermissibility of suicide have typically centered on the question of whether suicide violates one or more of three obligations: to oneself, to others, and to God. Their essays on suicide are both structured specifically to answer these questions. Aquinas's answers rely almost exclusively on the use of the Principle of Human Worth and the Theological Principle, while Hume's answers rely almost exclusively on the other two fundamental principles discussed above—the principles of Utility and of Autonomy. Virtually everything asserted by Aquinas is disputed by Hume, because each relies heavily on a different set of these principles.

§11 THE POSITION OF ST. THOMAS AQUINAS

During the medieval period, many arguments using a theological basis were developed to demonstrate the immorality of suicide. These arguments became the dominant view of the most influential theologians of the Christian Church, and they continue today to exert powerful influence on the views of religious persons. Their arguments range from straight Biblical injunctions against killing, as in the Sixth Commandment ("Thou shall not kill") to the rather more reasoned arguments on which we shall concentrate. St. Augustine (A.D. 354–430) was an early and influential Christian writer against suicide, but St.

Thomas Aquinas's views ultimately prevailed in influence and power.

Aquinas advances three primary moral arguments against suicide—or, as he himself says (*Summa Theologica,* II–II, Q. 64, Art. 5), three "reasons" that show that it is "altogether unlawful to kill oneself." Here are slightly abbreviated versions of his arguments, as found in the *Summa Theologica:*

> It is altogether unlawful to kill oneself, for three reasons:
> [1] because everything naturally loves itself, the result being that everything naturally keeps itself in being. . . . Wherefore suicide is contrary to the inclination of nature, and to charity whereby every man should love himself. Hence, suicide is . . . contrary to the natural law and to charity.
> [2] because . . . every man is part of the community, and so, as such, he belongs to the community. Hence by killing himself he injures the community. . . .
> [3] because life is God's gift to man, and is subject to His power. . . . Hence whoever takes his own life, sins against God. . . . For it belongs to God alone to pronounce sentence of death and life. . . .

How are we to understand these cryptic arguments? The first Thomistic argument may be reconstructed in the following form.

1. It is a natural law that everything loves and seeks to perpetuate itself.
2. Suicide is an act contrary to self-love and self-perpetuation.
3. (Therefore) suicide is contrary to natural law.
4. Anything contrary to natural law is morally wrong.
5. (Therefore) suicide is morally wrong.[17]

It is easy to misapprehend this argument. Here is one common misunderstanding by a careful writer on suicide, the English legal thinker Glanville Williams:

> The first argument . . . is, in fact, an application of the usual Catholic method of arguing from an assumed "nature" to morals. Actually, the assumption here is wrong; if suicide were always contrary to man's inclinations, it would not occur. The moral question arises because the individual is, in some circumstances, tempted to suicide. . . . Not every disregard of a fundamental instinct is wrong . . .[18]

This interpretation overlooks the fact that Thomas and his followers have never held that *all* natural tendencies or instincts ought to be pursued. Thomistic philosophers have always drawn an important distinction between laws of nature and natural laws. Presumably the former are descriptive statements derived from scientific knowledge of universal regularities in nature (for example, the law of gravity or Charles's law), while the latter are prescriptive statements derived from philosophical knowledge of the essential properties of human nature (for example, the law "Thou shalt not kill"). In this theory, natural laws do not empirically *describe* behavior; they do not tell us how we *do* behave; rather, they delimit the behavior that is morally appropriate for a human being; they tell us how we *ought* to behave. What is proper for a human differs from what is to be expected from other creatures insofar as their "natures" differ; and their natures differ because they possess different essences with different potentialities. In particular, while humans share with animals a natural tendency toward sexual reproduction, only through human reason can there be a tendency toward universal goods, such as concern about the interests of others. Suicide is thus regarded as wrong precisely because it violates a natural inclination to the conservation of one's own existence and well-being (and as we shall see, because the suicide does not exclusively intend a truly good outcome). This theory also permits the Thomist to admit that it is an empirical psychological fact that powerful inclinations to suicide do occur, while denouncing them as unnatural deprivations.[19]

Aquinas's second argument, by comparison to the first, is quite simple. It is an argument from social obligations and asserts that every individual belongs to family and neighbors and thus has obligations that are violated by an act of suicide. While Aquinas does not believe that society is sovereign over the individual, he does believe that individual decisions cannot be properly made in even so personal a matter as suicide without reference to the interests of other persons in the State. He effectively regards an act of suicide as undermining social authority and human relations and therefore as harming all those affected by the action. Surprisingly, this argument is basically utilitarian.

Aquinas's third argument has exerted massive influence among Christian believers, perhaps because it is squarely rooted in the Theological Principle. According to this argument, each human life is a gift from God, and all individuals therefore belong to their creator, much as a piece of property belongs to its owner. To commit suicide, then, is tantamount to the sin of theft, for it deprives God of that which He created and is rightfully His.

We should also note that throughout Thomas's arguments, attention to right motives is essential. He excuses suicide if (and perhaps only if) one takes one's life because divinely commanded to do so. The so-called Principle of Double Effect allows him this conclusion.[20] This principle may be formulated as follows: Whenever from an action there occur two effects, one good and the other evil, it is morally permissible to perform the action and to permit the evil if and only if:[21]

1. The intention is to bring about the good effect and not to bring about the evil effect (which is merely foreseen).
2. The action intended must be truly good or at least not evil.
3. The good effect must bring at least as much good into the world as the evil effect brings evil into the world.

Aquinas apparently thinks that the suicide always intends evil effects except when specifically commanded by God to perform the act.[22]

§12 THE POSITION OF DAVID HUME

In his essay "On Suicide,"[23] David Hume presented perhaps the strongest set of arguments in the classical history of the subject for the moral permissibility of suicide. He offered arguments against the Thomistic contention that suicide is morally condemnable and was especially critical of St. Thomas's theological views.

Hume's Antitheological Arguments   Hume's strategy in opposing St. Thomas's theological arguments is not that of challenging belief in the existence of God. Rather, he critically analyzes the following general theological proposition: The act of suicide violates an obligation to God and provokes divine indignation *because it encroaches on God's established order for the universe.*[24] This proposition is a general paraphrase of Aquinas's third argument. Hume serially rejects several possible theological meanings of the above phrase—a sensible approach since it is not clear in Aquinas's philosophy precisely what this phrase might mean. Each of Hume's arguments begins by specifying a meaning of 'God's established order'. Hume then argues that on the particular interpretation in question, the theology underlying it is either deficient or is perfectly compatible with the moral acceptance of suicide. While I have somewhat reordered Hume's presentation, the following are the three main theological interpretations that he considers and subsequently rejects:[25] (1) The Divine-Ownership Interpretation; (2) The Natural-Law Interpretation; and (3) The Divine-Appointment Interpretation.

 1. THE DIVINE-OWNERSHIP INTERPRETATION   Hume first considers the possibility that encroaching on God's established order is wrong because "the Almighty has reserved to himself . . . the disposal of the lives of men, and has not submitted that event . . . to the general laws by which the universe is governed" (154). This interpretation seems directly parallel to Aquinas's claim that "it belongs to God alone to provide sentence of death and life," while death "is subject not to man's free will but to the power of God." Presumably Aquinas believed that human life is God's property because He created it, for he specifically likens the "sin against God" to the sin committed against the master of a slave when the slave is killed by a third party.

 Hume sweeps aside these Thomistic claims as unworthy. He argues that since persons die of *natural* causes—as in the cases of being poisoned or swept away by a flood—there is no reason to believe that there is an additional, nonnatural divine cause. That is, since such events can be easily explained by general causal laws, without reference to the notion of particular divine volition, appeal to divine intervention is not needed in order to explain the event. Hume also dismisses the divine-ownership thesis (as distinct from a right-of-disposal thesis): "If my life be not my own, it [would be] criminal for me to put it in danger, as well as to dispose of it. . . ." (156)

Hume's argument is not very convincing. It may be appropriately replied that natural causes are simply God's chosen means for the taking of human lives, yet the taking itself is a right God reserves and is an integral aspect of divine providence. Moreover, it does not follow from God's ownership of human lives that we ought not to endanger them any more than it follows from my entrusting of my life's savings to a speculative broker that the broker ought not to risk it.[26] Hume may have recognized a weakness in his first argument, for without belaboring it he shifts to a different accounting of the phrase "encroaching on God's established order." This shift introduces both his second and third arguments, which, as we shall see, partially overcome the deficiency just mentioned.

2. THE NATURAL-LAW INTERPRETATION Hume's second accounting of the possible meanings of "encroaching on God's established order" —and of the wrongfulness of encroachment—is that it is wrong to disturb the operation of any general causal law, since all causal laws taken together constitute the divine order. Hume construes this natural-law thesis to mean that human beings must be absolutely passive in the face of natural occurrences, for otherwise they would disturb the operations of nature by their actions. Hume ridicules this theology as absurd, since unless we resisted some natural events by counteractions, we "could not subsist for a moment." Hume means that diseases or exposure to the weather or some other "natural" event would destroy us. But if it is morally permissible to disturb *some* operations of nature, Hume reasons, then would it not also be morally permissible to avert life itself by diverting blood from its natural course in human vessels? Does not this action relevantly resemble turning one's head aside to avoid a falling stone, since both alike simply divert the course of nature? Hume thinks it arbitrary to permit stone avoidance while condemning suicide: "It would be no crime in me to divert the Nile or Danube from its course, were I able to effect such purposes. Where then is the crime of turning a few ounces of blood from their natural channel?" (155)

Hume's argument seems to me to fail as an argument against Thomists (as do R. B. Brandt's and Sidney Hook's similar arguments[27]), because the Thomistic contention that laws of nature and natural laws are distinct is not confronted. As we previously noted, according to Thomists natural laws do not describe behavior but rather delimit the natural behavior that is morally appropriate for a human being; suicide is wrong precisely because it violates a natural inclination to live in this sense of 'natural'. While it is true that the Thomistic distinction between laws of nature and natural laws is obscure, it is an essential feature of natural-law ethics; and if the distinction is allowed, then there arguably is a morally relevant difference between diverting the

Nile from its normal course and taking one's life by diverting blood from its normal channel, for human nature is different from river nature. Hume's central contention—that it is arbitrary to permit resistance to the effects of some laws while prohibiting intervention against the effects of others—would be acceptable *if the accusation of arbitrariness were demonstrated.* That is, his argument would be conclusive if he successfully showed the arbitrariness of accepting some law-governed natural processes as authoritative while excluding others. But Hume's conviction to this effect is only asserted, not argued, and hence fails to refute the Thomist.

3. THE DIVINE-APPOINTMENT INTERPRETATION Hume's third accounting of "encroaching on God's established order" rests on the theological view that nothing in the universe happens without providential "consent and cooperation." (157) He outlines this interpretation as follows:

> You are placed by Providence, like a sentinel, in a particular station; and when you desert it without being recalled, you are equally guilty of rebellion against your Almighty Sovereign, and have incurred his displeasure. . . . (157)

With this interpretation, Hume strikes at the heart of the theological matter. His "rebellion" is Aquinas's "sin," and in general Hume's statement is a paraphrase of a theology prominent in his time. The argument had appeared in John Locke (1632–1704), and would later appear in strikingly similar form in Kant.[28] But its popularity fails to impress Hume. He pronounces the argument absurd as an objection to suicide: If God so completely controls life, then *nothing* in life happens without divine consent and "neither does my death, however voluntary, happen without its consent." He concludes that whenever one no longer has a wish to live because of pain or exhaustion and wants to die, then one is being recalled from one's station "in the clearest and most express terms." (157)

Despite the importance and insightfulness of Hume's three arguments, even in combination they seem to me unsuccessful as a case against all possible theological objections to suicide. According to many moral philosophers, including both Hume and Aquinas, it is possible for humans to act both freely and in accordance with God's instituted order. Let us agree with them that all events, including all human choices, are caused, while free human actions still occur whenever one acts out of one's own reason or motive (while uncoerced). Thus, human death and, most importantly, a rational decision to commit suicide, are caused; but it does not follow either that a human death need happen with God's moral approval, or that the suicide is being recalled by God from his or her station. The reason is presumably simple: the suicide may be acting out of the wrong motive. For Hume to make good on his third antitheological argument, he would have to argue that no motive is morally better or worse than any other motive, since all motives are caused and in turn are the causes of action. Hume cannot consistently espouse this position, for he himself insists that some motives are blameworthy and others praiseworthy, even though all motives are caused. If this objection is sound, then Hume's first three antitheological arguments all fail. These arguments may provide a powerful case against some theologies, but not against all possible theologies. And if Aquinas's theology can accommodate the above argument, Hume's contentions fail to refute his thesis that suicide performed from certain motives is immoral (or, as some Thomists prefer to say, that all suicides are immorally motivated).

This criticism of Hume may, however, be overly stringent, for he does suggest one antitheological argument based on the importance of motives. Quoting Seneca, he observes that it is not inconsistent that a man should take his life in virtue of his misery, while at the same time expressing sincere gratitude to God "both for the good which I have already enjoyed, and for the power which I am endowed of escaping the ills that threaten me." (156) This one-sentence suggestion seems to me to constitute an important objection to Aquinas's theological arguments. It is powerful precisely because it challenges the moral and theological roots of the Thomistic position. The following is a reconstruction of Hume's argument, framed specifically as an objection to Aquinas: The removal of misery is a truly good effect and the intention to produce it cannot by itself be a condemnable motive, even if suicide is the unfortunate means to the end of the misery; additionally, it cannot be regarded as evil or sinful in intent if accompanied by a sincere expression of gratitude to God.

Under my previous interpretation of Aquinas's views, this argument has moral force, but the exact force depends on further specification of Aquinas's account. If one construes his position narrowly, so as to allow only a severely restricted set of motives to excuse suicide (fulfillment of a divine command as the sole allowed motive, e.g.), then the Humean objection seems powerful. But the more broadly one construes Aquinas's position as allowing a range of excusing intentions, the more one blunts the force of Hume's counterargument. On an extreme liberal interpretation of acceptable Thomistic intentions and effects, it would no longer be possible to say that Hume and Aquinas have a principled disagreement at all.

I do not conclude, then, either that Aquinas or Hume is right or that either is wrong. My conclusion is weaker: Hume's antitheological arguments fail to refute Aquinas, except insofar as Hume's gratitude-in-death argument is reconstructed in terms of motives. It would be hard to reach a more critical or decisive conclusion, since the arguments of neither philosopher contain the requisite specificity. Still, it is disappointing to reach this conclusion, since so many writers have been so heavily influenced by both philosophers. For example, in one of the best essays on the moral justification of suicide in recent years, Brandt completely defers to Hume's antitheological arguments, claiming that Hume's arguments are "perspicacious" and that they "discuss at length" the difficulties and contradictions in theological arguments.[29] I cannot agree. To the extent Hume's arguments are perspicacious, the detail of argument is lacking; and to the extent there is detailed argument, perspicacity is lacking. If one accepts an explicitly theological basis for a position on suicide (as St. Thomas and other defenders of the Theological Principle do), and if one also assumes that God exists (as Hume does for the sake of the argument), then it is virtually impossible to refute or "falsify" such a theological position from a philosophical perspective. It is therefore somewhat surprising that so many thinkers have thought Hume so completely refutes St. Thomas.

Hume's Constructive Position   In addition to criticizing St. Thomas's position, Hume argues positively in support of the moral permissibility of suicide. His argument is based almost exclusively on the principles of Utility and Autonomy. Hume first tries to show that in some cases resignation of one's life from the community "must not only be innocent, but laudable." The strategy of the argument is that of analyzing hypothetical cases[30] that stand as counterexamples to St. Thomas's claim (in his second argument) that "by killing himself (a person) injures the community." Hume begins with an analogy: Suppose a man retires from his work and from all social intercourse. He does not thereby harm society; he merely ceases to do the good he formerly did by his productivity and amiability. Hume advances a general claim about the reciprocity of obligations that launches his argument:

> All our obligations to do good to society seem to imply something reciprocal. I receive the benefits of society, and therefore ought to promote its interests; but when I withdraw myself altogether from society, can I be bound any longer? But [even] allowing that our obligations to do good were perpetual, they have certainly some bounds; I am not obliged to do a small good to society at the expense of a great harm to myself: when then should I prolong a miserable existence, because of some frivolous advantage which the public may perhaps receive from me? (158)

Hume immediately considers a series of both hypothetical and actual cases of suicide. Each case contains some new element not contained in previous cases that increases the personal or social value of death. In his first hypothetical case, Hume envisages a person still marginally productive in society. If his social contribution is small in proportion to the largeness of his misery, then Hume thinks there is no social obligation to continue in existence. The claim is utilitarian: If the value of removing misery by taking one's own life is greater than the value to the community of one's continued existence, then suicide is justified.

Hume then moves to his second and third hypothetical cases.[31] In the second, the potential suicide's existence is so bleak that he is not only miserable and relatively unproductive but a complete burden to society. In the third, a political patroit spying in the public interest is seized by enemies and threatened with the rack, and is aware that he is too weak to avoid divulging all he knows. In both cases, Hume stipulates that these unfortunates shall remain miserable for the remainder of their days. He then proclaims suicide under such conditions praiseworthy because it is in the larger public interest. He even maintains that "most people who live under any temptation to abandon existence" act from such lofty motives. (159) These examples of different suicides point to the empirical possibility that a person might be so situated that everyone in society actually benefits from the suicide. Whether the State is advantaged or disadvantaged by citizen involvement is relative to the citizen's situation, and Hume thinks that there are cases where suicide not only promotes the interest of the dying individual but in fact honors and shows respect for his family. These moral views clearly exhibit an emphasis on autonomy, but with a sharp utilitarian twist.

Can St. Thomas Refute Hume?　　What we have seen, then, is that Hume's defense of suicide can also be read as a critique of St. Thomas's second (nontheological) argument against suicide. We can now ask whether Hume's general claims about the reciprocity of obligations, his hypothetical cases, and his utilitarian arguments succeed in refuting Aquinas.

Aquinas's views depend on the thesis that the State actually is *injured* by removal of the part from the whole. Hume's carefully contrived examples point to the possibility that a person might be so situated that everyone actually benefits from his suicide. Should this result occur, then the Thomist would seem compelled in principle to *require* suicide in order to avoid injury to the State, or at the very least to *permit* suicide. More specifically, Hume's counterexamples show the Thomistic premises to be too feeble to support the desired conclusion in prohibition of suicide. Whether the State is advantaged or disadvantaged by citizen involvement is relative to the citizen's situation, and it is implausible to insist that the State is always advantaged by the participation of all its members under all circumstances. Aquinas's real grounding principle, it seems, is the absolutistic one that it is *always* illegitimate to take one's own life when the motive is self-regarding. This is probably a rather strong variant of what we earlier called the Principle of Human Worth. Thomas gives this principle much greater weight than either of the principles employed by Hume, including Utility. But if the Thomist presupposes this principle —or even the Theological Principle—as a basis for his second argument, then the argument must probably be judged evasive at best.

§13 A DEFENSE OF THE UTILITARIAN POSITION

Anyone who inferred from the previous section that my own sympathies in matters of the morality of suicide lie with Hume would have made a correct inference. In general, the position defended by Hume, and the one that I would defend as well, gives predominant weight in matters of the morality of suicide to the principles of Utility and Autonomy. Suicide is then judged permissible (and even on occasion laudable) if, on balance, more value is produced for the individual and for society by the action than would be produced by not performing the act of taking one's own life.[32] But at this point a certain problem arises. Hume is not only a utilitarian but a particular *type* of utilitarian, *viz.*, a rule-utilitarian. That is, he believes that the Principle of Utility justifies the moral rules that should be operative in society, and that particular acts are right if and only if they conform to these rules. And so the question arises whether there are substantial objections to rule-utilitarianism that have direct implications for suicide.

Donagan's Objections   At least one such objection should be considered, an objection advanced by the American philosopher Alan Donagan.[33] His is a *general* attack on rule-utilitarianism, and there can be little doubt that he would regard Hume's arguments—and mine as well—as subject to his criticism.

Donagan starts off by constructing a general theoretical objection to rule-utilitarianism by appealing to the distinction between (1) *morally obligatory actions* (those required by a moral duty) and (2) *supererogatory actions* (those over and above the call of moral duty and done from one's own personal ideals). His strategy is that of imagining situations where it is clearly our moral conviction that an action would be supererogatory rather than obligatory and yet where it is equally obvious that utilitarians must see the action as a duty because "there would be more good and less evil in society as a whole if the rule were adopted."[34] Donagan does not specifically consider a case of suicide, but he does imagine a society in which a rule sanctioning judicial murders in extreme circumstances would be required by rule-utilitarianism. That is, he constructs cases where, for the good of society, a judge sentences innocent persons to be killed. He takes this imagined society to be one in which rule-utilitarianism dictates that "one man should die for the people."[35] Similarly, Donagan would regard suicide solely for the sake of other persons as a near perfect illustration of a supererogatory act. He also would regard a society where "one man should die for the people" by committing a suicide as equal in demerit to his society that sanctions judicial murder. Suicide thus seems a remarkably good example for Donagan's objection to rule-utilitarianism. Moreover, Donagan argues that his very similar cases present the most difficult "kinds of consideration" that must be faced by *all* utilitarians.

Donagan's criticism of rule-utilitarianism can be given further support by constructing it as a *direct* reply to Hume's essay on suicide, as follows: As Hume's reciprocity-of-obligations thesis acknowledges, utilitarianism generates not only individual rights but also social obligations. It requires a code of rules that determines everyone's moral and social obligations. According to Hume, there are occasions when human existence has become personally and socially burdensome and has ceased to benefit that person or others. He argues that in such dire circumstances, suicide sets "an example, which, if imitated, would preserve to everyone his chance for happiness in life." Even more strongly, he argues that "both prudence and courage *should* engage us to rid ourselves at once of existence when it becomes a burden." (160, italics added) It follows that for reasons of utility we should adopt a moral rule that obliges every person so situated to commit suicide[36]—e.g., the rule that "Suicide ought to be performed whenever it is the case both that one has become more of a burden than a benefit to society and that there is more intrinsic disvalue than value in one's personal life."[37] Not only is this requirement counterintuitive, it is blatantly violative of our deepest moral convictions about autonomy and "the right to life," for one might *want* to live even if, by living, personal disvalue outweighs personal and even social value. This outcome seems a perfect instance of Donagan's claim that utilitarians cannot account for the distinction between morally obligatory acts and supererogatory acts.

If this Donagan-style criticism is sound, it shows that Hume's prosuicide argument, as it stands, is too broad, for it justifies too much: It dictates a moral rule *requiring* suicide, not a moral rule that merely grants a *right* to commit suicide. (Hume's argument would presumably also dictate rules requiring various forms of euthanasia, abortion, cessation of livesaving therapy, etc.)

A Reply to Donagan's Objection   Though there may be other ways to defend utilitarianism against Donagan's criticism, I shall dispute his criticism in the following way only: Against Donagan, I shall try to show why it is a mistake to suppose that utilitarian thinking dictates that a *rule* requiring suicide ought to be made current in our moral code. I shall also argue that it is a mistake to suppose that Hume's essay justifies too much by requiring such a rule. My argument will take this guarded route to the defense of a utilitarian position on suicide, as well as a defense of Hume.[38]

Donagan's argument assumes that a rule-utilitarian position requires the acceptance of moral rules that are so formulated that they *directly require* such bizarre obligations as suicide and judicial murder. There is no reason, however, that a rule-utilitarian must accept this characterization of the position. Here a distinction must be introduced between actions that fulfill what may be called *direct* obligations and those that fulfill what may be called *indirect* obligations—

where the obligations in both cases are rule governed. An action of the sort that fulfills a direct obligation is itself specifically described in and required by a valid rule in the moral code. The rule is universalizable for actions of that type. Truth-telling rules, for example, require that we tell the truth when faced with the temptation of lying, and they specifically govern truth-telling contexts. An action that fulfills an indirect obligation, by contrast, is not itself specifically described in and required by a valid rule referring to actions of that type; yet it is required in order to be in conformity with some valid rule, and the operative rule is not universalizable *for actions of that action type.* For example, we presumably do not have a duty to be sterilized, for there is not and ought not to be a moral rule in our code specifically requiring actions of that type. Still, circumstances can arise where the obligation to be sterilized is acquired in order to fulfill, for example, a promise to one's spouse. This raises the question whether (1) there *ought to be* a rule that itself refers to and requires suicide *or* (2) there *ought not to be* such a rule, even though suicide *might* be required as a means to the fulfillment of moral obligations generated by other moral rules. A rule-utilitarian like Hume must allow for the possibility of both (1) and (2)—as Hume and Donagan both recognize[39]—since the acceptance or rejection of any rule in such theories depends upon actual social conditions. Because (2) is intuitively more acceptable than (1), I shall begin with (2) and return later to a consideration of (1).

INDIRECT OBLIGATIONS TO SUICIDE Consider Hume's case of the pliable spy, a case Hume believes historically genuine, in the figure of Strozi of Florence. The spy possesses secrets "in the public interest" that could be extorted because of his own weakness and so commits suicide. This case is similar to Kant's fascinating case of Frederick the Great, who carried a quick-acting poison into battle. He intended to use the poison, if captured, in order to protect the nation from having to pay an intolerably burdensome ransom for his release.[40] In these two striking cases, it is plausible to invoke the Donagan doctrine that these actions are both supererogatory, though utilitarians make them matters of moral duty. But before capitulating to Donagan, we ought to build on these cases in order to see if his thesis can withstand a tougher trial. Suppose that the first two men on the moon had returned to earth with an incurable, deadly, and perilously contagious microorganismic disease with a forty-eight-hour incubation period. If the two do not die within forty-eight hours of their return (or are not sent into space exile), the disease will be incubated, and the human species will be annihilated. But if the two do die, then so will the microorganisms of disease. I would say that, under the circumstances, these two astronauts, who are themselves doomed to certain death, have a moral *obligation* to commit suicide.

A less fanciful, and indeed nonhypothetical, case can be used to reach the same conclusion. At the Treblinka concentration camp, some of those incarcerated were ordered to exterminate their fellow prisoners by opening the gas valves. Many so ordered committed suicide rather than carry out the order. Their reasons for suicide were that they had an obligation not to kill innocent persons and that suicide at their own hands was a better, or at least less cruel, fate than death by Nazi extermination. One might say that they committed suicide for the instrumental purpose of preserving their own moral integrity, which could be maintained only by fulfilling their moral obligations. However, the principled or rule-governed reason for the obligation to suicide (let us suppose suicide is here the only morally satisfactory alternative) is the requirement *to protect* (themselves and others) *from harm* and *not* a rule that itself requires suicide.

DIRECT OBLIGATIONS TO SUICIDE It has now been shown that from a Humean rule-utilitarian perspective, an indirect obligation to commit suicide is sometimes generated by some valid moral rules. But should there also be a rule that specifically mentions suicide and that requires it under certain circumstances? That is, should the moral code be such that there are rules specifically to commit suicide? To this question, I think the answer is almost certainly no, at least under social circumstances as we presently know them. There is a point of diminishing returns in any moral code concerning how many rules can be or ought to be publicly promulgated. There ought not to be so many rules that people cannot acquaint themselves with all the rules, or rules that apply only infrequently, or rules that are so heavily qualified that their interpretation is difficult. Since moral rules restrict human freedom, the social value derived from the having of a rule must be greater than the value of the freedom that would be gained by not having the rule. Moreover, it is doubtful that any rule directly requiring suicide could achieve any positive end that indirect-obliging rules could not. In short, it is doubtful that the public utility gained by having direct-obliging rules about suicide would exceed the disutility produced by confusion, insecurity, and misunderstanding.[41]

These reasons make it possible to see the germ of truth in the antiutilitarian argument offered by Donagan as well as its deficiencies. Generally, other-regarding or altruistic suicides *are* supererogatory, not morally obligatory. They are supererogatory because they confer a benefit on others, but not the sort of benefit that it would seem in general either significant enough or valuable enough to require. Thus we say such suicides are beyond the *normal* call of duty.[42] It is most doubtful that having a direct-obliging rule in our code that required suicide as a service to others would produce actions with better consequences than would be produced by leaving the choice of suicide generally up to one's personal ideals (the instruments of supererogatory actions) and to rules that indirectly require it in such highly dilemmatic situations as those previously mentioned.

On the other hand, any rule-utilitarian following Hume's lead must leave it an open question whether *under some social conditions* a rule requiring suicide *might validly be made current*. A rule-utilitarian must, for example, applaud the Eskimo rule that required suicide by the elderly. Survival at a decent level of human existence depended upon the institutionalization of the rule in their moral code, and it was fairly applied.[43] One can also imagine dire social circumstances into which any of us might fall that would similarly demand such a rule.[44] Consider, for example, those recent cases where a large plane has been forced down in a remote snowy region that is invisible from the air, and outsiders do not know where the plane has crashed, thus precluding rescue efforts. (Hume himself considers similar cases of shipwreck.) Now imagine a moral code being devised in such a minisociety. Suppose it were freely decided by all that in order for some to attempt escape after the spring thaw, cannibalism was necessary, that those who would die and be devoured would be chosen by a random method, that one so selected must commit suicide (so that none could later be prosecuted), and that normal rules against murder would prevail. Here I think rule-utilitarians must hold that under these and other unaccustomed circumstances, *a rule requiring suicide should control everyone's conduct and ought to be given a prominent place in the moral code.* Under these exotic circumstances, not committing suicide would encourage and perhaps even produce a general breakdown in the orderly system such that none could live—clearly the greatest disutility. It seems to me that any utilitarian who took this line—Hume included—would not in the least be subject to Donagan's censure, for what in other cases is either supererogatory or excusably wrong (because beyond a *normal* obligation) is here *obligatory, even if desperate.*

A general point of theoretical interest follows from this discussion. Those who attack utilitarianism often do so by adducing Donagan-type counterexamples. Cases of broken promises made in secret and cases of killing the innocent are legion in the antiutilitarian literature. But once the distinction between direct obligations and indirect obligations is recognized, it becomes obvious that unpalatable *rules* are not dictated except in unpalatable circumstances, such as the cannibalism case just mentioned. Thus, a Donagan-type objection fails to make any advance against either Hume's rule-utilitarianism or his position on suicide.

IV. PROBLEMS OF SUICIDE INTERVENTION

If the Principle of Autonomy is strongly relied upon for the justification of suicide, as it has been thus far, then it would seem that there is a *right* to commit suicide, so long as a person acts autonomously and without seriously affecting the interests of others. Yet we certainly do not always act as if the suicide has such a right, for we often intervene to prevent a person from committing suicide. In days past, for example, it was not uncommon for several persons to place themselves at risk of death in order to prevent a person from lying down on the subway tracks in New York in the path of an oncoming train. It is easy to understand why such interventions occur, as acts of humanity. And the Principle of Human Worth may incline one to believe that we are justified in intervening in the lives of such individuals. But if they have a *right* to commit suicide, are we really justified? In the case of almost any other similarly intrusive action, the person interfered with could sue those who intervene. A physician, for example, might be sued for malpractice by a similarly coercive treatment of patients. Yet in the case of suicide, some feel strongly inclined to say that we have obligations to suicidal human persons, even when they are acting autonomously. These are obligations both to prevent suicide and to intervene to stop it. Can we morally justify this conviction that intervention in the name of human worth and beneficence is better than nonintervention in the name of autonomy?

One account of our obligations, by a strong advocate of the principle of autonomy, is the following by Glanville Williams:

> If one suddenly comes upon another person attempting suicide, the natural and humane thing to do is to try to stop him, for the purpose of ascertaining the cause of his distress and attempting to remedy it, or else of attempting moral dissuasion if it seems that the act of suicide shows lack of consideration for others, or else again from the purpose of trying to persuade him to accept psychiatric help if this seems to be called for. Whatever the strict law may be (and authority is totally lacking), no one who intervened for such reasons would thereby be in danger of suffering a punitive judgment. But nothing longer than a temporary restraint could be defended. I would gravely doubt whether a suicide attempt should be a factor leading to a diagnosis of psychosis or to compulsory admission to a hospital. Psychiatrists are too ready to assume that an attempt to commit suicide is the act of a mentally sick person.[45]

Many do not agree with Williams's estimate. There are two main reasons for disagreement. First, failure to intervene may indicate both a lack of concern about others and a diminished sense of moral responsibility in a community. Attempts to save persons from suicide in subways are now comparatively rare, and this seems to indicate how times have changed in large cities—how disastrous the change has been. Second, many believe that most suicides are mentally ill or at least seriously disturbed and therefore are not capable of autonomous action. Notoriously, suicidal persons are often under the strain of temporary crises, under the influence of drugs or alcohol, and beset with considerable ambivalence (or they simply wish to reduce or interrupt anxiety, while not wishing to die). Let us consider this latter class of suicides first.

§14 NONAUTONOMOUS SUICIDES

Many psychiatric and legal authorities can be cited in support of the belief that suicides are almost always the result of maladaptive attitudes needing therapeutic attention. Their underlying conviction is that the suicidal person suffers from some form of disease or irrational drive toward self-destruction, and that it is the business of medicine or behavioral therapy to cure the illness and prevent the patient from taking this action. While no single theory presently suffices for the understanding of the motivation to suicide, many such accounts characterize suicide as substantially nonvoluntary and therefore as nonautonomous. Also, there exist other suicidal persons who are not ill but nonetheless are not in a position to act autonomously, because they are either immature, ignorant, coerced, or in a vulnerable position in which they might be exploited by others.

These nonautonomous persons are of course due all the same protections of moral rules afforded to autonomous persons. One way of respecting them as persons is by direct intervention in their lives, which is intended to protect them against harms resulting from their illness, immaturity, psychological incapacitation, ignorance, coercion, or possible exploitation. We might directly intervene, for example, by coercively preventing their suicides. Medical interventions, coercive institutionalizations, or some other method of prevention might be used. Those who are defenders of the Principle of Autonomy have never denied that this interference is valid, because they regard such suicidal actions as nonautonomous. They regard the Principle of Autonomy and the derivative right to commit suicide as extending only to persons capable of autonomous choice. For these reasons virtually everyone is agreed that nonautonomous suicidal actions should be prevented by intervention. The only controversial question is whether *autonomous* suicides should be similarly prevented.

§15 PATERNALISM AND AUTONOMOUS SUICIDES

This issue properly falls under the problem of paternalism, and we must begin with an understanding of this problem and of the options available in suicide intervention. 'Paternalism' is used in current moral philosophy to refer to practices that restrict the autonomy of individuals without their consent, where the justification for such actions is either the prevention of some harm they will do to themselves or the production of some benefit for them that they would not otherwise secure. The *Paternalistic Principle* asserts that limiting people's liberty is justified if through their own actions they would produce serious harm to themselves or would fail to secure important benefits. Many kinds of actions, rules, and laws are commonly justified by appeal to the Paternalistic Principle. Examples include laws that protect drivers by requiring seat belts, rules that do not permit a subject of biomedical research voluntarily to assume a risk when it is too great, court orders for blood transfusions when it is known that patients do not wish them, and various forms of involuntary commitment to mental hospitals. Laws both allowing intervention to stop autonomous suicides and permitting the resuscitation of patients who have asked not to be resuscitated have been claimed to be justified on similar, and even identical grounds.

Any supporter of a paternalistic principle that would justify suicide intervention should specify with care precisely which goods, needs, and interests warrant paternalistic protection. In most recent formulations, it has been said that the State is justified in interfering with a person's liberty if by its interference the person is protected against either (1) his or her own extremely and unreasonably risky actions, or (2) those actions not in the person's own best interest when such a person's best interest is knowable by the State, or (3) those actions that are potentially dangerous and irreversible in effect. Some believe that acts of suicide fit all of these categories, and therefore that intervention is justified. A general justification of this view has been offered by the British legal philosopher H. L. A. Hart:

> Paternalism—the protection of people against themselves—is a perfectly coherent policy. . . . No doubt if we no longer sympathise with [John Stuart Mill's] criticism this is due, in part, to a general decline in the belief that individuals know their own interest best, and to an increased awareness of a great range of factors which diminish the significance to be attached to an apparently free choice or to consent. . . . Harming others is something we may still seek to prevent by use of the criminal law, even when the victims consent to or assist in the acts which are harmful to them.[46]

Careful proponents of this view usually maintain that, at least in the case of suicide, paternalism is justified only if (1) the evil prevented from occurring to the person (death) is greater than the evils (if any) caused by limiting the person's autonomy; and (2) it is universally justified under relevantly similar circumstances to treat other persons in this same way.

By contrast, some moral philosophers believe that paternalism to prevent suicide is never justified after an initial temporary intervention to ascertain the cause (as mentioned by Williams). This position is the one classically supported by the nineteenth-century English philosopher John Stuart Mill (1806–1873) in *On Liberty,* though it can be supported on grounds other than the utilitarian ones offered by Mill. The following passage is Mill's own summary of his central theses:

> The only purpose for which power can be rightfully exercised over any member of a civilized community, against his will, is to prevent harm to others. His own good, either physical or moral, is not a sufficient warrant. He cannot rightfully be compelled to do or forebear because it will be better for him to do so, because it will make him happier, because in the opinion of others, to do so would be wise, or even right. These are good reasons for remonstrating with him, or

reasoning with him or persuading him, or entreating him, but not for compelling him, or visiting him with any evil in case he does otherwise.... His independence is, of right, absolute.[47]

Mill supposed he had articulated a general ethical principle that properly restricted social control over individual liberty, regardless whether such control is legal, religious, economic, or of some other type. Autonomous suicide would certainly seem to be covered—much as Hume would defend it by a similar argument.

Those who support this *antipaternalist* case, which is rooted in the Principle of Autonomy, would argue that it is legitimate to remonstrate with, to counsel, and to use other noncoercive measures to attempt to persuade the suicide not to perform the contemplated action —especially when the suicidal person appears voluntarily at a physician's office seeking help. But they would also maintain that in some cases it might be wise to counsel persons in favor of suicide. An analogy is often made between committing a "mentally disturbed" person against his or her will and performing the same act for someone who is suicidal. It is clearly illegal and immoral to cause the involuntary committal of someone capable of autonomous actions merely on grounds that he or she is suicidal. Similarly, it is argued, it would be immoral and should be illegal to coercively prevent someone from carrying out an intention to commit suicide. If people are autonomous, then they have the right to be left alone and to do with their lives as they wish, so long as they are sufficiently free of responsibilities to others. From this perspective, the intervention in the life of a suicide is simply an unjust deprivation of liberty.[48]

§16 UTILITARIANISM AND SUICIDE INTERVENTION

What now should be concluded about the justifiability of paternalistic intervention to prevent suicide? Clearly we are once again witnessing a dispute in ethics where the four principles earlier adduced have come into conflict. Autonomy and Utility generally incline us toward nonintervention, while Human Worth and the Theological Principle suggest intervention. Consistent with the positions previously maintained, the sympathies of this author are for the noninterventionist position, once it has been *established* that the suicide's act is an autonomous one. There is, however, a moral reason in addition to those previously mentioned for now accepting the noninterventionist position. In my view, paternalism to limit autonomy is never justified, whether in cases of suicide or elsewhere. The general reason is that paternalism gives to the State or to other authorities, in the cloak of a morally justified reason, a principle that would warrant unduly extensive intrusions into our personal lives. Paternalism in principle empowers authorities to prevent dangerous rafting on public rivers, to require that one not drink or smoke (even in private), and to preclude performing dangerous experiments on oneself (such as Walter Reed's famous yellow-fever experiments). This worry is not purely a theoretical and disembodied one. Prison environments and medical settings have sometimes thrived on the use of paternalistic justifications. Paternalism potentially gives prison wardens, medical professionals, and state officials a good reason for using all sorts of means to achieve ends they believe are in the interests of those affected. This argument is again rule-utilitarian. It is an objection to social *rules* that would allow (more than temporary) suicide intervention.[49]

V. CONCLUSION

Although Hume's convictions about the permissibility of suicide have been supported in this paper, we should note in conclusion that a suicidal action may be cowardly and even morally wrong. More strongly put, there are occasions on which one has moral obligations not to commit suicide, and there could be occasions on which one has moral obligations to commit suicide, though the latter are extremely rare. But merely because one has *some* obligation not to commit suicide, it does not follow that when all interests are taken account of, the overriding obligation will be to abstain from suicide. On the contrary, weak duties are sometimes overridden not only by stronger duties but also by strong prudential interests. Even though a dependent daughter might beg her terminally ill father to stay alive for his last remaining month, his agony may nonetheless be sufficiently great to override the daughter's interest in his remaining alive.

It is of course true that in calculating whether or not to commit suicide, it is easy to be mistaken in one's assessment by taking an unconsidered view. One's desires, sufferings, and hopes in the present moment generally tend to overwhelm consideration of what one's desires, sufferings, and joys may be at future times. In the case of known terminal illness, which provides one of the strongest justifications of suicide, one is not likely to change to a more optimistic frame of mind. Indeed, the matter is likely to become worse daily. But in the event of depression (where there is not a terminal physiological illness), during which the majority of suicides are committed, it is easy to miscalculate by substituting present feelings for rational calculations of future possibilities. Depression not only tends to foreclose consideration of the future, but even to render it impossible to project an adequate picture of future possibilities and probabilities. Without depression, persons might make quite different calculations, even when their situation is dire. The reason for this speculation about depression is the following: It is one thing to reach the conclusion, as I have, that autonomous suicide sometimes is justified. It is another to frame a realistic appraisal of the circumstances and of the actual state of mind of persons who perform allegedly autonomous suicides. It would be hoped that a suicide would take account of all relevant variables and future possibilities, but it is known that this often does not occur. Thus, questions about our obligations to prevent suicide will always be difficult because of our uncertainty as to whether the suicides are or are not truly autonomous.

However, in any final assessment of the wrongness of an act of suicide, it is important to distinguish two different judgments that might be reached. First, we might say that a suicide is seriously mistaken, and even morally wrong, but not blameworthy. Second, we might say that the suicide is both blameworthy and morally wrong. Use of this distinction turns on whether some wrong suicides may be excused.[50] We can excuse some suicides if they act on false information, if they are of temporarily unsound mind, or when depression or some other psychological state overwhelms someone of an ordinarily even disposition. The case of false information is the most interesting, as the latter two are somewhat obvious. Suicides often do act on information that is false or radically incomplete. This might occur if a physician concealed information, if one had a false belief about one's medical condition, if a person felt mistakenly spurned by a lover, etc. The most fascinating cases are those where a person acts altruistically in committing suicide, but bases the act on false information. For example, one might falsely believe that one is ill with a dreadful disease that will produce prolonged agony and leave one's family in financial ruin. Here it is reasonable to say that such a person not only acted wrongly though excusably, but even that he or she acted commendably though wrongly. One problem with the discussion of suicide found in St. Thomas and similar thinkers is that they do not distinguish the objective wrongness of an action from the moral excusability and even praiseworthiness of that same action. It is hoped that one virtue of the analysis of suicide offered throughout this paper is that it permits us to make these important distinctions and to adjust our moral judgments about suicide accordingly.

NOTES

1. Ronald Maris, "Sociology," in S. Perlin, ed., *A Handbook for the Study of Suicide.* New York: Oxford University Press, 1975, p. 101.
2. Cf. R. B. Brandt, "On the Morality and Rationality of Suicide," in S. Perlin, ed., *A Handbook for the Study of Suicide, op. cit.*, p. 61. Eike-Henner W. Kluge, *The Practice of Death.* New Haven: Yale University Press, 1975, p. 101. The article on suicide in *The Encyclopedia of Bioethics* is jointly authored by David Smith and Seymour Perlin. In fairness to Brandt, he does preface his definition with the word "assuming." Effectively he *assumes* this definition in order to discuss the morality and rationality of suicide. So I shall not be criticizing Brandt *per se*, but rather the definition that he assumes.

3. Emile Durkheim, *Suicide: A Study in Sociology,* trans. John A. Spaulding and George Simpson. New York: Free Press, 1966, p. 44.
4. Maris, *op. cit.*, p. 100.
5. E. Stengel, in *Proceedings of the VI International Congress for Suicide Prevention.* Ann Arbor, Mich.: Edwards Publishing, 1972.
6. It seems to me that some active but involuntary killings of the self can correctly be described as suicide—as when a frustrated lover heavily under the influence of LSD plunges through a sixteenth-floor window. Perhaps, then, we should speak here only about rational suicides.
7. Joseph Margolis, "Suicide," in Chapter 2 of *Negativities: The Limits of Life.* Columbus, Ohio: Charles E. Merrill Co., 1975, pp. 23f.
8. Important problems for the definition of suicide are presented by the indefinite meaning of the term 'cause'. Unfortunately, this difficult concept cannot be analyzed here and must be left as an undefined term.
9. Henderson Smith and Glanville Williams have coined the term 'voluntary death' as a surrogate. Cf. Williams's essay, "Euthanasia," *Medico-Legal Journal,* 41 (1973, Part 1), p. 30.
10. I do not think it would be correct, however, to hold that such justifying reasons *must be moral ones* or even must be thought to be moral ones, though they can be moral ones. Religious martyrs may act from the reason that an action being demanded of them is a violation of their religious convictions, and they may be willing to die for them, because they regard them, or at least their nonviolation of them, as more important than life. The political patriot is in a similar situation.
11. Joel Feinberg, "Introduction" to "The Sanctity of Life," in Tom L. Beauchamp, William T. Blackstone, and Joel Feinberg, eds., *Philosophy and the Human Condition.* Englewood Cliffs, N.J.: Prentice-Hall, 1980.
12. See Robert S. Scott, *Scott's Last Expedition.* London: 1935, Vol. I, p. 462.
13. R. F. Holland, "Suicide," in J. Rachels, ed., *Moral Problems.* New York: Harper and Row, 1971, pp. 352–353.
14. Perhaps a harder case is found in Eskimo societies, where the elderly take a small amount of food and leave the village expecting death in a short period of time but do not directly force death upon themselves as did Oates.
15. Margolis, *op. cit.*, pp. 27–28. Cf. his final definition on p. 33.
16. 'Arrangement' here *excludes* a refusal of treatment.
17. Premise (2) commits the Thomist to agreement with Hume that some suicides are rational and avoidable. Many philosophers and psychiatrists would deny this, of course, yet would use an argument similar to (1)–(3). Premises (1)–(2) would be acceptable to them if and only if (1) is construed as a law of human nature that denies that there can exist a natural internal impulse to self-destruction, while it is admitted that "external" forces such as physical causes or psychological compulsion can cause suicide.
18. Glanville Williams, *The Sanctity of Life and the Criminal Law.* New York: Alfred Knopf, 1957, p. 264.
19. This reading of Aquinas is based primarily on selected passages in the *Summa Theologica* other than the suicide passages. Cf., e.g., I–II. 90–97 and II–II. 94. Some Thomists place more emphasis on the importance of essential properties and/or rational intuition, but it makes little difference for our purposes.
20. Cf. Aquinas, Reply to Objection 4 in Article 5 and Reply to Objection 1 in Article 6 for his excusing condition. Article 7 in Question 64 contains a rough formulation of the Principle of Double Effect. Below I

consider the possibility that a Thomist would regard killing oneself for the sake of others as morally justified, while maintaining that it is not a case of suicide.

21. It is sometimes said that a fourth condition must obtain: The evil result must not be the cause of or means to the good effect. Whether this condition is a necessary condition of the principle is a substantive moral controversy into which we cannot here delve. Fortunately, it is irrelevant to any controversy pertaining to Hume's criticisms and probably is not found in Aquinas's text in any event.

22. Aquinas discusses the case of Samson as follows: " . . . not even Samson is to be excused . . . except the Holy Ghost . . . had secretly commanded him to do this." Reply Obj. 4.Cf. Reply Obj. 1 in Art. 6.

23. Throughout I shall use page references to the reprinting of Hume's essay in *Of the Standard of Taste and Other Essays,* ed. John Lenz (Indianapolis: Bobbs-Merrill, 1965). Hume's essay has been widely reprinted in textbooks of philosophical ethics (as a classic deserving equal consideration with writings on suicide by Seneca, Aquinas, Kant, Schopenhauer, and others), though its main influence may have come as a contribution to both late eighteenth-, nineteenth-, and twentieth-century English discussions of the morality of suicide and the acceptability of its legalization. The history of the English debate on suicide through Hume's early critics is discussed in S. E. Sprott, *The English Debate on Suicide from Donne to Hume* (LaSalle, Illinois: Open Court, 1961).

24. Hume's exact words are: "What is the meaning of that principle, that a [suicide] . . . has incurred the indignation of his Creator by encroaching on the office of divine providence, and disturbing the order of the universe?" (154)

25. Hume's choice of these three arguments is probably related to the Thomistic theories that were influential during his time.

26. However, Hume's theory of property, if correct, would render the Thomistic claim nonsensical. For Hume, the notion of property has no meaning prior to the establishment of rules of justice, and both are matters of human convention. (Cf. Hume's *Treatise,* pp. 484–514, Selby-Bigge edition.)

27. Brandt, *op. cit.,* p. 66. Cf. Sidney Hook's distinctly Humean approach in "The Ethics of Suicide," *Ethics,* 37 (1927), and reprinted in Marvin Kohl, ed., *Beneficent Euthanasia* (Buffalo: Prometheus Books, 1975), p. 62.

28. John Locke, *Second Treatise of Government* (Indianapolis: Bobbs-Merrill, 1952), p. 6. Immanuel Kant, *Lectures on Ethics,* trans. Louis Infield (New York: The Century Co., 1942 and reprinted by Harper Torchbooks, 1963), pp. 148–154, esp. 153f.

29. Brandt, *op. cit.,* p. 66.

30. His hypothetical cases have actual analogues. Many suicide notes reflect a belief that the suicide has become an unavoidable social burden.

31. Hume imagines still other cases, such as that of a prisoner condemned to die and the presumably historical case of Strozi of Florence. But these cases do not constitute types of cases relevantly different from the third case.

32. The reverse, however, does not follow from any argument thus far presented. That is, it does not follow that suicide *should* or *must be* performed if the utilitarian calculus indicates that it would maximize value in the circumstances. Autonomy should not be overridden by utility—at least no argument thus far addressed commits either me or Hume to this claim.

33. Donagan's objection is pressed in particular against R. B. Brand t's rule-utilitarianism, but that fact is of little concern for our purposes. Cf. Richard B. Brandt, "Toward a Credible Form of Utilitarianism," and Alan Donagan, "Is There a Credible Form of Utilitarianism?" both in *Contemporary Utilitarianism,* ed., Michael D. Bayles (Garden City: Doubleday & Co., 1968).
34. Donagan, *op. cit.*, p. 196.
35. *Ibid.*
36. In the context of Hume's essay it is left unclear whether the "should" in the previous sentence is merely a matter of what he calls a "duty to ourselves" or is a moral matter and hence a matter of a "duty to our neighbors." By reference to the constraints of his rule-utilitarianism, it can plausibly be argued that Hume cannot consistently believe that it is merely a matter of self-duty. Following this interpretation, which is favorable to Donagan, Hume is committed to saying the following: Whenever a person regards his life as "not worth keeping" and is a social burden, utility would be maximized in this single circumstance by committing suicide. An act-utilitarian might stop here, but a rule-utilitarian would go on to say that if adoption of a general rule to this effect would maximize utility, then a society ought to make such a rule current.
37. That is, if social utility would be maximized by having such a rule, as it often would be, then the rule ought to be adopted. Donagan actually formulates a similar rule intended to govern judicial murder (p. 196) and one that governs unusual welfare payments (p. 194).
38. My defense is not a full defense of rule-utilitarianism, of course, since the perplexing problem of distributive justice is not considered.
39. Hume, *Second Enquiry,* Pars. 147, 149. Donagan, *op. cit.*, p. 195f.
40. Kant, *The Metaphysics of Morals,* Part II, published as *The Metaphysical Principles of Virtue,* trans. J. Ellington (Indianapolis: Bobbs-Merrill, 1964), pp. 84f.
41. The above analysis is indebted to both Brandt, "Toward a Credible Form of Utilitarianism," *op. cit.*, p. 158, and to Hume.
42. Drawn from Joel Feinberg, "Supererogation and Rules," *Ethics,* Vol. 71 (1961), pp. 276–88, esp. 280.
43. For an interesting presentation of the Eskimo rule, cf. Margolis, *op. cit.*
44. Hume specifically considers such cases, using the example of a shipwreck. However, his case is the more radical one, where social order breaks down completely and "the strict laws of justice are suspended." He also considers famines, but his comments are not insightful (*Enquiries,* pars. 147 and 165).
45. Williams, "Euthanasia," *op. cit.*, p. 27.
46. H. L. A. Hart, *Law, Liberty, and Morality.* Stanford: Stanford University Press, 1963, pp. 31–33.
47. *On Liberty,* as reprinted in *Essential Works of John Stuart Mill.* New York: Bantam Books, 1961, p. 263.
48. For one influential statement of this view, cf. Thomas Szasz, "The Ethics of Suicide," *Antioch Review,* 31:1 (Spring 1971), pp. 7–17.
49. Since I have elsewhere defended this case against paternalism at length, I shall not further elaborate the argument here. Cf. "Paternalism and Biobehavioral Control," *The Monist,* Vol. 60 (January 1977), pp. 62–80.
50. This analysis draws heavily on Brandt's useful discussion of the subject in "The Morality and Rationality of Suicide," *op. cit.*, p. 124.

SUGGESTIONS FOR FURTHER READING

On the question of how suicide is to be defined (§§1–6), the following readings are especially noteworthy:

Douglas, Jack D., *Social Meanings of Suicide.* Princeton, N.J.: Princeton University Press, 1967.

Durkheim, Emile, *Suicide: A Study in Sociology,* trans. John A. Spaulding and George Simpson. New York: Free Press, 1966.

Holland, R. F., "Suicide," as reprinted in James Rachels, ed., *Moral Problems,* 2nd ed. New York: Harper and Row, 1975.

Margolis, Joseph, *Negativities: The Limits of Life.* Columbus, Ohio: Charles E. Merrill Co., 1975. Chapter 2.

St. Thomas's position (§11) and related positions are set forth in representative primary and secondary works, including the following:

Augustine, *The City of God,* trans. Marcus Dods. New York: Modern Library, Random House, 1950. Bk. I, sections 17–27, esp. sections 21–22, 26.

Novak, David, *Suicide and Morality: The Theories of Plato, Aquinas, and Kant and Their Relevance for Suicidology.* New York: Scholars Studies Press, 1975.

St. John-Stevas, Norman, *Life, Death and the Law: Law and Christian Morals in England and the United States.* Bloomington: Indiana University Press, 1961.

Thomas Aquinas, *Summa Theologica,* trans. English Dominican Fathers. New York: Benziger Brothers, 1947. Q. 64, A. 5 and Q. 76, A. 4.

David Hume's position (§12) and related positions are found in commentaries or other sources where Hume's position plays a central role. These sources include:

Beauchamp, Tom L., "An Analysis of Hume's Essay 'On Suicide'," *Review of Metaphysics,* 30 (September 1976), 73–95.

Hume, David, "On Suicide." Reprinted widely.

Mossner, Ernest Campbell, "Hume's *Four Dissertations:* An Essay in Biography and Bibliography," *Modern Philology,* 48 (1950), 37–57.

Sprott, S. E., *The English Debate on Suicide.* LaSalle, Ill.: Open Court, 1961.

Important readings relevant to the problem of suicide intervention (§§14–16) include:

Chodoff, Paul, "The Case for Involuntary Hospitalization of the Mentally Ill," *American Journal of Psychiatry,* 133 (1976), 496–501.

Greenberg, David F., "Involuntary Psychiatric Commitments to Prevent Suicide," *New York University Law Review,* 49 (1974), 227–269.

Szasz, Thomas, "The Ethics of Suicide," *The Antioch Review,* 31 (Spring 1971), 7–17.

Williams, Glanville, *The Sanctity of Life and the Criminal Law.* New York: Knopf, 1957.

The following are important classical writings on problems of suicide:

Kant, Immanuel, *Lectures on Ethics,* trans. Louis Infield. New York: Harper and Row, 1963, pp. 148–154.

————,*The Metaphysics of Morals,* Part II, published as *The Metaphysical Principles of Virtue,* trans. James Ellington. Indianapolis: Bobbs-Merrill, 1964.

Montaigne, Michel de, "A Custom of the Isle of Cea," *Essays,* trans. John F. Florio. 3 vols. London: Dent, 1928. Bk. 2, Chapter 3.

Schopenhauer, Arthur, "On Suicide," *Studies in Pessimism,* trans. T. B. Saunders. London: George Allen & Unwin, 1890, 1962.

Seneca, "On Suicide," *Epistles,* trans. E. Barker. Oxford: Clarendon Press, 1932.

The following are important books and anthologies on suicide:

Beauchamp, Tom L., and Seymour Perlin, eds., *Ethical Issues in Death and Dying.* Englewood Cliffs, N.J.: Prentice-Hall, Chapter 2.

Perlin, Seymour, ed., *A Handbook for the Study of Suicide.* New York: Oxford University Press, 1975.

Shneidman, Edwin S., ed., *Suicidology: Contemporary Developments.* Seminars in Psychiatry, ed. Milton Greenblatt. New York: Grune & Stratton, 1976.

Stengel, Erwin, *Suicide and Attempted Suicide.* Studies in Social Pathology. Hamondsworth, England: Penguin Books, 1973. Reprint, New York: J. Aronson, 1974.

The following are especially important articles on moral problems of suicide:

Brandt, R. B., "The Morality and Rationality of Suicide," as reprinted in James Rachels, ed., *Moral Problems.* New York: Harper and Row, 1975. Second Edition.

Hook, Sidney, "Ethics of Suicide," *International Journal of Ethics,* 37 (1927), 173–189.

Kluge, Eike-Henner W., *The Practice of Death.* New Haven: Yale University Press, 1975. Chapter 2.

Important reference works include the following:

Bibliographies

Farberow, Norman L., *Bibliography on Suicide and Suicide Prevention, 1897–1957, 1958–1970.* DHEW Publication No. (HSM) 72-9080. Rockville, Md.: National Institute of Mental Health. Washington: U.S. Government Printing Office, 1972.

Sollitto, Sharmon, and Veatch, Robert M., comps., *Bibliography of Society, Ethics, and the Life Sciences.* Hastings-on-Hudson, N.Y.: Institute of Society, Ethics, and the Life Sciences, 1973—Issued annually. See "Death and Dying: Suicide."

Walters, LeRoy, ed., *Bibliography of Bioethics.* Vols. 1—. Detroit: Gale Research Co., 1975—. Issued annually. See "Suicide."

Encyclopedia of Bioethics *Articles*

AGING AND THE AGED: *Health Care and Research in the Aged*—Ernlé Young

LIFE: *Value of Life*—Peter Singer

LIFE: *Quality of Life*—Warren T. Reich

4

Violence and War

JAN NARVESON

§1 INTRODUCTION

War is a depressing subject. Its evils are manifest, and it is hard to think of anything good to say on its behalf. After all, people are killed, maimed, disabled for life, their lives thoroughly disrupted, their property ruined or taken over by strangers whom they probably dislike, and they are likely to be subject to autocratic rule for the duration and perhaps long after that if they are on the losing side. And in the end, what difference does it make? Probably just that the people who rule over certain stretches of terrain are different from the former rulers; apart from that, the main difference is that some of the people involved in the conflict are now dead. Given all this, one can well wonder how anything positive can be said about war.

But things are not so simple. For one thing, not everyone has been so uniformly impressed with the negative aspects of war. Immanuel Kant (1724–1804) said that war is "sublime," and Hegel (1770–1831) taught that wars are required by the world spirit. Politicians—not necessarily just tyrannical ones at that—have often undertaken wars with enthusiasm. And then, when we condemn wars we probably have in mind only those who start them, the aggressors. But what about the side that is attacked? Do we condemn it as well, for fighting back? Interestingly enough, some have said yes to this, holding that all use of violence, whether defensive or otherwise, is morally wrong. That is a view that surely commands our attention. And if we reject it in the end, there remains the knotty question of just when we are justified in fighting back, and what we may do when we do so.

These are the subjects we shall be concerned with in the following pages. I will explore, if sketchily, what I regard as the major reasonable options in moral theory, applying them to the subjects of violence and war. We start with the use by individuals of violence, then move to war, which is violence as used by large, organized groups on a grand scale. In between, we discuss in depth the theory of pacifism, which condemns all violence however used. The aim is to be fundamental, to work from the ground up. But while I am by no means austerely neutral on all subjects—some views being roundly rejected—no one view is presented as definitive. Rather, the reader, I hope, will be left with a sense of there being reasonable options.

This is not entirely to my liking. I should prefer to have been able to present the Truth about these matters. But I simply do not see my way clear to narrowing the "reasonable options" down to just one.

§2 DEFINITIONS: 'WAR' AND 'VIOLENCE'

'War' We use the word 'war' mainly to refer to large-scale armed conflicts between politically organized states. But not always, for we also speak of "tribal war," "gang war," and "race war," in which the groups aren't formally political units; and we even speak of war between individuals—"Lydia, this means war!" or more seriously, the condition of a "universal war of all against all" envisaged by Thomas Hobbes (1588–1679). We even speak of "price wars" and "wars of nerves." In all cases, though, what makes it a case of war is the same: there is a conflict in which the parties resort to violence, or (in the nonliteral cases) they resort to means that amount to violence in that they involve abuse and flout the usual rules of procedure, in the attempt to impose their will on the other side. War, then, is the coercive use of violence by opposed parties, primarily politically organized states. The most important part of this definition is the concept of violence. Let us consider that.

'Violence' Sometimes 'violence' is simply a synonym for 'force', as when we say "the volcano exploded with great violence." Sometimes we mean by it the likelihood of injury or pain, as when football and ice hockey are called "violent" sports. Again, we speak of "violating" rules or principles, as in "doing violence to the English language." And sometimes violence is defined as being wrong, as the *wrongful* infliction of injuries, etc. For our purposes, however, 'violence' will be used in the narrower way, to refer to the intentional infliction of damage, pain, injury, or death by forcible means. We need not worry too much about trying to arrive at a precise definition, so long as we are careful to avoid two pitfalls. First, since we are inquiring into the issue of when, if ever, violence is wrong, we must not adopt a meaning of 'violence' in which it is simply defined as "wrong," since that would make the inquiry into its justification nonsensical. Second, we must not use the term so broadly that any and all bad things are meant by it.

Those who argue that violence is the supreme evil, for instance, must be understood to be saying that there are also other evils, and that violence is worse than they are. Armed robbery involves violence, but embezzlement does not. Stabbing a person is a violent act, but defaming his or her character is not. Rape and arson are cases of violence; poverty and malnutrition are not (though they could result from it). But we shall, by and large, leave the details to common sense.

§3 VIOLENCE BY GROUPS AND INDIVIDUALS

War is violence on the grand scale, by large groups. But large groups, however they are organized, consist of individuals. Whether the politically organized nature of war affects the morality of violence will be considered in part III. But if violence by individuals is always wrong, for instance, then the immorality of war would follow, since wars can only be fought if some individuals use violence. We treat individual violence first, therefore—in part I generally, and in part II with special reference to pacifism. In part III only do we discuss war as such, with some further reflection on political violence in general.

I. MORALITY AND VIOLENCE

§4 VALUES AND VALUING

Philosophers have differed greatly on such subjects as what 'good' means, what if anything the Good is, and what is the best way or ways to live. Fortunately, we do not need to resolve any of those matters here. Instead, we need merely fix on one obvious point about values, namely that a person's values are his or her *preferences,* more especially his or her considered ones. They are what one wants and continues to want even when one thinks carefully about it.

There are two features of values that are crucial for purposes of moral philosophy. First, they guide our behavior. Thus, when different people have conflicting values, this is likely to lead to conflicting actions as well. Second, values are held by rational beings. They are subject to criticism, reflection, argument from oneself or others, and thus to change in the light of reasons.

Rational *behavior* is closely connected with values. The rational person is one who (a) thinks about his or her values, seeking out relevant facts and shaping the values in the light of those facts; and (b) is a rational *agent,* acting in such a way as to do one's best in terms of one's own values. Not, notice, the values others have, but the values he or she has. The importance of this will emerge at many places in the following pages, especially in §6. One immediate implication to note is that this definition may make it sometimes rational to use violence in the promotion of what one values.

§5 MORALITY

Which of a person's values and principles are *moral* ones? For present purposes, we shall answer this much-argued question by saying that they are those that concern how everyone, the person included, ought to deal with others in general. Moral principles are those by which everyone ought to guide his or her dealings with others. A given person's moral principles are the ones that he or she believes ought to guide everyone's behavior toward others. One's principles might not be formed in words, but it is important that principles could, in principle, be formulated that way.

What kind of guidance do we have in mind in saying that our principles do or should "guide" our behavior? First, such principles are to override contrary desires. This is essential. A person who acts simply on desires, however whimsical, has no principles. Second, insofar as we talk about moral guidance, the guidance is "internal": moral principles are internal behavior controls. Insofar as others control us and we have no will of our own, we do not act morally. Sometimes, to be sure, we profess principles that we fail to act on. If so, we may be insincere or we may have misunderstood something or we may be "morally weak," unable to do as we believe we ought. These, necessarily, are moral defects.

Morality includes the principles by which governments, as well as individuals, ought to act, for it concerns how individuals always ought to act, including when they are acting in governmental roles. But more of this in part III (§§18 ff.).

§6 MORAL THEORY

Moral principles and rules are generalizations about what we ought to do. Moral *theories,* however, are organized sets of beliefs that include not only the most general principles of morality but also explanations of what morality is and why just those principles, rather than others, are properly part of it. Anyone might have such a theory, but the moral philosopher makes certain to do so, and to subject proposed theories of morality to criticism. Theories aim to be true: so if two theories are incompatible with each other, then we can rationally believe at most one of them, for at most one can be true. Aiming at truth, they are subject to all the demands of any rational activity; they are to be rejected, or at least temporarily shelved, if shown to be inconsistent, insufficiently evidenced, obscure, or at odds with the facts.

What we seek as philosophers, and indeed as rational beings, is a rational moral theory, one that compels our acceptance upon careful consideration. What will such a theory look like? The answer, we may conjecture, is that it will appeal to *rational agents.* A rational agent, recall, is one whose actions are guided by his or her values—whatever they are. So a rational moral theory, we may plausibly suppose, will be one whose principles can be rationally accepted by people pursuing many *different* values. Now, moral principles involve values, and values are, of course, preferences. However, a principle about how everyone is to behave need not be founded upon a sheer preference. I may happen to like everyone's doing so-and-so. But I have no reason to *expect* others to do something simply because I prefer them to do it, for people act on their own preferences, not on mine. Thus, if my proposal for a uniform way of behaving by all is to be rational, it will have to be based on something much more substantial than my sheer preferences. It must be based on two things: the whole ensemble of my own values—i.e., my preferences for all sorts of things, not just my preferences for others' behavior—*and* the fact that there are other people with whom I come in contact, people who have their own peculiar value schemes in the light of which they act, and rationally act.

Already certain popular ideas of morality can be rejected. For instance, any that simply invoke authorities whose commands are not to be questioned will not do. The "authority" has to show us reason why we should act as ordered; that another being tells us to do something is, by itself, no good reason at all. Or again, a theory might invoke ideas that are simply too obscure to be capable of giving us any reasons for anything. But morality is for everyone. It cannot invoke notions that make no sense to the ordinary person.

Morality, then, will be a sort of agreement among rational agents. In the next section, I present three views about what the basic terms of such an "agreement" might be. Meanwhile, one last point. Theorizing and discussing and criticizing are, of course, basically peaceable and cooperative activities. It might be thought, then, that war, being a species of conflict, will automatically be condemned on any moral theory, just by virtue of its nature as a *moral* theory—i.e., a theory expressing a rational agreement on what all are to do. But this is not so. For we conceivably might agree on principles that *call for* conflict. To take an obvious example from a limited sphere, consider the players in a competitive game, such as football or chess. The players agree perfectly on the rules. Yet even though they break no rules at all, they are still in conflict—each is trying to defeat the other, and each not only knows but approves of the fact that the other is trying to do so. It is an important question whether war—or, for that matter, life!—is like that. If it is, we may all be morally justified in engaging in conflict. Obviously, it is important to know whether this is so. The point, at the moment, is that our conception of morality does not automatically rule it out.

§7 THREE THEORIES

It would be too lengthy to explore, or even to list, all the theories of morality that have been seriously advocated and that would have implications for our subject. Anyway, many of them would, I believe, be ruled out by the basic theory begun above. However, that conception does not narrow the field down to just one option. What we must reject, so far, are theories that take some values, the values of some people (or perhaps gods), and try to erect on them rules for everyone's conduct. A proper theory, however, must leave everyone *in.* Many theories might do this. Here I present three. Each meets our requirements and each is of special interest in its own way. In addition, though it may not be obvious, each has had many adherents and has been very influential in (at least) Western thought and action. (Each, I think, is also mirrored in influential Eastern thought and certainly action. But we cannot pursue that here.) At any rate, here they are:

a. Libertarianism   The basic requirement of morality is noninterference with others in what belongs to them. And what "belongs" to each of us is: our body and mind, whatever we have made, whatever has been given to us either as a free gift or in voluntary exchange, and whatever we take possession of that is not already someone else's. Each of us may do exactly as we wish with what is ours, but with what is anyone else's, no one may do anything except by consent of the owner. Hence, the theory's name: we are to respect absolutely the liberty of others to do as they please with what is theirs.

b. Contractarian Egoism   Ethical egoism is the view that each individual ought to do whatever promotes his or her values to the maximal degree; relations with others are governed entirely by viewing them as means to one's own ends. As a theory of what constitutes rational behavior, this has much to recommend it; but as a moral theory it seems hopeless, as it stands. For it is not in general in the interest of any given person to have other people doing whatever is in *their* maximal interest, since their interests often conflict with one's own. And yet, that is what the theory seems to require us to approve. But an interesting modification makes this into a more plausible moral theory. What constraints in relation to others will we adopt to promote our own long-run interests? Those that are beneficial to us, of course. But others will not adopt them unless they benefit them as well. So we will rationally adopt mutually beneficial constraints: we will agree to do things for each other where we would be worse off acting independently. These agreements require trust, of course, for if one party tries to do still better—collecting the benefits without sharing in the work —the other's agreement and cooperation would have been in vain. Morality, then, consists in respecting reasonable agreements. This includes not only agreements that have been explicitly made but also behavior that is so obviously of mutual benefit that no prior agreement should be necessary. Moral praise and blame will be distributed so as to reinforce these mutually advantageous patterns of behavior. But where mutual advantage is not possible, each is allowed to act independently according to his or her own values.

c. Utilitarianism   Each individual is to count a given amount of value realization by anyone as equal in value to a like amount by anyone else. Morality consists in promoting the satisfaction (i.e., value realization) of everyone as much as possible. For any given choice of actions, then, we are to estimate the positive effects of each alternative on all affected parties, then the negative, subtracting the bad from the good. The right action is the one with the highest net "score" of utility promotion. ('Utility' equals 'value realization'.)

Each of these theories, in its own way, uses only the values that individuals separately have, selecting different methods of accommodating the fact of other people's existence. Libertarianism allows each of us to do as we like within our own sphere. Contractarianism tells each of us to maximize our own long-range utility, morality being a means to this. And utilitarianism asks the greatest accommodation to others but promises the greatest average reward as well. Each has had important advocates, past and present. But rather than discuss them further in the abstract, let us see what each has to say about violence.

§8 IMPLICATIONS OF THE THREE THEORIES CONCERNING VIOLENCE

a. Libertarianism   To use violence against someone is to "cross that person's boundaries" without permission, inflicting things on the person that he or she does not want—injury, damage, pain, and harm. Since each of us has the right to do with our own body, mind, and property as we wish, violence is therefore absolutely wrong when done against persons who have done no wrong themselves. However, once someone has committed an infringement against another, the latter has the right to restoration or compensation. The aggressor forfeits freedom insofar as necessary to make this compensation. And everyone has the right to self-defense, insofar as reasonably necessary, against such depredations. Violence that is necessary to rectify injustices, if used only against guilty parties, is justified (in which case it usually would not be *called* "violence," of course). All other violence is wrong.

b. Contractarianism   Contractarianism is somewhat different. First, if there is no reasonable, mutually advantageous agreement possible, then each party may do as he or she pleases, including commit violence. Of course, that situation of no agreement, which Hobbes calls the "State of Nature," would be extremely dangerous, since everyone would have good reason to engage in warfare for self-protection: the best defense may be a good offense! Clearly, for almost everyone it will be worthwhile exchanging one's freedom to do violence in return for everyone else's abstention from violence toward oneself. Might there be a few who enjoy fighting so much that they won't agree? Yes. But remember: since nothing is wrong outside of the areas of agreement, it follows that the rest of us may, without any injustice, kill these few or imprison them or whatever we like, and they can have no moral complaint. Moral condemnation of violence will therefore be unanimous among everyone who counts for moral purposes. Of course, by the same reasoning, the use of violence if necessary for defensive purposes will be approved, for it was in the interest of safety that we surrendered the liberty to be violent in the first place.

There is one important divergence between the contractarian and libertarian views worth noting here. Suppose that the only way one can stay alive is by using violence: one's neighbors refuse to help. It would not be rational to renounce the use of violence in such cases. And it would be in the interests of the better off to be willing to help those in desperate need, rather than fighting them. So the condemnation of violence will extend to every case where it is not necessary to preserve one's life, but not to cases where it is necessary. Libertarianism, on the other hand, condemns such violence as well.

c. Utilitarianism Utilitarianism nearly agrees with the other two theories. Violence is the infliction of injuries, damage, etc., and these are "disutilities." So it would be wrong to use violence unless the benefits to all concerned, counting the victims equally with the aggressors, outweigh the net benefit of *any* alternative action. It is overwhelmingly likely that violent acts will not meet this condition. Pain, injury, death—these are great losses to us. But the would-be aggressor who refrains from violence does not suffer such losses. So when the potential victim is "innocent," that is, has no reason to be punished, then it is virtually certain that more net good to all concerned can be realized without violence. Again, however, self-defense is an exception. For to allow people to get away with violence cannot be utility promoting, for one thing. And for another, when there is an aggressor, some violence is going to be done in *any* case; so it is obviously going to be utility promoting to allow violence, if necessary, for self-defense. And there will be the same kind of exception possible for people in desperate need. In the utilitarian view, others ought to help them, and if they do not, then it may come down to a choice between death by starvation (say) for some and the threat of violence to others, who can easily avoid it by being just slightly helpful. Violence in such extreme cases could not easily be condemned. But in all other nondefensive cases, it will be.

The area of agreement among these theories, as we see, is very substantial. All agree that violence against people who have not themselves committed wrongs against others is to be virtually always condemned. The theories differ somewhat about when violence would not be condemned, and in part III we shall consider whether that makes enough difference to allow certain nondefensive wars to be justly fought. Meanwhile, the thought may nag us that perhaps our theories are excessively "soft on violence." Doesn't life have supreme value, for instance? Has it not been lost sight of? The idea that violence is supremely wrong and always to be refrained from, no matter what the circumstances, is among the most fascinating ones in this area. It behooves us to give this idea the most serious attention as we proceed to part II, consisting of the next eight sections of this essay.

II. PACIFISM

§9 WHAT PACIFISM IS

By 'pacifism', in what follows, I shall mean adherence to the rule that one is to refrain from using violence under all circumstances, none of the usual excuses or justifications being permitted. This is an "extreme" rule, and many less extreme ones have been called "pacifist." But the extreme rule is of great interest, and in examining it we will perhaps shed light on the "milder" doctrines as well.

Our definition leaves open the question *why* the rule is to be adopted. This is because there are many different ways of defending it. We shall be examining just these below; the next seven sections deal with various arguments for pacifism. I am sure that not all have been examined, but I am hopeful that all of the most important ones have. In §16, I turn to positive criticism, summarizing my results in §17.

§10. THE WRONGNESS OF VIOLENCE—A DISTINCTION

One reason that someone might adopt pacifism is the feeling that violence is wrong, wrong in itself. What could be simpler? And surely true morality can allow no exceptions to this?

But indeed it can. Those who advocate pacifism because violence is "wrong in itself" may be making a mistake. Their reasoning is evidently something like this:

1. Violence is wrong in itself.
2. Violence in self-defense (etc.) is still violence.

Therefore,

3. Violence in self-defense (etc.) is still *wrong*.

The argument is unsatisfactory because the somewhat unusual expression 'wrong in itself' is unclear. What does it mean? I suggest this: If we take into account only that it is that *kind* of act (in this case, a violent one), ignoring all else about the circumstances in which it may be performed, then we have reason to disapprove of it, morally. Now this means, really, that acts of that kind are wrong "other things being equal," or as recent philosophers say, *prima facie* wrong. But its being wrong, other things being equal, does not mean that other things cannot *count*. Acts are complex. Some of an act's features in a given case may suggest that it is wrong, while others suggest that it is right. It is wrong, other things being equal, to strike a child; yet sometimes striking the child might be necessary for its long-run well-being. This fact must be weighed against the fact that striking causes pain. So, turning to the argument above, we note that its first premise (1) would usually mean that violence is wrong "other things being equal"; but the conclusion (3) apparently means that violent acts are still wrong, even after all other facts have been taken into account. But this conclusion does not follow from that premise. The pacifist needs a further premise: namely, that other things *have no weight* as compared to violence—that once we know an act is violent, then we know it is wrong no matter what else is true about it. But what if the harm done by the violence is very small, while the evils avoided because of it are very great? If these other facts have any real weight, they can sometimes outweigh the fact that violence was involved. So the pacifist must show that they have *no* weight. Just saying that violence is wrong in itself will not do the job. Can the pacifist *show* that?

§11 "ABSOLUTE" EVILS

One way to support the claim that nothing else counts by comparison to violence is to maintain that violence is not only evil "in itself," but that it is "absolutely" evil, meaning that it is *irredeemable:* that the degree of evil involved in any amount of violence, however small, exceeds the degree of compensating good that could be accomplished by such an act, however great. There are two questions to raise: (a) Is this true? and (b) Does it actually support pacifism? Let us consider these in turn.

a. Is violence "absolutely" evil? How do we assess a belief like this? One way is to look at the evils involved from the point of view of those who suffer them, i.e., the victims of violence. Indeed, this would seem by far the best way to look at it, for how could anything except the effects on those it hurts be the basis of the wrongness of violence? (Some—Plato, for instance—say that violence harms the *perpetrator:* "to do evil is worse than to suffer it." But how could it be rational to think this if what violence did to the *victim* was not evil?)

But if we consider the victim's point of view, we surely find that violence is *not* absolutely evil. For if violence were absolutely evil, it would mean that no matter what a life might otherwise be like, so long as it contains any suffering caused by violence, it is worse than *any* other possible life. To be the victim of violence, in this view, would be incomparably worse than anything else that could happen to you. But no sensible person actually believes such a thing. Few residents of New York would move to a remote corner of North Dakota merely because they would thus considerably reduce their chances of being mugged. No one of us would give up what we find a wonderfully satisfying life for what we would expect to be a thoroughly dreary one just because we were somewhat safer from violence in the latter. For my part, even if it was *certain* that I would suffer some violence in the former, I still would not trade. Would you? And suppose, to fix on a slightly different aspect of this, that one had a choice between being the victim of human violence or of natural disaster. The latter is not necessarily preferable. Better a mugger taking one's wallet and leaving one sore for a couple of days than a tornado mangling one's limbs and destroying one's house and family—isn't it?

b. But even if we accept that violence is, in the sense defined, an "absolute" evil, does pacifism follow? It does not! Its being an absolute evil means that nothing else can compare to it in moral importance. Very well. But suppose that we had a situation in which we had to choose between two actions, either of which would lead to violence, though one would produce *more* violence than the other. Nothing about the notion of absoluteness prevents this kind of choice from being possible. Well, if violence is absolutely evil, then the reasonable thing to do would seem to be to minimize it—to do what produces least of this irredeemable evil. But suppose that what does this is a violent action of my own: I must shoot B in order to prevent B from killing C, D, and E. Surely killing B is what I should do, rather than allowing the greater violence of B's multiple murders? Indeed it is what I should do *if* violence's being an absolute evil *commits us to minimizing it.* Therefore, violence's being absolutely evil does not commit me to the rule of always avoiding it myself.

§12 ABSOLUTE WRONGS AND THE PRIMACY OF THE SELF

At this point, it may be felt by the defender of pacifism that something has gone wrong. In saying that violence is "absolutely evil," perhaps he or she didn't mean that we should do what we can to cause as little and prevent as much of it as possible, no matter who brings it about. A better statement of it would be that violence is absolutely *wrong,* meaning by this that one is not to do any of it oneself, no matter what the consequences—even if the consequence is that greater violence *by others* will result. Of course, this comes very close to simply reaffirming the rule of pacifism, rather than supporting it. Even so, it runs into problems.

First, a small point. The idea that consequences are irrelevant, that it is the "act of violence itself" rather than what it brings about that is objectionable, is very strange when one thinks about it. For after all, part of what we *mean* by 'violence' is the production of certain consequences, namely harm, suffering, injury, pain, or death in some other person, isn't it? It makes no sense to think that violence is wrong and yet that consequences do not matter! What must be meant is something different, namely, that *I* am never responsible for *other* people's violence. If I am in one of those desperate situations where some madman will murder several people unless I shoot him, it is quite true that if *I* squeeze this trigger, then I will have brought it about that a person dies, whereas if I don't, then he, not I, will have brought it about that people die. And that, I might say, will be his fault, not mine. I did not do it—he did. And I am responsible for the consequences of only *my* actions. Of course, the pacifist will add that I ought to prevent evil actions of others *if* I can do so without violence. That is another matter.

This question of responsibility for the actions of others is tricky. Is it a "consequence" of my inaction that all those people die whom the madman shoots if I do not act? Of course it is not as if I shot them. He did. But equally, we must admit that I could have prevented it, and I did not. It certainly was a *result* of my nonaction that those people died, in the circumstances. And can't I be blamed for that?

At least it is not true that one can be blamed only for action rather than inaction. Suppose I am an engineer in a power station, and it is my duty to pull a certain switch at a certain time. If I don't, thousands will be inconvenienced and some imperiled. At the crucial moment, however, I am napping or playing parcheesi in the back room. Clearly I am to blame for the resulting harms. It cannot sensibly be maintained that only actions rather than inactions are blamable.

Nor can it be maintained that we can never affect the actions of others. Obviously we can. Why, then, should we think it wrong to prevent the wrongs of others by violent means? The pacifist cannot say "because one wrong cannot be used to prevent another," for this is begging the question. The question is whether it *would* be wrong to use violence in the case where we must use it to prevent violence by others.

What it seems to come down to is that pacifists want, so to speak, to keep their own hands clean. Never mind how many others will be murdered, raped, tortured by their refusal to use violence if it is necessary to prevent that. The interests of their own souls come first! There are two things wrong with this attitude. First, of course, it sounds utterly myopic and self-centered. And in view of the very idea of morality, how can it be *self-centered?* Second, and less rhetorically, we have to point out that this is again to beg the question. *Is* it a mark of "cleanliness" to refrain from violence when doing so allows great and terrible evils to happen that one could have prevented? Why isn't it instead an abject failure to meet one's moral responsibilities?

§13 VIOLENCE AND THE VALUE OF LIFE

We still lack a clear and convincing basis for pacifism. Having considered the "absolute evil" of violence and found it wanting, perhaps we should turn to the other side of that coin, as it were, namely, recognition of the good that violence destroys: the value of life. Perhaps it is recognition of the supreme value of every life that commits us to total abstention from violence. For obviously, to commit violence is to damage a life. Even violence against property does this, for in destroying a person's property, I destroy what he or she values (even if only as an investment), and thus do damage to that person's life: it would, all things considered, be preferable from his or her point of view if that hadn't happened.

The idea that *life* has supreme value is very unclear, and we must plainly begin by trying to give it a definite meaning. Is it *all* life that is supremely valuable and not to be damaged? Evidently not, for plants, worms, and paramecia, as well as higher animals and humans, are living things. If the supreme value of life meant that we could damage no living thing, then we would not be allowed to eat, apparently, for in eating we certainly damage living things! But let us suppose that it is only human life that is meant, setting aside even the question of animals. And then, not even all human life; for an unconscious human who could never awaken would be no better than a vegetable. We will suppose, then, that it is "fully human" life—conscious experience, imbued with thought, awareness, and emotion—that is supposed to be supremely valuable.

Yet even this needs more refinement. For many parts of our experience are not valuable, but the reverse: pain, boredom, fear, and many other conditions are surely to be avoided rather than valued. So let us say that it is the *valuable* experience of all persons that is to be supremely valued.

But now we have an oddity. Why should we *supremely* value the valuable experience of all people? For after all, much of this experience is only modestly valuable from the point of view of the very person whose experience it is. I like the experience of sipping Darjeeling tea, but only moderately. And if that is all the value *I* attach to it, why on earth should *you* attach more, indeed *infinitely* more?

Perhaps what we should say is that we ought to value the experience of others just as much as they do themselves. Here we would have one way of incorporating the kind of equality of regard for others that may be felt to be basic to morality. But at this point, let us note, we have lost contact with any support for pacifism. For the view we now have, in case the reader has not already noticed, seems to be simply utilitarianism again! That view, we recall, simply consists in granting equal value to the equal utility of all persons. And that view, as we also saw, is incompatible with pacifism. On some occasions, the amount of valuable experience that will be brought about by doing some violence may be greater than what would be promoted by any alternative.

If we relax this very startling valuation of others in a direction that is more in accord with what people really do think of each other, we will probably arrive at one of our other two theories. For instance, we may take it that we should value others in the sense that we should allow them to live their lives as they please, without interference. We should, in short, not *value,* but rather *respect,* their lives. But this, carefully followed out, will give us libertarianism. Or if we relax things still more and say merely that we ought to respect others by respecting mutually beneficial agreements, then we have contractarianism— though we also have a view that cannot reasonably be characterized as involving commitment to the "supreme value of life." And in any case, neither of these two views, as we saw in §8, will support pacifism either.

Finally, let us ask what the status of the claim that "life has supreme value" might be. Is this supposed to be a statement of what we *do* think, or only what we *ought to* think? It seems very clear that it would be false if it were the former, for plainly people do not, characteristically, value all people to anything like the degree apparently called for in this view. But if it is what we ought to think, then how is that to be supported? It might, of course, be offered as a sheer statement of faith; and indeed, this kind of view has characteristically been advocated by religious people. But that will not do, if we seek a rational morality. For we cannot accuse someone of irrationality just for refusing to accept a claim of faith! We need principles that are acceptable to people as they are, except in their irrational moments. We cannot base a rational morality on things that at most very few rational people accept.

And now, taking the values we do have, can we try to show that we would do better to attach "supreme value" to life? I suspect not. That other people's lives are to be *respected* is certainly supportable, and indeed, our three theories are each ways of interpreting that idea. But "supremely valued"? This would seem to be something more like love—universal love. And is it sensible to insist on that? I think not. Even if it were possible to love everyone, which one can doubt, it is, in the first place, logically impossible to love each person *supremely,* for to love a thing supremely is to love it above all else, and at most one thing can be loved *above* all else. And anyway, as the philosopher Friedrich Nietzsche (1844–1900) observed, the situation of universal love would be "... An agonizing and ridiculous state of affairs.... Everyone gushed over, pestered and sighed for, not as at present by one lover, but by thousands...." (*Human, All Too Human,* sect. 39). A few is enough!

We have to conclude, then, that this notion of the supreme value of life is either simply a restatement of one of the theories we have already considered or else a rather obscure hypothesis that scarcely anyone could really accept. In either case, it will not give us a basis for pacifism.

§14 "BUT WHAT IF EVERYONE DID IT?"

One way of interpreting the idea that violence is supremely evil, we saw, is that we ought to do all we can to minimize or if possible eradicate it. It was not clear, however, that practicing pacifism is the best way to do that. If pacifism is viewed as a means to reducing the evil of violence, then it would seem to be essentially a question of fact whether it is the most effective means. But some people who accept the idea that pacifist behavior is a means rather than an end in itself still might think that we ought to be pacifists. Their argument is as follows. Moral principles, they note, must be the same for everyone. They are general, or universal. And since they are, we must not just ask what would result if *I* were to adopt a given principle in *my* case. Instead, we must ask what would happen if *everyone* were to adopt it. But clearly if everyone were to adopt pacifism, then violence would indeed be minimized, for in fact there could not be any at all if each person correctly practiced pacifism.

This is an appeal to a very interesting idea in ethics, that of "universalizability" (in one of its forms). Although we cannot discuss that idea at length here—and much has been written about it—I will show that its use in this argument is fallacious, as well as founded on a misconception. Let us start with the fallacy, which lies in the fact that pacifism is not the *only* principle whose universal adoption would lead to total nonviolence. For there is at least one other principle that would have the same effect, if correctly practiced by everyone: the policy of using violence *only defensively.* If all observed this, then there would be no aggressive violence, since that is what it forbids. But then there could be no defensive violence either, for this principle permits that only if there is aggression to defend people from. Thus, we get the *same* presumably desirable outcome as with pacifism. And therefore, the argument does not give us reason to adopt pacifism *rather than* the other policy.

There is also a misconception to note in connection with the argument. Suppose someone says, "But wait a minute! Always refraining from violence is the sort of thing I mean by a 'universal' rule. The rule of refraining from it *except* when necessary for defense has an exception in it; so it is not really *universal.*" But this misconceives the notion of universality, by confusing it with a quite distinct idea, that of simplicity. Both the rule never to use violence *and* the rule never to use it except defensively are equally universal: both give us a rule to be followed in all cases. But the former is less complicated than the latter. The way it calls upon us always to act is more simply described than the way the other does.

The fact is, however, that there is no need for moral rules to be extremely simple, though no doubt if they were too complicated people would not be able to follow them. But the rule "no violence except for defense" is not nearly *that* complicated. And it is easy to see that rules can be too simple. Consider such actions as crossing bridges or entering elevators. If "everybody" were to try to get on the bridge or the elevator at once, it would collapse. But it would be silly to conclude that nobody should ever use a bridge or an elevator—indeed, given modern life, that would be disastrous too! Clearly, the correct rule for all to follow always is not to get on a structure that is already occupied by as many people as it can safely carry. More complicated, to be sure —but far more sensible!

As a final observation, we should note that if the correct moral rules are those whose universal observance would give the best consequences, then there is one general rule—a very simple one to state, too—that, if correctly followed, ensures the best consequences of all, namely "Maximize good!" Of course, people would not always follow this correctly. But that is a different question from whether it would be best *if* they did. And then, there is no rule that *cannot* be incorrectly applied. Now the rule 'Maximize good!' derives from utilitarianism, which, as already noted, does not support pacifism. So this new argument gets nowhere.

§15 "POSITIVE NONVIOLENCE" AND THE QUESTION OF CHARISMA

Some who advocate pacifism regard it as a way of life and an active method of improving the world. Their idea is that nonviolence, if practiced "positively," will influence others to renounce their violent tendencies and thus promote the cause of peace. Why do they think that pacifism in particular will have these good effects?

Everyone agrees that *Homo sapiens* has a strong inclination to use violence, not only defensively but in other situations too. We do not know just why this is; some say that it is a basic instinct, others that it is due to the socioeconomic system, still others that it is due to early childhood training. Whatever the reason, the tendencies are very strong in many cases. To counteract them will take powerful methods, things being what they are. And it will be a rare person indeed who has the kind of charismatic or hypnotic personality that would stop evil people in their tracks and make them lay down their guns. To suppose that just anyone can do this is implausible. It is all very well for people like Christ or Gandhi to "turn the other cheek" when their enemies smite them. But who are they to tell us ordinary mortals to do the same? (Especially when we take into account how each of them met his end!) We who lack extraordinary powers, saintly courage, or great persuasive ability will be hard put to understand why the way to deal with threats to our lives is to surrender rather than put up a fight. Why shouldn't the aggressor be the one to surrender?

Indeed, when we reflect further on this kind of advocacy of pacifism, we come face to face with the disconcertingly real possibility that pacifism might actually prove self-defeating. For there might be sadistic people in the world who would inflict tortures on people precisely because they do not resist. Many contemporary Jewish writers have argued that the near extinction of European Jews in World War II was due partly to their very tendency to go meekly along with their captors. Trying to resist the Nazis's peculiarly hideous brand of violence with nonviolent methods was surely an enormous mistake from the evidence we have; and contemporary Israel is understandably determined not to repeat it. This brings us to another vital point, which is that we cannot speak here of the mere abstract possibility of there always being a nonviolent method that would ward off aggression better than any violent one. For we act in the real world, and in this world there is not always time to seek out such methods even if they exist. By the time we hit upon the right, nonviolent way to deal with *this* murderer, *this* rapist, *this* armed robber, their victims will long since have been left bleeding in the alleyway. Pacifism in the here and now will, on all the evidence we have, sometimes fail. And if it is said that we must fix our vision on the long run, then surely this is the place to quote John Maynard Keynes's (1883–1946) acid observation that "in the long run, we are all dead!"

At very least, we demand extreme sacrifices of people if we ask them to become pacifists—not only of themselves but perhaps also of their friends, loved ones, and neighbors, who may have been relying on them for help in the face of violent enemies. And it is questionable whether we have the *right* to demand such sacrifices. The idea that people have a right to be protected from violence, with the assurance of enforcement if need be, presents itself here. We shall consider that matter in our concluding section on pacifism, which follows.

§16 PACIFISM AND JUSTICE

To speak of justice is to speak of rights. But what is it to speak of rights? What does it mean to say that someone "has a right"? I shall consider four ideas about this, going from "weakest" to "strongest." 'A', 'B', and 'C' stand for persons, 'x' for acts.

i. 'A has a right to do x' = 'It is not wrong for A to do *x*'.

On this definition, skeptics who think that nothing is right or wrong would have to be said to believe that people have rights. This is absurd. The proposed definition is uselessly weak.

ii. 'A has a right to do x' = 'It would be wrong for others to interfere with A's doing of x, if A wants to'.

This is more like it, for surely the main point of talk of rights is to indicate what people may or may not do in relation to those who have them: namely, they may not interfere. But what does this 'may not' amount to? One who believes that A has the right to do x is thereby disapproving the behavior of B, if B interferes with A's attempts to do x. But is this enough either? No. It does not capture a vital element in the notion of rights, namely, that they are claims to protection. The question is just how this claim is to be incorporated. Here are two ideas, the first weaker than the second.

iii. 'A has a right to do x' = 'If B attempts to interfere with A's attempts to do x, and C attempts to prevent B from such interference, then C is doing what is right. If B does interfere, then if C forces B to compensate A for the interference, C does what is right'.

On this view, to agree that A has a right is to approve of efforts, forcible if need be, to protect A or to restore his or her loss if others interfere. This, I believe, is the minimum necessary to have a genuine notion of rights. But we must carefully distinguish this from a still "stronger" notion:

iv. 'A has the right to do x' = 'Others have a duty to protect A from interference and to help restore his or her loss from such interference with A's attempts to do x'.

The difference between iii and iv is the difference between its being merely all right to prevent or rectify invasions of rights and its being positively wrong *not* to try to do that. An important case illustrating these differences is that of a young woman, Kitty Genovese, who was assaulted, raped, and murdered in an entryway while some thirty-eight people in nearby buildings and walks looked on. None of them even tried to phone the police, let alone intervene personally. Were they acting wrongly? According to view iii they may not have been: presumably they would have approved if someone *had* called the police, so their action was consistent with their acknowledging that Kitty had the right not to be assaulted. But view iv would condemn them, for it requires those who acknowledge that someone has a right to do something to help secure it.

When we move from rights of type iii to rights of type iv we cross the line dividing "negative" from "positive" rights. Negative rights are those that may be fulfilled by doing nothing whatever. If my duty is simply not to kill or harm people, then I can completely live up to its requirements by doing nothing at all.

Positive rights are another matter, for the duties that they impose on others do require that we do something, rather than that we merely refrain from doing something. In the case of type iv, what they require us to do is to assist others whose negative rights are being violated or threatened.

Type iv rights are still pretty minimal. For the positive duties that they impose on others will be imposed only in case of prior threats to rights of type iii. But there is still another level of possible rights that goes beyond this minimum, potentially in very significant ways. These rights are definable as follows:

v. 'A has a right to x' = 'Others have a duty to supply x to A, if A is unable to get x by A's unaided efforts and the unforced activities of others'.

Note that I have here changed from 'right to do x' to 'right to x', x now being something that can be given to or had by A, rather than something A does. But we could also have defined it as follows:

v¹. 'A has a right to do x' = 'Others have the duty to help A do x, if A is unable to do x by unaided effort or the unforced assistance of others'.

Since positive-right claims are usually made in regard to such things as food, medical care, and income, the first of these two formulations is more convenient, but I believe that rights to have are always translatable into rights to do. In any case, the effect of such rights is to create duties on the part of others to go out of their way to do things for other people, duties that are *enforceable.* It is this feature that makes it legitimate for governments to come into the act. For governments have the power to make people do things, whether they want to or not. If we stop with rights of type iii only, then, governments are illegitimate. Rights of type iv would allow "minimal" governments, while rights of type v usher in more extensive governments—how extensive depends on how substantial a schedule of positive rights the theorist proposes.

However, we need not concern ourselves with these positive rights, for even negative rights in what I have argued is the minimal sense, type iii, are plainly incompatible with pacifism. If we are to maintain that there are any genuine rights at all, then pacifism must be rejected. Pacifism, incidentally, would also entail *anarchism,* that is, the illegitimacy of government. For a purely voluntary "government" is not a government in the sense that defines a state at all.

§17 CONCLUDING NOTE: THE INCOHERENCE OF PACIFISM

As we saw in part I, none of our three theories supports the pacifist. Each allows a right of freedom from violence at least as strong as that defined in view iii in the foregoing section. If these have the truth among them somewhere, then the pacifist's claim that violence is always wrong must be firmly rejected. Whether it is admirable as a personal attitude is debatable. But that it tells us the truth about the rights and wrongs of violence must be denied.

Indeed, pacifism is a strange view—strange, even, to the point of incoherence. It is founded on the supreme wrongness of violence and the inviolability of persons. Yet at the same time as it holds the infliction of pain or injury on people to be supremely wrong, it is opposed to the securing of persons from violence when to do so requires the use of violence itself. But just as fire must sometimes be employed to help put out fire, so violence is sometimes necessary to prevent violence. If they wish to deny that violence is ever necessary, pacifists may be accused of unrealism. But if they go further and refuse to approve the use of violence even when they agree that it *is* necessary to counter violence, then their view verges on incoherence. For in saying this, they lose touch with the basic point that violence is a source of evils that ought to be minimized. And they seem to be saying that the person who forcibly prevents a murder is no better than an actual murderer. Finally, if the pacifist wishes to say that the rule of total nonviolence is founded on the right of all people to be free from violence, then this view is inconsistent with the central, protection-claiming function of rights.

The upshot of our first two parts, then, is to deny that no one may ever legitimately employ violence, though it is also to agree that violence against the innocent is virtually always wrong. We must now move on to the question of group use of violence—in short, war. This we do in our next and last part.

III. VIOLENCE AND THE STATE: WAR

Thus far we have been discussing the morality of violence at the level of relations between individuals. Now we must ask what, if any, difference it makes if the subject of our appraisals is a large, politically organized group—that is, a state. The first question is whether such an entity is subject to moral appraisal at all. We consider that in §18. Replying in the affirmative, we can then divide our problems into three important areas. First, of course, is the relations of a state to other states: When, if ever, is a state's engaging in war with another state legitimate? For example, may a state, unlike an individual, legitimately engage in "aggressive" as distinct from purely defensive war? This also, of course, brings up the question of how you distinguish the two, which is not quite so easy at this level. Second, there will be questions about how a state relates to its own citizens in wartime. May it, for instance, conscript them into the army? And third, there are questions concerning a state's conduct in relation to citizens elsewhere, in particular to private citizens of the enemy's state. We deal with these in §§19–22. Finally, in §23 we consider some general issues hanging over the whole idea of the "just war." I close with a note on the Bomb and an epilogue.

§18 THE MORAL STATUS OF STATES

States are not individuals. They are not superindividuals, godlike and Olympian, any more than they are ordinary individuals like ourselves. But they do, in some sense, consist of individuals; they are organized groups of individuals. Now, only individuals literally have minds, intentions, and decision-making faculties. Some have argued that because of this, we cannot literally hold states responsible for their actions, since they do not literally act. If this were right, then to accuse states of immorality, or praise them for generosity, would be silly and meaningless. But we need not agree with that view. Of course it makes sense to say "Yesterday, the Elaphians declared war on the Mohamians"; and if that makes sense, so too does the additional observation that they did so unjustly, wisely, imprudently, and so on. Further, the net effect of supposing that it makes no sense to attribute moral qualities to states is to allow them to do whatever they please: for states do act, whatever philosophers might say!

It has also been suggested, by Thomas Hobbes for instance, that states are in a "State of Nature" with each other, because there is no supreme power over them all to make them obey reasonable rules. And there is certainly something to that. But it does not follow that no moral judgments may be made about their behavior. Nations have interests and can make agreements, and often we can see what a universally rational agreement among them would be, whether made or not. So even in our most "hardheaded" theory, contractarianism, a basis for moral appraisal of their behavior exists. And as to enforcement, it is wrong to think that moral judgments depend for their validity on their being enforced; or insofar as they do, it is up to us to "enforce" them by our expressions of praise and blame. Obviously, such expressions are not of decisive influence all the time. But they often make a difference, as any politician knows. States do care what people, and other states, think of them.

That states consist of individuals without being individuals poses an interesting problem of analysis. My own view is that whenever a state or any group is said to "do" something, then we can identify individuals, perhaps numerous, whose actions are what the group action consists in. Moral praise or blame filters, in complicated ways, down to these agents. And influence on these individuals—as any lobbyist can tell us—in turn influences what the group does. But we need not resolve this problem in detail. It is enough to see that the moral principles that hold for individuals can also hold for groups and states. The differences made by states are not such as to leave morality out of it, but merely to make its application more complicated.

§19 AGGRESSIVE WAR?

The argument for condemning violence by one individual against another who is innocent of previous wrong or aggressive actions is, as we saw in part I, very strong in all of our theories. Is there any reason to think the same will not be true of states? In the case of two of our theories, there plainly is none. The aggressions of states visit terrible harms upon individuals, and libertarianism will condemn this regardless of what sort of alleged goods the aggressor state aims at, while utilitarianism appears to be a very close second. But contractarianism may seem to be another matter. Its condemnation of individual aggression stems from contemplation of the consequences of the "war of all against all," which Hobbes depicts in memorable language:

> ... there is no place for Industry. ... no Arts; no Letters; no Society; and which is worst of all, continuall feare, and danger of violent death; and the life of man, solitary, poore, nasty, brutish, and short. (*Leviathan* I, xiii)

The "price" of peace, which is to refrain from aggression, is well worth it. But will this same reasoning apply in the case of states? This, after all, is *not* a "universal war of all against all," but a quite restricted war of some against some. A small percentage of the populace goes off to the front, and those who remain behind may not face much danger. Those who engage in the fighting will be told that they are fighting for a noble cause and are held in high esteem by their nation—and, in any event, will get paid for it, which might even make it better than unemployment or a more boring job back home. And if its generals are efficient, a state might even "win," which might be worth something. Most important of all, though, is the fact that those in power, who get the war going, may stand little chance of personal loss, while those who do stand such a chance may have no choice, being forced to fight and having no influence. So those in power will take the prospect of war more lightly than, say, the wives of common soldiers.

Yet all this makes for no argument in favor of war. Instead, it may make an argument against bureaucracy and the bureaucratic temperament that puts up with just about anything the "machine" asks us to do. In the case of war, the machine—one's state or nation—asks one to go out and kill people, or to help make weapons for those who do. The plain fact that it *is* one's state or nation surely makes no difference to the morality of this. Even if your mother asks you to go out and kill some innocent person, that hardly makes it right. And why should the State's asking us to do this have any more effect? Some may say that it is a matter of loyalty: but why should we be more "loyal" to an immoral state than to our mothers? If aggressive wars are, as they seem to be, just the same sort of thing as aggressive actions by individuals (only more so, because on a larger scale), then on the face of it, such wars are wrong. And if they are wrong, then no sort of "authority" claimed by the State will make any difference.

Is aggressive war immoral, then? It will be, on the contractarian view, only if it would be rational to join in an agreement with all others to condemn it. On the individual level, as we have seen, that is rational. Is it on the state level as well? Indeed it is. Not to be willing to join in such an agreement would be to say that war against oneself, for example, is morally permissible if sufficiently in the interests of the aggressor. But overwhelmingly, the likelihood is against being in a position to gain from war. Most people will lose, whether or not they are on the "winning" side. It was not always so. Long ago, and in some isolated cases today, tribes and even nations have occasionally been able to make real gains by means of aggressive warfare. But no more. There is, for one thing, scarcely any *point* in trying to dominate other nations nowadays. Today slavery is just too impractical: one does much better by engaging in reasonable free trade with others than by trying to enslave them. And few resources are worth the price of oppressing the people who own them: better simply to pay for them! Besides, any taxpayer can testify that being on the "winning" side in a war is no bed of roses either. So it comes out to be the same story as in the case of the individual. Overwhelmingly, the argument tells in favor of peace. But because this is overwhelming, the few remaining ones who might gain from aggression could be readily overpowered by the rest of us; it would then be in their interest to accept the agreement to be peaceable. It is therefore in the interest of everyone who counts. Aggressive war, therefore, will be condemned.

To say that aggression is wrong is to say that there is a right of defense. But just what is this? It is the right, of course, to prevent others from engaging in violence against one. But just when are they doing that? Sometimes it is clear enough: a large number of armed troops cross the clearly marked borders of some other country, shooting at whoever tries to resist, occupying buildings without permission from their owners, and so on. But what if the country attacked has recently been very hostile indeed? Suppose, in fact, that the attacker has a good deal of evidence that the other country is just waiting until its armaments, which it has been assiduously increasing for some time, are superior to those of our attackers, at which point *it* will march into *their* country? Under these circumstances, to strike first may be literally the only means of defense—defense, in that the aim, and the result, is simply to prevent the other country from carrying out its intentions. We cannot clearly say that a nation resorting to such "preemptive war" is engaging in "aggression."

Formulating a clear principle to deal with such situations is no easy matter. We could take the view that any nation that builds up a standing army is ripe for preemptive attack—an idea that turns into the major snag that whoever does the preemptive attacking would have to have already built up *its* armies in order to mount its attack! Again, one might suggest that any nation not surrounded by armed neighbors will be viewed as aggressive if it increases its armaments. But then, the preemptive attack would have to be mounted by a more distant friendly state, whose own neighbors, then, would presumably have armed because of *its* putative "aggressiveness." Here is food for thought—and some insight into why the United Nations is not an easy place to work. I do not pretend to have solutions to these difficult problems, other than the obvious one that we must all do our best to get the contending sides to negotiate if at all possible. But this, as recent experience shows, is at best a necessary rather than a sufficient condition for peace. Further reflections on that subject will be found in §23.

§20 THE RIGHT OF DEFENSE—OR THE DEFENSE OF RIGHTS?

One problem with the notion of defense, as we have just seen, is that it is not easy, in many cases, to say just what constitutes an "aggressive action" on the part of another person. Even if we know just what it is that we have the right to defend, that is a problem. But now we face a far deeper one, and one that leads to the most far-reaching divisions among theorists and among the various people who act more or less in the light of those theories. The problem got started back in §8 when we noted that two of our theories may generate what, in the terminology of §16, I called "positive" rights. All genuine rights, according to my analysis, are enforceable. If there are positive rights, that means that coercive action in support of something more than the endeavor to prevent people from inflicting certain harms on others is justifiable. And if this is true on the individual level, then why should it not also be so on the group level? Indeed, positive rights, as noted in §16, are precisely what are required to justify that bastion of allegedly legitimate coercion, the State. And if we allow the nose of this particular camel into the tent of "defense," we may soon find our condemnation of aggression condemning very little.

Let us start with the nose. Suppose that the rains cease to fall on country A, and that its more fortunate neighbor, B, refuses to help in various ways that it could without too great difficulty. If the starving As now make war on the well-off Bs, is this aggression? Or is it, in view of the fact that their only alternative is starvation, really "self-defense"? We might be inclined to say that it is not, at any rate, defense against threats offered by other humans. But why not? The As need food; the Bs have it, and they refuse to give any to the As. Some theorists will simply call this refusal by the As "aggression." They may talk, for instance, of "implicit" or perhaps "institutional" violence: social arrangements and systems of ideas implanted in people that result in poverty, disease, and death for others even though they do not overtly hit people over the head or shoot them. Others will agree that there is a line to draw between positive harms and mere refusals of aid but will insist that there is no serious difference.

Libertarians will insist that there is a serious difference, and that our rights fall entirely on the negative side of this line: the Bs, they will agree, are being ungenerous, perhaps even real rotters—very bad Samaritans, shall we say—but they are not violating the As' rights. It is tough for them, and one can understand why they would go to war, but still, the war in question is unjust. But contractarians, I argued in §8, cannot so easily take this line. For would it be rational for all to agree to live on terms of peace with others if the terms included no provision at all for assistance against natural catastrophes? People must eat. If they cannot eat where they are, they must, rationally must, go elsewhere. They cannot be expected to agree to others' blocking the way without even any reasons being required to justify the blockage. A very modest dose of positive rights seems indicated. How much is unclear: perhaps just enough to keep people alive, beyond which they are on their own.

Utilitarianism, however, would appear to be another kettle of fish altogether. According to it, after all, a given amount of utility for X counts the same as a given amount for Y, no matter who X and Y may be, or what they have done; and nothing but utility counts as justifications for actions, morally speaking. Well, could not the substantial benefit of many outweigh a fair amount of violence done to some few? And is this not equivalent to asserting positive rights? For if only the use of some violence will enable many to get substantial benefits, and if indeed the total utility thus brought about, even when you count in the considerable negative utility produced by the needed violence, exceeds the utility available from the next-best alternative, then that violence is justified, by definition, given utilitarian premises.

It is interesting that many philosophers consider utilitarianism inimical to rights; for the problem seems to be that it grants too many, rather than too few or none. It may seem, given the foregoing argument, that the theorist equipped with utilitarian principles is on the high road to positive rights: rights to food, medical care, education, and perhaps even to an equal standard of living with all others.

I do not think this is so, in fact. But it is important to see just what the proponent of positive rights is implying. To have such rights is for it to be the case that those in a position to give people whatever they have those rights to may be *compelled* to give it to them. And if they may, then it is not obvious that groups of people going to war with better-off others in order to get "their share" are not justified in doing so. And that means that we are going to have to accept a great deal of violence as possibly justified. Our negative rights, *if* there are also positive ones, stand in constant peril. They can be at best *prima facie*, in the sense of §10: one's right not to have violence done one may be overridden quite easily, *viz.*, by refusing to assist others to the degree required by their positive rights, whatever they are. The State, e.g., may take your money to enable these things to be done, and it may put you in jail if you try to evade the tax.

The question of what, if any, positive rights we have is obviously a major—indeed, *the* major—question of social philosophy. We can hardly hope to settle it in the present essay. But since we now see that these questions are supremely relevant to our subject of violence and war, I shall conclude this section by arguing, very briefly, that even on the utilitarian theory the case for positive rights of any considerable extent is not forthcoming. There are philosophers who claim to have nonutilitarian theories, different from any of our three, in support of such rights. I believe that no such theory is coherent: if utilitarianism won't do it, then nothing will. But this last claim is one I cannot take the space to argue for here.

Well, then: the claim was that if violence was necessary to secure a major benefit, then if that benefit was great enough, the total utility to all, even counting in the negative utility of the violence, might exceed the total utility available on any other alternative, and if so, there would be a positive right to the type of benefit in question, at least in the circumstances in question. True enough. But is there any reason to think that all these conditions can realistically be supposed ever to obtain? For if they would not obtain in the world as we know it, especially on the biggish scale required for helpful assertion of a general "right," then the case for this positive right is not made out.

Among the considerations that make a negative answer to these questions plausible are two major ones. In the first place, there is very good reason for thinking that in a free-market system, "positive rights" will be unnecessary. The system will work well enough that the disutility of violent intervention will exceed that of any gains made possible by its use. A main reason for thinking this is that if interferences with persons and their property are ruled out (and this includes all forms of violence), then all reasonable actions will be in furtherance of the interests of all concerned. If A and B make a deal, then it is legitimate only if it interferes with no third parties; and they will not make it unless it is advantageous from the point of view of each. So long as people are being rational, the system will work to the benefit of all who are willing to act in their interests

And what of those who cannot or will not? It seems implausible to argue that there is utility to be gained by rewarding the latter. And as to the former, here is where the other major consideration, namely human generosity and love, comes into play. Those who meet with misfortune may well be adequately taken care of by their friends and by the generosity of others—a generosity surely much promoted by the confidence that violence will never be approved in the effort to fulfill the needs of those in need.

That is the general case. In detail, what is needed is an argument about the relative disutilities of violence as compared with, say, poverty. It is plausible to suppose that most people would prefer a life of poverty to one of considerable wealth at the price of a constant threat of violent death, imprisonment, and robbery. If this is so, then how are such threats justified merely in order to relieve poverty? And why, then, should we think a country is justified in making war on another one in order to obtain the second one's oil—especially when they can get it anyway, by simply offering a reasonable price for it?

In brief, it is one thing to say that the net utility of society would be greater if everyone were middle-class than if some, in addition, were rich and some poor. But it does not follow that the net utility of despoiling the rich in order to relieve the poverty of the poor is greater than that of securing everyone, rich or poor, against violence in all forms, whatever (within some quite great extreme) the resulting distribution of wealth. And similarly, then, for international relations. No one is justified in making war on the wealthy nations, e.g., simply in order to force them to relieve the poverty of the poor nations. (The more so, in view of the fact that the wealthiest nations have also been the most generous, by and large.)

The upshot of all this is that violence is not justified in support of supposed rights to equality, welfare, and the like. The latter are, in brief, not really rights. They are desirable things that everyone has the right, and of course usually also the desire, to work for within the limits of the stronger right of nonviolence to persons and their fairly acquired property.

If this is correct, it of course follows that many currently popular types of revolution are also unjustified, as well as the terrorist activities sometimes launched on their behalf. But we will have a further word on those matters later on.

§21 CONSCRIPTION AND CONSCIENTIOUS OBJECTION

Thus far, we have argued for a right of defense, not a duty—a negative right, not a positive one. Self-defense is not a duty in any case: If Smith is attacked, he may elect not to resist, and we cannot force him to do so. But do we have the duty to defend other people who do want to be defended, such as our fellow countrymen in time of war? When a soldier volunteers to fight, he may believe that he is nobly doing his duty to his country, and many will encourage him in that belief. Others, however, may not share his enthusiasm. Is it a matter of moral duty for them too, that they be willing to defend their neighbors with their own lives? An enforceable duty? In short, is there a right to conscript?

One view on this matter to which many people have at least claimed to subscribe is that conscription is all right if it is done by a democratically elected government. But they can hardly mean this. For presumably nobody thinks that it is all right for a government, however popularly elected, to use some randomly selected person for target practice in the public square tomorrow noon. But if not, why then is it all right for such a government to take 100,000 randomly selected young men and expose them to target practice at the hands of the enemy? Surely we need an argument, one that is independent of the sheer fact of a majority's favoring the practice, to justify this extreme step of threatening people with deprivation of liberty or perhaps life unless they participate in an extremely dangerous activity, one of which they may not even approve.

Here the divergence of our three theories seems to become acute. Since libertarianism, to begin with, seems scarcely able to justify the State at all, how will it manage to justify conscription? But with the other two, things would seem to be different. For the contractarian, the question is whether it would be rational to subscribe to a principle of mutual assistance when subject to attack. For limited assistance, it seems clear, the answer will be in the affirmative. If A can assist B without serious danger to A, then A ought to assist. For what A has to gain from everyone else's similar willingness is much more than what he or she stands to lose by being willing to do so, at least so long as the likelihood of being frequently called on to do so is low in proportion to the likelihood of being attacked. But if the danger in rendering such assistance is very great, then it will probably not be worth the risk, unless the likelihood of being attacked is proportionately great. In the latter case, however, it will be worth undertaking very dangerous defenses in return for others' willingness to do the same. But of course, in a defensive war this is presumably the case: the danger *is* very great. Better, of course, to have volunteers do the fighting, and to pay them to do so. But if there are not enough to do the job, then a fair system of conscription—one that distributed the chances of being called up equally among the able-bodied populace—could not be objected to. (Or could it? Shortly we will examine conscientious objection, which might seem to be a counterinstance to this view.)

Turning to utilitarianism, it would appear that it has an easier job of it. For neither of the two conditions that the contractarian imposes is ultimately essential to the utilitarian's view. Whether or not each person stands to gain by the imposition of a conscription system, and whether or not it is fair in the sense indicated, are not crucial; the question is: Is the war better undertaken, all things considered, using conscription than not using it? If it is, then conscription is justified. If not, not.

The conditions imposed by the latter two theories are certainly not easy to meet, but they seem in principle possible. But the libertarian view is another matter, since one could hardly justify conscripting people to go to war for the State if, as the libertarian arguably holds, the State itself cannot be justified. But things are simply not that clear-cut. The lack of justification for the State, in particular, may be a red herring. For wars need not be carried on by states. In a particular region under attack by some external group, a "defensive agency" might exist whose business it was to protect all those who subscribed to it. If we can show that even such an agency could possibly be justified in something amounting to conscription, then if I am right that the truth lies somewhere in the region of these three theories, it will follow that conscription could in principle be justified.

This sounds like a very tall order, but let us consider. Suppose this agency can demonstrate that if its defensive activities did not take place, then everyone in that territory would be either killed or enslaved by the common enemy. If that were literally true, then those people would literally owe their lives or their freedom to the defensive agency. And if that were so, then the agency could be justified in threatening to collect on this debt from those who refused to assist in the defensive effort when asked. But that is all that conscription amounts to: telling the conscriptee that he has his choice between joining the army and being imprisoned or killed.

If the conditions required by the other two theories were difficult to meet, this one would be still more so. But it does seem conceivable that it could be met. Everything depends, of course, on the credibility of the argument that the conditions in question really do obtain. We shall consider problems related to that in §25 below.

Meanwhile, we should note that none of these conditions has any direct connection with such things as the religious or moral beliefs of the persons whose conscription is in question. And some will object violently to this omission. They may insist that there is a "right of conscience," such that those whose conscience tells them that the war in question is unjustified may not justly be required to participate in it. Is there such a right? Indeed there is not! Let us see why.

One's moral beliefs are about what everyone is to do, not just oneself. Moreover, they are about what is enforceable: about what people may be compelled to do, as well as what they may be induced or persuaded to do. This being so, it is incoherent to maintain that people have the right to do whatever they think is right. If A thinks that duty requires that B be put to death, while B thinks that nobody may kill anybody, then in order to respect the supposed "right of conscience," we must both prevent everyone from preventing A from killing B, thus respecting A's "right of conscience," and prevent A from killing B, in order to respect B's "right of conscience"—and so on, for every case where consciences differ on what is right. And this is, of course, absurd. A genuine, full-blooded right of conscience is therefore impossible. The most we can do is to have a much weakened version. A given moral theory can frame some area of permissible actions, actions that the theory neither condemns nor requires, and then allow others to act on their consciences *within that permissible area.* Thus we allow Mohammedans to pray five times a day, but we do not allow them to lop the heads off non-Mohammedans who will not voluntarily convert. Yet it was once the understanding of Mohammedans that to do precisely that was their sacred duty! In short, any moral theory must, in effect, say that those who disagree may act on their beliefs, *except where it matters!* Only liberalized Mohammedans are tolerated. All may have whatever beliefs they wish, so long as they do not *act* on them! But this is no "fault" of liberalism. No moral theory can do better, unless you count nihilism, which says that nothing is right or wrong.

In principle, then, if conscription in a particular war is justified, then the fact that some disagree with that is no grounds for exemption any more than would be the fact that the person in question did not feel like fighting. Still, "in principle" is not enough for practical purposes. One who has strong conscientious objections to fighting will, no doubt, make an ineffective soldier. It may well be impossible to make such a person fight; and it may be possible to get that person to do other useful things that in one way or another promote the war effort. So there might be good practical reason for not conscripting certain people. But that is not the same as allowing a right of conscientious objection. There is no such right.

Is there something we do owe conscientious objectors? Yes: It is the same that is owed to anyone who is subjected to coercion—namely, a decent explanation. If a clear and compelling explanation is given just why this war must be fought and why conscription is justified, then it would also be true, no doubt, that the individual in question would go gracefully. Doubtless the person would not be convinced. But a decent try would surely be better than what is usually done, which is simply to tell the draftee that the government demands his or her services and no questions will be tolerated. (And to this, alas, it will be correctly replied that in the press of war, there may be no time for talk. This, unfortunately, is just one more of the evils of war.)

§22 JUST CONDUCT OF JUST WAR

In war, a lot of people are trying to kill or enslave us, and we have the right to prevent them from doing that. But just what may we do in order to prevent them? It might be thought that we may do just anything: for after all, war seems to be a situation in which the most elementary principle of morality—that it is wrong to kill—is suspended.

But this is not so. In the first place, wars are between states, and yet the fighting takes place among individuals. The other state is the enemy, but only some of its citizens are trying to kill us. Others are not. Some may even have opposed the war bitterly and may even be trying to sabotage the war effort. The principle of defense certainly does not allow us to ignore these distinctions. And in the second place, it may not be true that we can do just *anything* to the enemy's combatants. Let us consider these problems in turn.

Rights of Noncombatants   If some person, even though a citizen of the enemy state, is not among those who are trying to kill us, it is at least *prima facie* wrong to inflict damage on that person. The circumstances of war, unfortunately, raise two serious problems: (a) the question of just exactly who is and who is not a "combatant"; and (b) the likelihood that noncombatants, if any, will be damaged in the process of trying to get at the combatants.

(a) Who is an "innocent" person, a noncombatant, and who is not? Obviously, those bearing and aiming the weapons aimed at us are proper targets. But consider the range of others. There will be planners, perhaps thousands of miles away, who go off to work in their civilian suits like you and I and who may have no idea how to pull a trigger, let alone be ready to pounce on suspected enemies. Yet their planning may result in thousands of us being killed. And then there are workers in weapons factories. What about them? Of course, they all must eat, so what about all who grow more than enough food to feed themselves, those who make shoes, or even those who teach arithmetic in schools, thus training future warmakers or, at a minimum, enabling their mothers to work in the munitions factories? It seems impossible to say just who is and who is not contributing to the enemy's war effort. At the extreme, of course, we could simply take the line that all who are not actually doing their best to hinder the enemy's war effort are promoting it, thus assimilating those who merely do not go out of their way to prevent killing with the killers themselves.

Now there is, I believe, no reason to expect an exact answer to this question. Instead, we must bear in mind what is clearly the fundamental principle: that the use of force, even in war, is to be kept to the minimum compatible with securing a just ultimate peace. Do we contemplate obliterating the civilian population? But is there any reason to think this *necessary?* If it is not, then all of our principles will converge on refraining from doing it. By and large, arguments asserting its necessity tend not to be based on the facts. But if it is necessary, then what?

(b) At this point, our question shades into the other one: When, if ever, may we kill the enemy's noncombatants? There are, broadly speaking, three options. (1) We may take the strict line: Refrain from any military operation that significantly endangers innocents, irrespective of military consequences. (2) A middle line would have us minimize the killing of innocents in relation to military objectives: If operation 0_1 promises modestly more military gains than 0_2, but at greatly increased danger to civilians, we prefer 0_2; but if 0_1 promises enormously greater military returns than 0_2, though at some increased risk to civilians, we prefer 0_1. And (3), there is the militarist's option: We ignore this factor entirely, choosing whichever operation promises greatest military advantage, regardless of civilian endangerment.

Surely the second is the only reasonable option, though. If the war can be justified at all, then it is reasonable to reckon that one's own soldiers, as well as civilians, are just as innocent as the enemy's civilians: for *we* didn't start this war—*they* did! Why, then, must our soldiers risk their lives still more than they are already doing in order to avoid taking lives that are, after all, no more innocent than their own? This rules out option 1 as unreasonable. But option 3 is equally unreasonable, especially in inviting retaliation. No rational person can approve such dangerous behavior: If there is any chance of our being in that situation, we would not wish the enemy's armies to ignore utterly the factor of civilian safety. The civilians will be sometimes endangered, and justly as well; that is inevitable in modern war and is a significant part of what makes war an evil. But a high "price" of this kind is not worth paying. It is too dangerous. So we are left with the middle policy. And although the reasoning just given is stated in contractarian terms, both other theories would, I think, agree on this point—the utilitarian obviously, and the libertarian because the war is defensive (otherwise it would not be justified). Thus, the innocents endangered by military operations that will save the lives of us who are under attack are in the situation of people caught in the crossfire: it is tragic, but justified by the right of defense.

Thus, without erasing the line between innocents and noninnocents, it still turns out that military means that result in danger to innocents will have to be reckoned as part of the price of modern war. The instruments of contemporary war are often indiscriminate. Of course, they ought not to be used if possible. But if the attacker uses them, the defender has no option but to use them in return or face obliteration. To maintain that efficient weapons ought not to be used is really simply to say that wars ought not to be fought. All of which is perfectly true, but pointless. For the question before us is what to do by way of defense against people who have not taken note of that point!

Rights of Combatants What are the limits, if any, to what we can legitimately do to the very people who are trying to kill us? Since we may, if necessary, kill them, it may seem that there are no such limits. But in the first place, some things might be worse than death. May we use a weapon that paralyzes our victims from the neck down, for life? May we torture them hideously?

There are at least two principles that all of our theories would, I think, accept. The first is that we may do no more than is necessary to bring about the just end to the fighting that we seek. That it is often not obvious what is necessary is true. Yet it often will be, and to require all to bear in mind the distinction between what is and what is not necessary is entirely reasonable, and likely to have results. The principle is to respect any agreements to which the enemy's state is a party, at least so long as there is not very clear evidence both that the enemy has broken them *and* that there would be genuine military advantage in breaking them ourselves. Treating enemy prisoners humanely, for example, may be required by a treaty one's State has signed, and in any case, it offers a clear inducement to enemy soldiers to surrender willingly, whereas the prospect of hideous treatment would induce the enemy to fight to the bitterest possible end.

Neither of these principles will guarantee that awful things are not permitted, though. And when do we reach the point where no amount of "military necessity" will justify a given practice?

It is not easy to answer the latter, nor the question that our discussion of the rights of noncombatants also leaves hanging, *viz., how many* noncombatants may be sacrificed to the just ends of the war? Here again, we may expect divergence among our theories. And it seems that only utilitarianism clearly could require an upper limit independently of such considerations. For if the sum of human happiness will be lessened by our infliction of severe damages to either combatants or noncombatants, then however wrong their conduct in starting the war may have been, we must desist, even at the expense of our own lives. Contractarianism, on the other hand, obviously does not impose any upper limit. It must leave the matter to individual values, in the end. But what of libertarianism? This is problematic. Yet if all rights are in principle absolute, it is hard to see how limits may be drawn.

So we can get somewhere, without fundamentally deciding in favor of one theory, but we cannot get to the bottom of the matter. I commend this set of melancholy problems to the reader.

§23 REVOLUTIONS, INTERVENTIONS, AND TERRORISM

Wars are by no means the only uses of violence for political ends. Among the others are some that have recently become depressingly popular. Revolutions and interventions in other people's revolutions are perennials, but terrorism, kidnapping, and political murder are showing something of an upsurge nowadays. One is tempted to lay down a sweeping principle to the effect that all of these are illegitimate ways of pursuing moral and political ends, even if the ends are legitimate. But that would be to speak too quickly. For even if we confine the justification of violence to its use for strictly defensive purposes, it can hardly be denied that both revolutions and interventions might be justified on precisely such grounds. Whether the other acts mentioned also could be justified might be a different matter. But since both revolutions and interventions in support of them will involve killings, and quite possibly killings of innocent people, it is at least open to question whether assassinations or even kidnappings might not be similarly justified. These are large questions, and we cannot pretend to do justice to them in a few paragraphs. But still, a few observations can be made. I offer three.

a. Positive Rights, Again   Recent revolutionary activity has usually proceeded from more or less Marxist premises. These premises rest on Marx's economic analysis, which I believe is demonstrably faulty, a matter we cannot go into here. But I think it will be seen that such revolutions are usually not really defensive in the sense I have argued to be definitely legitimate. Rather, they tend to be on behalf of positive rights, which I believe are not. "The Ys are oppressing the Xs" too often turns out to mean merely that the Ys are not doing as well by the Xs as they might. However, we must concede that sometimes this erasing of the important line between positive and negative rights is not necessary for the justification of the revolution in question. Suppose that the regime against which a revolution is contemplated has been violating people's negative rights as well—i.e., their *rights simplicitur.* Then what? In that case, revolutions could possibly be in order, to be sure. Of course, the first question to ask is whether the grievances could not be rectified by some other means. Violence should come approximately last on our list of methods. Still, it may be the only way. If so, there are two other relevant considerations. The first I shall call moral arithmetic.

b. Moral Arithmetic   Let us suppose that the regime to be overthrown does in fact visit death and other kinds of violence upon its citizens. And let us suppose, what is often not obvious, that the regime by which it is proposed to replace them would do better in this regard. Let us also suppose, what is also very often far from obvious, that we can identify who the bad guys are—just which individuals are guilty of these crimes. Now the question is whether our revolution is going to extend the hand of violence to others besides those individuals, to the innocent as well as the guilty. What now? It might be argued that no harm to innocent individuals is justified. But if harm is ever justified in war, then why couldn't it be here as well? Well, it might. It is possible that in the process of defending ourselves from the regime's forces we must use weapons that unfortunately will hurt some innocents next door; or it may be that bystanders on their way to the post office unfortunately get in the way of the bullets before we can stop firing. But this will not, for instance, justify kidnapping the dictator's 10-year-old son and threatening to send pieces of him, bit by bit, to the dictator in the mail. It is not easy to say just when the harming of some innocent is genuinely necessary in order to mount a particular revolution; nor is it clear that just any sort of harms can be justified however necessary to the revolution they might be. At the very least, we have a problem of moral arithmetic: How many persons will be killed or otherwise unjustly used if the regime carries on, and how many innocents will be killed or damaged in the process of deposing it? What is the proper ratio? Is it 1:1? Or should we insist that it be quite a bit more than that? Not a few revolutionists have acted as though it could be quite a bit *less.*

An example from history might not be out of place to illustrate the issue. Was the American Revolution justified? Or ought the Americans to have taken the more boring course of the Canadians, who were content with colonial status for another ninety years after the American Revolution, and who then were quite peaceably promoted to independent status? There is little reason to believe that the number of people unjustly killed, taxed, etc., by the British in the American colonies would have come close to the number actually killed in the war of revolution—indeed, there is no very good reason for supposing it would have much exceeded, if at all, the number of people thus used by the Americans themselves in the decades during which British rule would probably have lasted had there been no revolution. I leave it to the reader's reflection to consider whether the moral of this story is that moral arithmetic of the type described is irrelevant to the justification of revolution, whether the ratio I have mentioned should be much smaller than the 1:1 that may well strike us as an absolute minimum, or whether we should concede that the colonists were rather impatient. Nor will it be easy to apply such reasoning to, say, the French Revolution. However, I do not see how the arithmetic in question can conceivably be thought irrelevant. And if this much is granted, then we should address ourselves to one more matter, which I will call moral sanity.

c. Moral Sanity The recent history of the world has been darkened by terrorism. Typical terrorists feel free to kidnap industrialists, to murder athletic teams, and to threaten the lives of airline passengers (not to mention the airplanes belonging to the airlines in question), in order to promote the supposed liberation of some group. Might such activity be justified? There are two pertinent questions. Of course, the first is whether the cause in question is justified anyway. It is no good saying, as terrorists sometimes do, that we are all part of the plot against whatever group they are acting on behalf of, that we are all guilty, and therefore that it is not a question of their acting against "innocent" people. To do that one must invoke the entirely unacceptable idea that "he who is not with us is against us"—an idea that obliterates the distinction between negative and positive rights, and ultimately renders all theories of rights incoherent. Nor, we may note, are terrorists given to producing clearly reasoned arguments in support of their causes. But in addition, there is a second question—*viz.,* whether it could ever be rational to promote their causes in this *way?* We have, of course, long since parted with libertarianism, which plainly says no without even inquiring into the matter of efficacy. But even on a theory that would allow consideration of such tactics, the question of efficacy, of whether these methods could conceivably be thought to promote the object in question to any nontrivial degree, is surely relevant. And here, I think, is where the question of the sanity of terrorists is open to question. By what conceivable stretch of the imagination can it be supposed that stealing an airliner or kidnapping Patricia Hearst will do anything at all to liberate Transylvania, or loosen the "capitalist grip on America"? Is it to be supposed that the publicity will help? And how can one expect public *support* on the basis of such tactics? Moral sanity is a matter of acting on credible beliefs about the probable efficacy of one's actions towards morally justified ends. Quite apart from the fact that their ends are usually dubious, terrorists do not usually pass this test. We are usually justified in regarding them as sick. And while this leaves the terrible practical problem of how to deal with them, it does not leave the terrible moral problem of whether they might be right.

§24 SOME SOBER REFLECTIONS

The habit of regarding it as a privilege of the State to make war on whomever it likes for any reason it sees fit has happily become extinct. Wars of recent vintage are fought by parties both of whom, with few exceptions, have grievances that, if their version of the facts were correct, might really justify war. Both sides claim to be defending themselves, in one way or another; or at least both claim that the other has violated some of its rights. From the rational point of view, then, there will be wars until such time as publicly agreed tests of such claims exist. The tests are of two kinds: first, tests of the factual claims made. *Were* the Xs there first? Did the Ms bomb that village? But second, there must be agreement on the principles of justice, at least to the extent that they concern matters in which the use of violence is appropriate. This is a tall order. Philosophers, who are quite probably more rational than political leaders, have not reached such agreement. Small wonder, then, that it has not been attained by practical men caught up in the press of affairs.

In many areas of life we can "agree to disagree," and resorting to war is irrational and unjustified when that is so. But agreeing to disagree about what is fundamentally right and wrong is quite a different matter from, say, agreeing to disagree about the merits of Horowitz's interpretation of the Emperor Concerto. For if I think that you have *morally* wronged me, then I will also think I am justified in exacting compensation for the wrong, by force if need be. On such matters, agreeing to disagree is agreeing to go to war!

Let us take an example—an important one indeed in today's world. Consider the question of the legitimacy of "internal interference in the affairs of other nations." Is it reasonable to reject such interference in principle? Not obviously. No one will accuse me of injustice if I rush into my neighbor's house to stop him from murdering his wife. Why, then, should they do so on the international scene? We know, of course, what the answer is: It would be dangerous and likely to exacerbate tensions. True, but this is not the same as its being wrong in principle. Rather, it indicates the prudence of political compromise.

It is widely felt that the main general threat to peace in the past few decades has been caused by the ideological division between socialist and nonsocialist countries. Why is this? Because each thinks the other's system *unjust.* The belief that socialism is unjust is not, indeed, so widespread as it once was, but the belief that capitalism is unjust is a central tenet of socialist-sector countries. And that is enough. For if socialists are committed to the belief that capitalists are mounting a sort of international conspiracy—wittingly or unwittingly—against the working classes of the world, and that they pursue this goal by any and all means and hence are not to be trusted in anything they do; and if, to compound matters, socialists believe that forcible overthrow of capitalism is entirely justified—the only question being whether it would work if attempted—then it is no wonder that we are all sitting on a tinderbox. Were both parties to agree that the other's view is not really wicked but merely erroneous, not unjust but merely silly, then things would be comfortable. I don't make war on you merely because I think you a fool. That response is reserved for injustice.

War, of course, is not an entirely rational phenomenon. But neither is it entirely nonrational. No nation will publicly agree that its cause is unjust yet pursue it violently anyway. It may be that appeals to justice are partly rationalizations. But a nation whose proposed rationalization is shot full of holes by everyone else will not so readily go forth to war. Agreement on what constitutes justice, and on the facts of particular cases, is probably necessary, and may also be sufficient, to prevent war: Without it, war is almost certain; with it, war is quite unlikely.

§25 THE BOMB

We are constantly being reminded that this is an age when the potential for destruction is of a wholly different order than before. This undoubtedly gives a new urgency to the avoidance of major wars, at least, and also to the technological task of devising ways of making sure that the weapons are not used by mistake or by cranks. Does it also mean, as might be supposed, that all such deliberations as the foregoing are rendered irrelevant? I think not.

The potential consequences of atomic wars, while undoubtedly enormously greater in size, are just the same in kind as before, with minor variations. Each of us has just one life to live, and that life is threatened no more by the prospect of H-bomb obliteration than it was by people with spears and torches. The reasons for avoiding wars are the same as always. What differs is only the far greater likelihood of the "accidental" production of these horrors and the much greater number of those affected. There is no reason to revise our entire conception of what makes wars morally wrong, if they are wrong.

There is an important moral of these developments. As the stakes get bigger, it becomes more and more rational to reduce, if we can, the probability that these evil consequences will ensue. It becomes, for example, increasingly rational to permit inspectors from the other side to monitor one's own weapons deployment in exchange for similar permission on their part for our inspectors to monitor theirs. And perhaps it will become also clearer that visions of capitalist wickedness and socialist revolution, or vice versa, are of less importance than simply allowing us all to live in peace. Perhaps we can hope for the day when the leaders of great powers will take the view that these extremely dangerous and extremely expensive toys are simply not worth the money or the danger, and they will reach sensible agreement to bury them safely back in the earth from which their exotic components originally sprang. That view has, after all, one important recommendation: It is true!

IV. EPILOGUE

The main burden of this essay has been to explore the case for and against the morality of war. The conclusions defended are unsurprising, and I hope have been well supported. The grounds for regarding aggressive war as immoral are solid, rationally speaking. But where violence is used in defense, it often cannot be condemned at all. What can be condemned is the use of violence when other ways of reaching agreement are available, as they nearly always are. There are those who resort to violence too readily, and to political systems and attitudes that encourage it. What needs to be done with people who participate in such systems and share such attitudes is not only to persuade them that violence is evil. It is, in addition, to persuade them that violence, even if it "works," is too *poor* a thing for humans. This is a matter not merely of morality but of values. We return to the importance of accepting the value of life—of accepting it as part of our vision of life. What is wrong with most violence is not just that it is wrong, but also that it is barbaric, mindless, and contemptible; and those who resort easily to it are bullies, paranoiacs, or fanatics. That the world should be dominated by such people is depressing in the extreme.

This is not a view that I can impartially urge upon all rational people. It is, instead, a view that I partially urge as a civilized person. There is, alas, no certainty that we friends of civilization—we nice guys, in short—will win. Indeed, the nasties and the bullies among us have a terrible advantage, and a tragically unfair one. For by taking up arms against us, which they apparently enjoy, they force us to do likewise, which we do *not* enjoy. The strategy of being as ready to retaliate as the others are to attack is forced upon us, and it lowers the quality of our lives.

Almost equally depressing is the thought that probably the causes of belligerence are as ignoble or trivial as the temperament itself. Perhaps it will turn out that the incalculable suffering that people have inflicted on each other is due to some aberration in their infancy that was nobody's fault at all. Their parents, perhaps, failed to pick them up at some unknowably crucial moment, or fed them the wrong sort of vegetables. Rationality is of limited avail against this sort of thing. Yet, reason is the most important weapon we have in our arsenal. And who knows? Perhaps it will ultimately prove sufficient.

SUGGESTIONS FOR FURTHER READING

An enormous amount has been written about the subjects touched upon in this essay. The suggestions below are strictly to get you started; they are not comprehensive.

Introduction
§§1–3 J. A. Shaffer, ed., *Violence* (David McKay, 1971). See especially the essay by Ronald Miller, "Violence, Force and Coercion."

Newton Garver, "What Violence Is," reprinted in R. Wasserstrom, ed., *Today's Moral Problems* (Macmillan, 1975).

I. Morality and Violence
§§4–6   General: Paul W. Taylor, *Principles of Ethics* (Dickenson, 1975). Kurt Baier, *The Moral Point of View* (Random House, 1965).

§§7–8   The Three Theories:

1. Contractarianism: Thomas Hobbes, *Leviathan*, Book I (many editions); David Gauthier, "Reason and Maximization," *Canadian Journal of Philosophy*, March 1975.

2. Libertarianism: John Locke, *Essay on Civil Government*; Robert Nozick, *Anarchy, State and Utopia* (Basic Books, 1974).

3. Utilitarianism: Jeremy Bentham, *Principles of Morals and Legislation*; Henry Sidgwick, *The Methods of Ethics* (Macmillan, 1906, 1962, etc.); Jan Narveson, *Morality and Utility* (John Hopkins Press, 1967); S. Gorovitz, ed., *Mill: Utilitarianism—Text and Critical Essays* (Bobbs-Merrill, 1971).

II. Pacifism
Anthology: Peter Mayer, ed., *The Pacifist Conscience* (Gateway, paperback, 1967).

§§9–16   Donald A. Wells, *The War Myth* (Pegasus, paperback, 1967).
Two interesting pamphlets: A. D. Lindsay, "Pacifism as a Principle and Pacifism as a Dogma," S.C.M. Press, London, 1939; and Ronald Sampson, "The Anarchist Basis of Pacifism" (Peace Pledge Union, 6 Endsleigh St., London W.C.1, 1970).
Raghaven N. Iyer, *The Moral and Political Thought of Mahatma Gandhi* (Oxford University Press, 1973). See the discussion of this book by Jan Narveson, "Morality and Non-Violence," *Philosophia* (Israel), November 1978.

§17   Jan Narveson, "Pacifism—A Philosophical Analysis," *Ethics*, vol. 75, 1965. This essay is reprinted in the Wasserstrom anthologies listed above and below; the former also contains the reply by Tom Regan, "A Defense of Pacifism," *Canadian Journal of Philosophy*, Sept. 1972.

III. Violence and the State
Count Carl von Clausewitz, *On War* (new edition by Howard & Paret, Princeton, 1976).

§§18–25   R. Wasserstrom, ed., *War and Morality* (Belmont, Calif.: Wadsworth, paperback, 1970); *Philosophy and Public Affairs Reader: War and Moral Responsibility* (Princeton, 1973).
Ted Honderich, *Political Violence* (Ithaca: Cornell University Press, 1977).
J. Glenn Gray, *The Warriors* (New York: Harcourt, Brace and World, 1959) (selection also in Wasserstrom, *Today's Moral Problems*).
Jan Narveson, "Nationalism," in Shea and King-Farlow, eds., *Contemporary Issues in Political Philosophy* (New York: Science History Publications, 1976).
Immanuel Kant, *Perpetual Peace* (Bobbs-Merrill, Library of Liberal Arts, paperback).
R. Wasserstrom, "On the Morality of War: A Preliminary Inquiry," in *War and Morality, op. cit.*

5
Capital Punishment

HUGO ADAM BEDAU

§1 INTRODUCTION

When we confront the task of evaluating punishments from the moral point of view, a host of questions immediately arise. Who should be punished? What offenses and harms should be made liable to punishment? What is involved in making the punishment fit the crime? Are some punishments too cruel or barbaric to be tolerated no matter how effective they may be in preventing crime? Are some criminals so depraved or dangerous that no punishment is too severe for them? What moral principles should govern our thinking about crime and punishment? In order to give reasonable answers to such questions, we need to appeal to a wide variety of empirical facts. We will want to know, for example, what would happen to the crime rate if no one were punished at all, or if all offenders were punished more leniently than is usual. We would want to know whether the system of criminal justice operates with adequate efficiency and fairness when it metes out severe punishments, or whether the severest punishments tend to fall mainly upon some social or racial classes. But we will want to settle other things besides these matters of fact. Social values, moral ideals, ethical principles are also involved, and we will want to know which values and which ideals they are and how to evaluate them as well. Central among these ethical considerations are the value, worth, and dignity of persons—the victims of crime, the offenders, and the general public. How, exactly, does our belief in the value of human life, the worth of each person, our common humanity and our common dignity, bear on the nature and methods of punishment as seen from the moral point of view?

There is no better setting in which to examine these questions than the one provided by the controversy over the morality of capital punishment (the death penalty). From an historical perspective, the earliest and most enduring form that these basic ethical values take is in the idea of *the sanctity of life* and, subsequently, *the right to life.* The fundamental idea of the sanctity of human life derives from some of the earliest passages in the Old Testament. The central Biblical text is *Genesis* 1:27, where we are told that "God created man in his own image." Other peoples of antiquity—the Homeric Greeks, the ancient Egyptians, Persians, and Babylonians—showed interest in and concern for the value of human life. But the idea that human life is of transcendent worth, independent of the value that can be placed on a person by virtue of efforts, accomplishments, talents, or any other measure, and that this worth is equal for all and owing to something divine in human beings—this is an inescapably religious notion and it is Biblical in origin.

With the rise of rationalist thought in European culture during the Renaissance and the Enlightenment, and the concurrent decline in an exclusively religious foundation for moral principles, philosophers increasingly lent their support to the doctrine of "the rights of man" as the foundation for constitutional law and public morality. This doctrine took many forms, and it is a prominent part of the moral, political, and legal thinking of the most influential European, British, and American writers. These thinkers differ in their views about the nature of rights, but all agree that first and foremost among these rights is "the right to life."

Distinct as the sanctity of human life and the right to life are, they are bound together by a common bond. Each idea is an attempt to express the view that it is morally wrong to take a purely instrumental view of human life. By 'instrumental view of human life' I mean any view that makes it permissible to kill persons in order to protect some other value (e.g., property) or in order to advance some social or political goal (e.g., national liberation). If every human life is sacred or if every person has a right to life, then the murder of an insignificant peasant is just as heinous as the assassination of a king. Likewise, deliberately killing thousands in order to advance the welfare of millions is forbidden. On an instrumental view of human life, however, when other things are assumed to be more "valuable" or "worthy" than the lives of some people, the deaths of many persons often can be justified as necessary to the accomplishment of various social goals. For example, in the eyes of the Nazis, the triumph of the "master race" justified the murder of millions of Jews and other "inferior" peoples. But if everyone has a right to life, or if everyone's life is sacred, then genocidal murder cannot be justified and stands condemned as a grave crime against humanity.

So far as the death penalty is concerned, it might seem that once it is granted that human life is sacred or that everyone has an equal right to life, the death penalty is morally indefensible. Such a punishment seems obviously inconsistent with these ideals of human worth and value. The opposite, however, is true if we let history be our guide. Chief among the traditional defenders of capital punishment have been those religious and secular thinkers who sincerely believe in these ideals. In fact, they usually invoked the sanctity of human life and the right to life as part of their defense and justification of death for murderers and other criminals. To see how such a seemingly paradoxical doctrine can be maintained, as well as to begin our examination of the major issues involved in the moral evaluation of the death penalty, we must scrutinize the traditional doctrine of the right to life.

I. THE RIGHT TO LIFE AND CAPITAL PUNISHMENT

§2 THE DOCTRINE OF NATURAL RIGHTS

The right to life can be thought of, first, as underlying the prohibition against murder common to the criminal law of all countries. The general idea shared by many philosophers, beginning in the seventeenth century, was that each person by nature—that is, apart from the laws of the state and simply by virtue of being born a human being —had the right to live. It followed from this that it was a violation of that right to be killed by another person, and that it was the responsibility of government to protect human rights, prohibit murder, and convict and punish anyone guilty of this crime. On some versions of the theory, God was thought to be the source of this and other "natural rights." Still, few philosophers assumed a necessary connection between everyone's having the right to life and the existence of God as the creator. Hence, the right to life can be understood without significant distortion as a secular notion, free of any essential religious overtones, and thus available to the moral philosophy of theist, atheist, and agnostic alike.

In addition to being *natural,* the right to life was traditionally understood to be *universal* and *inalienable.* A universal right is a right that everyone everywhere has, regardless of where he or she is born or lives, and regardless of sex or race. An inalienable right is a right that the possessor cannot transfer, sell, or give away to another person. Thus, killing one person is as much a violation of the right to life as killing any other person, and no one of us can authorize another to kill us by giving up to that person our right to life.

The right to life seems to pose a problem for a policy of capital punishment. Even if a person has committed murder (so the argument runs), and has therewith violated another's right to life, the criminal still has his or her own right to life. Would it not be a violation of that right for the murderer to be put to death as punishment, and if so, must not capital punishment be morally wrong? A few philosophers, notably Thomas Hobbes (1588–1679), Jean-Jacques Rousseau (1712–1778), and Cesare Beccaria (1738–1794), show signs of having been troubled by this argument, but they are the exceptions. Most philosophical proponents of the doctrine of a natural right to life were not troubled by it at all, because they adopted one or another variant of the position influentially expressed by John Locke (1632–1704). It will suffice for our purposes to examine his views.

§3 FORFEITING THE RIGHT TO LIFE

Locke argued that although a person's right to life is natural and inalienable, it can be "forfeited" and *is* forfeited whenever one person violates that right in another. A recent philosopher has put the point clearly: "The offender, by violating the life, liberty, or property of another, has lost his own right to have his life, liberty, or property respected . . ."[1] The idea is a familiar one, although there are troubling and unanswered questions, such as whether this right once forfeited can ever be restored and if so by whom and under what conditions. Thanks to the doctrine of forfeiture, it was possible for Locke to assert without apparent contradiction both that everyone has a natural right to life and that the death penalty for a murderer does not violate that right.

Locke's actual reasoning was slightly different and less plausible but more revealing than the account of it so far given. What Locke said was that a person forfeits his right to life whenever he or she commits some criminal act "that deserves death."[2] The obvious objection to this formulation is that it allows the doctrine of forfeiture of the right to life to permit the use of capital punishment not only for murderers but for almost any crime whatever. Not only treason and the other traditional felonies (arson, rape, robbery, burglary), but relatively minor offenses against property and public order could be said to be properly punished by death. All that is required is some good argument to show that crime x "deserves" such punishment. It will then follow that anyone guilty of x has "forfeited" the natural right to life. (It should be noted that Locke himself seems to have given no thought at all to what should be the criterion for crimes that "deserve" death, apart from murder.)

It is this very sweeping doctrine of forfeiture as Locke formulated it that proved to be the influential one, at least in Anglo-American criminal law, where it was carried over intact a century after Locke by the jurist Sir William Blackstone in his monumental *Commentary on the Laws of England* (1776). Thus, the seeming inconsistency of English legal philosophy being founded on a doctrine of natural rights, including the right to life, and English criminal law authorizing capital punishment for dozens of minor offenses against property—by 1800, there were some 200 capital offenses, ranging from arson in the dockyards to theft of goods from a bleaching ground—disappears. Locke's doctrine of forfeiture shows why the idea of a natural, universal, and inalienable right to life was not, historically, a rigid moral barrier to capital punishment.

§4 DIFFICULTIES IN LOCKE'S THEORY

There are various objections to the classic theory of the right to life, two of which deserve to be mentioned here. First, underlying Locke's doctrine of natural rights and wholly independent of it are two important assumptions. One is that punishment under law is necessary for social defense.[3] The other is that justice requires retribution—crime must be punished, and the punishment must fit the crime. The result of these beliefs is that the punishment for murder and other crimes should be death, and they force Locke to make some accommodation in his theory of natural rights. The device he hit upon, and one that generations of later thinkers have also adopted, is to declare that the right to life could be forfeited under certain conditions. But the conclusiveness of the doctrine of forfeiture is no greater than whatever general reasons can be brought forward to show that retributive justice and social defense are themselves free of moral objections and that they jointly can be satisfied at least in some cases only by the death penalty. If it cannot be shown that retributive justice in general requires the death penalty for murderers, and that social defense in general does likewise, then Locke's argument for the conclusion that a murderer (or any other criminal) forfeits his or her right to life collapses. It is extremely important to grasp this criticism. There is no intrinsic feature of any right, including the natural right to life, that makes it subject to loss through forfeiture. The only basis for supposing that any right is forfeited rather than grossly violated by society when it punishes an offender by death is that just retribution and social defense together require the death penalty for offenders of this sort. If this requirement turns out to be false or unsubstantiated or doubtful, then the claim that a criminal's right to life has been forfeited turns out to be equally false, unsubstantiated, or doubtful. As so much turns, therefore, on these questions of the necessity of the death penalty for just retribution and social defense, we shall return to examine them in more detail later (in §§19–28).

Even if it is concluded that a murderer or other felon does forfeit the natural right to life, it does not follow that a murderer *must* be put to death. This is the second objection. The doctrine of forfeiture does not involve the idea that once a person forfeits a right to *x*, then the one to whom it is forfeited has a *duty* to take *x* away from that person. This is often overlooked by those who insist that the death penalty is justified because murderers forfeit their lives. Forfeiting one's *right* to life is not identical with forfeiting one's life. Also, forfeiting one's right to life does not confer upon anyone else the *duty* to take the forfeited life. Just as a person may in fact continue to possess something for which he or she has forfeited the right of possession (by, say, failing to renew the lease on a house he or she still occupies), so the government may decide to let a person live who under the doctrine of forfeiture "deserves" to die. In such a case, it may be that nothing wrong is being done—to the criminal's victims, to the rest of society, or even to the criminal. Another way of putting it is this: Although a person may have forfeited the right to life, it is within *our* rights to let him or her live; in doing so we do not invariably violate any duty, and it may be that there is nothing morally wrong in what we do. What is true is that if a person who has forfeited the right to life nevertheless continues to live, he or she cannot claim to do so on the ground of that right. Whether or not we do the right thing in not killing someone who has forfeited the right to life is, of course, a further question. But enough has been said to show that the fact (if it ever is a fact) that someone forfeits the right to life does not morally require that he or she be put to death.

§5 THE DIGNITY OF PERSONS

Kant's doctrine of the supreme worth or dignity of persons may be treated more briefly, because it adds little to what we have already examined. The most famous single passage in which this doctrine and Kant's views on the punishment of murder are brought together is the following:

> If . . . he has committed a murder, he must die. In this case, there is no substitute that will satisfy the requirements of legal justice. There is no sameness of kind between death and remaining alive even under the most miserable conditions, and consequently there is no equality between the crime and the retribution unless the criminal is judicially condemned and put to death. But the death of the criminal must be kept entirely free of any maltreatment that would make an abomination of the humanity residing in the person suffering it. Even if a civil society were to dissolve itself by common agreement of all its members (for example, if the people inhabiting an island decided to separate and disperse themselves around the world), the last murderer remaining in prison must first be executed, so that everyone will duly receive what his actions are worth and so that the bloodguilt thereof will not be fixed on the people because they failed to insist on carrying out the punishment; for if they fail to do so, they may be regarded as accomplices in this public violation of legal justice.[4]

In this passage, the idea of the dignity of man enters only to rule out any aggravations and brutality attended upon the sentence of death and its execution. For Kant, the dignity of man underlies the whole idea of a society of free and rational persons choosing to submit themselves to a common rule of law that includes the punishment of crimes. Accordingly, in punishment, "a human being can never be manipulated merely as a means to the purposes of someone else . . . His innate personality protects him against such treatment . . ."[5]

Of most importance for our purposes is the way the above passage shows that a principle of just retribution underlies Kant's belief in the appropriateness of punishing murder with death. This is reminiscent of Locke's view (recall the weight Locke attached to the idea of crimes that "deserve" the punishment of death), and it is probably also an echo of the ancient law of retaliation, *lex talionis* ("a life for a life"). The chief difference between Kant and Locke is that Locke thinks it is proper to take into account not only just retribution but also social defense to determine proper punishments, whereas Kant unequivocally rules out the latter. What Kant has done is to present us with two moral principles—the dignity or worth of each person as a rational creature, and the principle of just retribution—that he regards as inextricably tied together. The latter of these two principles he formulated in the following way:

> What kind and what degree of punishment does public legal justice adopt as its principle and standard? None other than the principle of equality . . . , that is, the principle of not treating one side more favorably than the other. Accordingly, any undeserved evil that you inflict on someone else among the people is one that you do to yourself. Only the Law of retribution . . . can determine exactly the kind and degree of punishment . . . All other standards fluctuate back and forth and, because extraneous considerations are mixed with them, they cannot be compatible with the principle of pure and strict legal justice.[6]

§6 THE MIND OF THE MURDERER

Although Kant does not stress the point in the passages we have quoted, he must have realized that in actual practice, apportioning punishments to crimes is not so simple as his principle of retribution seems to imply. A person deserves to be punished, by Kant's reasoning, only when there is no excuse or justification for the criminal conduct, i.e., by virtue of one's "inner viciousness," as when one has "rationally willed" to kill another person who is entirely innocent and undeserving of any harm.

If modern criminologists are correct, however, most murders are not committed by persons whose state of mind can be described as Kant implies. Empirical (clinical, experimental) criminology requires us to test and verify our assumptions regarding the psychology (motivation, intention, state of mind) of each person who kills, whereas Kant's theory is formulated from beginning to end without regard to empirical assumptions at all. Kant's position is more abstract and theoretical. He argues, in effect, that *if* anyone rationally wills the death of an innocent party and acts on that decision, *then* such a person deserves to be put to death. Such an abstract doctrine is quite consistent with the reality described by social and clinical scientists that few if any who perpetrate violent crimes act in such a coolly deliberate and rational fashion. Consequently, it is theoretically possible to accept Kant's doctrine of just punishment and the death penalty for murder, and at the same time to oppose the actual execution of every convicted murderer—a possibility that Kant seems to have entirely overlooked, owing perhaps to his unfamiliarity with criminal psychopathology and to the primitive state of the social, behavioral, and clinical sciences of his day. Whether we should accept Kant's doctrine of just retribution even in the abstract remains an open question, and one difficult to answer. In later sections (§§24–28), we shall examine some of the most important retributive principles that bear on the death-penalty controversy.

§7 DIFFICULTIES IN KANT'S THEORY

In the course of presenting Kant's views, we have already identified three respects in which his theory is vulnerable. One is that, like Locke's, it assumes that just retribution requires capital punishment for murder, an assumption that may be unnecessary and in any case is not proved. Another difficulty is that, unlike Locke's theory, Kant's seems to make no room whatever for the role of social defense in the justification of punishment. Because Kant's theory excludes this, one cannot argue that if social defense does not require capital punishment for murderers or other criminals, then it is to that extent morally wrong to inflict this punishment on them. But one should be able to argue against a mode of punishment in this way, even if one concedes to Kant that social defense cannot be the only consideration in a system of just punishment.

Finally, a third objection follows from the fact that Kant's theory is so obviously abstract and unempirical from beginning to end. If we really take seriously the idea of the dignity of man, then it may be that we will be led in case after case of actual crime to reject Kant's reasoning on the ground that it is inapplicable in light of the actual facts of the case before us. It is an objection to Kant's theory that it tells us what to do only with ideally rational killers, when what we need is a theory that tells us how to cope with the actual persons who kill, and to do that in a way that acknowledges our common humanity with both the victim and the offender, the injustices to which all social systems are prone, and the wisdom of self-restraint in the exercise of violence, especially when undertaken in the name of justice.

§8 CONCLUSION

We have so far examined two different versions of the special worth of human life as it bears on the problem of capital punishment, the idea of the right to life (especially Locke's theory), and the idea of the dignity of man (especially Kant's). In each case, we have seen how the doctrine in question helps explain why murder is a heinous crime and should be condemned and punished, how it is not an absolute barrier to capital punishment, and how it makes room for the death penalty as a morally proper and socially necessary punishment. This accommodation is provided in part by the role of other moral principles alongside the right to life and the dignity of man.

The underlying considerations in favor of the death penalty turn out to be considerations of justice and social defense. Death for murderers and other felons, it is assumed, is a necessary mode of punishment, necessary on the ground either of just retribution or of social defense and public safety. Since these necessities leave no alternative to the punishment of death, it cannot be morally wrong, and any moral ideal or moral principle that seems to forbid the death penalty cannot really do so and must be reinterpreted so that it is consistent with the practice of capital punishment.

The consequence is that either we must give up any attempt to found a principled opposition to the death penalty on the idea of the special worth or unique value of human life, or we must reinterpret these ideas in a more subtle manner. It is now time to begin this latter task.

II. THE MORALITY OF CAPITAL PUNISHMENT

As a first step toward providing a fresh setting for the rest of our discussion, it is useful to have a general sketch before us of why it is rational for society to have a system of punishment at all, quite apart from whether or not the death penalty is used as one of the modes of punishment. We are not likely to assess the morality of capital punishment correctly unless we understand the morality of punishment in general. Accordingly, we need to have a general conception of why society should have a system of punishment, a conception that takes into consideration the value of human life.

§9 THE NATURE OF PUNISHMENT

We may start with the fact that a punishment, by its very nature, is unpleasant, often painful, frequently humiliating, and in any case either a deprivation of something deemed to be of value or the imposition of something deemed to be a hardship. Freedom of bodily movement and assembly with others, disposing of one's money and property as one pleases, having one's body (and one's life) intact—all these it is good to have and to have free of interference. Why, then, does society always insist on a system of punishment when this means inflicting so much suffering and deprivation upon persons? Punishment is in need of justification because it is always the deliberate infliction of deprivation or hardship on a person, and is thus the sort of thing no one would freely consent to have imposed on oneself.

The justification must begin with the fact that we cannot avoid regarding some kinds of human conduct as harmful to innocent persons. This leads society to prohibit and condemn such conduct. Condemnation is achieved by the imposition of punishment. The next step is to establish degrees of severity in the punishments as a function of such factors as the community's judgment of the gravity of the offense, the difficulty and cost in detecting offenders, and so forth. In a society such as ours, where individual freedom is so highly prized, there is a tendency to make punishments somewhat more severe than otherwise in order to compensate for having restricted the police and the courts to a role that hampers them in bringing offenders to justice lest they invade what we regard as our justifiable privacy.

§10 THE RIGHT TO PUNISH

Society is organized by reference to common rules that forbid anyone and everyone to engage in certain sorts of harmful conduct. When anyone does deliberately, willfully, and knowingly violate such rules, and therewith harms the innocent, the offender has violated the rights of others and therewith immediately becomes liable to a punitive response. Since the rules were originally designed to provide protection to every person, and since (so we also assume) the culprit knew in advance that his or her conduct was prohibited and would be injurious to others, and since he or she freely and knowingly chose nevertheless to violate the prohibition and injure another, society cannot simply ignore the violation and continue to treat the offender as if no wrong had been done. It must attempt to bring the offender to judgment. But the reason is not mainly to give a lesson to the offender or to set an example for others who might be inclined to imitate such lawless conduct. The reason is twofold. First, it is simply inconsistent for society to establish a set of fair rules, with penalties for their violation, and then when actual violations occur to ignore them. Second, it is simply unfair for the law-abiding to have to suffer the harms inflicted on them by lawbreakers, as well as the inconvenience of their own self-discipline, and for the criminals to indulge their lawless inclinations and to suffer nothing in return.

Crime, on the model being developed here, can always be seen as an attempt to take more than one's fair share of something. Theft of material goods is an obvious example. Murder and other crimes of violence against the person can be seen in the same way as conduct in which the offender takes more than a fair share of liberty with the bodies of others and disregards the lack of the victim's consent. Punishment, therefore, serves the complex function of reinforcing individual compliance with a set of social rules deemed necessary to protect the rights of all the members of society. Once it has been determined that society needs rules to guide the conduct of its members, when one of these rules has been deliberately violated, then there is no alternative but to set in motion the system of punishment.

The chief contentions of the doctrine of just retribution are two: Crime must be punished, and the punishment must fit the crime. On the theory being developed here, the first of these contentions is certainly acknowledged. Punishment by its nature is retributive; it pays back to an offender suffering and indignity akin to what the offender inflicted on the innocent victim. Justice, more than any other consideration (social defense, reform of the offender), dictates that in principle all crimes be liable to punishment, and that a reasonable portion of social resources (public expenditures) be allocated to the arrest and conviction of offenders.

§11 MODES OF PUNISHMENT

The retributive principle that punishments must fit crimes is more difficult to implement, and we shall discuss it in detail later (in §§24–28). A prior and related problem concerns the sorts of punishments that are available to society to inflict on offenders. What is needed, if we are to be fair and effective, is some common denominator. What are the sorts of things any person could be deprived of that would count as punishment? Obviously, one could lose one's money or property, or the right to future earnings or an inheritance. But because so much crime against property and against the person is committed by the poor and untalented, by persons with no property and no prospects of any, it is often pointless to levy punishments in the form of fines or confiscations. Also, if the crime in question is not against property but against the person, there is insufficient affinity between the offense and the punishment. If society were to punish assault and battery by, say, a fine of $1,000, it would be impossible for the poor to be punished for the crime, and it would be seen merely as a tariff on the conduct of the very rich, like higher taxes on yachts and private planes—an inconvenience, but not much more. In either case, the victim of the assault and battery would have suffered injury quite incommensurate with the punishment (especially if the $1,000 were to go to the State rather than to the victim).

It is for reasons such as this that society has long preferred to take other things of value from persons in the name of punishment—notably, their freedom and their bodily integrity. Everybody, rich and poor, young and old, male and female, has life and some degree of liberty to lose. Historically, the objection to making punishments mainly a deprivation of liberty was that considerable tax revenues were needed to build and staff prisons. It was in part for such economic reasons that the earliest punishments were neither pecuniary nor incarcerative, but corporal: flogging, branding, maiming, and killing. Inexpensive and quick to administer, acutely painful for the offender—

it is hardly any wonder that every society today is heir to punitive practices involving widespread and varied use of corporal punishments.

What our discussion shows is that there is an argument on grounds of fairness for a system of punishment in the first place (given the fact that not everyone will always abide by rules that prohibit injury to others, and that it is necessary to have such rules), and an argument on grounds of equality for modes of punishment that all can pay and that impose similar deprivations on all concerned. It is also clear from this sketch that there is no intrinsic necessity or requirement for the use of capital punishment. It is simply one possible mode of punishment among others, even if in the case of murder it is the one punishment most like the injury the victim has suffered.

§12 THE VALUE OF HUMAN LIFE AND MORAL PRINCIPLES

We have had occasion to notice earlier that there is an important tie among the religious idea of the sanctity of human life and the secular ideas of the right to life and the dignity of man. That common factor is the way each of these ideas rules out as immoral the taking of a person's life on grounds of social usefulness and nothing more. From the standpoint of moral theory, this amounts to the claim that when the moral principle of overall social welfare conflicts with the moral principle of the individual's right to life, the latter shall prevail. We have also seen how the right to life and the dignity of man generate the requirement that society must forbid and punish severely the crime of murder. From the standpoint of moral theory, this is an instance where a moral ideal is the source of a social or legal rule.

With a little reflection it is possible to connect several other moral principles with the idea of the worth of human life. We may regard these principles as corollaries or theorems of that ideal taken as an axiom or first principle of morality. Each of these principles bears on the moral desirability or permissibility of the death penalty. Some of these subsidiary principles we have already encountered; others will emerge in the discussions that follow. Here, for future reference, is the full set:

1. An untimely or an undignified death is morally objectionable.
2. Taking the life of anyone as a punishment is not justified if it is not necessary, i.e., as long as there is a feasible alternative.
3. Unless there is a good reason to punish a crime severely, a less severe penalty is to be preferred.
4. The more severe a penalty is, the more important it is to inflict it fairly and equally, i.e., on all and only those who deserve it.
5. Death is a more severe punishment than long-term imprisonment, even life imprisonment without parole.

6. If human lives are to be risked, risking the life of the guilty is morally preferable to risking the life of the innocent.

All of the above principles can be seen, in one way or another, as expressive of ideas that have their origin in the worth of human life. In addition to the above principles, two others have emerged that express aspects of the idea of retribution, or justice in punishment. These are:

7. Crimes should be punished.
8. Punishments should be graded in their severity according to the gravity of the crimes for which they are imposed.

Our task is to determine the scope and application of these several principles so that we may render, so far as it is possible, a final judgment on capital punishment from the moral point of view. These eight principles are not, of course, of equal weight or scope; some are much more important than others. Nothing short of a full-scale moral theory could incorporate each of these principles to the exact extent that is proper, and there is no opportunity here for the development of such a theory. Instead, we will attempt to show how each of these principles enters into a line of reasoning relevant to the morality of capital punishment and thus how each can be accorded something like its proper weight, so that by the time we are finished, we will have found a role for each principle that seems plausible. Most of these principles have no specific reference to the morality of capital punishment. That should not be surprising, and it is certainly no defect that they lack such reference. In general, one wants moral principles of wide application, to cover as many different kinds of cases and situations as possible. If such broad generalizations can withstand criticism and counterexamples to test their plausibility, then to that extent they are likely to be sound principles.

III. THE INDIGNITY AND SEVERITY OF THE DEATH PENALTY

§13 IS CAPITAL PUNISHMENT AN UNTIMELY AND UNDIGNIFIED DEATH?

Some critics of the opposition to capital punishment have complained that such opposition involves an overestimation of the value of human life, for it tends to ignore the fact that we are all bound to die eventually. According to these critics, all that capital punishment does is to schedule a person's death at a definite time and place, by a definite mode and for a definite reason. This raises a new question for us, namely, whether the ideas of the value, worth, dignity, or sanctity of human life can be made consistent with the fact of human mortality.

Even though death is a fact of life, emphasizing the worth of human life is a way of giving sense to the familiar notions of an "untimely" death and of an "undignified" death. These terms are no doubt vague, and have application in a wide variety of settings, but they also have a place where crime and punishment are concerned. Other things being equal, if a death is brought about by one person killing another, as in murder, then it is an untimely death. If a death is brought about in a way that causes terror during the dying and disfigurement of the body, then it is an undignified death. This, of course, is exactly what murder and capital punishment typically do. (The French film "We Are All Murderers" (1956) rendered this theme vividly.) Only when the person being killed does not know, and does not believe, he or she is dying, and only when the lethal agent is painless and leaves no mark or scar, would a murder or a legal execution be free of the objection that it is "undignified."

Historically, however, the most brutal methods of execution have been practiced in public, despite any objection that might be brought on these grounds. The reason was that such brutality was thought necessary to enhance the deterrent effect of the execution and to pay back the guilty offender, with interest, for the crime that had been committed. Stoning, crucifixion, impalement, beheading, even hanging and shooting, have often been hideously painful, terrifying to anticipate and experience, and they have left the executed person in various degrees of bodily disfigurement. In principle, of course, there is no medical or technical barrier to the development of modes of inflicting the death penalty that do not conspicuously affront human dignity. The gas chamber was introduced in this country in the 1920s as an improvement on the electric chair, much as the electric chair itself had been introduced in the 1890s in the belief that it was a humane improvement upon hangings. During the 1970s, several state legislatures enacted bills to impose the death penalty by painless lethal injection.

Confronted by these considerations, what should be the reply of the defender of the death penalty? One can argue in any of several ways: (a) Neither retribution nor social defense, each of which does require brutal methods or administering the death penalty, is part of the purpose or justification of capital punishment; (b) neither retribution nor social defense really requires any of the brutalities still characteristic of capital punishment; or (c) the idea that death should be neither untimely nor undignified is a moral principle of little weight, and other moral principles favoring the death penalty easily outweigh it. It is difficult to imagine any defender of the death penalty resting content with alternative (a). Alternative (b) is more promising, but for reasons to be given below (in §§20 and 27), it really will not withstand close scrutiny. It is most likely that the defender of capital punishment would prefer to stand on alternative (c). If so, the dispute between defenders and critics of the morality of capital punishment will turn on how that punishment fares when measured by the requirements of just retribution and social defense. Accordingly, the bulk of our discussion will eventually need to be devoted to resolving this dispute (see parts IV and V).

§14 GRADING THE SEVERITY OF PUNISHMENTS

Punishments can be plausibly graded into three categories of relative severity: Fines (loss of property) are the least severe, imprisonment (loss of liberty) is much more severe, and death (loss of life) is the most severe of all. Fines, as we noted earlier, are often like a tax on conduct, and relatively little social disgrace is attached to illegal conduct if the main consequence for the offender is to incur a fine. Loss of liberty, however, not only curtails freedom of association and movement; it is also a stigma, as well as a reminder hour by hour to the offender that he or she is undergoing punishment and that he or she has become (at least for the time being) literally a social outcast. As for the death penalty, most of those who oppose it as well as those who favor it believe it is far more severe than imprisonment. Why it is so severe, however, is often in dispute. Because opposition to the death penalty rests largely on the belief that this unusual severity is unnecessary and unjustified, it is important to examine this issue with some care.

Prolonged imprisonment without hope of release except by natural death has figured in dozens of novels and stories as the ultimate horror, and this is hardly surprising, especially if the incarceration is compounded by wretched living conditions and solitary confinement. Thus, life imprisonment without the possibility of parole can verge on the borderline that normally divides imprisonment from death as the less from the more severe punishment. Occasionally, prisoners under life sentence will commit suicide rather than face their bleak future any longer. "Lifers" also occasionally report that if they had known what it would be like to serve thirty or forty years in prison, they would have made no effort to avoid a death sentence at their trial. For those of us with just enough experience of prison life to be appalled by the thought of undergoing it, and with imaginations vivid enough to know what we would be deprived of once we were imprisoned behind bars, it is understandable that we might reach the sober conclusion that we would rather die than be imprisoned for life.

But do these considerations really show that death is not a more severe punishment even than life imprisonment? Do they indicate that life imprisonment can be as great or even a greater affront to the dignity of a person than the death penalty? Mainly at issue is whether personal preference of one penalty over another shows that the latter is more severe than the former. It does not. First of all, it is not really possible to tell which of two penalties one prefers, where the one is death and the other life, the way it is possible to tell which of two vacations one prefers, a week at the seashore or a week in the mountains. One can try different vacations and then, on the basis of actual experience, determine which is the preferable. But where death and life imprisonment are concerned, at most one can hope to *imagine* which of the two one would like the least. Any comparative judgment, in the nature of the case, must be based on no experience of the one (death) and very incomplete experience of the other (life imprisonment). If the severity of these two alternative punishments had to be judged in this way, we would never be able to tell which is the more severe. Or we would have to conclude that severity of punishments is not a matter for objective evaluation, but only of arbitrary preference or guesswork.

§15 WHY DEATH IS MORE SEVERE THAN IMPRISONMENT

If we reflect further on the matter, we will see that the issue of the severity of a punishment is a complex idea in which there are identifiable factors that permit clear comparison between modes of punishment. Roughly, of two punishments, one is more severe than the other depending its duration and on its interference with other things a person so punished might do. Death is interminable, whereas it is always possible to revoke or interrupt a life sentence. Death also makes compensation impossible, whereas it is possible to compensate a prisoner for wrongful confinement even if it is not possible to give back any of the liberty that was taken away. Of most importance, death permits of no concurrent experiences or activities, whereas even a life-term prisoner can read a book, watch television, perhaps even write a book or repair a television set, and experience social relations of some variety with other people. Death eliminates the presupposition of all experience and activity: life itself. For these reasons, the death penalty is unquestionably the more severe punishment, no matter what any despondent life-term prisoner or sentimental observer may prefer (or thinks he or she prefers), and no matter how painless and dignified the mode of execution may be.

It is of course true that it is possible to make even short-term imprisonment a living hell for the prisoner. No doubt, methods of imprisonment have been designed that would make death a blessed relief. Opponents of the death penalty, however, need favor no such brutal alternatives. It is true that Europe's first outspoken opponent of the death penalty, the young Italian nobleman Cesare Beccaria, recommended imprisonment over the death penalty because of "the perpetual example" that life-term prisoners afforded the public of what could happen if one committed a felony. Beccaria thought this would make long imprisonment a better deterrent than death because of the "much stronger impression" on the imagination of a whole life in prison as opposed to a few moments on the gallows.[7]

Today most opponents of the death penalty would favor as an alternative punishment a prison term of relatively brief duration (say, ten years) and then eligibility for parole release, with actual release depending upon the likelihood of further violent offenses and upon the public acceptability of the offender's release. Thus, a Charles Manson might never be released, whereas an armed robber who shot a gas station attendant during a holdup might be released in fifteen years (as, in fact, happens today in many such cases). The day-to-day prison regimen, while it need not approximate a country club—as it is cynically described by those who have never been there—also need not involve mistreatment, neglect, and brutality of a sort to delight the Spanish Inquisition, either.

We should also not forget that, as history shows, it is possible to aggravate the severity of the death penalty by any of several well-known techniques. Burning at the stake, for instance, would do very nicely as a more severe mode of execution than the electric chair. However, even if it could be established that such severe methods accomplished a marvelous improvement in the deterrent effect over less brutal methods, or that they were superbly fitted to repay the criminal for the kind of murder he committed, indignation at such cruelties would prohibit their use. They would be widely if not universally seen as a dangerous throwback to more savage times, in which respect for our common humanity was less prominent and less widespread than it is today. Thus we see that even retribution and deterrence have their moral limits, limits imposed in the name of human dignity.

§16 THE INDIGNITY OF CORPORAL PUNISHMENTS

In addition to the severity of the death penalty, killing persons as punishment shares certain important features with other modes of corporal punishment once widely practiced in our society—maiming, flogging, branding—but now abandoned. All these other methods of corporal punishment have been abandoned in part because they are now seen to violate the dignity of the person being punished. It is undignified to carry for the rest of one's life the visible stigma of having been convicted of a crime. But this is exactly what branding and maiming (such as cutting off the hand of a thief) did. Since the Freudian revolution earlier in this century, informed and reflective persons have become uneasy whenever violent physical abuse is inflicted by one person upon another who is helpless to do anything about it. Yet this is exactly what flogging involves. (By 'flogging' I do not mean the paddling a mother might administer to the bottom of her wayward child. I mean tying a person to a post or a railing and then beating him on the naked back with a whip so that bloody welts are raised that leave scars for life, a standard form of punishment only a few decades ago and still in use within prisons until fairly recently.) Any attempt by the authorities to revive such modes of punishment would be denounced as an unacceptable return to primitive techniques of punishment, and as needless physical violence that only hardens both those who undergo it and those who inflict it.

Why has death as a punishment escaped the nearly universal social and moral condemnation visited on all these other punishments with which it is historically and naturally associated? In part, it may be owing to a failure of imagination. Whereas we all know or can easily and vividly imagine the pain and humiliation involved in other corporal punishments, an execution is carried out away from public view, it is quickly over, and the person punished by death is no longer in our midst as a constant reminder. There are other factors, too. One is the belief that in some cases there is truly no alternative, because if the criminal were not killed there would be too much risk that he or she would repeat the crime. If so, then neither retribution nor deterrence, but rather prevention turns out to be the last line of defense. We shall examine this line of reasoning more closely below (§§18–22).

IV. CAPITAL PUNISHMENT AND SOCIAL DEFENSE

§17 THE ANALOGY WITH SELF-DEFENSE

Capital punishment, it is sometimes said, is to the body politic what self-defense is to the individual. If the latter is not morally wrong, how can the former be morally wrong? In order to assess the strength of this analogy, we need to inspect rather closely the morality of self-defense.

Except for the absolute pacifists, who believe it is morally wrong to use violence even to defend themselves or others from unprovoked and undeserved aggression, most of us believe that it is not morally wrong and may even be our moral duty to use violence to prevent aggression. The law has long granted persons the right to defend themselves against the unjust aggressions of others, even to the extent of killing a would-be assailant. It is very difficult to think of any convincing argument that would show it is never rational to risk the death of another in order to prevent death or grave injury to oneself or to others. Certainly self-interest dictates the legitimacy of self-defense. So does concern for the well-being of others. So also does justice. If it is unfair for one person to attempt violence on another, then it is hard to see why morality compels the victim to acquiesce in the attempt by another to hurt him or her, rather than to resist it, even if that resistance may involve injury to the assailant.

The foregoing account assumes that the person acting in self-defense is innocent of any provocation of the assailant. It also assumes that there is no alternative to victimization except resistance. In actual life, both assumptions—especially the second—are often false, because there may be a third alternative: escape, or removing oneself from the scene of danger and imminent aggression. Hence, the law imposes on us the so-called "duty to retreat." Before we use violence to resist aggression, we must try to get out of the way, lest unnecessary violence be used to resist aggression. Now suppose that unjust aggression is imminent, and there is no path open for escape. How much violence may justifiably be used to ward off aggression? The answer is: No more violence than is necessary to prevent the aggressive assault. Violence beyond that is unnecessary and therefore unjustified. We may restate the principle governing the use of violence in self-defense in terms of the use of "deadly force" by the police in the discharge of their duties. The rule is this: Use of deadly force is justified only to prevent loss of life in immediate jeopardy where a lesser use of force cannot reasonably be expected to save the life that is threatened.

In real life, violence in self-defense in excess of the minimum necessary to prevent aggression is often excusable. One cannot always tell what will suffice to deter or prevent becoming a victim, and the law looks with a certain tolerance upon the frightened and innocent would-be victim who turns upon a vicious assailant and inflicts a fatal injury even though a lesser injury would have been sufficient. What is not justified is deliberately using far more violence than is necessary to prevent becoming a victim. It is the deliberate, not the impulsive, use of violence that is relevant to the death-penalty controversy, since the death penalty is enacted into law and carried out in each case only after ample time to weigh alternatives. Notice that we are assuming that the act of self-defense is to protect one's person or that of a third party. The reasoning outlined here does not extend to the defense of one's property. Shooting a thief to prevent one's automobile from being stolen cannot be excused or justified in the way that shooting an assailant charging with a knife pointed at one's face can be. In terms of the concept of "deadly force," our criterion is that deadly force is never justified to prevent crimes against property or other violent crimes not immediately threatening the life of a person.

The rationale for self-defense as set out above illustrates two moral principles of great importance to our discussion (recall §12). One is that if a life is to be risked, then it is better that it be the life of someone who is guilty (in our context, the initial assailant) rather than the life of someone who is not (the innocent potential victim). It is not fair to expect the innocent prospective victim to run the added risk of severe injury or death in order to avoid using violence in self-defense to the extent of possibly killing his assailant. It is only fair that the guilty aggressor run the risk.

The other principle is that taking life deliberately is not justified so long as there is any feasible alternative. One does not expect miracles, of course, but in theory, if shooting a burglar through the foot will stop the burglary and enable one to call the police for help, then there is no reason to shoot to kill. Likewise, if the burglar is unarmed, there is no reason to shoot at all. In actual life, of course, burglars are likely to be shot at by aroused householders because one does not know whether they are armed, and prudence may dictate the assumption that they are. Even so, although the burglar has no right to commit a felony against a person or a person's property, the attempt to do so does not give the chosen victim the right to respond in whatever way he or she pleases in retaliation, and then to excuse or justify such conduct on the ground that he or she was "only acting in self-defense." In these ways the law shows a tacit regard for the life of even a felon and discourages the use of unnecessary violence even by the innocent; morality can hardly do less.

§18 PREVENTING CRIME *VERSUS* DETERRING CRIME

The analogy between capital punishment and self-defense requires us to face squarely the empirical questions surrounding the preventive and deterrent effects of the death penalty. Let us distinguish first between preventing and deterring crime. Executing a murderer in the name of punishment can be seen as a crime-*preventive* measure just to the extent it is reasonable to believe that if the murderer had not been executed he or she would have committed other crimes (including, but not necessarily confined to, murder). Executing a murderer can be seen as a crime *deterrent* just to the extent it is reasonable to believe that by the example of the execution other persons are frightened off from committing murder. Any punishment can be a crime preventive without being a crime deterrent, and it can be a deterrent without being a preventive. It can also be both or neither. Prevention and deterrence are theoretically independent because they operate by different methods. Crimes can be prevented by taking guns out of the hands of criminals, by putting criminals behind bars, by alerting the public to be less careless and less prone to victimization, and so forth. Crimes can be deterred only by making would-be criminals frightened of being arrested, convicted, and punished for crimes—that is, making persons overcome their desire to commit crimes by a stronger desire to avoid the risk of being caught and punished.

§19 THE DEATH PENALTY AS A CRIME PREVENTIVE

Capital punishment is unusual among penalties because its preventive effects limit its deterrent effects. The death penalty can never deter the executed person from further crimes. At most, it can prevent him or her from committing them. Popular discussions of the death penalty are frequently confused and misleading because they so often involve the assumption that the death penalty is a perfect and infallible deterrent so far as the executed criminal is concerned, whereas nothing of the sort is true. It is even an exaggeration to think that in any given case of execution the death penalty has proved to be an infallible crime preventive. What is obviously true is that once a person has been executed, it is physically impossible for him or her to commit any further crimes. But this does not prove that by executing a murderer society has in fact prevented any crimes. To prove this, one would need to know what crimes the executed criminal would have committed if he or she had not been executed and had been punished only in some less severe way (e.g., by imprisonment).

What is the evidence that the death penalty is an effective crime preventive? From the study of imprisonment, and parole and release records, it is clear that in general, if the murderers and other criminals who have been executed are like the murderers who were convicted but not executed, then (a) executing all convicted murderers would have prevented few crimes, but not many murders (less than one convicted murderer in a hundred commits another murder); and (b) convicted murderers, whether inside prison or outside after release, have at least as good a record of no further criminal activity as does any other class of convicted felon.

These facts show that the general public tends to overrate the danger and threat to public safety constituted by the failure to execute every murderer who is caught and convicted. While one would be in error to say that there is no risk such criminals will repeat their crimes —or similar ones—if they are not executed, one would be equally in error to say that by executing every convicted murderer we know that many horrible crimes will never be committed. All we know is that a few such crimes will never be committed; we do not know how many or by whom they would have been committed. (Obviously, if we did we could have prevented them.) This is the nub of the problem. There is no way to know in advance which if any of the incarcerated or released murderers will kill again. It is useful in this connection to remember that the only way to guarantee that no horrible crimes ever occur is to execute *everyone* who might conceivably commit such a crime. Similarly, the only way to guarantee that no convicted murderer ever commits another murder is to execute them all. No society has ever done this, and for 200 years our society has been moving steadily in the opposite direction.

These considerations show that our society has implicitly adopted an attitude toward the risk of murder rather like the attitude it has adopted toward the risk of fatality from other sources, such as automobile accidents, lung cancer, or drowning. Since no one knows when or where or upon whom any of these lethal events will befall, it would be too great an invasion of freedom to undertake the severe restrictions that alone would suffice to prevent any of them from occurring. It is better to take the risks and keep our freedom than to try to eliminate the risks altogether and lose our freedom in the process. Hence, we have lifeguards at the beach, but swimming is not totally prohibited; smokers are warned, but cigarettes are still legally sold; pedestrians may be given the right of way in a crosswalk, but marginally competent drivers are still allowed to operate motor vehicles. Some risk is therefore imposed on the innocent; in the name of our right to freedom, our other rights are not protected by society at all costs.

§20 THE DEATH PENALTY AS A CRIME DETERRENT

Determining whether the death penalty is an effective deterrent is even more difficult than determining its effectiveness as a crime preventive. In general, our knowledge about how penalties deter crimes and whether in fact they do—whom they deter, from which crimes, and under what conditions—is distressingly inexact. Most people nevertheless are convinced that punishments do deter, and that the more severe a punishment is the better it will deter. For more than a generation, social scientists have studied the question of whether the death penalty is a deterrent and of whether it is a better deterrent than the alternative of imprisonment. Their verdict, while not unanimous, is fairly clear. Whatever may be true about the deterrence of lesser crimes by other penalties, the deterrence achieved by the death penalty for murder is not measurably greater than the deterrence achieved by long-term imprisonment. In the nature of the case, the evidence is quite indirect. No one can identify for certain any crimes that did not occur because the would-be offender was deterred by the threat of the death penalty and that would not have been deterred by a lesser threat. Likewise, no one can identify any crimes that did occur because the offender was not deterred by the threat of prison even though he would have been deterred by the threat of death. Nevertheless, such evidence as we have fails to show that the more severe penalty (death) is really a better deterrent than the less severe penalty (imprisonment) for such crimes as murder.

If the conclusion stated above is correct, and the death penalty and long-term imprisonment are equally effective (or ineffective) as deterrents to murder, then the argument for the death penalty on grounds of deterrence is seriously weakened. One of the moral principles identified earlier comes into play and requires us to reject the death penalty on moral grounds. This is the principle that unless there is a good reason for choosing a more rather than a less severe punishment for a crime, the less severe penalty is to be preferred. This principle obviously commends itself to anyone who values human life and who concedes that, all other things being equal, less pain and suffering is always better than more. Human life is valued in part to the degree that it is free of pain, suffering, misery, and frustration, and in particular that it is free of such experiences when they serve no purpose. If the death penalty is not a more effective deterrent than imprisonment, then its greater severity than imprisonment is gratuitous, purposeless suffering and deprivation.

§21 A COST/BENEFIT ANALYSIS OF THE DEATH PENALTY

A full study of the costs and benefits involved in the practice of capital punishment would not be confined solely to the question of whether it is a better deterrent or preventive of murder than imprisonment. Any thoroughgoing utilitarian approach to the death-penalty controversy would need to examine carefully other costs and benefits as well, because maximizing the balance of social benefits over social costs is the sole criterion of right and wrong according to utilitarianism. Let us consider, therefore, some of the other costs and benefits to be calculated. Clinical psychologists have presented evidence to suggest that the death penalty actually incites some persons of unstable mind to murder others, either because they are afraid to take their own lives and hope that society will punish them for murder by putting them to death, or because they fancy that they, too, are killing with justification analogously to the justified killing involved in capital punishment. If such evidence is sound, capital punishment can serve as a counter-preventive or an incitement to murder, and these incited murders become part of its social cost. Imprisonment, however, has not been known to incite any murders or other crimes of violence in a comparable fashion. (A possible exception might be found in the imprisonment of terrorists, which has inspired other terrorists to take hostages as part of a scheme to force the authorities to release their imprisoned comrades.) The risks of executing the innocent are also part of the social cost. The historical record is replete with innocent persons indicted, convicted, sentenced, and occasionally legally executed for crimes they did not commit, not to mention the guilty persons unfairly convicted, sentenced to death, and executed on the strength of perjured testimony, fraudulent evidence, subornation of jurors, and other violations of the civil rights and liberties of the accused. Nor is this all. The high costs of a capital trial, of the inevitable appeals, the costly methods of custody most prisons adopt for convicts on "death row," are among the straightforward economic costs that the death penalty incurs. No scientifically valid cost/benefit analysis of capital punishment has ever been conducted, and it is impossible to predict exactly what such a study would show. Nevertheless, based on such evidence as we do have, it is quite possible that a study of this sort would favor abolition of all death penalties rather than their retention.

§22 WHAT IF EXECUTIONS DID DETER?

From the moral point of view, it is quite important to determine what one should think about capital punishment if the evidence clearly showed that the death penalty is a distinctly superior method of social defense by comparison with less severe alternatives. Kantian moralists, as we have seen, would have no use for such knowledge, because their entire case for the morality of the death penalty rests on the way it is thought to provide just retribution, not on the way it is thought to provide social defense. For a utilitarian, however, such knowledge would be conclusive. Those who follow Locke's reasoning would also be gratified, because they defend the morality of the death penalty both on the ground that it is retributively just and on the ground that it provides needed social defense.

What about the opponents of the death penalty, however? To oppose the death penalty in the face of incontestable evidence that it is an effective method of social defense seems to violate the moral principle that where grave risks are to be run, it is better that they be run by the guilty than by the innocent. Consider in this connection an imaginary world in which by executing a murderer the victim is invariably restored to life, whole and intact, as though the murder had never occurred. In such a miraculous world, it is hard to see how anyone could oppose the death penalty on moral grounds. Why shouldn't a murderer die if that will infallibly bring the victim back to life? What could possibly be morally wrong with taking the murderer's life under such conditions? It would turn the death penalty into an instrument of perfect restitution, and it would give a new and better meaning to *lex talionis,* "a life for a life." The whole idea is fanciful, of course, but it shows better than anything else how opposition to the death penalty cannot be both moral and wholly unconditional. If opposition to the death penalty is to be morally responsible, then it must be conceded that there are conditions (however unlikely) under which that opposition should cease.

But even if the death penalty were known to be a uniquely effective social defense, we could still imagine conditions under which it would be reasonable to oppose it. Suppose that in addition to being a slightly better preventive and deterrent than imprisonment, executions also have a slight incitive effect (so that for every ten murders an execution prevents or deters, it also incites another murder). Suppose also that the administration of criminal justice in capital cases is inefficient, unequal, and tends to secure convictions of murderers who least "deserve" to be sentenced to death (including some death sentences and a few executions of the innocent). Under such conditions, it would still be reasonable to oppose the death penalty, because on the facts supposed more (or not fewer) innocent lives are being threatened and lost by using the death penalty than would be risked by abolishing it. It is important to remember throughout our evaluation of the deterrence controversy that we cannot ever apply the principle (recall §12) that advises us to risk the lives of the guilty in order to save the lives of the innocent. Instead, the most we can do is weigh the risk for the general public against the execution of those who are *found* guilty by an imperfect system of criminal justice. These hypothetical factual assumptions illustrate the contingencies upon which the morality of opposition to the death penalty rests. And not only the morality of opposition; the morality of any defense of the death penalty rests on the same contingencies. This should help us understand why, in resolving the morality of capital punishment one way or the other, it is so important to know, as well as we can, whether the death penalty really does deter, prevent, or incite crime, whether the innocent really are ever executed, and whether any of these things are likely to occur in the future.

§23 HOW MANY GUILTY LIVES IS ONE INNOCENT LIFE WORTH?

The great unanswered question that utilitarians must face concerns the level of social defense that executions should be expected to achieve before it is justifiable to carry them out. Consider three possible situations: (1) At the level of a hundred executions per year, each additional execution of a convicted murderer reduces the number of murder victims by ten. (2) Executing every convicted murderer reduces the number of murders to 5,000 victims annually, whereas executing only one out of ten reduces the number to 5,001. (3) Executing every convicted murderer reduces the murder rate no more than does executing one in a hundred and no more than a random pattern of executions does.

Many people contemplating situation (1) would regard this as a reasonable trade-off: The execution of each further guilty person saves the lives of ten innocent ones. (In fact, situation (1) or something like it may be taken as a description of what most of those who defend the death penalty on grounds of social defense believe is true.) But suppose that, instead of saving 10 lives, the number dropped to 0.5, i.e., one victim avoided for each two additional executions. Would that be a reasonable price to pay? We are on the road toward the situation described in situation (2), where a drastic 90 percent reduction in the number of persons executed causes the level of social defense to drop by only 0.0002 percent. Would it be worth it to execute so many more murderers at the cost of such a slight decrease in social defense? How many guilty lives is one innocent life worth? In situation (3), of course, there is no basis for executing all convicted murderers, since there is no gain in social defense to show for each additional murderer executed after the first out of each hundred murderers has been executed. How, then, should we determine which out of each hundred convicted murderers is the unlucky one to be put to death?

It may be possible, under a complete and thoroughgoing cost/benefit analysis of the death penalty, to answer such questions. But an appeal merely to the moral principle that if lives are to be risked then let it be the lives of the guilty rather than the lives of the innocent will not suffice. (We have already noticed, in §22, that this abstract principle is of little use in the actual administration of criminal justice, because the police and the courts do not deal with the guilty as such but only with those *judged* guilty.) Nor will it suffice to agree that society deserves all the crime prevention and deterrence it can get by inflicting severe punishments. These principles are consistent with too many different policies. They are too vague by themselves to resolve the choice on grounds of social defense when confronted with hypothetical situations like those proposed above.

Since no adequate cost/benefit analysis of the death penalty exists, there is no way to resolve these questions from this standpoint at the present time. Moreover, it can be argued that we cannot have such an analysis without already establishing in some way or other the relative value of innocent lives versus guilty lives. Far from being a product of a cost/benefit analysis, this comparative evaluation of lives would have to be brought into any such analysis. Without it, no cost/benefit analysis can get off the ground. Finally, it must be noted that we have no knowledge at present that begins to approximate anything like the situation described above in (1), whereas it appears from the evidence we do have that we achieve about the same deterrent and preventive effects whether we punish murder by death or by imprisonment. Therefore, something like the situation in (2) or in (3) may be correct. If so, this shows that the choice between the two policies of capital punishment and life imprisonment for murder will probably have to be made on some basis other than social defense; on that basis the two policies are equivalent and therefore equally acceptable.

V. CAPITAL PUNISHMENT AND RETRIBUTIVE JUSTICE

As we have noticed earlier in several contexts, there are two leading principles of retributive justice relevant to the capital-punishment controversy. One is the principle that crimes should be punished. The other is the principle that the severity of a punishment should be proportional to the gravity of the offense. (A corollary to the latter principle is the judgment that nothing so fits the crime of murder as the punishment of death.) Although these principles do not seem to stem from any concern over the worth, value, dignity, or rights of persons, they are moral principles of recognized weight and no discussion of the morality of capital punishment would be complete without them. Leaving aside all questions of social defense, how strong a case for capital punishment can be made on the basis of these principles? How reliable and persuasive are these principles themselves?

§24 CRIME MUST BE PUNISHED

Given the general rationale for punishment sketched earlier (§§9–10), there cannot be any dispute over this principle. In embracing it, of course, we are not automatically making a fetish of "law and order," in the sense that we would be if we thought that the most important single thing society can do with its resources is to punish crimes. In addition, this principle is not likely to be in dispute between proponents and opponents of the death penalty. Only those who completely oppose punishment for murder and other erstwhile capital crimes would appear to disregard this principle. Even defenders of the death penalty must admit that putting a convicted murderer in prison for years is a punishment of that criminal. The principle that crime must be punished is neutral to our controversy, because both sides acknowledge it and comply with it.

It is the other principle of retributive justice that seems to be a decisive one. Under the principle of retaliation, *lex talionis,* it must always have seemed that murderers ought to be put to death. Proponents of the death penalty, with rare exceptions, have insisted on this point, and it seems that even opponents of the death penalty must give it grudging assent. The strategy for opponents of the death penalty is to show either (a) that this principle is not really a principle of justice after all, or (b) that although it is, other principles outweigh or cancel its dictates. As we shall see, both these objections have merit.

§25 IS MURDER ALONE TO BE PUNISHED BY DEATH?

Let us recall, first, that not even the Biblical world limited the death penalty to the punishment of murder. Many other nonhomicidal crimes also carried this penalty (e.g., kidnapping, witchcraft, cursing one's parents). In our own recent history, persons have been executed for aggravated assault, rape, kidnapping, armed robbery, sabotage, and espionage. It is not possible to defend any of these executions (not to mention some of the more bizarre capital statutes, like the one in Georgia that used to provide an optional death penalty for desecration of a grave) on grounds of just retribution. This entails that either such executions are not justified or that they are justified on some ground other than retribution. In actual practice, few if any defenders of the death penalty have ever been willing to rest their case entirely on the moral principle of just retribution as formulated in terms of "a life for a life." Kant seems to have been a conspicuous exception. Most defenders of the death penalty have implied by their willingness to use executions to defend limb and property, as well as life, that they did not place much value on the lives of criminals when compared to the value of both lives and things belonging to innocent citizens.

§26 ARE ALL MURDERS TO BE PUNISHED BY DEATH?

Our society for several centuries has endeavored to confine the death penalty to some criminal homicides. Even Kant took a casual attitude toward a mother's killing of her illegitimate child. ("A child born into the world outside marriage is outside the law . . . , and consequently it is also outside the protection of the law.")[8] In our society, the development nearly 200 years ago of the distinction between first- and second-degree murder was an attempt to narrow the class of criminal homicides deserving of the death penalty. Yet those dead owing to manslaughter, or to any kind of unintentional, accidental, unpremeditated, unavoidable, unmalicious killing are just as dead as the victims of the most ghastly murder. Both the law in practice and moral reflection show how difficult it is to identify all and only the criminal homicides that are appropriately punished by death (assuming that any are). Individual judges and juries differ in the conclusions they reach. The history of capital punishment for homicides reveals continual efforts, uniformly unsuccessful, to identify before the fact those homicides for which the slayer should die. Benjamin Cardozo, a justice of the United States Supreme Court fifty years ago, said of the distinction between degrees of murder that it was

> ... so obscure that no jury hearing it for the first time can fairly be expected to assimilate and understand it. I am not at all sure that I understand it myself after trying to apply it for many years and after diligent study of what has been written in the books. Upon the basis of this fine distinction with its obscure and mystifying psychology, scores of men have gone to their death.[9]

Similar skepticism has been registered on the reliability and rationality of death-penalty statutes that give the trial court the discretion to sentence to prison or to death. As Justice John Marshall Harlan of the Supreme Court observed a decade ago,

> Those who have come to grips with the hard task of actually attempting to draft means of channeling capital sentencing discretion have confirmed the lesson taught by history. . . . To identify before the fact those characteristics of criminal homicide and their perpetrators which call for the death penalty, and to express these characteristics in language which can be fairly understood and applied by the sentencing authority, appear to be tasks which are beyond present human ability.[10]

The abstract principle that the punishment of death best fits the crime of murder turns out to be extremely difficult to interpret and apply.

If we look at the matter from the standpoint of the actual practice of criminal justice, we can only conclude that "a life for a life" plays little or no role whatever. Plea bargaining (by means of which one of the persons involved in a crime agrees to accept a lesser sentence in exchange for testifying against the others to enable the prosecutor to get them all convicted), even where murder is concerned, is widespread. Studies of criminal justice reveal that what the courts (trial or appellate) decide on a given day is first-degree murder suitably punished by death in a given jurisdiction could just as well be decided in a neighboring jurisdiction on another day either as second-degree murder or as first-degree murder but without the death penalty. The factors that influence prosecutors in determining the charge under which they will prosecute go far beyond the simple principle of "a life for a life." Nor can it be objected that these facts show that our society does not care about justice. To put it succinctly, either justice in punishment does not consist of retribution, because there are other principles of justice; or there are other moral considerations besides justice that must be honored; or retributive justice is not adequately expressed in the idea of "a life for a life."

§27 IS DEATH SUFFICIENTLY RETRIBUTIVE?

Given the reality of horrible and vicious crimes, one must consider whether there is not a quality of unthinking arbitrariness in advocating capital punishment for murder as the retributively just punishment. Why does death in the electric chair or the gas chamber or before a firing squad or on a gallows meet the requirements of retributive justice? When one thinks of the savage, brutal, wanton character of so many murders, how can retributive justice be served by anything less than equally savage methods of execution for the murderer? From a retributive point of view, the oft-heard exclamation, "Death is too good for him!" has a certain truth. Yet few defenders of the death penalty are willing to embrace this consequence of their own doctrine.

The reason they do not and should not is that, if they did, they would be stooping to the methods and thus to the squalor of the murderer. Where criminals set the limits of just methods of punishment, as they will do if we attempt to give exact and literal implementation to *lex talionis,* society will find itself descending to the cruelties and savagery that criminals employ. But society would be deliberately authorizing such acts, in the cool light of reason, and not (as is often true of vicious criminals) impulsively or in hatred and anger or with an insane or unbalanced mind. Moral restraints, in short, prohibit us from trying to make executions perfectly retributive. Once we grant the role of these restraints, the principle of "a life for a life" itself has been qualified and no longer suffices to justify the execution of murderers.

Other considerations take us in a different direction. Few murders, outside television and movie scripts, involve anything like an execution. An execution, after all, begins with a solemn pronouncement of the death sentence from a judge, is followed by long detention in maximum security awaiting the date of execution, various appeals, perhaps a final sanity hearing, and then "the last mile" to the execution chamber itself. As the French writer Albert Camus remarked,

> For there to be an equivalence, the death penalty would have to punish a criminal who had warned his victim of the date at which he would inflict a horrible death on him and who, from that moment onward, had confined him at his mercy for months. Such a monster is not encountered in private life.[11]

§28 DIFFERENTIAL SEVERITY DOES NOT REQUIRE EXECUTIONS

What, then, emerges from our examination of retributive justice and the death penalty? If retributive justice is thought to consist in *lex talionis*, all one can say is that this principle has never exercised more than a crude and indirect effect on the actual punishments meted out. Other principles interfere with a literal and single-minded application of this one. Some murders seem improperly punished by death at all; other murders would require methods of execution too horrible to inflict; in still other cases any possible execution is too deliberate and monstrous given the nature of the motivation culminating in the murder. Proponents of the death penalty rarely confine themselves to reliance on this principle of just retribution and nothing else, since they rarely confine themselves to supporting the death penalty only for all murders.

But retributive justice need not be thought to consist of *lex talionis*. One may reject that principle as too crude and still embrace the retributive principle that the severity of punishments should be graded according to the gravity of the offense. Even though one need not claim that life imprisonment (or any kind of punishment other than death) "fits" the crime of murder, one can claim that this punishment is the proper one for murder. To do this, the schedule of punishments accepted by society must be arranged so that this mode of imprisonment is the most severe penalty used. Opponents of the death penalty need not reject this principle of retributive justice, even though they must reject a literal *lex talionis*.

§29 EQUAL JUSTICE AND CAPITAL PUNISHMENT

During the past generation, the strongest practical objection to the death penalty has been the inequities with which it has been applied. As Supreme Court Justice William O. Douglas once observed, "One searches our chronicles in vain for the execution of any member of the affluent strata of this society."[12] One does not search our chronicles in vain for the crime of murder committed by the affluent. Every study of the death penalty for rape has confirmed that black male rapists (especially where the victim is a white female) are far more likely to be sentenced to death (and executed) than white male rapists. Half of all those under death sentence during 1976 and 1977 were black, and nearly half of all those executed since 1930 were black. All the sociological evidence points to the conclusion that the death penalty is the poor man's justice; as the current street saying has it, "Those without the capital get the punishment."

Let us suppose that the factual basis for such a criticism is sound. What follows for the morality of capital punishment? Many defenders of the death penalty have been quick to point out that since there is nothing intrinsic about the crime of murder or rape that dictates that only the poor or racial-minority males will commit it, and since there is nothing overtly racist about the statutes that authorize the death penalty for murder or rape, it is hardly a fault in the idea of capital punishment if in practice it falls with unfair impact on the poor and the black. There is, in short, nothing in the death penalty that requires it to be applied unfairly and with arbitrary or discriminatory results. It is at worst a fault in the system of administering criminal justice (and some, who dispute the facts cited above, would deny even this).

Presumably, both proponents and opponents of capital punishment would concede that it is a fundamental dictate of justice that a punishment should not be unfairly—inequitably or unevenly—enforced and applied. They should also be able to agree that when the punishment in question is the extremely severe one of death, then the requirement to be fair in using such a punishment becomes even more stringent. Thus, there should be no dispute in the death penalty controversy over these principles of justice. The dispute begins as soon as one attempts to connect these principles with the actual use of this punishment.

In this country, many critics of the death penalty have argued, we would long ago have got rid of it entirely if it had been a condition of its use that it be applied equally and fairly. In the words of the attorneys who argued against the death penalty in the Supreme Court during 1972, "It is a freakish aberration, a random extreme act of violence, visibly arbitrary and discriminatory—a penalty reserved for unusual application because, if it were usually used, it would affront universally shared standards of public decency."[13] It is difficult to dispute this judgment, when one considers that there have been in the United States during the past fifty years about half a million criminal homicides but only about 4,000 executions (all but 50 of which were of men).

We can look at these statistics in another way to illustrate the same point. If we could be assured that the 4,000 persons executed were the worst of the worst, repeated offenders without exception, the most dangerous murderers in captivity—the ones who had killed more than once and were likely to kill again, and the least likely to be confined in prison without imminent danger to other inmates and the staff— then one might accept half a million murders and a few thousand executions with a sense that rough justice had been done. But the truth is otherwise. Persons are sentenced to death and executed not because they have been found to be uncontrollably violent, hopelessly poor parole and release risks, or for other reasons. Instead, they are executed for entirely different reasons. They have a poor defense at trial; they have no funds to bring sympathetic witnesses to court; they are immigrants or strangers in the community where they were tried; the prosecuting attorney wants the publicity that goes with "sending a killer to the chair"; they have inexperienced or overworked counsel at trial; there are no funds for an appeal or for a transcript of the trial record; they are members of a despised racial minority. In short, the actual study of why particular persons have been sentenced to death and executed does not show any careful winnowing of the worst from the bad. It shows that the executed were usually the unlucky victims of prejudice and discrimination, the losers in an arbitrary lottery that could just as well have spared them as killed them, the victims of the disadvantages that almost always go with poverty. A system like this does not enhance respect for human life; it cheapens and degrades it. However heinous murder and other crimes are, the system of capital punishment does not compensate for or erase those crimes. It only tends to add new injuries of its own to the catalogue of our inhumanity to each other.

§30 CONCLUSION

Our discussion of the death penalty from the moral point of view shows that there is no one moral principle the validity of which is paramount and that decisively favors one side to the controversy. Rather, we have seen how it is possible to argue either for or against the death penalty, and in each case to be appealing to moral principles that derive from the worth, value, or dignity of human life. We have also seen how it is impossible to connect any of these abstract principles with the actual practice of capital punishment without a close study of sociological, psychological, and economic factors. By themselves, the moral principles that are relevant are too abstract and uncertain in application to be of much help. Without the guidance of such principles, of course, the facts (who gets executed, and why) are of little use, either.

My own view of the controversy is that on balance, given the moral principles we have identified in the course of our discussion (including the overriding value of human life), and given the facts about capital punishment and crimes against the person, the side favoring abolition of the death penalty has the better of the argument. And there *is* an alternative to capital punishment: long-term imprisonment. Such a punishment is retributive and can be made appropriately severe to reflect the gravity of the crime for which it is the punishment. It gives adequate (though hardly perfect) protection to the public. It is free of the worst defect to which the death penalty is liable: execution of the innocent. It tacitly acknowledges that there is no way for a criminal, alive or dead, to make amends for murder or other grave crimes against the person. Finally, it has symbolic significance. The death penalty, more than any other kind of killing, is done in the name of society and on its behalf. Each of us has a hand in such a killing, and unless such killings are absolutely necessary they cannot really be justified. Thus, abolishing the death penalty represents extending the hand of life even to those who by their crimes have "forfeited" any right to live. It is a tacit admission that we must abandon the folly and pretence of attempting to secure perfect justice in an imperfect world.

Searching for an epigram suitable for our times, in which governments have launched vast campaigns of war and suppression of internal dissent by means of methods that can only be described as savage and criminal, Camus was prompted to admonish: "Let us be neither victims nor executioners." Perhaps better than any other, this exhortation points the way between forbidden extremes if we are to respect the humanity in each of us without trespassing on the humanity of others.

NOTES

1. W. D. Ross, *The Right and the Good* (1930), pp. 60–61.
2. John Locke, *Second Treatise of Government* (1690), §§23, 172.
3. By 'social defense' is meant the prevention of crime, including deterrence, and the avoidance of incentives and opportunities for the commission of crimes. Thus, prisons, police forces, controlling the sale of firearms, locks on doors, and threats of punishment can all be regarded as methods of social defense.
4. Immanuel Kant, *The Metaphysical Elements of Justice* (1797), tr. John Ladd, p. 102
5. *Ibid.*, p. 100.
6. *Ibid.*, p. 101.
7. Cesare Beccaria, *Of Crimes and Punishments* (1764), tr. Henry Paolucci, p. 50.
8. Immanuel Kant, *op. cit.*, p. 106.
9. Benjamin Cardozo, "What Medicine Can Do for Law" (1928), reprinted in Margaret E. Hall, ed., *Selected Writings of Benjamin Nathan Cardozo* (1947), p. 204.
10. *McGautha* v. *California*, 402 U.S. 183 (1971), at p. 204.
11. Albert Camus, *Resistance, Rebellion, and Death* (1961), p. 199.
12. *Furman* v. *Georgia*, 408 U.S. 238 (1972), at pp. 251–252.
13. NAACP Legal Defense and Educational Fund, Brief for Petitioner in *Aikens* v. *California*, O.T. 1971, No. 68–5027, reprinted in Philip English Mackey, ed., *Voices Against Death: American Opposition to Capital Punishment, 1787–1975* (1975), p. 288.

SUGGESTIONS FOR FURTHER READING

Further readings are mentioned below in connection with the section (§) of the essay to which they are most pertinent.

§§2–4 For a general discussion of natural or human rights, see the essays collected in A. I. Melden, ed., *Human Rights,* Belmont, Calif., Wadsworth

Publishing Co., 1970. A discussion of the right to life as it bears on capital punishment will be found in chapter 5 of Norman St. John-Stevas, *The Right to Life*, New York, Holt, Rinehart and Winston, 1964. For an examination of the views of Locke and Blackstone on this right and the death penalty, see H. A. Bedau, "The Right to Life," *The Monist*, vol. 52 (1968), pp. 550–572. The best discussions by legal thinkers of rights and of the value of life, Ronald Dworkin's *Taking Rights Seriously*, Harvard University Press, 1977, and Glanville Williams's *Sanctity of Life and the Criminal Law*, New York, Knopf, 1957, ignore the death penalty.

§§5–7 On the moral and political philosophy of Kant, see H. B. Acton, *Kant's Moral Philosophy*, New York, St. Martin's Press, 1970, and Jeffrie G. Murphy, *Kant: The Philosophy of Right*, New York, St. Martin's Press, 1970.

§§9–11 See in general H. L. A. Hart, *Punishment and Responsibility*, Oxford University Press, 1968; Ted Honderich, *Punishment: The Supposed Justifications*, London, Hutchinson, 1969; H. B. Acton, ed., *The Philosophy of Punishment*, London, Macmillan, 1969; Gertrude Ezorsky, ed., *Philosophical Perspectives on Punishment*, Albany, N.Y., SUNY Press, 1972; Andrew von Hirsch, *Doing Justice: The Choice of Punishments*, New York, Hill and Wang, 1976; Joel Feinberg and Hyman Gross, ed., *Punishment: Selected Readings*, Belmont, Calif., Dickenson Publishing Co., 1975; Milton Goldinger, ed., *Punishment and Human Rights*, Cambridge, Mass., Schenkman Publishing Co., 1974; J. B. Cederblom and W. L. Blizek, eds., *Justice and Punishment*, Cambridge, Mass., Ballinger Publishing Co., 1977.

§17 On the use of force in self-defense and in defense of property, see the cases and materials in T. C. Fischer and R. F. Zehnle, *Introduction to Law and Legal Reasoning*, St. Paul, Minn., West Publishing Co., 1977, chapters 1 and 2.

§§19–29 The literature in social science relevant to the factual issues surrounding the death-penalty controversy is extensive. See especially H. A. Bedau, ed., *The Death Penalty in America*, Chicago, Aldine Publishing Co., revised ed., 1967; Thorsten Sellin, ed., *Capital Punishment*, New York, 1967; William J. Bowers, *Executions in America*, Lexington, Mass., D.C. Heath, 1974; and H. A. Bedau and C. M. Pierce, eds., *Capital Punishment in the United States*, New York, AMS Press, 1976.

§20 The best general discussion of deterrence and related issues is in Jack Gibbs, *Crime, Punishment, and Deterrence*, New York, Elsevier, 1975. The best and most recent discussion relevant to the death penalty is Hans Zeisel, "The Deterrent Effect of the Death Penalty: Facts v. Faith," in P. B. Kurland, ed., *The Supreme Court Review 1976*, University of Chicago Press, 1977, pp. 317–343.

§22 On the defective administration of criminal justice where the death penalty is involved, see Charles L. Black, Jr., *Capital Punishment: The Inevitability of Caprice and Mistake*, New York, W. W. Norton, 1974.

§§24–27 For a strong retributivist theory of punishment that does not defend the death penalty, see Claudia Card, "Retributive Penal Liability," *American Philosophical Monographs*, No. 7 (1973), pp. 17–35. See also David A. J. Richards, *The Morality of the Criminal Law*, Belmont, California, Dickenson Publishing Co., 1977; and H. A. Bedau, "Retribution and the Theory of Punishment," *The Journal of Philosophy*, 55 (1978), pp. 601–620.

Discussions of the death-penalty controversy by other philosophers may be found in various essays and chapters of books. An influential utilitarian criticism of capital punishment will be found in chapter 3 of Hart's *Punish-*

ment and Responsibility, cited above. Qualified defenses of the death penalty may be found in essays by Jacques Barzun and by Sidney Hook, reprinted in H. A. Bedau, ed., *The Death Penalty in America,* cited above; in chapters 18 and 19 of Ernest van den Haag's *Punishing Criminals,* New York, Basic Books, 1974; in chapter 8 of Burton M. Leiser's *Liberty, Justice, and Morals,* 2nd ed., New York, Macmillan, 1979; and Walter Berns, *For Capital Punishment,* New York, Basic Books, 1979.

Information and arguments of interest for moral reflection on the death penalty may be found in the opinions of the United States Supreme Court in several death-penalty cases since 1972. See especially *Furman* v. *Georgia,* 408 U.S. 238 (1972), *Gregg* v. *Georgia,* 428 U.S. 153 (1976), *Woodson* v. *North Carolina,* 428 U.S. 280 (1976), and *Coker* v. *Georgia,* 45 U.S.L.W. 4584 (1977). For a general discussion, see H. A. Bedau, *The Courts, the Constitution, and Capital Punishment,* Lexington, Mass., D. C. Heath, 1977.

6

Abortion

JOEL FEINBERG

Abortion can be defined as the deliberate causing of the death of a fetus, either by directly killing it or (more commonly) by causing its expulsion from the womb before it is "viable," that is before it is capable of surviving outside its mother's body. The word 'fetus' in this definition refers to a human offspring at any stage of its prenatal development, from conception to birth. There is a narrower medical sense of the word 'fetus' in which it refers to the unborn entity from roughly the eighth week of pregnancy (when brain waves can first be monitored) until birth, normally at nine months. In this technical sense the word 'fetus' is used to contrast the relatively mature unborn being with its earlier stages when it is called a "zygote" (from conception to implantation a week later in the uterine wall) or an "embryo" (from implantation until the eighth week). I shall use the word 'fetus' as a convenient general term for the unborn at all phases of its development, except when the contrast between fetus and embryo or zygote becomes central in the argument.

A number of serious practical questions are raised by the practice of abortion. Two in particular stand out. The first is a question of personal conscience: Under what conditions, if any, is abortion morally justified? The second is a question of public policy: What, if anything, should be done to increase or decrease the opportunities for abortion? Despite its importance, we will not be able to consider this second question in the present essay.

The question of the moral permissibility of abortion demands that we answer two very hard philosophical questions. The first requires us to consider which traits of the developing fetus are relevant to deciding what morally may and may not be done to it. The general problem discussed in this regard is often called "the problem of the status of the fetus." This question will be discussed in the first part of this essay. The second question that demands our attention can be classified under the general heading "the problem of the conflict of claims." The problem here is that, even granting that the fetus is a person, the fetus is not the only person involved; there is also the mother, the father, possibly other family members, etc. The needs and interests of all the affected parties, not just those of the fetus, seem to have a bearing on the question of the moral permissibility of abortion. Therefore, we must determine *whose* claims are the strongest, if they happen to clash. This problem is explored in the second part of this essay.

I. THE STATUS OF THE FETUS

The problem of the status of the fetus can be formulated as follows: At what stage, if any, in the development between conception and birth do fetuses acquire the characteristic (whatever it may be) that confers on them the appropriate status to be included in the scope of the moral rule against homicide—the rule 'Thou shalt not kill'? Put more tersely: At what stage, if any, of their development do fetuses become people? A variety of familiar answers have been given—for example, that fetuses become persons "at the moment of conception," at "quickening" (that is, at the moment of their first self-initiated movement in the womb), at viability (that is, when the fetus is able to survive independently outside the mother's womb). Debates about *when* the fetus becomes a person, however, are premature unless we have first explored *what* a person is. Answers to the question 'When does the fetus become a person'? attempt to draw a *boundary line* between prepersons and persons; however, even if correctly drawn, a boundary line is not the same thing as a *criterion* of personhood and indeed, until we have a criterion, we cannot know for sure whether a given proposed boundary is correct. Let us mean by 'a criterion of personhood' a specification of the characteristic (or set of characteristics) that is such that (1) no being can be a person unless he or she possesses that characteristic, (2) any being who possesses that characteristic is a person, and (3) it is precisely that characteristic that directly confers personhood on whoever possesses it. The person-making characteristic, in brief, is that characteristic (or set of characteristics) that is common and peculiar to all persons and in virtue of which they are persons. 'A criterion of personhood', as we shall understand the phrase, is some statement (true or false) of what the person-making characteristic is.

The statement of a mere boundary line of personhood, in contrast, may be correct and useful even though it mentions no person-making characteristic at all. Such a statement may specify only some theoretically superficial characteristic that happens to be invariably (or perhaps only usually and roughly) correlated with a person-making characteristic. For example, even if it is true that all persons can survive outside the mother's womb, it does not follow that being able to survive outside the mother's womb is what makes someone a person or that this is even partially constitutive of what it is to be a person. The "superficial characteristic" then can be used as a clue, a test, or an indication of the presence of the basic personhood-conferring characteristic and therefore of personhood itself, even though it is in no sense a *cause* or a *constituent* of personhood. An analogy might make the point clearer. What makes any chemical compound an acid is a feature of its molecular structure, namely that it contains hydrogen as a positive radical. But it also happens that acids "typically" are soluble in water, sour in taste, and turn blue litmus paper red. The latter three characteristics then, while neither constitutive nor causative of acidity, can nevertheless be useful and reliable indexes to, or tests of, acidity. The litmus test in particular draws a "boundary" between acids and nonacids. The question now to be addressed is whether a reasonable criterion for personhood can be found, one that enables us to draw an accurate boundary line.

§1 HUMAN BEINGS AND PERSONS

The first step in coming to terms with the concept of a person is to disentangle it from a concept with which it is thoroughly intertwined in most of our minds, that of a human being. In an influential article, the young American social philosopher Mary Anne Warren has pointed out that the term 'human' has two "distinct but not often distinguished senses."[1] In what she calls the "moral sense," a being is human provided that it is a "full-fledged member of the moral community," a being possessed (as Jefferson wrote of all "men"—did he mean men and women?) of inalienable rights to life, liberty, and the pursuit of happiness. For beings to be humans in this sense is precisely for them to be people, and the problem of the "humanity" of the fetus in this sense is that of determining whether the fetus is the sort of being —a person—who has such moral rights as the right to life. On the other hand, a being is human in what Warren calls the "genetic sense" provided he or she is a member of the species *Homo sapiens,* and *all* we mean in describing someone as a human in the genetic sense is that he or she belongs to that animal species. In this sense, when we say that Jones is a human being, we are making a statement of the same type as when we say that Fido is a dog (canine being). Any fetus conceived by human parents will of course be a human being in this sense, just as any fetus conceived by dogs will of course be canine in the analogous sense.

It is possible to hold, as no doubt many people do, that all human beings in the moral sense (persons) are human beings in the genetic sense (members of *Homo sapiens*) and *vice versa,* so that the two classes, while distinct in meaning, nevertheless coincide exactly in reality. In that case all genetically human beings, including fetuses from the moment of conception, have a right to life, the unjustified violation of which is homicide, and no beings who are genetically nonhuman are persons. But it is also possible to hold, as some philosophers do, that some genetically human beings (for example, zygotes and irreversibly comatose "human vegetables") are *not* human beings in the moral sense (persons), and/or that some persons (for example, God, angels, devils, higher animals, intelligent beings in outer space) are *not* members of *Homo sapiens.* Surely it is an open question to be settled, if at all, by argument or discovery, whether the two classes correspond exactly. It is not a question closed in advance by definition or appeals to word usage.

§2 NORMATIVE *VERSUS* DESCRIPTIVE PERSONHOOD

Perhaps the best way to proceed from this point is to stick to the term 'person' and avoid the term 'human' except when we clearly intend the genetic sense, in that way avoiding the ever-present danger of being misunderstood. The term 'person', however, is not without its own ambiguities. The one central ambiguity we should note is that between purely *normative* (moral or legal) uses of 'person' and purely *descriptive* (conventional, commonsense) uses of the term.

When moralists or lawyers use the term 'person' in a purely normative way they use it simply to ascribe moral or legal properties—usually rights or duties, or both—to the beings so denominated. To be a person in the normative sense is to have rights, or rights and duties, or at least to be the sort of being who could have rights and duties without conceptual absurdity. Most writers think that it would be sheer nonsense to speak of the rights or duties of rocks, or blades of grass, or sunbeams, or of historical events or abstract ideas. These objects are thought to be conceptually inappropriate subjects for the attribution of rights or duties. Hence we speak of them as "impersonal entities," the types of beings that are contrasted with objects that can stand in personal relationships to us, or make moral claims on us. The higher animals—our fellow mammalian species in particular—are borderline cases whose classification as persons or nonpersons has been a matter of controversy. Many of them are fit subjects of right-ascriptions but cannot plausibly be assigned duties or moral responsibilities. These ideas are examined in considerable detail in Peter Singer's essay in the present volume. In any case, when we attribute personhood in a purely normative way to any kind of being, we are attributing such moral qualities as rights or duties, but not (necessarily) any observable characteristics of any kind—for example, having flesh or blood, or belonging to a particular species. Lawyers have attributed (legal) personhood even to states and corporations, and their purely normative judgments say nothing about the presence or absence of body, mind, consciousness, color, etc.

In contrast to the purely normative use of the word 'person' we can distinguish a purely empirical or descriptive use. There are certain characteristics that are fixed by a rather firm convention of our language such that the general term for any being who possesses them is "person." Thus, to say of some being that he is a person, in this sense, is to convey some information about what the being is like. Neither are attributions of personhood of this kind essentially controversial. If to be a person *means* to have characteristics *a, b,* and *c,* then to say of a being who is known to have *a, b,* and *c* that he or she is a person (in the descriptive sense) is no more controversial than to say of an animal known to be a young dog that it is a puppy, or of a person known to be an unmarried man that he is a bachelor. What make these noncontroversial judgments true are conventions of language that determine what words mean. The conventions are often a bit vague around the edges but they apply clearly enough to central cases. It is in virtue of these reasonably precise linguistic conventions that the word 'person' normally conveys the idea of a definite set of descriptive characteristics. I shall call the idea defined by these characteristics "the commonsense concept of personhood." When we use the word 'person' in this wholly descriptive way we are not attributing rights, duties, eligibility for rights and duties, or any other normative characteristics to the being so described. At most we are attributing characteristics that may be a *ground* for ascribing rights and duties.

These *purely* normative and *purely* descriptive uses of the word 'person' are probably unusual. In most of its uses, the word both describes or classifies someone in a conventionally understood way *and* ascribes rights, etc., to him or her. But there is enough looseness or flexibility in usage to leave open the questions of whether the classes of moral and "commonsense" persons correspond in reality. Although some may think it obvious that all and only commonsense persons are moral persons, that identification of classes does not follow simply as a matter of word usage, and must, therefore, be supported independently by argument. Many learned writers, after all, have maintained that human zygotes and embryos are moral persons despite the fact that they are almost certainly not "commonsense persons." Others have spoken of wicked murderers as "monsters" or "fiends" that can rightly be destroyed like "wild beasts" or eliminated like "rotten apples." This seems to amount to holding that "moral monsters" are commonsense persons who are so wicked (only *persons* can be wicked) that they have lost their moral personhood, or membership in our moral community. The English jurist Sir William Blackstone (1723–1780) maintained that convicted murderers forfeit their rights to life. If one went further and maintained that moral monsters forfeit all their human rights, then one would be rejecting the view that the classes of moral and commonsense persons exactly coincide, for wicked persons who are answerable for their foul deeds must first of all be persons in the descriptive sense, but as beings without rights, they would not be moral persons.

§3 THE CRITERION OF COMMONSENSE PERSONHOOD

A criterion of personhood in the descriptive sense would be a specification of those characteristics that are common and peculiar to commonsense persons and in virtue of which they are such persons. They are necessary conditions for commonsense personhood in the sense that no being who lacks any one of them can be a person. They are sufficient conditions in the sense that any being who possesses all of them is a person, whatever he or she may be like in other respects. How shall we formulate this criterion? If this question simply raises a matter of fixed linguistic convention, one might expect it to be easy enough to state the defining characteristics of personhood straight off. Surprisingly, the question is not quite that simple, and no mere dictionary is likely to give us a wholly satisfactory answer. What we must do is to think of the characteristics that come at least implicitly to mind when we hear or use such words as 'person', 'people', and the personal pronouns. We might best proceed by considering three different classes of cases: clear examples of beings whose personhood cannot be doubted, clear examples of beings whose nonpersonhood cannot be doubted, and actual or hypothetical examples of beings whose status is not initially clear. We probably will not be able to come up with a definitive list of characteristics if only because the word 'person' may be somewhat loose, but we should be able to achieve a criterion that is precise enough to permit a definite classification of fetuses.

Undoubted Commonsense Persons Who are undoubted persons? Consider first your parents, siblings, or friends. What is it about them that makes you so certain that they are persons? "Well, they look like persons," you might say; "They have human faces and bodies." But so do irreversibly comatose human vegetables, and we are, to put it mildly, not so certain that they are persons. "Well then, they are males and females and thus appropriately referred to by our personal pronouns, all of which have gender. We can't refer to any of them by use of the impersonal pronoun 'it', because they have sex; so perhaps being gendered is the test of personhood." Such a reply has superficial plausibility, but is the idea of a "sexless person" logically contradictory? Perhaps any genetically human person will be predominately one sex or the other, but must the same be true of "intelligent beings in outer space," or spirits, gods, and devils?

Let's start again. "What makes me certain that my parents, siblings, and friends are people is that they give evidence of being conscious of the world and of themselves; they have inner emotional lives, just like me; they can understand things and reason about them, make plans, and act; they can communicate with me, argue, negotiate, express themselves, make agreements, honor commitments, and stand in relationships of mutual trust; they have tastes and values of their own; they can be frustrated or fulfilled, pleased or hurt." Now we clearly have the beginnings, at least, of a definitive list of person-making characteristics. In the commonsense way of thinking, persons are those beings who are conscious, have a concept and awareness of themselves, are capable of experiencing emotions, can reason and acquire understanding, can plan ahead, can act on their plans, and can feel pleasure and pain.

Undoubted Nonpersons   What of the objects that clearly are not persons? Rocks have none of the above characteristics; neither do flowers and trees; neither (presumably) do snails and earthworms. But perhaps we are wrong about that. Maybe rocks, plants, and lower animals are congeries of lower-level spirits with inner lives and experiences of their own, as primitive men and mystics have often maintained. Very well, that is possible. But if they do have these characteristics, contrary to all appearance, then it would seem natural to think of them as persons too, "contrary to all appearance." In raising the question of their possession of these characteristics at all, we seem to be raising by the same token the question of their commonsense personhood. Mere rocks are quite certainly not crowds of silent spirits, but if, contrary to fact, they are such spirits, then we must think of them as real people, quite peculiarly embodied.

Hard Cases   Now, what about the hard cases? Is God, as traditionally conceived, a kind of nonhuman—or better, superhuman—person? Theologians are divided about this, of course, but most ordinary believers think of Him (note the personal pronoun) as conscious of self and world, capable of love and anger, eminently rational, having plans for the world, acting (if only through His creation), capable of communicating with humans, of issuing commands and making covenants, and of being pleased or disappointed in the use to which humans put their free will. To the extent that one believes that God has these various attributes, to that extent does one believe in a *personal* God. If one believes only in a God who is an unknown and unknowable First Cause of the world, or an obscure but powerful force sustaining the world, or the ultimate energy in the cosmos, then, it seems fair to say, one believes in an *impersonal* deity.

Now we come to the ultimate thought experiment. Suppose that you are a space explorer whose rocket ship has landed on a planet in a distant galaxy. The planet is inhabited by some very strange objects, so unlike anything you have previously encountered that at first you don't even know whether to classify them as animal, vegetable, mineral, or "none of the above." They are composed of a gelatinous sort of substance much like mucus except that it is held together by no visible membranes or skin, and it continually changes its shape from one sort of amorphous glob to another, sometimes breaking into smaller globs and then coming together again. The objects have no appendages, no joints, no heads or faces. They float mysteriously above the surface of the planet and move about in complex patterns while emitting eerie sounds resembling nothing so much as electronic music. The first thing you will wish to know about these strange objects is whether they are extraterrestrial *people* to be respected, greeted, and traded and negotiated with, or mere things or inferior animals to be chopped up, boiled, and used for food and clothing.

Almost certainly the first thing you would do is try to communicate with them by making approaches, gesturing by hand, voice, or radio signals. You might also study the patterns in their movements and sound emissions to see whether they have any of the characteristics of a language. If the beings respond even in a primitive way to early gestures, one might suspect at least that they are beings who are capable of perception and who can be *aware* of movements and sounds. If some sort of actual communication then follows, you can attribute to them at least the mentality of chimpanzees. If negotiations then follow and agreements are reached, then you can be sure that they are rational beings, and if you learn to interpret signs of worry, distress, anger, alarm, or friendliness, then you can be quite confident that they are indeed people, no matter how inhuman they are in biological respects.

A Working Criterion of Commonsense Personhood   Suppose then that we agree that our rough list captures well the traits that are generally characteristic of commonsense persons. Suppose further (what is not quite as evident) that each trait on the list is necessary for commonsense personhood, that no one trait is by itself sufficient, but that the whole *collection* of traits is sufficient to confer commonsense personhood on any being that possesses it. Suppose, that is, that consciousness is necessary (no permanently unconscious being can be a person), but that it is not enough. The conscious being must also have a concept of a self and a certain amount of self-awareness. But although each of these last traits is necessary, they are still not enough even in conjunction, since a self-aware, conscious being who was totally incapable of learning or reasoning would not be a person. Hence rationality is also necessary, though not by itself sufficient. And so on through our complete list of person-making characteristics, each one of which, let us suppose, is a necessary condition, and all of which are jointly a sufficient condition of being a person in the commonsense, descriptive sense of 'person'. Let us call our set of characteristics *c*. Now at last we can pose the most important and controversial question about the status of the fetus: What is the relation, if any, between having *c* and being a person in the normative (moral) sense, that is, a being who possesses, among other things, a right to life?

§4 PROPOSED CRITERIA OF MORAL PERSONHOOD

It bears repeating at the outset of our discussion of this most important question that formulating criteria of personhood in the purely moral sense is not a scientific question to be settled by empirical evidence, not simply a question of word usage, not simply a matter to be settled by commonsense thought experiments. It is instead an essentially controversial question about the possession of moral rights that cannot be answered in these ways. That is not to say that rational methods of investigation and discussion are not available to us, but only that the methods of reasoning about morals do not often provide conclusive proofs and demonstrations. What rational methods can achieve for us, even if they fall short of producing universal agreement, is to list the various options open to us, and the strong and weak points of each of them. Every position has its embarrassments, that is, places where it appears to conflict logically with moral and commonsense convictions that even its proponents can be presumed to share. To point out these embarrassments for a given position is not necessarily to refute it but rather to measure the costs of holding it to the coherence of one's larger set of beliefs generally. Similarly, each position has its own peculiar advantages, respects in which it coheres uniquely well with deeply entrenched convictions that even its opponents might be expected to share. I shall try in the ensuing discussion to state and illustrate as vividly as I can the advantages and difficulties in all the major positions. Then I shall weigh the cases for and against the various alternatives. For those who disagree with my conclusion, the discussion will serve at least to locate the crucial issues in the controversy over the status of the fetus.

A proposed criterion for moral personhood is a statement of a characteristic (or set of characteristics) that its advocate deems both necessary and (jointly) sufficient for being a person in the moral sense. Such characteristics are not thought of as mere indexes, signs, or "litmus tests" of moral personhood, but as more basic traits that actually confer moral personhood on whoever possesses them. All and only those beings having these characteristics have basic moral rights, in particular the right to full and equal protection against homicide. Thus, fetuses must be thought of as having this right if they satisfy a proposed criterion of personhood. The main types of criteria of moral personhood proposed by philosophers can be grouped under one or another of five different headings, which we shall examine in turn. Four of the five proposed criteria refer to possession of c (the traits we have listed as conferring *commonsense* personhood). One of these four specifies actual possession of c; the other three refer to either actual or potential possession of c. The remaining criterion, which we shall consider briefly first, makes no mention of c at all.

a. The Species Criterion "All and only members of the biological species *Homo sapiens*, 'whoever is conceived by human beings', are moral persons and thus are entitled to full and equal protection by the moral rule against homicide." The major advantage of this view (at least for some) is that it gives powerful support to those who would extend the protection of the rule against homicide to the fetus from the moment of conception. If this criterion is correct, it is not simply because of utilitarian reasons (such that it would usefully increase respect for life in the community) that we must not abort human zygotes and embryos, but rather because we owe it to these minute entities themselves not to kill them, for as members of the human species they are already possessed of a full right to life equal in strength to that of any adult person.

The species criterion soon encounters serious difficulties. Against the view that membership in the species *Homo sapiens* is a *necessary* condition of membership in the class of moral persons, we have the possibility of there being moral persons from other planets who belong to other biological species. Moreover, some human beings—in particular, those who are irreversibly comatose "vegetables"—*are* human beings but doubtfully qualify as moral persons, a fact that casts serious doubt on the view that membership in the species *Homo sapiens* is a *sufficient* condition of being a moral person.

The species criterion might be defended against these objections if some persuasive reason could be given why moral personhood is a unique feature of all and only human beings. Aside from an arbitrary claim that this is "just obvious," a position that Singer argues amounts to a pernicious prejudice against nonhuman animals comparable to racism and sexism, the only possible way to defend this claim to uniqueness is by means of some *theological* argument: *All* human beings (including human fetuses) and *only* human beings (thereby excluding all nonhuman animals and possible beings from other planets) are moral persons *because God has made this so.*[2] Now, if one already believes on faith that God had made it true that all and only humans are moral persons, then of course one has quite conclusive reason for believing that all and only humans are moral persons. But if we leave faith aside and confine our attention to reasons, then we shall have to ask what grounds there are for supposing that "God has made this so," and any reason we might have for doubting that it *is* so would count equally as a reason against supposing that God made it so. A good reason for doubting that $7 + 5 = 13$ is an equally good reason for doubting that God made it to be the case that $7 + 5 = 13$; a good reason for doubting that cruelty is morally right is, if anything, a better reason for denying that God made it to be the case that cruelty is right.

b. The Modified Species Criterion "All and only members of species generally characterized by *c*, whether the species is *Homo sapiens* or another, and whether or not the particular individual in question happens to possess *c*, are moral persons entitled to full and equal protection by the moral rule against homicide." This modification is designed to take the sting out of the first objection (above) to the unmodified species criterion. If there are other species or categories of moral persons in the universe, it concedes, then they too have moral rights. Indeed, if there are such, then *all* of their members are moral persons possessed of such rights, even those individuals who happen themselves to lack c because they are not yet fully developed or because they have been irreparably damaged.

The major difficulty for the modified species criterion is that it requires further explanation why c should determine moral person-hood when applied to *classes* of creatures rather than to individual cases. Why is a permanently unconscious but living body of a human or an extragalactic person (or for that matter, a chimpanzee, if we should decide that that species as a whole is characterized by c) a moral person when it lacks as an individual the characteristics that determine moral personhood? Just because opposable thumbs are a characteristic of *Homo sapiens,* it does not follow that this or that particular *Homo sapiens* has opposable thumbs. There appears to be no reason for regarding right-possession any differently, in this regard, from thumb-possession.

c. The Strict Potentiality Criterion "All and only those creatures who either actually or potentially possess c (that is, who either have c now or would come to have c in the natural course of events) are moral persons now, fully protected by the rule against homicide." This crite-rion also permits one to draw the line of moral personhood in the human species right at the moment of conception, which will be counted by some as an advantage. It also has the undeniable advan-tage of immunity from one charge of arbitrariness since it will extend moral personhood to all beings in *any* species or category who possess c, either actually or potentially. It may also cohere with our psycholog-ical attitudes, since it can explain why it is that many people, at least, think of unformed or unpretty fetuses as precious. Zygotes and em-bryos in particular are treasured not for what they are but for what they are biologically "programmed" to become in the fullness of time: real people fully possessed of c.

The difficulties of this criterion are of two general kinds, those deriving from the obscurity of the concept of "potentiality," which perhaps can be overcome, and the more serious difficulties of answer-ing the charge that merely potential possession of any set of qualifica-tions for a moral status does not logically ensure actual possession of that status. Consider just one of the problems raised by the concept of potentiality itself.[3] How, it might be asked, can a mere zygote be a potential person, whereas a mere spermatozoon or a mere unfertil-ized ovum is not? If the spermatozoon and ovum we are talking about are precisely those that will combine in a few seconds to form a human zygote, why are they not potential zygotes, and thus potential people, *now*? The defender of the potentiality criterion will reply that it is only at the moment of conception that any being comes into existence with exactly the same chromosomal makeup as the human being that will later emerge from the womb, and it is *that* chromosomal combination that forms the potential person, not anything that exists before it comes together. The reply is probably a cogent one, but uncertainties about the concept of potentiality might make us hesitate, at first, to accept it, for we might be tempted to think of both the germ cell (spermatozoon or ovum) and the zygote as potentially a particular person, while holding that the differences between their potentials, though large and significant to be sure, are nevertheless differences in degree rather than kind. It would be well to resist that temptation, however, for it could lead us to the view that some of the entities and processes that combined still earlier to form a given spermatozoon were themselves potentially that spermatozoon and hence potentially the person that spermatozoon eventually became, and so on. At the end of that road is the proposition that everything is potentially everything else, and thus the destruction of all utility in the concept of potentiality. It is better to hold this particular line at the zygote.

The remaining difficulty for the strict potentiality criterion is much more serious. It is a logical error, some have charged, to deduce *actual* rights from merely *potential* (but not yet actual) qualification for those rights. What follows from potential qualification, it is said, is potential, not actual, rights; what entails actual rights is actual, not potential, qualification. As the Australian philosopher Stanley Benn puts it, "A potential president of the United States is not on that account Commander-in-Chief [of the U.S. Army and Navy]."[4] This simple point can be called "the logical point about potentiality." Taken on its own terms, I don't see how it can be answered as an objection to the strict potentiality criterion. It is still open to an antiabortionist to argue that merely potential commonsense personhood is a ground for *duties* we may have toward the potential person. But he cannot argue that it is the ground for the potential person's *rights* without committing a logical error.

d. The Modified or Gradualist Potentiality Criterion "Potential possession of *c* confers not a right, but only a claim, to life, but that claim keeps growing stronger, requiring ever stronger reasons to override it, until the point when *c* is actually possessed, by which time it has become a full right to life." This modification of the potentiality criterion has one distinct and important advantage. It coheres with the widely shared feeling that the moral seriousness of abortion increases with the age of the fetus. It is extremely difficult to believe on other than very specific theological grounds that a zygote one day after conception is the sort of being that can have any rights at all, much less the whole armory of "human rights" including "the right to life." But it is equally difficult for a great many people to believe that a full-term fetus one day before birth does not have a right to life. Moreover, it is very difficult to find one point in the continuous development of the fetus before which it is utterly without rights and after which it has exactly the same rights as any adult human being. Some rights in postnatal human life can be acquired instantly or suddenly; the rights of citizenship, for example, come into existence at a precise moment in the naturalization proceedings after an oath has been administered and a judicial pronouncement formally produced and certified. Similarly, the rights of husbands and wives come into existence at just that moment when an authorized person utters the words 'I hereby pronounce you husband and wife'. But the rights of the fetus cannot possibly jump in this fashion from nonbeing to being at some precise moment in pregnancy. The alternative is to think of them as growing steadily and gradually throughout the entire nine-month period until they are virtually "mature" at parturition. There is, in short, a kind of growth in "moral weight" that proceeds in parallel fashion with the physical growth and development of the fetus.

An "immature right" on this view is not to be thought of simply as no right at all, as if in morals a miss were as good as a mile. A better characterization of the unfinished right would be a "weak right," a claim with some moral force proportional to its degree of development, but not yet as much force as a fully matured right. The key word in this account is 'claim'. Elsewhere I have given an account of the difference between having a right (which I defined as a "valid claim") and having a claim that is not, or not quite, valid. What would the latter be like?

> One might accumulate just enough evidence to argue with relevance and cogency that one has a right ... although one's case might not be overwhelmingly conclusive. The argument might be strong enough to entitle one to a hearing and fair consideration. When one is in this position, it might be said that one "has a claim" that deserves to be weighed carefully. Nevertheless the balance of reasons may turn out to militate against recognition of the claim, so that the claim is not a valid claim or right.[5]

Now there are various ways in which a claim can fail to be a right. There are many examples, particularly from the law, where *all* the claims to some property, including some that are relevantly made and worthy of respect, are rejected, simply because none of them is deemed strong enough to qualify as a right. In such cases, a miss truly is as good as a mile. But in other cases, an acknowledged claim of (say) medium strength will be strong enough to be a right *unless* a stronger claim appears on the scene to override it. For these conflict situations, card games provide a useful analogy. In poker, three-of-a-kind is good enough to win the pot unless one of the other players "makes claim" to the pot with a higher hand, say a flush or a full house. The player who claims the pot with three-of-a-kind "has a claim" to the pot that is overridden by the stronger claim of the player with the full house. The strongest claim presented will, by that fact, constitute a right to take the money. The player who withdrew with a four-flush had "no claim at all," but even that person's hand might have established a right to the pot if no stronger claim were in conflict with it.

The analogy applies to the abortion situation in the following way. The game has at least two players, the mother and the fetus, though more can play, and sometimes the father and/or the doctor are involved too. For the first few weeks of its life, the fetus (zygote, embryo) has hardly any claim to life at all, and virtually any reason of the mother's for aborting it will be strong enough to override a claim made in the fetus's behalf. At any stage in the game, any reason the mother might have for aborting will constitute a claim, but as the fetus matures, its claims grow stronger requiring ever-stronger claims to override them. After three months or so, the fact that an abortion would be "convenient" for the mother will not be a strong enough claim, and the fetus' claim to life will defeat it. In that case, the fetus can be said to have a valid claim or right to life in the same sense that the poker player's full house gives him or her a right to the pot: It is a right in the sense that it is the strongest of the conflicting claims, not in the sense that it is stronger than any conflicting claim that could conceivably come up. By the time the fetus has become a neonate (a newborn child), however, it has a "right to life" of the same kind all people have, and no mere conflicting claim can override it. (Perhaps more accurately, only claims that other human persons make in self-defense to their own lives can ever have an equal strength.)

The modified potentiality criterion has the attractiveness characteristic of compromise theories when fierce ideological quarrels rage between partisans of more extreme views. It shares one fatal flaw, however, with the strict potentiality criterion: Despite its greater flexibility, it cannot evade "the logical point about potentiality." A highly developed fetus is much closer to being a commonsense person with all the developed traits that qualify it for moral personhood than is the mere zygote. But being almost qualified for rights is not the same thing as being partially qualified for rights; nor is it the same thing as being qualified for partial rights, quasi-rights, or weak rights. The advanced fetus is closer to being a person than is the zygote, just as a dog is closer to personhood than a jellyfish, but that is not the same thing as being "more of a person." In 1930, when he was six years old, Jimmy Carter didn't know it, but he was a potential president of the United States. That gave him no claim *then,* not even a very weak claim, to give commands to the U.S. Army and Navy. Franklin D. Roosevelt in 1930 was only two years away from the presidency, so he was a potential president in a much stronger way (the potentiality was much less remote) than was young Jimmy. Nevertheless, he was not actually president, and he had no more of a claim to the prerogatives of the office than did Carter. The analogy to fetuses in different stages of development is of course imperfect. But in both cases it would seem to be invalid to infer the existence of a "weak version of a right" from an "almost qualification" for the full right. In summary, the modified potentiality criterion, insofar as it permits the potential possession of c to be a *sufficient condition* for the actual possession of claims, and in some cases of rights, is seriously flawed in the same manner as the strict potentiality criterion.

e. The Actual-Possession Criterion "At any given time t, all and only those creatures who actually possess c are moral persons at t, whatever species or category they may happen to belong to." This simple and straightforward criterion has a number of conspicuous advantages. We should consider it with respect even before examination of its difficulties if only because the difficulties of its major rivals are so severe. Moreover, it has a certain tidy symmetry about it, since it makes the overlap between commonsense personhood and moral personhood complete—a total correspondence with no loose ends left over in either direction. There can be no actual commonsense persons who are not actual moral persons, nor can there be any actual moral persons who are not actual commonsense persons. Moral personhood is not established simply by species membership, associations, or potentialities. Instead, it is conferred by the same characteristics (c) that lead us to recognize personhood wherever we find it. It is no accident, no mere coincidence, that we use the moral term 'person' for those beings, and only those beings, who have c. The characteristics that confer commonsense personhood are not arbitrary bases for rights and duties, such as race, sex, or species membership; rather they are the traits that make sense out of rights and duties and without which those moral attributes would have no point or function. It is because people are conscious; have a sense of their personal identities; have plans, goals, and projects; experience emotions; are liable to pains, anxieties, and frustrations; can reason and bargain, and so on— it is because of these attributes that people have values and interests, desires and expectations of their own, including a stake in their own futures, and a personal well-being of a sort we cannot ascribe to unconscious or nonrational beings. Because of their developed capacities they can assume duties and responsibilities and can have and make claims on one another. Only because of their sense of self, their life plans, their value hierarchies, and their stakes in their own futures, can they be ascribed fundamental rights. There is nothing arbitrary about these linkages.

Despite these impressive advantages, the actual-possession criterion must face a serious difficulty, namely that it implies that small infants (neonates) are not moral persons. There is very little more reason, after all, to attribute c to neonates than to advanced fetuses still *in utero*. Perhaps during the first few days after birth the infant is conscious and able to feel pain, but it is unlikely that it has a concept of its self or of its future life, that it has plans and goals, that it can think consecutively, and the like. In fact, the whole complex of traits that make up *c* is not *obviously* present until the second year of childhood. And that would seem to imply, according to the criterion we are considering, that the deliberate destruction of babies in their first year is no violation of their rights. And *that* might seem to entail that there is nothing wrong with infanticide (the deliberate killing of infants). But infanticide *is* wrong. Therefore, critics of the actual-possession criterion have argued that we ought to reject this criterion.

THE KILLING OF NORMAL INFANTS   Advocates of the actual-possession criterion have a reply to this objection. Even if infanticide is not the murder of a moral person, they believe, it may yet be wrong and properly forbidden on other grounds. To make this clearer, it is useful to distinguish between (i) the case of killing a normal healthy infant or an infant whose handicaps are not so serious as to make a worthwhile future life impossible, and (ii) the case of killing severely deformed or incurably diseased infants.

Most advocates of the actual-possession criterion take a strong stand against infanticide in the first (the normal) case. It would be seriously wrong for a mother to kill her physically normal infant, they contend, even though such a killing would not violate anyone's right to life. The same reasons that make infanticide in the normal case wrong also justify its prohibition by the criminal law. The moral rule that condemns these killings and the legal rule that renders them punishable are both supported by "utilitarian reasons," that is, considerations of what is called "social utility," "the common good," "the public interest," and the like. Nature has apparently implanted in us an instinctive tenderness toward infants that has proven extremely useful to the species, not only because it leads us to protect our young from death, and thus keep our population up, but also because infants usually grow into adults, and in Benn's words, "if as infants *they* are not treated with some minimal degree of tenderness and consideration, they will suffer for it later, as persons."[6] One might add that when they are adults, others will suffer for it too, at their hands. Spontaneous warmth and sympathy toward babies then clearly has a great deal of social utility, and insofar as infanticide would tend to weaken that socially valuable response, it is, on utilitarian grounds, morally wrong.

There are other examples of wrongful and properly prohibitable acts that violate no one's rights. It would be wrong, for example, to hack up Grandfather's body after he has died a natural death, and dispose of his remains in the trash can on a cold winter's morning. That would be wrong not because it violates *Grandfather's* rights; he is dead and no longer has the same sort of rights as the rest of us, and we can make it part of the example that he was not offended while alive at the thought of such posthumous treatment and indeed even consented to it in advance. Somehow acts of this kind if not forbidden would strike at our respect for living human persons (without which organized society would be impossible) in the most keenly threatening way. (It might also be unhygienic and shocking to trash collectors—less important but equally relevant utilitarian considerations.)

THE KILLING OF RADICALLY DEFORMED INFANTS   The general utilitarian reasons that support a rather rigid rule against infanticide in the case of the normal (and not too abnormal) infant might not be sufficiently strong to rule out infanticide (under very special and strict circumstances) when the infant is extremely deformed or diseased. Very likely, a purely utilitarian-based rule against homicide would have exceptive clauses for extremely abnormal neonates. In this respect such rules would differ sharply from rules against infanticide that derive from the ascription to the newborn infant of a full-fledged right to life. If the deformed neonate is a moral person, then he or she is as fully entitled to protection under the rule forbidding homicide as any reader of these words; if the neonate is not a moral person, then in extreme cases there may be a case on balance for killing him or her. The partisan of the actual-possession criterion of moral personhood actually takes this consequence of nonpersonhood to be an advantage of his view rather than an embarrassment for it. If his view is correct, then we can destroy hopelessly malformed infants *before* they grow into moral persons, thus saving them from a longer life that would be so horrible as to be "not worth living," and this can be done without violating their rights.

Indeed, *failure* to kill such infants before they reach moral personhood may itself be a violation of their rights, according to this view. For if we permit such children to grow into moral personhood knowing full well that the conditions for the fulfillment of their most basic future interests have already been destroyed, then we have wronged these persons before they even exist (as persons), and when they become persons, they can claim (or it can be claimed in their behalf) that they have been wronged. I have argued elsewhere that an extension of the idea of a birthright is suggested by this point: If we know that it will never be possible for a fetus or neonate to have that to which he or she has a birthright and we allow him or her nevertheless to be born or to survive into personhood, then that fetus or neonate is wronged, and we become a party to the violation of his or her rights.[7]

Not just any physical or mental handicaps, of course, can render a life "not worth living." Indeed, as the testimony of some thalidomide babies[8] now growing into adulthood shows, it is possible (given exceptional care) to live a valuable life even without arms and legs and full vision. But there may be some extreme cases where deformities are not merely "handicaps" in the pursuit of happiness but guarantees that the pursuit must fail. A brain-damaged, retarded child born deaf, blind, partially paralyzed, and doomed to constant pain might be such a case. Given the powerful general utilitarian case against infanticide, however, the defender of the "right to die" position must admit that in cases of doubt, the burden of showing that a worthwhile life is impossible rests on the person who would elect a quick and painless death for the infant. And there is almost always some doubt.

IMPLICATIONS FOR THE PROBLEM OF ABORTION The implications of the actual-possession criterion for the question of the status of the fetus as a moral person are straightforward: Since the fetus does not actually possess those characteristics (*c*) that we earlier listed as necessary and sufficient for possessing the right to life, the fetus does not possess that right. Given this criterion, therefore, abortion never involves violating a fetus' right to life, and permitting a fetus to be born is never anything we *owe* it, is never something that is *its* due.

It does not follow, however, that abortion is never wrong. As we saw earlier, despite the fact that infants fail to meet the actual-possession criterion and thus are not moral persons, reasons can be given, of a utilitarian kind, why it is wrong to kill them, at least if they are not radically deformed. It is possible, therefore, that similar reasons can be given in opposition to aborting fetuses at later stages in their development, if they are likely not to be radically deformed when born.

Utilitarian reasons of the sort we have considered are so very important that they might suffice to rule out harsh or destructive treatment of *any* nonperson whose resemblance or similarity to real persons is very close: not only deceased ex-persons and small babies, but even adult primates and human fetuses in the final trimester of pregnancy. Mr. Justice Blackmun may have had such considerations in mind when in his majority opinion in *Roe* v. *Wade* he declared that even though no fetuses are legal persons protected by the law of homicide, nevertheless during the final trimester, "The State in promoting its interest in the potentiality of human life, may if it chooses, regulate, and even proscribe, abortion . . ."[9] Whatever interest the State has in "the *potentiality* of human life" must be derivative from the plain interest it has in preserving and promoting respect for *actual* human life. It is not potential persons as such who merit our derivative respect but all *near-persons* including higher animals, dead people, infants, and well-developed fetuses, those beings whose similarity to real persons is close enough to render them sacred symbols of the real thing.

In the light of these considerations, it seems that a gradualist approach similar to that discussed earlier is a more plausible solution to the general problem of the moral justifiability of abortion than it is to the narrow problem of the criterion of moral personhood. Even if the fetus as a merely potential person lacks an actual right to life, and even if it would not be homicide therefore to kill it, its potential personhood may yet constitute a *reason* against killing it that requires an even stronger reason on the other side if abortion is to be justified. If that is so, it is not implausible to suppose that the more advanced the potential for personhood, the more stringent the case against killing.

As we have seen, there are reasons relevant to our moral decisions other than considerations of rights, so that sometimes actions can be judged morally wrong even though they violate no one's rights. Killing a fetus, in that case, could be wrong in certain circumstances, even though it violated no rights of the fetus, even though the fetus was not a moral person, even though the act was in no sense a murder.

§5 SUMMARY AND CONCLUSION

Killing human beings (homicide) is forbidden both by our criminal law and by the moral rules that are accepted in all civilized communities. If the fetus at any point in its development is a human being, then to kill it at that point is homicide, and if done without excuse or mitigation, murder. But the term 'human being' is subtly ambiguous. The fetus at all stages is obviously human in the genetic sense, but that is not the sense of the term intended in the moral rule against homicide. For a genetically human entity to have a right to life it must be a human being in the sense of a person. But the term 'person' is also ambiguous. In the commonsense descriptive meaning of the term, it refers to any being of any species or category who has certain familiar characteristics, of which consciousness of the world, self-concepts, and the capacity to plan ahead are prominent. In the purely normative (moral or legal) sense, a person is any being who has certain rights and/or duties, whatever his other characteristics. Whether or not abortion is homicide depends on what the correct criterion of moral personhood is.

We considered five leading formulations of the criterion of moral personhood and found that they are all subject to various embarrassments. One formulation in terms of species membership seemed both too broad and too narrow, and in the end dependent on an arbitrary preference for our own species. A more careful formulation escaped the charge of being too restrictive and the charge of arbitrariness but suffered from making the status of an individual derive from his membership in a group rather than from his own intrinsic characteristics. The two formulations in terms of potential possession of the characteristics definitive of commonsense personhood both stumbled on "the logical point about potentiality," that potential qualification for a right does not entail actual possession of that right. The modified or gradualist formulation of the potentiality criterion, however, does have some attractive features, and could be reformulated as a more plausible answer to another question, that about the moral permissibility of abortion. Even if the fetus is not a person and lacks a right to life, ever stronger reasons might be required to justify aborting it as it grows older and more similar to a person.

The weaknesses of the first four proposed criteria of moral personhood create a strong presumption in favor of the remaining one, the "actual-possession" criterion. It is clear that fetuses are not "people" in the ordinary commonsense meaning of that term, hence according to our final criterion they are not moral persons either, since this criterion of moral personhood simply adopts the criteria of common-sense personhood. The very grave difficulty of this criterion is that it entails that infants are not people either, during the first few months or more of their lives. That is a genuine difficulty for the theory, but a far greater embarrassment can be avoided. Because there are powerful reasons against infanticide that apply even if the infant is not a moral person, the actual-possession criterion is not subject to the devastating objection that it would morally or legally justify infanticide on demand.

II. THE PROBLEM OF THE CONFLICT OF CLAIMS

The problem of the status of the fetus is the first and perhaps the most difficult of the questions that must be settled before we can come to a considered view about the moral justifiability of abortion, but its solution does not necessarily resolve all moral perplexities about abortion. Even if we grant that the fetus is a moral person and thus has a valid claim to life, it does not follow that abortion is always wrong. For there are other moral persons, in addition to the fetus, whose interests are involved. The woman in whose uterus the fetus abides, in particular, has needs and interests that may well conflict with bringing the fetus to term. Do any of these needs and interests of the woman provide grounds for her having a genuine claim to an abortion and, if they do, which of the two conflicting claims—the woman's claim to an abortion or the fetus' claim to life—ought to be respected, if they happen to conflict? This is the second major moral question that needs to be examined with all the care we can muster. To do this, one very important assumption must be made—namely, that the fetus is a moral person and so has a valid claim to life. As we have seen in the previous section, this assumption might very well be unfounded and is unfounded in fact if we accept what appears to be the most reasonable criterion for moral personhood—namely, the actual-possession criterion. For purposes of the present section, however, we shall assume that the fetus is a moral person; this will enable us to investigate whose claim, the fetus' or the woman's, ought to be honored, if both have genuine but conflicting claims.

§6 FORMULATION OF THE "RIGHT TO AN ABORTION"

The right to an abortion that is often claimed on behalf of all women is a *discretionary right* to be exercised or not, on a given occasion, as the woman sees fit. For that reason it is sometimes called a "right to choose." If a pregnant woman has such a right then it is up to her, and her alone, whether to bear the child or to have it aborted. She is at liberty to bear it if she choses and at liberty to have it aborted if she chooses. She has no duty to bear it, but neither can she have a duty, imposed from without, to abort it. In respect to the fetus her choice is sovereign. Correlated with this liberty is a duty of others not to interfere with its exercise and not to withhold the necessary means for its exercise. These duties are owed to her, if she has a discretionary right to abortion, and she can claim their discharge as her due.

As a discretionary right, a right to an abortion would resemble the "right to liberty," or the right to move about or travel as one wishes. One is under no obligation to leave or stay home or to go to one destination rather than another, so that it is one's own choice that determines one's movements. But the right to move about at will, like other discretionary rights, is subject to limits. One person's liberty of movement, for example, comes to an end at the boundary of another person's property. The discretionary right to an abortion may be limited in similar ways so that the statement of a specific right of a particular woman in a definite set of concrete circumstances may need to be qualified by various exceptive clauses—for example, " . . . may choose to have an abortion *except* when the fetus is viable." Which exceptive clauses, if any, must be appended to the formulation of the right to an abortion depends on what the basis of this discretionary right is thought to be. For example, if a woman is thought to have a right to an abortion because she has a right to property *and* because the fetus is said to be her property, then the only exceptions there could be to exercising the right to an abortion would be those that restrict the disposing of one's property. What we must realize, then, is that the alleged right to an abortion cannot be understood in a vacuum; it is a right that can only be understood by the company it keeps, in particular by reference to the other, more fundamental rights from which it has often been claimed to be derived. Three of these rights and their possible association with the right to an abortion deserve our closest scrutiny. These are (1) the previously mentioned property rights, (2) the right to self-defense, and (3) the right to bodily autonomy. We shall consider each in its turn.

§7 POSSIBLE GROUNDS FOR THE WOMAN'S RIGHT

Property Rights over One's Body   Within very wide limits any person has a right to control the uses of his or her own body. With only rare exceptions, surgeons are required to secure the consent of the patient before operating because the body to be cut open, after all, is the patient's own, and he or she has the chief interest in it, and should therefore have the chief "say" over what is done to it. If we think of a fetus as literally a "part" of a woman's body in the same sense as, say, an organ, or as a mere growth attached to a part of the body on the model of a tumor or a wart, then it would seem to follow that the woman may choose to have it removed if she wishes just as she may

refuse to have it removed if she prefers. It is highly implausible, however, to think of a human fetus, even if it does fall short of moral
personhood, as no more than a temporary organ or a parasitic growth.
A fetus is not a constituent organ of the mother like her vermiform
appendix but rather an independent entity temporarily growing inside the mother.

It would be still less plausible to derive a maternal right to an
abortion from a characterization of the fetus as the *property* of its
mother and thus in the same category as the mother's wristwatch,
clothing, or jewelry. One may abandon or destroy one's personal property if one wishes; one's entitlement to do those things is one of the
"property rights" that define ownership. But one would think that the
father would have equal or near-equal rights of disposal if the fetus
were "property." It is not in his body, to be sure, but he contributed
as much genetically to its existence as did the mother and might
therefore make just as strong (or just as weak) a claim to ownership
over it. But neither claim would make very good conceptual sense. If
fetuses were property, we would find nothing odd in the notion that
they can be bought and sold, rented out, leased, used as collateral on
loans, and so on. But no one has ever seriously entertained such suggestions. Finally, we must remember the methodological assumption
that we shall make throughout this section, at least for the sake of the
argument, that the fetus is a full moral person, with a right to life like
yours and mine. On this assumption it would probably be contradictory to think of the fetus as *anyone's* property, especially if property
rights include what we might call "the right of disposal"—to abandon
or destroy as one chooses.

It is more plausible at first sight to claim that the pregnant woman
owns not the fetus but the body in which she shelters the fetus. On this
analogy, she owns her body (and particularly her womb) in roughly the
way an innkeeper owns a hotel or a homeowner his or her house and
garden. These analogies however are also defective. To begin with, it
is somewhat paradoxical to think of the relation between a person and
her body as similar to that of ownership. Is it possible to sell or rent
or lease one's body without selling, renting, or leasing oneself? If one's
body were one's property the answer would be affirmative, but in fact
one's relationship to one's own body is much more intimate than the
ownership model suggests. More important for our present purposes,
the legal analogies to the rights of innkeepers and householders will
not bear scrutiny. One cannot conceive of what it would be like for
a fetus to enter into a contract with a woman for the use of her womb
for nine months, or to fall in arrears in its payments and thus forfeit
its right of occupancy. Surely that cannot be the most apt analogy on
which to base the woman's abortion rights! Besides, whatever this,
that, or the other legal statute may say about the matter, one is not
morally entitled, in virtue of one's property rights, to expel a weak

and helpless person from one's shelter when that is tantamount to consigning the person to a certain death, and surely one is not entitled to shoot and kill a trespasser who will not, or cannot, leave one's property. In no department of human life does the vindication of property rights justify homicide. The maternal right to an abortion, therefore, cannot be founded on the more basic right to property.

Self-Defense and Proportionality Except for the most extreme pacifists, moralists agree that killing can be justified if done in self-defense. If, for example, one man (A) is attacked with a lethal weapon by another (B), we think that A has a right to defend himself against B's attack. Sometimes, in fact, we think that A would be justified in killing B, if this were the only way for A to defend himself. Now, some of those who urge the maternal right to an abortion believe that this right is associated with the more basic right to self-defense. There are many difficulties standing in the way to rational acceptance of this view. In particular, the innocence and the nonaggressive nature of the fetus need our special attention. We shall turn to these matters shortly. First, though, it is important to realize what reasons would not count as morally good reasons for an abortion, if the right to an abortion were supposed to be founded on the more basic right of self-defense.

All parties to the abortion dispute must agree that many women can be harmed if they are required to bring an unwanted fetus to term. Unwanted sexual intercourse imposed on a woman by a rapist can inflict on its victim severe psychological trauma of a sort deemed so serious by the law that a woman is entitled under some rules to use deadly force if necessary to prevent it. Similarly, an unwanted pregnancy in some circumstances can inflict equally severe psychological injury on a woman who is forced to carry her child to birth. There are various familiar examples of such harm. To borrow an example from Judith Thomson, a philosophy professor at the Massachusetts Institute of Technology: A terrified fourteen-year-old high school girl whose pregnancy has been caused by rape has already suffered one severe trauma. If she is now required, over her protests, to carry the child to full term despite her fear, anguish, deep depression, and fancied public mortification, the harmful ramifications may be multiplied a hundredfold. The forty-year-old housewife who has exhausted herself raising a large family in unfavorable economic circumstances while dependent upon an unreliable and unsympathetic husband may find herself to her horror pregnant again, and rightly feel that if she is forced to give birth to another child, she will forfeit her last opportunity to escape the intolerably squalid conditions of her life. A man must be morally blind not to acknowledge the severe harms that enforced continuance of unwanted pregnancies can inflict on women. An unwanted child need not literally cost the woman her life, but it can effectively ruin her life from her point of view, and it is a useful moral exercise for men to put themselves imaginatively in the woman's place to share that point of view.

At this stage in the argument the antiabortionist has a ready rejoinder. A woman need not keep her child, assume the responsibilities of raising it to adulthood, and forfeit her opportunities for self-fulfillment, he might reply, simply because she foregoes an abortion. She can always put the child up for adoption and be assured in the process that it will find loving foster parents who will give it a good upbringing. All she really has to suffer, the rejoinder concludes, is nine months of minor physical inconvenience. This is an argument that comes easily to the lips of men, but it betrays the grossest sort of masculine insensitivity. In the first place, it is not always true that a woman can have her baby adopted. If she is married, that transaction may require the consent of her husband, and the consent might not be forthcoming. But waiving that point, the possibility of adoption does not give much comfort to the unhappily pregnant woman, for it imposes on her a cruel dilemma, and an anguish that far surpasses "minor inconvenience." In effect, she has two choices, both of which are intolerable to her. She can carry the child to term and keep it, thus incurring the very consequences that make her unwilling to remain pregnant, *or* she can nourish the fetus to full size, go into labor, give birth to her baby, and then have it rudely wrenched away, never to be seen by her again. Let moralistic males imagine what an emotional jolt that must be!

Still, on the scale of harms, mere traumas and frustrations are not exactly equal to death. Few women would choose their own deaths in preference to the harms that may come from producing children. According to a common interpretation of the self-defense rule, however, the harm to be averted by a violent act in self-defense need not be identical in severity to that which is inflicted upon one's assailant, but only somehow "proportional" to it. Both our prevailing morality and our legal traditions permit the use of lethal force to prevent harms that are less serious than death, so it is plausible to assume that the rule of "proportionality" can be satisfied by something less than equality of harms. But how much less? The late Jane English, a philosopher from the University of North Carolina, offers an answer that, though vague, is in accordance with the moral sentiments of most people when they think of situations other than that involving abortion:

> How severe an injury may you inflict in self-defense? In part this depends upon the severity of the injury to be avoided: you may not shoot someone merely to avoid having your clothes torn. This might lead one to the mistaken conclusion that the defense may only equal the threatened injury in severity; that to avoid death you may kill, but to avoid a black eye you may only inflict a black eye or the equivalent. Rather our laws and customs seem to say that you may create an injury *somewhat but not enormously greater* than the injury to be avoided. To fend off an attack whose outcome would be as serious as

rape, a severe beating, or the loss of a finger, you may shoot; to avoid having your clothes torn, you may blacken an eye.[10] [Emphasis added.]

Applying English's answer to the abortion case, and assuming that both the fetus and the woman have legitimate claims, we derive the conclusion that killing the "fetal person" would not be justified when it is done merely to prevent relatively trivial harms to the mother's interests. Not *all* cases of abortion, therefore, can morally be justified, even if there is a maternal right to abortion derived from the more basic right to self-defense.

Self-Defense: The Problem of the Innocent Aggressor   Suppose, however, that the harms that will probably be caused to the mother if the fetus is brought to term are not trivial but serious. Here we have a case where the mother's right to have her important interests respected clashes with the assumed right to life of the fetus. In these circumstances, don't the mother's claims outweigh the fetus'? Doesn't self-defense in these circumstances justify abortion?

There is a serious, previously undiscussed difficulty that calls out for attention. Consider a case where someone aggressively attacks another. The reason we think that, to use English's expression, we may in self-defense create a "somewhat but not enormously greater injury" than would have been caused by the aggressor is because we think of the aggressor as the party who is morally at fault. If he or she had not launched the aggression in the first place, there should have been no occasion for the use of force. Since the whole episode was the aggressor's fault, his interests should not count for as much as those of the innocent victim. It is a shame that anybody has to be seriously hurt, but if it comes down to an inescapable choice between the innocent party suffering a serious harm or the culpable party suffering a still more serious harm, then the latter is the lesser of the two evils. Aggressors of course, for all their guilt, remain human beings, and consequently they do not forfeit all their human rights in launching an attack. We still may not kill them to prevent them from stealing ten dollars. But their culpability does cost them their right to equal consideration; we may kill them to prevent them from causing serious harm.

But now suppose that the party who threatens us, even though he or she is the aggressor who initiates the whole episode, is not morally at fault. Suppose the person cannot act otherwise in the circumstances and thus cannot justly be held morally responsible. For example, he or she was temporarily (or permanently) insane, or it was a case of mistaken identity (he or she mistook you for a Gestapo agent to whom you bear a striking resemblance), or someone had drugged the person's breakfast cereal and his or her behavior was influenced by the drug. George Fletcher, a UCLA law professor, provides a vivid illustration of the problem in what he calls "the case of the psychotic aggressor":

Imagine that your companion in an elevator goes berserk and attacks you with a knife. There is no escape: the only way to avoid serious bodily harm or even death is to kill him. The assailant acts purposively in the sense that his means further his aggressive end . . . [but] he does act in a frenzy or a fit . . . [and] it is clear that his conduct is non-responsible. If he were brought to trial for his attack, he would have a valid defense of insanity. [11]

The general problem, as lawyers would put it, is "whether self-defense applies against an excused but unjustified aggression."[12] To *justify* an act is to show that it was the right thing to do in the circumstances; to *excuse* an act is to show that although it was unjustified, the actor didn't mean it or couldn't help it, that it was not, properly speaking, his or her doing at all. In the "excused but unjustified aggression" we have a more plausible model for the application of self-defense to the problem of abortion, for *the fetus is surely innocent* (not because of insanity but because of immaturity, and because *it* did not choose to threaten its mother—it did not "ask to be born").

Upon reflection, most of us would agree, I think, that one would be justified in killing even an innocent aggressor if that seemed necessary to save one's own life or to prevent one from suffering serious bodily injury. Surely we would not judge harshly the slightly built lady who shoots the armed stranger who goes berserk in the elevator. If we were in her shoes, we too would protect ourselves at all costs to the assailant, just as we would against wild animals, runaway trucks, or impersonal forces of nature. But while the berserk assailant, as well as those persons mentioned in the last paragraph, all are innocent—are not *morally* responsible for what they do—they all *are* assailants, and in this respect they differ in a quite fundamental respect from the fetus. For the fetus not only is innocent; the fetus also is not an aggressor. *It* didn't start the trouble in any fashion. Thus, it would seem that while we are justified in killing an innocent assailant if this is the only way to prevent him from killing us, it does not follow that we are similarly justified in killing a fetal person, since, unlike the innocent aggressor, the fetus is not an aggressor at all.

Judith Thomson has challenged this argument. She presents the following farfetched but coherent hypothetical example:

Aggressor is driving his tank at you. But he has taken care to arrange that a baby is strapped to the front of the tank so that if you use your anti-tank gun, you will not only kill Aggressor, you will kill the baby. Now Aggressor, admittedly, is in the process of trying to kill you; but that baby isn't. Yet you can presumably go ahead and use the gun, even though this involves killing the baby as well as Aggressor.[13]

The baby in this example is not only "innocent," but also the "innocent shield of a threat."[14] Still it is hard to quarrel with Thomson's judgment that you *may* (not that you *should*) take the baby's life if necessary to save your own, that it is morally permissible, even if it is not morally obligatory, to do so. After all, you are (by hypothesis) perfectly innocent too. This example makes a better analogy to the abortion situation than any we have considered thus far, but there are still significant dissimilarities. Unless the fetus is the product of rape, it cannot conceivably be the shield of some third-party aggressor. There is simply no interpersonal "aggression" involved at all in the normal pregnancy. There may nevertheless be a genuine *threat* to the well-being of the mother, and if that threat is to her very life, then perhaps she does have a right to kill it, if necessary, in self-defense. At any rate, if the threatened victim in Thomson's tank example is justified in killing the innocent shield, then the pregnant woman threatened with similar harm is similarly entitled. But all that this would establish is that abortion is justified only if it is probably required to save the mother's life. So not only could we not use the self-defense argument to justify abortion for trivial reasons, as was argued earlier; it appears that the only reason that authorizes its use is the one that cites the fact that the mother will probably die if the fetus is not aborted.

Bodily Autonomy: The Example of the Plugged-in Violinist The trouble with the use of self-defense as a model for abortion rights is that none of the examples of self-defense makes an *exact* analogy to the abortion situation. The examples that come closest to providing models for justified abortion are the "innocent aggressor cases" and these would apply, as we have seen, only to abortions that are necessary to prevent death to the mother. Even these examples do not fit the abortion case exactly, since the fetus is in no way itself an aggressor, culpable or innocent, but is at most a "nonaggressive, nonculpable threat," in some respects like an innocent shield.[15] And the more we change the examples to bring them closer to the situation of the fetus, the less clear is their resemblance to the central models of self-defense. Once we are allowed to protect ourselves (and especially to protect interests less weighty than self-preservation) at the expense of nonaggressive innocents, it becomes difficult to distinguish the latter from innocent bystanders whom we kill as means to our own good, and that in turn begins to look like unvarnished murder. The killing of an innocent person simply because his or her continued existence in the circumstances would make the killer's life miserable is a homicide that cannot be justified. It is not self-defense to kill your boss because he makes your work life intolerable and you are unable to find another job, or to kill your spouse because he or she nags you to the point of extreme misery and will not agree to a divorce,[16] or (closer to the point) to kill your shipwrecked fellow passenger in the lifeboat because there are provisions sufficient for only one to survive and he or she claims half of them, or to kill your innocent rival for a position or a prize because you can win only if he or she is out of the running. In all these cases the victim is either innocent or relatively innocent and in no way a direct aggressor.

Partly because of deficiencies in the hypothetical examples of self-defense, Thomson invented a different sort of example intended at once to be a much closer analogy to the abortion situation and also such that the killing can be seen to be morally justified for reasons less compelling than defense of the killer's very life:

> You wake up in the morning and find yourself back to back in bed with an unconscious violinist. A famous unconscious violinist. He has been found to have a fatal kidney ailment, and the Society of Music Lovers has canvassed all the available medical records and found that you alone have the right blood type to help. They have therefore kidnapped you, and last night the violinist's circulatory system was plugged into yours, so that your kidneys can be used to extract poisons from his blood as well as your own. The director of the hospital now tells you, "Look, we're sorry the Society of Music Lovers did this to you—we would never have permitted it if we had known. But still they did it, and the violinist now is plugged into you. To unplug you would be to kill him. But never mind, it's only for nine months. By then he will have recovered from his ailment, and can safely be unplugged from you." Is it morally incumbent on you to accede to this situation? No doubt it would be very nice of you if you did, a great kindness. But do you have to accede to it? . . . What if the director . . . says . . . "Granted you have a right to decide what happens in and to your body, but a person's right to life outweighs your right to decide what happens in and to your body. So you cannot . . . be unplugged from him." I imagine you would regard this as outrageous . . . [17]

Suppose that you defy the director on your own, and exercise your control over your own body by unplugging the unconscious violinist, thereby causing his death. This would be to kill in defense of an interest far less important than self-preservation or the prevention of serious injury to oneself. And it would be to kill an innocent nonaggressor, indeed a victim who remains unconscious throughout the entire period during which he is a threat. We have, therefore, an example that—if it works—offers far more encouragement to the proabortion position than the model of self-defense does. We must now pose two questions: (1) Would you in fact be morally justified in unplugging the violinist? and (2) How close an analogy does this bizarre example make to the abortion situation?

There is no way to argue conclusively that unplugging the violinist would be morally justified. Thomson can only make the picture as vividly persuasive as she can and then appeal to her reader's intuitions. It is not an easy case, and neither an affirmative nor a negative judgment will seem self-evident to everyone. Still the verdict for justification seems at least as strong as in any of the other examples of killing innocent threats, and some additional considerations can be brought to bear in its support. There is, after all, a clear "intuition" in support of a basic right "to decide what happens in and to one's own body," even though the limits of that right are lost in a fog of controversy. So unless there is some stronger competing claim, anyone has a right to refuse to consent to surgery or to enforced attachment to a machine. Or indeed to an unconscious violinist. But what of the competing claim in this example, the violinist's right to life? That is another basic right that is vague around the edges.

In its noncontroversial core, the right to life is a right not to be killed directly (except under very special circumstances) and to be rescued from impending death whenever this can be done without unreasonable sacrifice. But as Warren has pointed out, one person's right to life does not impose a correlative duty on another person to do "whatever is necessary to keep him alive."[18] And though we all have general duties to come to the assistance of strangers in peril, we cannot be forced to make enormous sacrifices or to run unreasonably high risks to keep people alive when we stand in no special relationship to them, like "father" or "lifeguard." The wife of the violinist perhaps would have a duty to stay plugged to him (if that would help) for nine months; but the random stranger has no such duty at all. So there is good reason to grant Thomson her claim that a stranger would have a right to unplug the violinist.

But how close an analogy after all is this to the normal case of pregnancy? Several differences come immediately to mind. In the normal case of pregnancy, the woman is not confined to her bed for nine months, but can continue to work and function efficiently in the world until the final trimester at least. This difference, however, is of doubtful significance, since Thomson's argument is not based on a right to the protection of one's interest in efficient mobility but rather on a right to *decide* on the uses of one's own body, which is quite another thing. Another difference is that the mother and her fetus are not exactly "random strangers" in the same sense that the woman and the violinist are. Again the relationship between mother and fetus seems to be in a class by itself. If the person who needs to use the woman's body for nine months in order to survive is her mother, father, sister, brother, son, daughter, or close friend, then the relationship would seem close enough to establish a special obligation in the woman to permit that use. If the needy person is a total stranger, then that obligation is missing. The fetus no doubt stands somewhere between these two extremes, but it is at least as close to the "special relationship" end of the spectrum as to the "total stranger" end.

The most important difference, however, between the violinist case and the normal pregnancy is that in the former the woman had absolutely nothing to do with creating the situation from which she wishes to escape. She bears no responsibility whatever for being in a state of "plugged-in-ness" with the violinist. As many commentators have pointed out, this makes Thomson's analogy fit at most one very special class of pregnancies, namely those imposed upon a woman entirely against her will, as in rape. In the "normal case" of pregnancy, the voluntary action of the woman herself (knowingly consenting to sexual intercourse) has something to do with her becoming pregnant. So once again, we find that a proabortion argument fails to establish an unrestricted moral right to abortion. Just as self-defense justifies abortion at most in the case where it is necessary to save the mother's life, the Thomson defense justifies abortion only when the woman shares no responsibility for her pregnancy, as, for example, when it has been caused by rape (force or fraud).

Voluntariness and Responsibility   If we continue the line of reasoning suggested by our criticism of the violinist example, we will soon reach a general principle, namely, that whether or not a woman has a duty to continue her pregnancy depends, at least in part, on how responsible she is for being pregnant in the first place, that is, on the extent to which her pregnancy is the consequence of her own voluntary actions. This formula, in turn, seems to be an application of a still more general moral principle, one that imposes duties on one party to rescue or support another, even a stranger and even when that requires great personal sacrifice or risk, to the degree that the first party, through his own voluntary actions or omissions, was responsible for the second party's dependence on him. A late-arriving bystander at the seaside has no duty to risk life or limb to save a drowning swimmer. If, however, the swimmer is in danger only because the bystander erroneously informed him or her that there was no danger, then the bystander has a duty to make some effort at rescue (though not a suicidal one), dangerous as it may be. If the swimmer is in the water only because the "bystander" has pushed him out of a boat, however, then the bystander has a duty to attempt rescue at any cost to personal safety,[19] since the bystander's own voluntary action was the whole cause of the swimmer's plight.

Since the voluntariness of an action or omission is a matter of degree, so is the responsibility that stems from it, as is the stringency of the duty that derives from that responsibility. The duty to continue a pregnancy, then, will be stronger (other things being equal) in the case where the pregnancy was entered into in a fully voluntary way than it will be in the case that fits the violinist model where the pregnancy is totally involuntary. But in between these two extremes is a whole range of cases where moral judgments are more difficult to make. We can sketch the whole spectrum as follows:

   i. Pregnancy caused by rape (totally involuntary).
   ii. Pregnancy caused by contraceptive failure, where the fault is entirely that of the manufacturer or pharmaceutical company.
   iii. Pregnancy caused by contraceptive failure within the advertised 1 percent margin of error (no one's fault).
   iv. Pregnancy caused by the negligence of the woman (or the man, or both). They are careless in the use of the contraceptive or else fail to use it at all, being unaware of a large risk that they *ought* to have been aware of.

v. Pregnancy caused by the recklessness of the woman (or the man, or both). They think of the risk but get swept along by passion and consciously disregard it.

vi. Pregnancy caused by intercourse between partners who are genuinely indifferent at the time whether or not pregnancy results.

vii. Pregnancy caused by the deliberate decision of the parties to produce it (completely voluntary).

There would be a somewhat hollow ring to the claim in case vii that one has no obligation to continue one's bodily support for a moral person whose dependence on that support one has deliberately caused. That would be like denying that one has a duty to save the drowning swimmer that one has just pushed out of the boat. The case for cessation of bodily support is hardly any stronger in vi and v than in vii. Perhaps it is misleading to say of the negligence case (iv) that the pregnancy is only partially involuntary, or involuntary "to a degree," since the parents did not *intentionally* produce or run the risk of producing a fetus. But there is no need to haggle over that terminological question. Whether wholly or partially involuntary, the actions of the parents in the circumstances were faulty and the pregnancy resulted from the fault (negligence), so they are to a substantial degree responsible (to blame) for it. It was within their power to be more careful or knowledgeable, and yet they were careless or avoidably ignorant. So they cannot plead, in the manner of the lady plugged to the violinist, that they had no control over their condition whatever. In failing to exercise due care, they were doing something else and doing *it* "to a degree voluntarily." In these cases—iv, v, vi, and vii— the woman and her partner are therefore responsible for the pregnancy, and on the analogy with the case of the drowning swimmer who was pushed from the boat, they have a duty not to kill the fetus or permit it to die.

Cases ii and iii are more perplexing. In case ii, where the fault was entirely that of the manufacturer, the woman is no more responsible for being pregnant than in case i where she is the unwilling victim of a rape. In neither case did she choose to become pregnant. In neither case was she reckless or negligent in respect to the possibility of becoming pregnant. So if she has no duty to continue to provide bodily support for the dependent fetus in the rape case, then equally she has no duty in the other case. To be sure, there is always *some* risk of pregnancy whenever there is intercourse, no matter how careful the partners are. There may be only 1 chance in 10,000 that a contraceptive pill has an undetectable flaw, but there is no chance whatever of pregnancy without intercourse. The woman in case ii, then, would seem to have *some* responsibility, even if vanishingly small, for her pregnancy. She could have been even more careful by abstaining from sex altogether. But notice that much the same sort of thing could be said of the rape victim. By staying home in a locked building patrolled round the clock by armed guards, she could have reduced the chances of bodily assault from, say, 1 in 50,000 to effectively nil. By staying off the dangerous streets, she would have been much more careful than she was in respect to the risk of rape. But surely that does not entitle us to say that she was "partially responsible" for the rape that made her pregnant. When a person takes all the precautions that she can *reasonably* be expected to take against a certain outcome, then that outcome cannot fairly be described as her responsibility. So in case ii, where the negligence of the manufacturer of the contraceptive is the cause of the pregnancy, the woman cannot be held responsible for her condition, and that ground for ascribing to her a duty not to abort is not present.

Case iii brings us very close to the borderline. The couple in this example do not choose to have a baby and indeed they take strong precautions against pregnancy. Still they know that there is a 1 percent danger and they deliberately choose to run that risk anyway. As a result a woman becomes pregnant against her will. Does she then have a right to abandon to a certain death a newly formed moral person who is even less responsible for his dependence on her than she is? When one looks at the problem in this way from the perspective of the fetus to whom we have suppositively ascribed full moral rights, it becomes doubtful that the pregnant woman's very minimal responsibility for her plight can permit her to abandon a being who has no responsibility for it whatever. She ran a very small risk, but the fetus ran no risk at all. Nevertheless, this is a borderline case for the following reason. If we extend to this case the rule we applied to case ii, then we might be entitled to say that the woman is no more responsible than the fetus for the pregnancy. To reach that conclusion we have to judge the 1 percent chance of pregnancy to be a *reasonable* risk for a woman to run in the circumstances. That appraisal itself is a disguised moral judgment of pivotal importance, and yet it is very difficult to know how to go about establishing it. Nevertheless, *if* it is correct, then the woman is, for all practical purposes, relieved of her responsibility for the pregnancy just as she is in cases i and ii, and in that event the fetus' "right to life" does not entail a duty on her part to make extreme sacrifices.

§8 SUMMARY AND CONCLUSION

Assuming that the fetus is a moral person, under what conditions, if any, is abortion justifiable homicide? If the woman's right to an abortion is derived from her right to own property in her body (which is not very plausible), then abortion is never justifiable homicide. Property rights simply can't support that much moral weight. If the right is derived from self-defense, then it justifies abortion at most when necessary to save the woman from death. That is because the fetus, while sometimes a threat to the interests of the woman, is an innocent and (in a sense) nonaggressive threat. The doctrine of proportionality, which permits a person to use a degree of force in self-defense that is likely to cause the assailant harm greater (within reasonable limits) than the harm the assailant would otherwise cause the victim, has application only to the case where the assailant is culpable. One can kill an "innocent threat" in order to save one's life but not to save one's pocketbook. The right of bodily autonomy (to decide what is to be done in and to one's own body) is a much solider base for the right to abortion than either the right to property of the right to self-defense, since it permits one to kill innocent persons by depriving them of one's "life-support system," even when they are threats to interests substantially less important than self-preservation. But this justification is probably available at most to victims of rape, or contraceptive failure caused by the negligence of other parties, to the risk of which the woman has not consented. That narrow restriction on the use of this defense stems from the requirement, internal to it, that the woman be in no way responsible for her pregnancy.

It does not follow automatically that because the victim of a homicide was "innocent," the killing cannot have been justified. But abortion can plausibly be construed as justifiable homicide only on the basis of inexact analogies, and then only (1) to save the mother from the most extreme harm, or else (2) to save the mother from a lesser harm when the pregnancy was the result of the wrongful acts of others for which the woman had no responsibility. Another possibility that was only suggested here is (3) when it can be claimed for a defective or diseased fetus that it has a right *not* to be born. These narrow restrictions on the right of the woman to an abortion will not satisfy many people in the proabortion camp. But if the assumption of the moral personhood of the fetus is false, as was argued in the first part of this essay, then the woman's right to bodily autonomy will normally prevail, and abortions at all but the later stages, at least, and for the most common reasons, at least, are morally permissible.

NOTES

1. Mary Anne Warren, "On the Moral and Legal Status of Abortion," *The Monist* 57 (1973), pp. 43–61. Reprinted in J. Feinberg and H. Gross (eds.), *Liberty: Selected Readings,* pp. 133–143. The quotation is from the latter source, p. 138.
2. See Paul Ramsey, "The Morality of Abortion," in D. H. Labby (ed.), *Life or Death: Ethics and Options* (Seattle and London: University of Washington Press, 1968), pp. 60–93.
3. These problems are discussed in more detail in Joel Feinberg, "The Rights of Animals and Future Generations" (Appendix: The Paradoxes of Potentiality), in W. T. Blackstone (ed.), *Philosophy and Environmental Crisis* (Athens, Ga.: University of Georgia Press, 1974), pp. 67–68.
4. Stanley I. Benn, "Abortion, Infanticide, and Respect for Persons," in J.

Feinberg (ed.), *The Problem of Abortion* (Belmont, Cal.: Wadsworth Publishing Co., 1973), p. 102.

5. Joel Feinberg, *Social Philosophy* (Englewood Cliffs, N.J.: Prentice-Hall, 1973), p. 66.

6. Benn, *op. cit.,* p. 102.

7. Joel Feinberg, "Is There a Right to Be Born?" in James Rachels (ed.), *Understanding Moral Philosophy* (Encino, Cal.: Dickenson Publishing Co., 1976), pp. 353–354.

8. 'Thalidomide' is the trade name of a potent tranquilizer once manufactured in Europe but never permitted in the United States. In the late 1950s, thousands of deformed babies were born to European women who had taken thalidomide during pregnancy.

9. From Mr. Justice Blackmun's opinion in *Roe* v. *Wade* 410 U.S. 113 (1973).

10. Jane English, "Abortion and the Concept of a Person," *Canadian Journal of Philosophy* 5 (1975), p. 242.

11. George Fletcher, "Proportionality and the Psychotic Aggressor: A Vignette in Comparative Criminal Law Theory," *Israel Law Review* 8 (1973), p. 376.

12. Fletcher, *loc. cit.*

13. Judith Jarvis Thomson, "Self-Defense and Rights," The Lindley Lecture, 1976 (Lawrence, Kansas: University of Kansas Philosophy Department, 1977).

14. The term comes from Robert Nozick, *Anarchy, State, and Utopia* (New York: Basic Books, 1974), p. 35.

15. Even when self-defense is acceptable as a defense to homicide in the case of forced killings of nonaggressive innocents, that may be because it is understood in those cases to be an excuse or a mitigation rather than a justification. If a criminal terrorist from a fortified position throws a bomb at my feet, and I can escape its explosion only by quickly throwing it in the direction of a baby-buggy whose infant occupant is enjoying a nap, perhaps I can be *excused* for saving my life by taking the baby's; perhaps the duress under which I acted mitigates my guilt; perhaps the law ought not to be too severe with me. But it is not convincing to argue that I was entirely justified in what I did because I was acting in self-defense. But the problem is a difficult one, and the case may be borderline.

16. See Ludwig Lewisohn's remarkable novel, *The Case of Mr. Crump* (New York: Farrar, Straus and Co., 1947).

17. Judith Jarvis Thomson, "A Defense of Abortion," *Philosophy and Public Affairs* 1 (1971), pp. 48–49.

18. Warren, *op. cit.,* p. 135.

19. The examples are Sissela Bok's. See her article "Ethical Problems of Abortion," *Hastings Center Studies* 2 (1974), p. 35.

SUGGESTIONS FOR FURTHER READING

Further readings are mentioned below in connection with the section (§) of the essay to which they are most pertinent.

§3.   A very helpful collection of articles on the concept of a person is *The Identity of Persons,* edited by Amélie O. Rorty (Berkeley, Los Angeles, London: University of California Press, 1976). In particular, the editor's Introduction and Postscript, and Daniel Dennett's "Conditions of Personhood" are especially useful. A very penetrating and original analysis of commonsense personhood (not in the Rorty collection) is Harry Frankfurt's "Freedom of the Will and the Concept of a Person," *Journal of Philosophy* 68 (1971), reprinted in J. Feinberg (ed.), *Reason and Responsibility,* Fourth Edition (Belmont, Cal.: Wadsworth Publishing Co., 1978). For articles that defend particular accounts of personhood in the context of the abortion problem, see especially Mary Anne Warren, "The Moral and Legal Status of Abortion," *The Monist* 57 (1973), and Joseph Fletcher, "Indicators of Humanhood: A Tentative Profile of Man," *The Hastings Center Report 2* (1972). See also Lawrence C. Becker's "Human Being: The Boundaries of the Concept," *Philosophy and Public Affairs* 4 (1975).

§4. The most influential recent defenses of a species criterion are probably those of the Catholic legal scholar John T. Noonan, Jr., and the Protestant theologian Paul Ramsey. See Noonan's "Abortion and the Catholic Church: A Summary History," *Natural Law Forum* 12 (1967), and his rejoinder to critics, "How to Argue About Abortion" (New York: Ad Hoc Committee in Defense of Life, Inc., 1974). Ramsey's views are well stated in "The Morality of Abortion," in *Life or Death: Ethics and Options,* edited by D. H. Labby (Seattle: University of Washington Press, 1968).

A nicely nuanced defense of a kind of synthesis of the strict potentiality and species principles can be found in Philip E. Devine's book, *The Ethics of Homicide* (Ithaca, N.Y.: Cornell University Press, 1978). Although Devine's conclusions differ from those of this essay, the methodology is very similar to that employed here.

A thorough presentation of a modified potentiality criterion can be found in Daniel Callahan's learned and thoroughly moderate book, *Abortion: Law, Choice, and Morality* (London and New York: Macmillan, 1970). See especially chapters 10 and 11.

The most uncompromising defense of an actual-possession criterion is that of Michael Tooley, "Abortion and Infanticide," *Philosophy and Public Affairs* 2 (1972). Tooley defends not only abortion but, under certain circumstances, infanticide as well. His view on the latter question is criticized on utilitarian grounds by Stanley Benn and Jane English in the articles mentioned in the text of this essay.

§7. An eloquent account of the serious psychological harms that can be done to women by enforced pregnancies can be found in Lorenne M. G. Clark's "Reply to Professor Sumner," *Canadian Journal of Philosophy* 4 (1974). Baruch Brody argues forcefully that "self-defense" cannot justify abortion in his *Abortion and the Sanctity of Human Life: A Philosophical View* (Cambridge, Mass., and London: M.I.T. Press, 1975). An authoritative and very accessible discussion of the application of "self-defense" and other justifications to borderline cases of justifiable homicide of all kinds is Sanford Kadish's "Respect for Life and Regard for Rights in the Criminal Law," *California Law Review* 64 (1976), reprinted in S. F. Barker (ed.), *Respect for Life in Medicine, Philosophy, and the Law* (Baltimore and London: The Johns Hopkins University Press, 1976).

Judith Thomson's use of the "plugged-in violinist" example is sharply criticized by John Finnis in his "The Rights and Wrongs of Abortion," in *Philosophy and Public Affairs* 2 (Winter 1973). Thomson's rejoinder to Finnis, "Rights and Deaths," is included in the same issue. Both articles can be found in *The Rights and Wrongs of Abortion,* edited by M. Cohen, T. Nagel, and T. Scanlon (Princeton, N. J.: Princeton University Press, 1973).

7

Animals and the Value of Life

PETER SINGER

"Thou shalt not kill," says the Sixth Commandment, and we all nod our heads in solemn agreement. *Whom* should we not kill? Why, *people, human beings,* of course, we all answer. If pressed we may narrow the scope of this answer still further, making exceptions for killing in self-defense and perhaps one or two other special cases; but we rarely think that our interpretation of the commandment could be too *narrow,* and that it could apply to living things other than human beings.

The topic of this essay is the value of life and not the interpretation of the Sixth Commandment; but it is significant that we think it so obvious that the killing of nonhuman beings is not wrong that we do not even bother to spell out this qualification when we say "Thou shalt not kill"—or its equivalent—in more up-to-date language. That it is an immensely important qualification cannot be denied.

Take, for instance, chickens—just one of many species of nonhuman animals that humans kill for food. In the United States—just one of the countries where chickens are killed for human food—around *3 billion* chickens are slaughtered every year. That is several times greater than the number of human beings killed in all the wars of the present century. In making this comparison I am not saying that the death of a chicken is as bad as the death of a human being. That is something we shall consider later in this essay. At this stage, my aim is only to draw attention to the significance of the exception we make to the general principle that killing is wrong, and thereby to indicate the importance of the question: 'Are we justified in making this exception? Is it morally all right to kill nonhuman animals?' That, basically, is the question we shall be discussing.

I. INTRODUCTION

Before we begin our discussion of the value of nonhuman life, there are two things that should be said by way of preliminaries.

§1 FIRST PRELIMINARY: OTHER ISSUES IN THE TREATMENT OF ANIMALS

While any conclusion we may come to about the value of the lives of nonhuman beings will obviously be relevant to the issue of how we ought to treat nonhuman beings, it is not the only thing that is relevant to this issue. To see this, let us for the moment assume that the lives of the 3 billion chickens killed in the United States each year are of no value at all. Would this mean that there could be no moral objection to buying one of these chickens at your local supermarket, taking it home, and eating it? Not necessarily; for it is still the case that during their brief lives these chickens suffer from overcrowding, from having their beaks cut off with a hot knife, from rough handling during transportation, and finally from being hung upside down on a conveyor belt before they are killed. We might consider this a reason for holding that current methods of raising chickens for food are wrong, and therefore that we should boycott chicken produced by these methods. We could think this even if we do not think that there is anything wrong with painlessly killing a chicken.

Similarly, one can quite consistently oppose hunting, the slaughter of seals for their fur, many of the 60 to 100 million experiments performed annually on animals in the United States, and a whole host of other practices involving animals, without holding that killing an animal is in itself wrong. The suffering inflicted by these practices is grounds enough.

In my book *Animal Liberation* I argued at great length against unrestricted experimentation on animals, against the exploitation of animals in modern "factory farms," and for a vegetarian diet; yet, I did not assert that killing an animal is wrong.[1] I based my arguments on the wrongness of making animals suffer, because this seemed to me the most straightforward argument against experimentation and factory farming. I used straightforward arguments that I hoped would have a wide appeal, because I wanted to increase public awareness of what is being done to animals. The argument about killing animals is a more difficult one, and I was (and remain) less certain about this issue than about the question of suffering. Despite my uncertainty about killing, I was not (and am not) at all uncertain about the wrongness of many of the things we do to animals.

Since we can make up our minds on many issues involving the treatment of animals without deciding whether it is wrong to kill animals, it might be thought that this latter issue becomes an idle one that can make no difference to what we ought to do, and hence, that it is not worth discussing. This suggestion—the exact opposite of the view that the wrongness of killing is the only thing relevant to our treatment of animals—is also mistaken. In some cases, we cannot decide what we ought to do without first making up our mind about the wrongness of killing. From my own experiences, three examples come to mind.

§2 THREE QUESTIONS

1. A reader of *Animal Liberation* once said to me: "You don't eat meat because of the suffering the animals are forced to go through before they die, especially in modern intensive farms. I wouldn't eat an animal that had been made to live under these conditions either. But I live on a farm. Mainly we grow vegetables, but we do raise a few pigs. The pigs have a good life, with plenty of room to roam about. We do the slaughtering ourselves, so we know that it is quick and virtually painless. Do you think that's wrong? Would *you* eat our pork?"

2. A friend of mine who lives in New York City cannot pass a stray dog without trying to do something for it. Very often, when the dogs are especially thin she will take them home to her apartment and feed them. Unfortunately there is a limit to the number of dogs one can keep in a small apartment. After a time my friend is forced to send the dogs back to the street, although she knows that they will soon be reduced to the miserable condition in which she found them. She does not take them to the dog pound, because she does not approve of the manner in which the animals are treated there. I once asked her whether it wouldn't be better to take her strays to a vet to have them killed painlessly by an intravenous injection. We were walking near the Bowery at the time, and by way of an answer she gestured toward a man slumped in a doorway, marked by his stubble and dirty overcoat as one of New York's derelicts. "He leads a miserable life," she said, "but we don't take him off for an intravenous injection. Why is a dog different?"

3. Working for a university as I do, I frequently meet researchers who perform experiments on animals. Some of these experiments involve suffering, but others do not. In physiology, for instance, many experiments are performed when the animal is under total anesthetic, and upon completion of the experiment the animal is killed before it recovers from the anesthetic. Provided it is properly looked after prior to the experiment, the animal suffers no more than if it had been taken to a vet to be killed painlessly. At the same time, many of these experiments are not really necessary. They are not urgent, lifesaving research. They may extend our knowledge of animal physiology in some small details, but this knowledge may not be applicable to human beings; or there may be alternative methods of finding these things out that do not use animals, but are a little more laborious and expensive. What attitude should we take to such experiments? Are they wrong because they involve the needless death of an animal, or are they permissible, because they do not cause suffering and because the life of a dog, cat, or mouse is of no value?

All these cases raise, in a practical form, the question we shall be discussing. Is it all right to raise animals for food if the animals lead a pleasant life and die painlessly? Should we "put to sleep" strays and other animals whose lives are likely to be miserable? Does the life of an animal count for more than the desire to further knowledge, when we cannot foresee any benefits for humans from the knowledge gained? Does the life of an animal count for more than the convenience of the researcher? We will return to these questions at the conclusion of our investigation into the value of animal life (§19).

§3 SECOND PRELIMINARY: THE VALUE OF HUMAN LIFE

If we could agree on exactly what value a human life has, and why it has that value, the task of deciding on the value of nonhuman life would be greatly simplified. We could then consider to what extent members of the various species of animals possess the characteristics that give human life its value, and evaluate their lives accordingly. For instance, if we were agreed that human life is valuable only because humans are self-conscious beings, aware of themselves and capable of evolving long-range purposes and plans of life, we could probably agree that the lives of animals like frogs, shrimps, fish, and lizards are of no value, since these animals appear not to be self-conscious or capable of making long-range plans. (There might be some valuable characteristic possessed by these animals and not possessed by humans, but it is not easy to see what it could be.) The lives of chimpanzees and whales, on the other hand, might well be regarded as worthy of protection, since there is now a good deal of evidence—details of which I shall give later—that these animals are self-conscious. In between these two groups of animals, some cases would be harder to decide, because it is difficult to be certain about what counts as evidence of self-consciousness and long-range planning; but at least we would know what we were looking for, because we had agreed that it is these characteristics that give value to life.

Similarly, if we were agreed that it is not self-consciousness but merely consciousness, or the capacity to experience pleasure or pain, that gives value to human life, we would know what to look for when trying to assess whether the lives of other animals have value. On this criterion we would have to proceed much further down the evolutionary scale before we came to beings whose lives have no value. Again, the exact cutoff point would not be easy to establish, but we would know that when we came to the boundary of consciousness, we had also reached the boundary of value.

Regrettably, as some of the other essays in this volume demonstrate, there are few ethical issues more hotly debated or more difficult to resolve than the question of why and when human life has value. Consider the differences of opinion that exist over the morality of abortion, euthanasia, and suicide. To a large extent, these differences of opinion can be traced to differing views about when human life is valuable or sacrosanct. Is the life of the human fetus worthy of protection simply because it is, biologically, a member of the species *Homo sapiens?* Or because of its potential for full rationality and self-consciousness? Or should we, instead, hold that if the fetus is not actually conscious, its life can be taken fairly lightly? Or take euthanasia: again we find deeply divergent views on the value of human life. If a dying person has nothing in store except six months of unbearable pain, is there any point in denying release from life if he or she should ask for death? What of the human being in an irreversible coma, or the defective infant who will never be able to walk, or talk, or recognize another human being?

The solution of these problems is beyond the scope of this essay; yet how can we proceed to discuss the value of animal life when we are so divided about the value of human life? We shall have to bear in mind the variety of opinion about the value of human life while we examine different proposals about the value of animal life, noting at the appropriate points the implications that adopting one particular view on the value of human life might have for one's position on the value of nonhuman life.

With these preliminaries out of the way, we can now make a start on our real task: the critical examination of the more important of the many possible views that have been held, or might be held, regarding the value of nonhuman life. I shall begin with the view that all human lives, and only human lives, possess some kind of special value or worth —sanctity, some have called it—that is not possessed by any other animals, and in comparison with which any value that animal lives might possess pales into insignificance.[2]

II. IS HUMAN LIFE OF UNIQUE VALUE?

Most people think that the lives of human beings are of special value. They believe that any human life is so much more valuable than the life of any nonhuman animal that faced with a choice between saving the lowliest member of our own species or any member of any other species, they would always choose to save the human. So widespread is this belief in the supreme value of human life that the slightest hesitation over this choice is likely to be regarded as a sign of a warped moral sense. Even if the choice were between a thousand animal lives or one human life, most people would not doubt that it is right to save the human.

We can see the practical consequences of the attitude I have just described in our own daily lives. Our society takes great pains to save human life, spending millions of dollars on elaborate medical care for everyone from premature babies to geriatrics. At the same time, we kill billions of animals and birds for the quite unnecessary purpose of providing ourselves with a diet containing large portions of animal flesh. If a dog is unwanted, it may be taken to a vet or the local pound to be destroyed; no one dreams of doing the same to unwanted humans. When a woman breaks her leg, the doctor will tell her not to worry because in a few weeks the leg will be as good as new again; when an animal fractures a bone, it is quite common to kill it in order to save the expense of medical treatment.

These dramatic contrasts in our attitudes to human and nonhuman animals do not show that our attitudes are wrong, but they do indicate a need for justification. I shall consider four distinct attempts to explain why all human life possesses unique value, incomparably greater than the value possessed by nonhuman life.

§4 IS CONSCIOUSNESS UNIQUELY HUMAN?

Although most people in our society are prepared to take the lives of animals very lightly, we still think that there is more to killing a cow than there is to pulling up a plant or smashing a clock. The reason for this is not difficult to find: the clock, though it may move and emit noises, is neither alive nor capable of feeling; and the plant, while alive, is also, we presume, incapable of feeling.[3] The cow, on the other hand, is a living, feeling creature, a being with a mental life of its own, capable of experiences like pleasure and pain. To cut off the life of a being of this nature seems more serious than to destroy a plant, which lacks consciousness, or a machine, which lacks both consciousness and life.

More than 300 years ago, the French philosopher, mathematician, and scientist René Descartes startled his contemporaries by denying, in his celebrated *Discourse on Method,* that animals have minds. Animals, he said, are machines. Their movements and sounds are no more signs of consciousness than the movements and sounds of a clock; more complicated, to be sure, but this is to be expected, since clocks are machines made by humans, and animals are machines made by God. Descartes did not, of course, number humans among the animals. What distinguishes humans, he thought, is their possession of an immortal soul. It is this immortal soul, he said, that is responsible for our feelings and mental experiences.

Descartes was aware of the convenient implications of his theory about animals. It is, he wrote,

> indulgent to men—at least to those who are not given to the superstitions of Pythagoras—since it absolves them from the suspicion of crime when they eat or kill animals.[4]

By 'the superstitions of Pythagoras' Descartes meant vegetarianism, for Pythagoras is said to have abstained from the eating of animals.

If the nonhuman animals truly are incapable of feeling anything, the gulf between humans and nonhumans is very great and the striking distinction commonly made between the value of a normal human life and an animal life can easily be defended. On the other hand, Descartes's view is so flagrantly contrary to common sense that it has never gained wide acceptance (except perhaps among those pioneer experimenters for whom, in view of their wish to cut open living animals—before the days of anesthetics—it was a most convenient doctrine.)[5] Still, as philosophers we should not assume that common sense is always right. What grounds do we have for believing that animals are conscious?

We can start by asking how we know if any being, human or animal, is conscious. Take your own case. You know that you can feel because you are directly aware of your own feelings. When someone pricks you with a pin, you feel pain. Suppose, though, that you prick someone else with a pin. How do you know that he or she feels anything? You observe the person draw his or her arm away sharply, rub the spot where it has been pricked, and say "Ouch." None of these observations is a direct observation of pain, for it would be possible for a very complex doll to be wired up so that it reacted to a pinprick in precisely this manner. To that extent, Descartes was right. Indeed his arguments go further than he thought, and can be applied to humans too. A skeptical position about the consciousness of other beings is always possible. In practice, though, we do believe that other people are conscious, and we believe it on the basis of a perfectly reasonable inference from the similarity of their behavior to ours when we are in pain. The analogy is strengthened by our knowledge that other people are not robots, but are similar to us in origin and in basic anatomical features, including those anatomical features that seem to be associated with pain, pleasure, and other mental states.

When we turn to nonhuman animals, we find that within those species most nearly related to our own, the situation is fundamentally the same as it is with humans. All the mammals and birds show by their behavior that they feel pain, as clearly as humans do. If you prick a dog with a pin it will jump away, yelp, and perhaps rub the spot where it was pricked. We know that all the mammals and birds have the same basic nervous system that we have, and scientists have observed that they respond physiologically to pain in much the same way that we do. We have a bigger brain than most other animals (although dolphins, whales, and elephants have larger brains than we do), but our large brain consists mainly of a more developed cerebral cortex. The cerebral cortex is the part of the brain that is associated with thinking functions and not with feelings and emotions. Feelings and emotions are associated with a part of the brain known as the diencephalon, which evolved long before the cerebral cortex and is well developed in many species of animals, particularly mammals and birds.

The common origin of our own and other species provides a further reason for believing that they are conscious as we are. The central features of our nervous systems were already in existence when the ancestors of our own species diverged from the ancestors of other modern species. The capacity to feel enhances an animal's prospects of survival, since it leads it to avoid contact with sources of danger. It is absurd to suppose that the nervous systems of animals function in a radically different way from our own, despite their common origin, evolutionary function, and anatomical structure, and the similar forms of behavior to which they lead. Hence, if we accept that human beings are conscious, we should accept that mammals and birds, at least, are also conscious.

So far as other animals are concerned—reptiles, fish, crustaceans, molluscs, and so on—the analogy between them and us becomes weaker the further down the evolutionary scale we go. This is true of both the anatomical and the behavioral similarities. Nevertheless, in the case of vertebrate animals, at least, the analogies are sufficiently close to make it reasonable to suppose that they too possess consciousness. Even crustaceans (lobsters, crabs, prawns, and the like) have complex nervous systems, and their nerve cells are very much like our own.

Expert opinion on this matter is now virtually unanimous on the side of common sense against Descartes. The author of a recent book on pain has written:

> Every particle of factual evidence supports the contention that the higher mammalian vertebrates experience pain sensations at least as acute as our own. To say that they feel less because they are lower animals is an absurdity; it can easily be shown that many of their senses are far more acute than ours—visual acuity in certain birds, hearing in most wild animals, and touch in others; these animals depend more than we do on the sharpest possible awareness of a hostile environment.[6]

Three separate expert committees appointed by the British government to look into different areas of cruelty to animals have agreed that animals are capable of suffering not only from physical pain but also from emotions like fear, anxiety, stress, and so on.[7]

Someone might object that all this talk of similarities between humans and other animals overlooks one vital difference: Humans can talk. Hence, humans can tell us what they feel and animals cannot. This alleged difference between humans and animals is too simply stated, for many species of animals do communicate in one way or another. There is evidence suggesting that whales and dolphins are able to communicate to each other precise descriptions of dangerous objects or of tasks to be performed.[8] Chimpanzees have now shown that they are capable of learning a form of sign language widely used by deaf and dumb people. Still, for present purposes, we may let that pass and agree that most nonhuman animals cannot tell us, in so many words, that they feel pain, or anything else.[9] But so what? What is the relevance of language to something as basic as feeling pain? We should not neglect nonverbal forms of communication. We ourselves are better at conveying our emotions—for instance love, joy, fear, anger, sexual desire—by a look or an action than by words. As Charles Darwin pointed out in *The Expression of the Emotions in Man and Animals,* many of the nonverbal means by which we convey our emotions are identical with or clearly related to those used by other species. Nonverbal communication crosses the species gap and provides as good a basis for belief in the existence of emotions in the nonhuman animals as it does in the human ones.

Descartes's attempt to show that animals are machines therefore fails; and with it fails the attempt to show that human life has unique value because human life is unique in possessing consciousness. Consciousness is something that we share with other animals, and if human lives possess unique value, it cannot be in virtue of our possession of consciousness alone.

§5 MORTAL LIVES AND IMMORTAL SOULS

Descartes thought that human beings are not machines because they have immortal souls We have seen that he was wrong to deny consciousness to nonhuman animals; but what of his assumption that the possession of an immortal soul is an attribute that marks out human beings from all the other species that inhabit our planet? In assuming this, Descartes was doing no more than expressing one of the cardinal tenets of orthodox Christianity.

According to orthodox Christian beliefs, humans alone among animals are made in the image of God and possess immortal souls. Hence, humans are not merely material beings, beings of this world, as the other animals are. Humans also have a spiritual side to their nature, a side that relates them to God and the angels. Christianity sees humans as the link between the material and the spiritual worlds.

When faced with the claim that human lives are infinitely more valuable than animal lives because only humans possess an immortal soul, there are two quite different questions we must ask. The first is: What is the basis for believing that humans, and only humans, have immortal souls? The second is: Why is the life of a being with an immortal soul so much more valuable than the life of a being without one?

To go into all the issues raised by the first of these questions would take us beyond the scope of the present essay (or the present book, for that matter). The first question can in turn be divided into two more questions: Does anyone have an immortal soul? and, If some beings do have immortal souls, and others don't, how do we know which ones do? Most atheists would deny that there is such a thing as an immortal soul at all. If there is no such thing, obviously we need not go on to consider which beings possess one. Orthodox Christians, on the other hand, would point to the Scriptures as the basis for their belief that humans have immortal souls. In my view, belief in the existence of immortal souls lacks rational justification, and we should not take things on faith when they cannot be defended on rational grounds. Since I cannot take the space to defend this view here, I shall simply refer the reader who disagrees to the works of those who have written specifically on this issue.[10]

Suppose, however, that we do believe that there is such a thing as an immortal soul. Which beings possess one? The orthodox Christian view is that of all material beings, only human beings are capable of immortality. This view is, again, one that is normally defended within the assumptions of Christianity. Even within those assumptions, there have been a few voices raised against it.[11] The Old Testament says very little about immortality at all, and although the New Testament, by contrast, says a great deal about the next world, it never says whether animals have any prospect of entering it. The doctrine that animals have no immortal souls seems to have become firmly entrenched in Christianity through the teachings of the great medieval theologian and philosopher Thomas Aquinas. Aquinas took over the views of the Greek philosopher Aristotle, who had held that only the rational part of the soul could be immortal, and only humans are capable of rationality. The argument by which Aristotle linked rationality and immortality has been regarded as fallacious by most philosophers, and his claim that only humans are capable of rationality is equally dubious. Thus, today's standard Christian position that only humans have immortal souls is, at least in part, based on the unsound arguments of a non-Christian philosopher. [12]

If, notwithstanding all the grounds for doubt, we persist in believing that there are immortal souls and that human beings are the exclusive possessors of them, we must still ask: Why is the life of a being with an immortal soul so much more valuable than the life of a being without one? To most theologians, the greater value of the life of the being with the immortal soul has seemed too obvious to require explanation; yet it can seem obvious only if we forget that it is the value of the *mortal* life that is at stake. If we believe that human beings really do survive the death of their bodies, then we cannot put an end to their lives, whatever we do; it is only their lives in this world, their lives as material beings, that we can end. Hence, the question at issue in any discussion of the wrongness of killing humans must be the wrongness of ending the life of a human being in this world. But why should the wrongness of killing a being in this world be increased by the fact that the being will live forever in another world? To put the matter another way: If we compare the value of the lives in this world of two different beings, one human and the other nonhuman, is it not a little odd to say that the life of the human being in this world is far more valuable than the life of the nonhuman in this world because the human's life in this world is only an infinitely small fraction of its entire existence, whereas the nonhuman's life in this world is the entirety of its existence? Might we not, with at least equal plausibility, draw exactly the opposite conclusion?[13]

What probably did so impress the early Christians about killing a being with an immortal soul was the idea that in so doing one consigned the person to his or her eternal fate. The early Christians had a particularly vivid appreciation of what this meant. They believed that to kill a person at a particular moment, when he or she might have committed a sin and not yet repented, could mean roasting in hell forever, instead of the eternity of heavenly bliss that might have been in store had he or she lived a little longer and died in a state of grace. Given these beliefs, it is understandable that the killing of a human being should have been regarded with much greater abhorrence than the killing of an animal. Nonetheless, this attitude is not entirely logical either, since for every murder that sends to hell an unrepentant sinner who would otherwise have repented and gone to heaven, there is presumably another murder that is responsible for adding one member to the heavenly choir who, while innocent at the time of death, would have sinned mortally had he or she lived to have the chance. So even this argument for respecting human life fails.

This last failure exhausts the line of argument that seeks to defend the idea of the unique value of human life by reference to immortal souls. We have not, however, exhausted Christian arguments for the special sanctity of human life, for there is another, quite distinct, line of argument that will be examined in the following section.

§6 GOD'S RIGHTS AND HUMANITY'S DOMINION

More than 2,300 years ago, the great Greek philosopher Plato wrote a work known as the *Phaedo.* Like Plato's other writings, the *Phaedo* is in dialogue form. Socrates is represented as one of the participants in the dialogue, and he is the one through whom Plato expresses his own views. At one point in the dialogue Socrates is asked by Cebes, another participant in the discussion, to explain his belief that suicide is wrong. Socrates replies that he believes that human beings are "chattels" of the gods, and then asks Cebes:

> If one of your own chattels, an ox or an ass, for example, took the liberty of putting itself out of the way when you had given no intimation of your wish that it should die, would you not be angry with it, and would you not punish it if you could?[14]

This argument against suicide is significant for our enquiry, because it implies that taking human life (whether one's own or that of another) is quite different from taking the life of one's ox or ass. According to Socrates, to kill a human is to risk the wrath of the gods, but to kill an animal is merely to risk the wrath of the animal's owner. Consequently, if you own the animal yourself, you kill it or not as you please.

Plato was not, of course, a Christian, but a doctrine very similar to his has repeatedly been expressed by Christian writers. No Roman Catholic philosopher has had greater influence on the thinking of the Church than Thomas Aquinas, and Aquinas held that taking a human life is a sin against God, in the same way that killing a slave would be a sin against the master to whom the slave belonged.[15] On this view, God is the master of us all, and to kill a human being is to usurp His right to decide when we shall live and when we shall die. Many Protestant philosophers have taken a similar view, foremost among them Immanuel Kant. Kant uses a different metaphor but to the same end: "Human beings are sentinels on earth and may not leave their posts until relieved by another beneficent hand." The suicide, Kant says, "arrives in the other world as one who has deserted his post; he must be looked upon as a rebel against God."[16] This kind of position retains its influence to the present day. When we hear those who advocate the legalization of euthanasia being accused of seeking to "play God," we are hearing the echoes of Plato, Aquinas, and Kant.

What about nonhuman animals? Are not pigs and chickens God's creatures too? Certainly the Bible states that God created all of the animals, not just humans, and so one might think that to kill any animal is to destory God's property, and thus to "play God." The catch, so far as animals are concerned, is to be found in the Biblical story of the Creation, where it is said that, after creating man and woman,

> God blessed them, and God said to them, 'Be fruitful and multiply, and fill the earth and subdue it; and have dominion over the fish of the sea and over the birds of the air and over every living thing that moves upon the earth.'

After the flood, God made the meaning of his gift of dominion more explicit still:

> And God blessed Noah and his sons, and said to them, 'Be fruitful and multiply, and fill the earth. The fear of you and the dread of you shall be upon every beast of the earth and upon every bird of the air, upon everything that creeps on the ground and all the fish of the sea; into your hand are they delivered. Every moving thing that lives shall be food for you; and as I gave you the green plants, I give you everything.'[17]

These verses have been understood by writers in the Judeo-Christian tradition to mean that God granted His rights over the nonhuman animals to humans. Humans are therefore in the same position vis-à-vis the "lower" animals as God is to humans. Augustine, for instance, refers to the "most just ordinance of the Creator" according to which "both their life and their death are subject to our use."[18] Aquinas quotes this opinion and concurs with it, adding that the very purpose for which animals exist is to serve human beings. He even goes beyond Augustine when he says: "It matters not how man behaves to animals, because God has subjected all things to man's power . . . and it is in this sense that the Apostle says that God has no care for oxen, because God does not ask of man what he does with oxen or other animals."[19]

We may call this view the *Dominion Theory.* It is not so much a view about the *value* of animal life as about the *right* of humans to take animal life when it suits them to do so. This distinction is important and will crop up again later in this essay. We can understand the difference between a view about the right to take life and a view about the value of life if we think for a moment about, for instance, the right that a soldier has—or is generally thought to have—to kill an enemy soldier in wartime. We may believe that soldiers have this right without believing that the value of the life taken will always be less than the value of the life of the soldier who takes it.

So we can distinguish between saying that human beings have a right to take the lives of animals and saying that the lives of human beings are more valuable than the lives of animals. Strictly speaking, the Dominion Theory is a theory about the right to kill and not a theory about the value of life. Nevertheless, we must remember that the Dominion Theory is a theory within the Judeo-Christian tradition, and it is a central tenet of that tradition that God is all-knowing and all-good. Hence, God would not have given humans the right to kill animals without good reason, and yet He must have known that humans do not need to kill animals for food to survive. It would therefore appear to be an implication of the Dominion Theory, in the Judeo-Christian context, that animal life is of little or no value—for why else would God have given humans dominion over the other animals and told us that we may kill them for food?

Some of the writers who espouse the Dominion Theory have realized that it does not provide a complete explanation of the differing status of humans and animals and have therefore offered reasons why God should be content to hand over the animals to human beings. Aquinas, for instance, adopts an argument from Aristotle to the effect that only reason or intellect is of intrinsic value, and God has made all those things whose nature is nonintellectual for the sake of those beings with intellectual natures. Animals, Aquinas holds, have no intellectual nature and therefore exist only for the sake of humans.[20] To prevent our discussion from becoming too complicated, however, we shall postpone discussion of this view, because it is logically distinct from the Dominion Theory. It is very close to the view of Immanuel Kant, and we shall discuss it when we come to consider his position.

Meanwhile, what can we say about the Dominion Theory itself?

Obviously it rests on a number of questionable beliefs. To take the Dominion Theory seriously we must believe: that God exists; that He has the right to decide which of His creatures shall live or die; that He has the right to delegate this right to others; and that He did delegate this right to human beings.

There are many who do take the Bible as authoritative, and within the limits of this assumption, the Dominion Theory is well founded. One can, of course, accept the Biblical account without going to quite the lengths to which Aquinas goes when he claims that because God has granted us dominion over the animals, it doesn't matter how we behave to them. In opposition to this interpretation of the Dominion Theory, which makes humans despots over other animals, one could advance the interpretation that God's gift of dominion puts us in the position of stewards, that is, guardians of the property of another, who must take care to manage it well and keep it in good condition.[21] Adopting this "stewardship" interpretation of the Dominion Theory would make a significant difference to the way in which we are entitled to treat animals, particularly in respect of human activities that threaten to exterminate entire species of animals. It would not, however, make a fundamental difference to the principal implication of the theory, which is that we are entitled to kill individual animals if we wish to do so.

My own view is that belief in the existence of God cannot be justified. There is a dearth of convincing argument or evidence for the existence of a being who corresponds to the Judeo-Christian conception of God, and there are several reasons, of which the most important stems from the existence of so much unnecessary suffering and misery in the world, for believing that the universe is not under the control of an all-powerful and all-good God.[22] Whether I am right about this is, like the issue of immortality, a question for philosophy of religion rather than for ethics, and so I shall not elaborate here; but if I am right, the Biblical account of the Creation must be rejected, and the Dominion Theory with it. We may then regard the Dominion Theory as an attempt to justify human attitudes and practices towards animals, including the killing of animals for food—a practice that was, no doubt, in existence long before *Genesis* was written.

§7 HUMAN ENDS AND ANIMAL MEANS

If animals are capable of experiencing pleasure and pain as humans are, and if we reject the religious grounds for treating human life differently from animal life, what else can be said in favor of the sharp distinction we commonly make between ourselves and all other species? A lot of things have been said, although it is not clear that any of them helps very much.

Two hundred years ago the influential German philosopher Immanuel Kant lectured to his students as follows:

Animals are not self-conscious and are there merely as a means to an end. That end is man. We can ask, 'Why do animals exist?' But to ask, 'Why does man exist?' is a meaningless question. Our duties towards animals are merely indirect duties towards humanity ... If a man shoots his dog because the animal is no longer capable of service, he does not fail in his duty to the dog, for the dog cannot judge, but his act is inhuman and damages in himself that humanity which it is his duty to show towards mankind.[23]

The most distinctively Kantian idea in this passage is the idea that human beings are "ends in themselves." As one contemporary philosopher has explained this, it amounts to saying, "Everything other than a person can only have value *for* a person ... Thus of everything without exception it will be true to say: if x is valuable and not a person, then x will have value for some individual other than itself."[24] Other philosophers have tried to make similar points in different words. They talk of "the intrinsic dignity of the human individual"[25] or the "intrinsic worth of all men."[26]

This kind of rhetoric is popular and meets with little opposition. After all, why should we not attribute "intrinsic dignity" or "intrinsic worth" to ourselves? Why should we not say that we are the only things in the universe that have intrinsic value? Our fellow human beings are unlikely to reject the accolades we so generously bestow upon them, and the other species to whom we deny the honor are unable to object. Indeed, if we think only of human beings it can be very liberal, very progressive, to talk of the dignity and worth of all humans. In so doing we implicitly condemn slavery, racism, and— if we eliminate the sexist references to the "intrinsic worth of all *men*"—the oppression of women. It is only when we recall that human beings are no more than one among the many species of animals living on this planet that we may realize that in elevating our own species we are at the same time degrading all other species.

Once we ask *why* it should be that all humans—including infants, mental defectives, criminal psychopaths, and tyrants like Adolf Hitler and Idi Amin—have some kind of dignity or worth that no whale, gorilla, cow, or dog can ever achieve, we can see that the rhetoric of "human dignity" does not tell us much. More argument is needed to justify the claim that all and only humans have some special kind of dignity or worth, or are ends in themselves. On the face of it, after all, shouldn't the mere fact that a being can experience pleasure or pain be sufficient to make it an "end in itself"? Isn't the experience of pleasure good in itself, and the experience of pain bad in itself? What this question really amounts to is: If, while everything else remained the same, we were able to increase the amount of pleasure experienced in the universe, or decrease the amount of pain experienced in the world, wouldn't both of these be improvements, things that make the world a better place? And isn't the answer to this question affirmative, irrespective of whether the beings whose pleasure is enhanced and whose pain is diminished are humans, gnus, or guinea pigs?

§8 SPECIESISM

It is important to understand that the *mere* fact that all human beings are members of our species, while other animals are not, does not provide a satisfactory justification for the view that all humans have greater moral worth than other animals. It is this view that I refer to as "speciesism" in my book *Animal Liberation,* and that is the main target of the philosophical arguments of that book. I use the term 'speciesism' to make the analogy between this attitude of preference for members of our own species, simply because they are members of our own species, and better-known attitudes like racism (preference for members of one's own race, simply because they are members of one's own race) and sexism (preference for members of one's own sex, simply because they are members of one's own sex).[27] Once the parallel between these attitudes has been recognized, it is easy to see why we cannot say that membership in our species alone is enough to give a being special worth. If we are prepared to say that a being has less worth because it is not a member of our own species, how can we object to the racist who says that a being has less worth if it is not a member of his race? If species is a morally significant criterion, why isn't race?

Someone might reply that the differences between species are more significant than the differences between races and sexes. After all, human beings can reason about abstract matters, use complex languages, plan for events in the distant future, make moral judgments, and so on. Perhaps this is what Kant had in mind when, in saying that animals are not ends, he asserted that they are not self-conscious, and when, in saying that a man does not fail in his duty to his dog if he shoots it when it can no longer serve him, he added that "the dog cannot judge." Nonhuman animals, it is commonly supposed, are not self-conscious and cannot judge, reason abstractly, use complex languages, plan for the future, etc. On the other hand, the differences that exist between humans and other animals in respect of these capacities do not exist between the different races and sexes of human beings.

The facts alleged by those who put forward this line of objection to the parallel between speciesism and racism may hold true when we compare normal adult humans with members of other species (though as we shall see, even this is not entirely true), but they clearly are not true of *all* human beings. Infants and mentally defective human beings are often not capable of abstract reasoning, using language, planning for the future, or judging morally. If, therefore, we think it is one of these capacities, or some combination of them, that gives human beings a worth or moral status that other animals do not have, we cannot hold that all human beings without restriction have this worth. Infants will have it only potentially, and some mental defectives whose brains have been irreparably damaged will not have it at all.

The view that beings with certain capacities, such as self-consciousness, the use of reason, or the capacity to make moral judgments, are of special worth is not a form of speciesism, for it is not the view that human beings have special worth *simply because* they are members of our species. It may be true that most human beings possess these capacities and most other animals do not, but the boundary of the class of specially worthy beings cannot be expected to run precisely along the boundary of our species. It is beyond dispute that there are nonhuman animals who are superior in terms of all mental capacities to some beings who are, in the biological sense, human. An adult chimpanzee, for instance, can solve problems that are beyond the reasoning capacity of most three-year-old children, and despite the special aptitude for language that humans are widely believed to have, chimpanzees have acquired language skills (using the sign language of the deaf and dumb) that are roughly equivalent to those of two-year-old human children. Many other species—baboons, dogs, dolphins, pigs, and others—are equally clearly superior in these respects to human infants under, say, one year old. Even if we decide that their potential for a higher level of rationality gives infants special value, we are still faced with the fact that some mental defectives are at the same mental level as human infants and have no potential to reach a higher level.

Thus, if we select any mental capacities as the basis of special worth, the class of special worthy beings will diverge considerably from the class of human beings. Those who attempt to eliminate this divergency by forging some logical link between these two classes will make themselves liable to the charge of speciesism. The alternative is to abandon belief that human life has unique value.

I think this widely accepted Western attitude does have to be abandoned. We have considered a number of attempts to defend it, and none of them has stood up to critical scrutiny. The accepted view must give ground. It is not yet clear, however, how much ground it has to give. The smallest possible modification would seem to be a shift from the idea that all *human* lives have unique value to the idea that it is the lives of *persons* that have unique value, where 'person' is defined in some manner not quite equivalent to 'human being'. It is this position that we shall examine next.

III. THE VALUE OF A PERSON'S LIFE

§9 WHAT IS A PERSON?

I have suggested that we may modify the idea that the lives of all humans have special value by substituting 'persons' for 'humans'. This may lead to some puzzlement, for 'person' and 'human being' are often used as if they meant the same thing. This usage masks a significant distinction. That the terms are not really equivalent can be seen from the fact that religious believers may describe God as a Divine

Person without implying that He is a human being. According to the *Oxford English Dictionary,* one of the current meanings of the word 'person' is "a self-conscious or rational being." It is in something like this sense that the word is often used by philosophers, and it will be used in roughly this sense—the details will be discussed shortly—in the present essay.

Some writers have used the word 'human' to describe the kind of being I shall refer to as a person. For instance, Joseph Fletcher, an eminent Protestant theologian and ethicist, includes the following in a list of "Indicators of Humanhood": minimal intelligence, self-aware-ness, self-control, a sense of the future, a sense of the past, the capacity to relate to others, concern for others, communication, and curiosity.[28] There is no great harm in using the word 'human' in this way, as long as it is clearly understood that 'human' is then not equivalent to 'mem-ber of the species *Homo sapiens*'. They are obviously not equivalent because a newborn infant, an accident victim whose brain has been so damaged that he is in an irreversible coma, and an old man in a state of advanced senility are all members of the species *Homo sapiens,* though none of them possesses all of Fletcher's "indicators," and the road-accident victim, at least, possesses none of them.

So there are three terms that people are liable to confuse: 'person', 'human being', and 'member of the species *Homo sapiens*'. The im-portant philosophical point is that the first and third of these be kept distinct. As for the middle term, 'human', it could be allowed to slop around between the other two, but it is more convenient to reject Fletcher's usage and treat 'human' as equivalent to 'member of the species *Homo sapiens*', since the former expression is so much briefer than the latter. We can then use the word 'person' to refer to the class of being for which Fletcher was suggesting indicators.

What, then, is it to be a person? What characteristics does a being have to possess to be a person? Let us start with the dictionary defini-tion. What is it to be self-conscious? What is it to be rational? The concepts themselves need further analysis if they are to be made clear.

When philosophers refer to 'self-consciousness' they are not using the term in the popular sense in which I may say that I felt self-conscious when I realized that I was the only person at the State Banquet not wearing a tie. 'Self-awareness' might be a better way of expressing what philosophers mean by 'self-consciousness'. A being is self-conscious if it is aware of itself as an entity, distinct from other entities in the world. We might add the requirement that the being be aware that it exists over a period of time, that it has a past and a future; for to be aware of oneself as an entity it may well be necessary to be aware of oneself as existing over some period of time, however brief. To be aware of oneself only in the instantaneous present is hardly to be aware of oneself as an entity at all, since an entity is something that exists over a period of time.[29]

Is the fact that a being is self-conscious in this sense enough to establish that the being is a person? Are there other characteristics one should add, like rationality, or the ability to feel pleasure or pain? Rationality is probably already included in our conception of self-consciousness, since a being would not attain self-consciousness without possessing at least a minimally rational understanding of the world. The capacity to feel pleasure and pain is something that we might be able to separate from self-consciousness in theory, but in the world as we know it a self-conscious being will always be a being capable of feeling pleasure and pain—that is, if we interpret this capacity broadly enough so as to include any form of positive feeling, such as approval or satisfaction as a form of pleasure, and any negative feeling, such as disapproval or dissatisfaction, as a form of pain. Hence, our definition is roughly adequate as it stands.

§10 UTILITARIANISM AND THE VALUE OF A PERSON'S LIFE

Let us, for simplicity's sake, define a "person" as a self-conscious being; and let us say that by 'self-conscious being' we mean a being aware of itself as a distinct entity, existing over time, with a past and a future. We can then ask: Is the life of a person especially valuable?

Let us put the question a little differently: Why might one think that taking the life of a person is more serious than taking the life of some other kind of being? One important line of argument runs as follows. If a being is aware of itself as a distinct entity, with a past and a future, it is capable of having desires about its own future. For example, a professor of philosophy may hope to write a book demonstrating the objective nature of ethics; a student may look forward to graduating; a child may want to go for a ride in an airplane. To take the life of any of these people, without their consent, is to thwart the victim's desires for the future, in a way that killing a snail or a day-old infant presumably does not.

This does not mean, of course, that when a person is killed, the dead person's desires are thwarted in the ordinary sense in which when I am hiking through dry country my desire for water is thwarted when I discover a hole in my water bottle. In this case, I have a desire that I cannot fulfill, and I feel frustration and discomfort because of the continuing and unsatisfied desire for water. When a person is killed, the desires he or she has for the future do not continue after death, and he or she does not suffer from their nonfulfillment. But does this mean that preventing the fulfillment of these desires does not matter?

Classical utilitarianism, as expounded by the founding father of utilitarianism, Jeremy Bentham, and refined by later philosophers like John Stuart Mill and Henry Sidgwick, judges actions by their tendency to maximize pleasure or happiness and minimize pain or unhappiness. Terms like 'pleasure' and 'happiness' are a little vague, but it is clear that they refer to something that is experienced, or felt—in other words, to states of consciousness. According to classical utilitarianism, therefore, there is no direct significance in the fact that a person's desires for the future go unfulfilled when he or she is killed. If death is instantaneous, whether he or she has any desires for the future makes no difference to the amount of pleasure or pain experienced. Thus for the classical utilitarian, the status of 'person' is not *directly* relevant to the wrongness of killing.

Indirectly, however, personhood may be important for the classical utilitarian. Its importance arises in the following manner. If I am a person, I have a conception of myself having a future. If I am also mortal, I am likely to realize that my future existence is liable to be cut short. If I think that this is likely to happen at any moment, my present existence will probably be less enjoyable than if I do not think it is likely to happen for some time. If I learn that people like myself are often the victims of unprovoked, murderous attacks, I will worry about the prospect of being killed; if I learn that people like myself are very rarely killed, I will worry less. Hence, the classical utilitarian can defend a prohibition on killing persons on the indirect ground that it will increase the happiness of people who would otherwise worry that they might be killed. I call this an *indirect* ground because it does not refer to any direct wrong done to the person killed, but rather to a consequence of it for other people. There is, of course, something odd about objecting to murder not because of the wrong done to the victim but because of the effect on others. Only an exceptionally tough-minded classical utilitarian will be prepared to stomach this oddness. For our present purposes, however, the main point is that this indirect ground does provide a reason for taking the killing of a person, under certain conditions, more seriously than the killing of a being that is not a person. If a being is incapable of conceiving of itself as existing over time, we need not take into account the possibility of its worrying about the prospect of its future existence being cut short. It can't worry about this, for it lacks the necessary understanding of itself.

I said that the indirect classical utilitarian reason for taking the killing of a person more seriously than the killing of a nonperson holds "under certain conditions." These conditions are that the killing of the person may become known to other persons, who derive from this knowledge a more gloomy estimate of their own chances of living to a ripe old age. It is of course possible that a person could be killed under other conditions, in which case this classical utilitarian reason against killing would not apply.

That is, I think, the gist of what the classical utilitarians would say about the distinction between killing a person and killing some other type of being (although we shall return to classical utilitarianism in the next section). There is, however, another version of utilitarianism that may give more weight to the distinction. This other version of utilitarianism judges actions not by their tendency to maximize pleasure or minimize pain but by the extent to which they are in accord with the preferences of any beings who have preferences about the action or its consequences. This version of utilitarianism is sometimes known as "economic utilitarianism," because it is the form of utilitarianism used by economists who work in the area known as "welfare economics"; but a more accurate name would be "preference utilitarianism."

According to preference utilitarianism, an action contrary to the preference of any being is, unless this preference is outweighed by stronger contrary preferences, wrong. Killing a person who prefers to continue living is therefore wrong, other things being equal. Unlike classical utilitarianism, preference utilitarianism makes killing a direct wrong done to the person killed, because it is an act contrary to his or her preferences. That the victim is not around after the act to lament the fact that his or her preferences have been disregarded is irrelevant.

To the preference utilitarian, taking the life of a person will normally be worse than taking the life of some other being, since a being that cannot see itself as a distinct entity with a possible future existence cannot have a preference about its own future existence. This is not to deny that such a being might struggle against a situation in which its life is in danger, as a fish struggles to get free of the barbed hook in its mouth; but this indicates no more than a preference for the cessation of a state of affairs that is perceived as painful or threatening. Struggle against danger and pain does not suggest that the fish is capable of preferring its own future existence to nonexistence. The struggle of a fish on a hook suggests a reason for not killing fish by that method, but does not suggest a preference-utilitarian reason against killing fish by some other method that kills them instantly.

Although preference utilitarianism does provide a direct reason for not killing people, some may find the reason—even when coupled with the important indirect reasons that any form of utilitarianism will take into account—is not sufficiently stringent. Even for preference utilitarianism, the wrong done to the person killed is merely one factor to be taken into account, and the preference of the victim could sometimes be outweighed by the preferences of others. We commonly feel that the prohibition on killing people is more absolute than this kind of utilitarian calculation implies. A person's life, it is often said, is something to which he or she has a *right*, and rights are not to be traded off against the preferences or pleasures of others.

I am not myself convinced that the notion of a moral right is a helpful or meaningful one, except when it is used as a shorthand way of referring to more fundamental moral considerations. Nevertheless, since the idea that we have a "right to life" is a popular one, it is worth asking whether there are grounds for attributing a right to life to persons, as distinct from other living beings.

§11 DO PERSONS HAVE A RIGHT TO LIFE?

Michael Tooley, a contemporary American philosopher, has argued that the only beings who have a right to life are those who can conceive of themselves as distinct entities existing over time—in other words, persons, as we have used the term. His argument—which he originally wrote as a contribution to the abortion debate—is based on the claim that there is a conceptual connection between the desires a being is capable of having and the rights that the being can be said to have. As Tooley puts it:

> The basic intuition is that a right is something that can be violated and that, in general, to violate an individual's right to something is to frustrate the corresponding desire. Suppose, for example, that you own a car. Then I am under a *prima facie* obligation not to take it from you. However, the obligation is not unconditional: it depends in part upon the existence of a corresponding desire in you. If you do not care whether I take your car, then I generally do not violate your right by doing so.[30]

Tooley admits that it is difficult to formulate the connections between rights and desires precisely, because there are problem cases like people who are asleep or temporarily unconscious. We do not want to say that such people have no rights because they have, at that moment, no desires. Nevertheless, Tooley holds, the possession of a right must in some way be linked with, if not actual desires, at least the capacity to have the relevant desires.

The next step is to apply this view about rights to the case of the right to life. To put the matter as simply as possible—more simply than Tooley himself does and no doubt *too* simply—if the right to life is the right to continue existing as a distinct entity, then the desire relevant to possessing a right to life is the desire to continue existing as a distinct entity. But only a being that is capable of conceiving itself as a distinct entity existing over time—that is, only a person—could have this desire. Therefore, only a person could have a right to life.

This argument is incomplete. The connection between having a right and having a capacity to desire whatever is the subject of the right should be clarified and defended. There are objections that need to be considered. For example, Tooley has admitted that a fetus or an animal like a newborn kitten, which does not, on his account, have a right to life because it is not capable of envisaging a future for itself, may nonetheless have a right not to be tortured, because it can have a rudimentary desire that a painful sensation cease. Very well; but then, as one critic has asked, why could not a fetus or a newborn kitten also have a rudimentary desire that some pleasant sensation continue? If it can, then could one not argue that there is a right analogous to the right not to be tortured, namely the right to experience pleasure? And is not this right violated by being killed?[31]

Notwithstanding this objection, there may be something in the view that the capacity to envisage one's own future is a necessary condition for possession of a right to life. Tooley's argument does at least merit further thought and discussion.

§12 WHICH ANIMALS ARE PEOPLE?

We have seen that if we accept either preference utilitarianism or Tooley's view of rights, it becomes important to know whether a being is a person—that is, whether it has the capacity to be aware of itself as a distinct entity existing over time. To establish the relevance of these views to the treatment of animals we must therefore ask: Are any nonhuman animals persons?

This question is more difficult than it may appear at first glance. We do not normally think of animals as people, but this may be because of the confusion between the terms 'person' and 'human being', which I have already discussed. It does sound a little odd to refer to, say, a chimpanzee as a person. This oddness, however, may be no more than a linguistic echo of an unjustifiable prejudice. In any case, the real issue is whether any animals, other than human beings, are capable of conceiving themselves as distinct entities existing over time.

That some animals, at least, are self-conscious appears to have been shown by recent experiments in teaching American Sign Language to apes. The ancient dream of communicating with another species was realized when two American scientists, Allen and Beatrice Gardner, guessed that the failure of previous attempts to teach chimpanzees to talk was due not to the chimpanzees' lacking the intelligence required for using language but to their lacking the vocal equipment needed to reproduce the sounds of human language. The Gardners therefore decided to treat a young chimpanzee as if she were a human baby without vocal cords. They communicated with her, and with each other when in her presence, by using American Sign Language, a language widely used by deaf and dumb people.

The technique was a striking success. The chimpanzee, whom they called Washoe, now understands about 350 different signs and is able to use about 150 of them correctly. She also puts signs together to form simple sentences. As for self-consciousness, Washoe does not hesitate, when shown her own image in a mirror and asked, "Who is that?" to reply, "Me, Washoe." She also uses signs expressing future intentions.[32]

Suppose that on the basis of such evidence we accept that Washoe and the other apes who have now been taught to use sign language are self-conscious. Are they exceptional among all the nonhuman animals in this respect, precisely because they can use language? Or is it merely that language enables these animals to demonstrate to us a characteristic that they, and other animals, possessed all along?

Some philosophers have argued that for a being to think, it must be able to formulate its thoughts in words. The contemporary English philosopher Stuart Hampshire, for example, has written:

> The difference here between a human being and an animal lies in the possibility of the human being expressing his intention and putting into words his intention to do so-and-so, for his own benefit or for the benefit of others. The difference is not merely that an animal in fact has no means of communicating, or of recording for itself, its intention, with the effect that no one can ever know what the intention was. It is a stronger difference, which is more correctly expressed as the senselessness of attributing intentions to an animal which has not the means to reflect upon, and to announce to itself or to others, its own future behavior . . . It would be senseless to attribute to an animal a memory that distinguished the order of events in the past, and it would be senseless to attribute to it an expectation of an order of events in the future. It does not have the concepts of order, or any concepts at all.[33]

If Hampshire is right, no being without language can be a person. This applies, presumably, to young humans as well as to animals. Only those animals who can use a language could be persons. Apart from chimpanzees and gorillas who have been taught to use sign language, the other most likely group would be whales and dolphins, for there is some evidence that their buzzes and squeaks constitute a sophisticated form of communication that may one day be recognized as language.[34] With these few exceptions, however, the claim that language is necessary for reflective thought consigns the nonhuman animals to the level of conscious, but not self-aware, existence. But is this claim sound? I do not believe that it is. Hampshire's defense of it contains more assertion than argument, and in this respect he is representative of others who have advanced the same view. Attempts to decide a question of this nature by armchair philosophizing should be regarded with a certain degree of suspicion.

There is nothing altogether inconceivable about a being possessing the capacity for conceptual thought without having a language and there are instances of animal behavior that are difficult to explain except under the assumption that the animals are thinking conceptually. In one experiment, for instance, chimpanzees were taught to select the middle object from a row of objects. Even when the objects were not spaced regularly, the chimpanzees could pick out the middle object from a row of up to eleven objects. The most natural way to explain this is to say that the apes had grasped the concept of the "middle object." It is worth noting that many three- and four-year-old children, though accomplished language users, cannot perform this task.[35]

Nor is it only in laboratory experiments that the behavior of animals points to the conclusion that they possess both memory of the past and expectations about the future, and that their behavior is intentional. Consider Jane Goodall's description of how a young wild chimpanzee she had named Figan secured for itself one of the bananas that Goodall, to bring the animals closer to her observation post, had hidden in a tree:

> One day, sometime after the group had been fed, Figan spotted a banana that had been overlooked—but Goliath [an adult male ranking above Figan in the group's hierarchy] was resting directly underneath it. After no more than a quick glance from the fruit to Goliath, Figan moved away and sat on the other side of the tent so that he could no longer see the fruit. Fifteen minutes later, when Goliath got up and left, Figan without a moment's hesitation went over and collected the banana. Quite obviously he had sized up the whole situation: if he had climbed for the fruit earlier, Goliath would almost certainly have snatched it away. If he had remained close to the banana, he would probably have looked at it from time to time. Chimps are very quick to notice and interpret the eye movements of their fellows, and Goliath would possibly, therefore, have seen the fruit himself. And so Figan had not only refrained from instantly gratifying his desire but had also gone away so that he could not 'give the game away' by looking at the banana.[36]

Goodall's description of this episode does, of course, attribute to Figan a complex set of intentions, including the intention to avoid "giving the game away" and the intention to obtain the banana after Goliath's departure. It also attributes to Figan an "expectation of an order of events in the future," namely the expectation that Goliath would move away, that the banana would still be there, and that he, Figan, would then go and get it. Yet there seems nothing at all "senseless" about these attributions, despite the fact that Figan cannot put his intentions or expectations into words.

There are other incidents, equally revealing of complex intentions, in Goodall's book, and many more in the scientific literature on animal behavior. The cumulative effect is to lead us to the conclusion that nonhuman animals do act intentionally and with expectations about the future. These observations are not limited to chimpanzees, nor are they all derived from efforts to obtain food.[37]

Finally, what of self-consciousness? I do not think that anything more is required as evidence for the existence of self-consciousness than the evidence already offered in support of the existence of intentional behavior. If an animal can devise a careful plan for obtaining a banana, not now but at some future time, and can take precautions against his own propensity to give away the object of the plan, that animal seems to be aware of himself as a distinct entity existing over time.

So some nonhuman animals are persons, as we have defined the term. If Tooley's argument about the right to life is sound, these animals have a serious right to life, of the same kind as the right to life of an adult human. We cannot know which animals possess this right until many other species have been observed with the same kind of care and patience that Jane Goodall gave to her study of chimpanzees in the Gombe Stream area of Tanzania; but there is no reason to suppose that the chimpanzee is the only nonhuman animal with a right to life.

We can see, then, that if we accept the view that *persons* have a right to life that other beings do not have, we have come a long way from the position that all and only human beings have a right to life. In contrast to this latter view we are now saying that many nonhuman animals have the same kind of right to life that normal humans have; and we are also saying that there are some human beings—newborn infants and gross mental defectives—who do not have this kind of right to life.

Some may regard the inclusion of infants in this category along with gross mental defectives as a mistake. Although newborn infants may not possess the actual capacity to conceive of themselves as entities existing over time, they do have the potential to conceive of themselves in this way, given normal development. In view of this potential, it may be suggested, infants should be regarded as having the same right to life as adult persons.

This issue is the same as that raised by the potential of the fetus in the debate about abortion; since it is more central to the issue of abortion than to the question of the treatment of animals, and is discussed by Joel Feinberg in his essay on abortion in this volume, I shall not discuss it here. My own view is that the mere potential to possess a capacity does not necessarily carry with it the rights that arise from actual possession of the capacity. For our purposes, however, it does not matter too much whether the reader accepts this conclusion. Even readers who do not accept it have to recognize that there are still some humans—those with irreparable gross mental defects—who are not persons and who do not have the same right to life that persons, including nonhuman persons, have, if it is true that all and only persons have this right.

Tooley's argument thus has radical consequences for the way we may treat animals. We shall consider these consequences more fully below (§18).

IV. ANIMAL LIFE

Although the arguments put forward in the preceding section would, if accepted, extend beyond our own species the respect for life that we now accord only to humans, it is doubtful that we have gone far enough. The sphere within which life is to be protected includes only the "higher" animals, possibly only mammals who, like ourselves, have the capacity to see themselves as distinct entities existing over time. Perhaps a lizard or a fish is not capable of seeing itself in this way. Perhaps a chicken is not either. Some may think that the less intelligent mammals, like rabbits and mice, are not self-conscious. Yet as we saw earlier, birds and mammals are, almost certainly, capable of experiencing pleasure or pain, and the same is very likely true of reptiles and fish. All these animals possess a central nervous system, as we do, and the behavior of these animals, in situations in which we might expect them to be suffering pain, parallels our own pain behavior in many respects. There may therefore be animals who are *conscious* and capable of feeling but not *self-conscious* or capable of conceiving themselves as distinct entities existing over time. We must now consider what value the lives of these animals have, and whether even though they are not persons, they might not have some right to life.

§13 A CRITIQUE OF REGAN'S ARGUMENT FOR EXTENDING THE RIGHT TO LIFE TO ANIMALS

One argument for attributing a right to life to all conscious living things can be derived from the implications that the arguments already discussed have for mentally defective human beings. We have seen that permanent mental defectives cannot be said to have a right to life merely because they are human beings. This would be speciesism. Nor can they be said to have a right to life because they are persons. Many of them are not persons. Therefore, if mental defectives are to have a right to life at all, it must be grounded on something else. What could this something else be? Tom Regan has suggested that the most plausible candidate is the fact that all humans, even mental defectives—or at least those who are conscious—have positive interests in the shape of desires, goals, or preferences, the satisfaction of which provides them with intrinsically valuable experiences. The intrinsic value brought into the life of any one human being by the satisfaction of his or her desires is, Regan claims, "just as good, judged in itself" as the intrinsic value brought into the life of any other human being by the satisfaction of that human being's desires. Since one can seek to satisfy one's desires only if one is still alive, it is possible to draw from this argument the conclusion that there is value in the life of any being that has desires, and that can derive some valuable experience from their satisfaction. One could also argue, on this basis, that any such being has a right to be left alive to seek to satisfy its desires, and hence has a right to life. Finally Regan points out that while this argument for a right to life does succeed in encompassing all human beings, it also encompasses all those nonhuman animals who are capable of having desires and seeking to satisfy them.[38]

One small qualification needs to be made to Regan's argument. It does not quite cover all human beings. There are some human beings who are permanently unconscious and therefore have no desires. Regan's argument does not suggest that these humans have a right to life. Perhaps, though, this is an advantage rather than a drawback—for what point is there in keeping alive a human being who does not have, and never again will have, any conscious experiences? From the point of view of the permanently unconscious being, this state would appear to be indistinguishable from death.[39]

Similarly, Regan's argument may not cover all animals. There is no reason to believe that the boundary between animals and plants (which is, in scientific terms, a very fine line) corresponds exactly to the boundary between conscious and nonconscious life. It is reasonable to believe that some relatively simple forms of animal life have no desires or conscious preferences. Perhaps animals like oysters and mussels fall into this category—or if they don't, there are still more simple animals, like the amoeba, that probably do. In any case, we can consider Regan's argument without knowing precisely to which animals it applies. If Regan's argument is sound, we can say this: Wherever the boundary of consciousness is to be found, there too is the boundary of the right to life.

But *is* Regan's argument sound? It seems to me that its fundamental weakness is the extent to which the argument relies on the assumption that all human beings—including those with severe mental defects—have an equal right to life. Regan is, of course, quite open about the extent to which his argument relies on this assumption, but he does not indicate how he would argue for animals having an equal right to life if he were addressing an audience who did not hold that all humans had this right.

If we come to consider a human who has such severe brain damage that he or she is not a person and can never become a person, it is plausible to hold that this human being does not have the same right to life as a normal adult human. If this seems shocking, recall the arguments we considered earlier in this chapter, to the effect that merely being a member of the species *Homo sapiens* cannot carry with it any special moral status. Once this conclusion is accepted, it places humans who are not persons in the same category as nonhuman animals. It is this conclusion that is "shocking" to our conventional attitudes, for it forces us to alter our attitudes to one or the other of these groups, or to both. In other words, we must adopt one of the following positions:

1. While retaining our present attitudes to mentally defective humans, we change our attitudes to animals who are not persons, so as to bring them into line with our attitudes to mentally defective humans. This involves holding that animals have a right to life, and therefore should not be killed for food or for the purposes of scientific experimentation.
2. While retaining our present attitudes to animals, we change our attitudes to mentally defective humans, so as to bring them into line with our attitudes to animals. This involves holding that mental defectives do not have a right to life, and therefore might be killed for food—if we should develop a taste for human flesh—or (and this really might appeal to some people) for the purpose of scientific experimentation.

3. We change our present attitudes to both mentally defective
humans and nonhuman animals, so as to bring them together
somewhere in between our present attitudes. This involves
holding that both mentally defective humans and nonhuman
animals have some kind of serious claim to life—whether we
call it a "right" does not matter much—in virtue of which, while
we ought not to take their lives except for very weighty reasons,
they do not have as strict a right to life as do persons. In accordance with this view, we might hold, for instance, that it is wrong
to kill either mentally defective humans or animals for food if
an alternative diet is available, but not wrong to do so if the only
alternative is starvation.

The first of these three positions is the one for which Regan is
arguing. His argument is incomplete, however, because he does not
consider either of the other positions.[40] One may, quite consistently,
avoid Regan's arguments by adopting either the second or the third
position. The plausibility of these two positions is enhanced by the fact
that Tooley's arguments, discussed in the previous section of this essay,
can be invoked to show why mentally defective humans and animals
who are not persons do not have the same right to life as humans and
animals who are persons.

§14 EQUALITY AND THE RIGHT TO LIFE

Acute readers may have noticed that there is a parallel between the
arguments I used earlier against speciesism and Regan's arguments for
attributing a right to life to animals. In attacking speciesism, I made
use of the assumption that my audience does not hold racist views,
arguing that if we are prepared to discriminate on the basis of species,
we have no ground to stand on when we accuse the racist of discrimi-
nating on the basis of race alone. This strategy parallels Regan's use
of the assumption that all humans have an equal right to life, in his
argument for the position that all animals have an equal right to life.
The reader may therefore wonder how, if I criticize Regan for relying
on the assumption that all humans have an equal right to life, I can
defend my own argument, which also relies on an assumption of human equality.

My reply to this objection is that the principle of equality upon
which my own argument rests is very different from the claim that all
humans have an equal right to life, and it can, if necessary, be defended by argument, in a way that the idea of an equal human right
to life cannot be. The argument against speciesism is based on the
principle of equal consideration of interests. This is a fundamental
moral principle, and a number of moral philosophers, both recent and
not so recent, have argued that it is part of the very nature of morality
itself. To depart from so basic a moral principle is to open the way not

only to racism of the most blatant and naked kind, but also to a whole host of other partial or sectional moral views.[41]

The idea of an equal human right to life, on the other hand, does not follow from the principle of equal consideration of interests, and is not as fundamental a moral principle. It does not follow from it because the principle of equal consideration of interests allows us to treat different beings differently, where their interests are different. It can plausibly be argued that a being who is capable of conceiving itself as a distinct entity existing over time has a greater interest in continuing to live than a being that cannot conceive of itself in this manner. This argument is compatible with equal consideration of interests and not akin to racist or any other partial restrictions on the applicability of this principle.

For these reasons, the claim that all animals ought to come within the scope of the principle of equal consideration of interests is, in my view, on firmer ground than Regan's claim that all animals have an equal right to life.

§15 CLASSICAL UTILITARIANISM AND THE VALUE OF ANIMAL LIFE

The conclusion reached in the preceding section does not settle the issue of the value of the life of an animal that is not a person. In that section we distinguished three possible views, all consistent and none of them speciesist, that one might take about both mentally defective humans and nonhuman animals. We have now found Regan's argument for the first of these positions to be inadequate, or at best incomplete. There remain the other two positions, one of which puts mentally defective humans in the same position as animals now are, while the other brings our attitudes to mentally defective humans and to animals together in some intermediate position between our present attitudes to the two. Assuming the foregoing is sound, we must choose between these two positions.

The first of these two positions asks us to think about something that is, for many people, utterly repulsive. The idea of killing mentally defective human beings, for food or to satisfy scientific curiosity, involves a radical break with the widespread belief in the value of human life. Yet if my arguments up to this point have been sound, we must make a radical break with our current ethical beliefs at some point: If we do not reject the belief that it is wrong to kill mentally defective humans for food, then we must reject the belief that it is all right to kill animals at the same level of mental development for the same purpose.

If we remain strictly within the classical utilitarian position, we will incline toward the former view and hold that killing is not in itself wrong. The utilitarian view would, of course, take account of a wide variety of external factors. It would note that many of the modes of

killing used on animals do not inflict an instantaneous death and involve considerable suffering. It would also take into account the effect
of the death of one animal on its mate or on other members of its social
group. There are many species of birds and animals in which the bond
between male and female lasts for a lifetime. Presumably in these
situations the death of one member of the pair causes something like
sorrow for the survivor.[42] The mother-child relationship is also strong
in most mammals and birds. In some species, too, the death of one
animal may be felt by a larger group. This is the case when, for
example, the leader of a wolf pack is killed.[43] All these factors would
lead utilitarians to oppose much of the killing of animals that now goes
on. They would not, however, lead them to oppose killing in itself.
Killing can be instantaneous and painless, and it can be of an animal,
or a mentally defective human being, who will not be missed by any
one else. In these special circumstances, killing will not increase the
amount of pain or diminish the amount of pleasure in the universe,
and hence it seems not, according to classical utilitarianism, to be
wrong.

There is, however, a further question: Should utilitarianism take
into account the pleasure that the human or animal would continue
to experience if it were not killed? In the classical utilitarian view, if
the chances are that the remainder of the lifespan of the being killed
would contain more pleasure than pain, then, other things being
equal, the killing diminishes the total surplus of pleasure over pain in
the universe, and is for that reason wrong, in the absence of counter-
vailing considerations. Before classical utilitarians seize on this as a
means of reconciling their theory with ordinary moral convictions,
however, there is something else that needs to be noticed: the loss of
pleasure associated with killing is, from a utilitarian point of view, of
no greater moral significance than the loss of pleasure associated with
failing to reproduce.

Let us look at this point more closely. Suppose that I am a utilitarian
and I am considering killing a young boy, X. Let us say that there are
no parents, friends, or relatives who will grieve over X's death, and the
killing will be quite painless, so there are no relevant external factors;
but I do, as a utilitarian, have to take into account the fact that X, living
as he does in a pleasant community in which his basic needs can be
satisfied, will probably experience a surplus of pleasure over pain in
his lifetime. Therefore, I decide that it would be wrong to kill X.

Now suppose that I am a (female) utilitarian and I am considering
whether to conceive and give birth to a child. We can call the possible
child Y. It is, we shall suppose, reasonable to believe that if Y is born,
he or she is likely to experience a surplus of pleasure over pain during
life—in fact, let us say that Y's prospects of a happy life, once conceived, are exactly as favorable as the prospects of X's life continuing
to be happy if he is not killed. Moreover as in the case of X, there are,

we shall say, no relevant external factors tipping the balance one way or the other. (The inconveniences of pregnancy are, for me, exactly balanced by the anticipated joys of becoming a parent.) Then, given all this, my reasons for not killing X are no more weighty than my reasons for conceiving Y, and my reason against killing X is, in utilitarian terms, equally a reason for conceiving Y. This means that the decision not to conceive Y is, other things being equal, as wrong as the decision to kill X.

All this is, again, very much at odds with our ordinary moral convictions. We do not ordinarily think that it is wrong to fail to conceive a child who would probably be happy. We certainly do not think that it is wrong in the way that killing a child is wrong. Someone might say that we do not think it wrong to fail to conceive a child because our world is already so overpopulated. This reply won't do; for why is killing a child a less acceptable way of reducing population than failing to conceive a child?

Essentially, the problem is that classical utilitarianism makes lives replaceable. Killing is wrong if it deprives the world of a happy life, but this wrong can be righted if another equally happy life can be created without any extra cost. Classical utilitarianism has this consequence because it regards sentient beings as valuable only insofar as they make possible the existence of intrinsically valuable experiences like pleasure. It is as if sentient beings were receptacles of something valuable, and it did not matter if a receptacle got broken, as long as another receptacle were available to which the contents could be transferred without any getting spilled in the process. The reasonableness of the classical utilitarian position turns on the reasonableness of this consequence. I shall have more to say on this matter shortly. First, though, it is worth noting that this argument has been used to justify meat eating. Leslie Stephen, for instance, once wrote:

> Of all the arguments for Vegetarianism none is so weak as the argument from humanity. The pig has a stronger interest than anyone in the demand for bacon. If all the world were Jewish, there would be no pigs at all.[44]

The thought here is that animals are replaceable, and that although meat eaters are responsible for the death of the animals they eat, they are also responsible for the creation of more animals of the same species. The benefit they thus confer on one animal cancels out the loss they inflict on the other. We shall call this the replaceability argument.

§16 THE REPLACEABILITY ARGUMENT

The first point to note about the replaceability argument is that even if it is valid when the animals in question have a pleasant life, it would not justify eating the flesh of animals reared in modern "factory farms," where the animals are so crowded together and restricted in their movements that their lives seem to be more of a burden than a benefit to them.[45]

A second point is that if the replaceability argument applies to animals, it must apply to humans at a comparable mental level as well. Situations in which the argument would apply to humans might not be common, but they could occur. Some people carry genes that mean that any children they produce will be severely mentally retarded. As long as the lives of these children are pleasant, it would not, according to the replaceability argument, be wrong to perform a scientific experiment on a child that results in the death of the child, provided another child could then be conceived to take its place. (Of course, one would need to consider the feelings of the parents—but then one should consider these feelings in the case of pigs too.)

A third point is that if it is good to create life, then presumably it is good for there to be as many people on our planet as it can possibly hold. With the possible exception of arid areas suitable only for pasture, the surface of our globe can support more people if we grow plant foods than if we raise animals.

These three points greatly weaken the replaceability argument as a defense of meat eating, but they do not go to the heart of the matter. Are sentient beings really replaceable? Henry S. Salt thought that the argument rested on a simple philosophical error:

> The fallacy lies in the confusion of thought which attempts to compare existence with non-existence. A person who is already in existence may feel that he would rather have lived than not, but he must first have the *terra firma* of existence to argue from: the moment he begins to argue as if from the abyss of the non-existent, he talks nonsense, by predicating good or evil, happiness or unhappiness, of that of which we can predicate nothing.[46]

When I wrote *Animal Liberation* I accepted Salt's view.[47] Now I am not so sure. To defend Salt's position more systematically, I attempted to formulate a plausible version of utilitarianism that accounts for the lack of symmetry in our attitudes to bringing a being into existence and putting a being out of existence. I ran into trouble as soon as I tried to apply this version of utilitarianism to situations in which the future population of the world is not fixed. In such a situation, a criterion for deciding upon the optimum population is required, and a plausible criterion is exceptionally difficult to find. An account of these difficulties would take us far beyond our present subject; it suffices to say that the adequacy of the reply that Salt and I have given to the replaceability argument must remain in doubt unless and until the difficulties are overcome.[48]

We must therefore conclude this section on a note of uncertainty. If the replaceability argument can be met, it would follow that from the classical utilitarian view the life of any being likely to experience more pleasure than pain is of value and not to be sacrificed without a very good reason. This would justify the third of the three possible positions outlined in §13, and would mean a radical change in our evaluation of the lives of animals. On the other hand, if the replaceability argument is sound, it would seem that in the absence of other considerations the second of the three positions is the one to take, and it is our attitudes to mentally defective human beings that are in need of reconsideration.

V. CONCLUSIONS

§17 THEORETICAL ISSUES

It is now time to draw the discussion together and see what conclusions we have reached. In the first substantive section of this essay (§2) we scrutinized the position, so fundamental to Western attitudes to animals and nature, that human life has a unique value far beyond that of any animal. We considered four grounds for believing this:

1. That humans alone are conscious.
2. That humans alone have immortal souls.
3. That human lives are God's property, whereas God has given humans dominion over animals.
4. That human beings are "ends in themselves" and animals mere means.

None of these grounds stood up to critical examination, and so I maintained that—unless some better arguments appeared—the traditional Western attitude would have to be abandoned. It would seem impossible to hold, without arbitrary and unjustifiable discrimination, that the life of every member of our species is of higher value than the life of every nonhuman animal.

Next we distinguished between the terms 'human being' and 'person', using the latter term to refer to a self-conscious being, aware of itself as a distinct entity existing over time. In this sense it is possible for a human being—a member of the species *Homo sapiens*—not to be a person, and also possible for a nonhuman animal to be a person.

We then asked if there were any reasons for holding that it was markedly more serious to take the life of a person than to take the life of a being that is not a person. We saw that this position can be defended on several grounds. The classical utilitarian can defend it only indirectly, in terms of the effects on others, but preference utilitarianism allows us to give direct weight to the desire for continued existence—a desire that only a self-conscious being can have. It is also possible to maintain, as Tooley does, that only a self-conscious being can have a *right* to life, in the fullest sense of the term.

If we accept that persons have a weightier claim to life than beings that are not persons, we still need to ask whether beings that are not persons have any kind of right to life at all, or whether their lives are of any value. We examined Regan's defense of an equal right to life for all sentient creatures but found it incomplete. We then considered the bearing of classical utilitarianism on this issue and found that a good deal depended on the very perplexing question of whether the loss of pleasure caused by the killing of one being can be made up for by the creation of another being. Only if a negative answer can be given to this question does classical utilitarianism allow the conclusion that killing is wrong in itself.

§18 THREE QUESTIONS ANSWERED

What do our theoretical conclusions mean in practical terms? If they are correct, in what respects should our treatment of animals be modified? What should we think about the three cases of killing animals mentioned in the first section of this essay?

a. Killing Animals for Food   Let us consider, first, whether it would be right to kill and eat a pig if the pig lived happily under pleasant conditions and was killed painlessly. The first problem is to decide whether pigs are self-conscious. This is not an easy matter to settle. Pigs may not be as intelligent as chimpanzees, but it was not for nothing that George Orwell made them the élite of *Animal Farm*. Pigs are comparable in intelligence to dogs, and if we are prepared to allow that self-consciousness is possible without language, it is possible that pigs are self-conscious. If this is so then both preference utilitarianism and Tooley's view of rights imply that we ought not to kill a pig, however painlessly it might be done, merely for the purpose of adding pork to our diet. Classical utilitarianism, on the other hand, would lead to this conclusion only if some justification exists for not setting against the loss of happiness occasioned by the death of the happy pig the happiness of future pigs that we will be able to raise only if we kill the one now alive.

My own position is that I am not certain that it would be wrong in itself to kill the pig; but nor am I certain that it would be right to do so. Since there is no pressing moral reason for the killing—the fact that one might prefer a dish containing pork to a vegetarian meal is hardly a matter of great moral significance—it would seem better to give the pig the benefit of the doubt.

There are also a number of other reasons why in most cases it is better not to raise and kill animals for food, even when they live happily and die painlessly. For a start, raising animals is an inefficient method of obtaining food for human consumption. Far more food— and more protein—can be produced by growing vegetables, grains, and soybeans than by raising animals—unless the land is not suitable for growing these crops. In a situation in which population growth is putting increasing pressure on all our resources, including food, it is important to encourage the most efficient possible use of the land we have available for agriculture.

Then there are some less tangible reasons against killing animals for food or for any other objective that is not a matter of life and death. For my own part, I cannot now, after being a vegetarian for about seven years, contemplate the killing and eating of an animal without a feeling of distaste amounting almost to revulsion. My meal would be tainted by the knowledge that I was dining on flesh from the corpse of an animal that was capable of relating to other animals, of caring for its young, and of having a pleasant or a miserable existence. This is an emotional attitude or perhaps an aesthetic judgment that would endure for some time even if I were to become convinced that on moral grounds the painless killing of a happy animal is not wrong. Moreover, there remains a doubt in my mind as to whether it is possible for those who kill animals for food to avoid slipping gradually into the attitude that animals are things for us to exploit for our convenience. If that attitude should take hold, the step to factory farming, with its ruthless sacrifice of the interests of animals to the dictates of commerce, is short indeed.

b. Euthanasia for Strays   The justifiability of euthanasia for stray dogs or cats, or for any animal whose future existence is likely to be wretched, is a very different matter. Here self-consciousness and the ability to understand and choose between alternatives is crucial. If an animal is not self-conscious and its future existence is likely to be wretched, utilitarian considerations and some views of rights agree that euthanasia is permissible. Instead of diminishing happiness, death then diminishes suffering. Even when self-consciousness is present, if the animal is not capable of understanding its future prospects and of choosing whether to live or die, it may be right for others to make this choice for the animal. Choosing on behalf of another can be defensible in situations in which one party understands the nature of a choice while the other party is totally incapable of appreciating what is at stake. Of course, such a choice is justifiable only if it is truly made in the interests of the being who is incapable of making the choice. But my New York friend with the small apartment would have been acting in the interests of the stray animals she could not look after if she had taken them to a vet to be killed by an intravenous injection; and while one can sympathize with her reluctance to take the animals to their death, it would not have been wrong to do so. We are responsible for the foreseeable consequences of our choices, whatever we choose, and we cannot escape responsibility for the fate of an animal by releasing it on the streets of New York and turning our back.

c. Experimenting on Animals   The third of the three cases with which this essay began is the case of animal experimentation. Again, it is not all animal experimentation with which we are here concerned, but only experiments that raise the question of killing in isolation from other factors like the infliction of suffering; for example, an experiment in which the animal is made unconscious by an anesthetic prior to the experiment being performed and is then killed before it regains consciousness.

Animal experimentation does, sometimes, serve important and worthwhile purposes. Although many experiments are trivial and a waste of time and money (quite apart from being an abuse of animals) others do lead to significant gains in our knowledge of biological processes and the prevention and treatment of disease. It may in the long run be possible to obtain this knowledge by alternative techniques not involving animals; but the prospect of such alternatives in the future does not negate the benefits now being obtained by some experiments. This places animal experimentation in a different category from raising animals for food. Except in some simple subsistence economies, the use of animals for food does not contribute to vitally important human objectives. It does not save lives or reduce suffering. The knowledge gained from some experiments on animals does save lives and reduce suffering. Hence, the benefits of animal experimentation exceed the benefits of eating animals and the former stands a better chance of being justifiable than the latter; but this applies only when an experiment on an animal fulfills strict conditions relating to the significance of the knowledge to be gained, the unavailability of alternative techniques not involving animals, and the care taken to avoid pain. Under these conditions the death of an animal in an experiment can be defended.

When the experimental animal may be self-conscious, the problem becomes more difficult. If Tooley's argument about the right to life is sound, it would appear that the lives of these animals should not be sacrificed in any experiments, no matter how important. Utilitarians, on the other hand, would be more flexible and would allow that some experimental goals are important enough to justify the death of even a self-conscious being. Preference utilitarians would require more in the way of likely benefits from the experiment than classical utilitarians, because they would take into account the animal's presumed desire to go on living. A utilitarian of either school would, in consistency, have to admit that an experiment important enough to justify the death of an animal would also justify the death of a mentally defective human at a similar mental level, if for some reason the human were a more suitable subject for the experiment than the nonhuman animal. That fact may temper the readiness of experimenters to assume that their own experiments are important enough to justify killing animals.

§19 CONCLUDING PRACTICAL POSTSCRIPT

Finally, it may be as well to remind the reader of the limitations on the scope of this essay and of the conclusions that, because of these limitations, do *not* follow from what I have said. We have been considering the issue of killing animals in isolation from other issues, like the infliction of suffering upon animals. This approach is necessary for a clear philosophical understanding of the separate issues involved, but it must not be taken as an indication of the way things are in the world. Killing animals for food normally means not only that the animals die, but that they must be exploited throughout their lives in order to reduce the costs of production. Thus, the case for vegetarianism is strong whatever view we take of the value of animal life. Using animals in experiments, even when the experiments are painless, means housing animals for long periods before the experiment takes place, often in closely confined conditions. Moreover, many experiments are not at all painless, and many more are of no real importance. Thus the case for stricter control of animal experimentation is also independent of the issue of the value of animal life. To maintain that the lives of most animals are of less value than the lives of most humans is not to excuse what humans do to animals or to diminish the urgency of the struggle to end the callous exploitation of other species by our own.

NOTES

1. *Animal Liberation* (New York, The New York Review 1975), ch. 1.
2. The reader may note, in what follows, the absence of any discussion of the view, associated with Eastern religions and with Albert Schweitzer, that *all* life, whether animal or plant, conscious or not, has value. I do not believe that it has; but since this issue is discussed in William Blackstone's essay in the present volume, I have not argued for my belief here.
3. For a brief discussion of the contrary view about plants, see *Animal Liberation, op. cit.,* pp. 261–263.
4. For Descartes's views, see the selections reprinted in *Animal Rights and Human Obligations,* ed. T. Regan and P. Singer (Englewood Cliffs, N.J., Prentice-Hall, 1976), pp. 60–66; for the passage quoted (from a letter to Henry More, February 5, 1649), see p. 66. Whether Descartes actually intended to deny that animals are *conscious* or merely that they can *think* is not altogether clear; but he has often been interpreted as making the stronger claim.
5. See L. Rosenfield, *From Beast-Machine to Man-Machine: The Theme of Animal Soul in French Letters from Descartes to La Mettrie* (New York, Oxford University Press, 1940).
6. Richard Sergeant, *The Spectrum of Pain* (London, Hart-Davis, 1969), p. 72.
7. See the reports of the Committee on Cruelty to Wild Animals (Command Paper 8266, 1951), paragraphs 36–42; the Departmental Committee on Experiments on Animals (Command Paper 2641, 1965), paragraphs 179–182; and the Technical Committee to Enquire into the Welfare of Animals Kept under Intensive Livestock Husbandry Systems (Command Paper 2836, 1965), paragraphs 26–28 (London, Her Majesty's Stationery Office).
8. John Lilly, *Man and Dolphin* (London, Gollancz, 1962), pp. 81–87. The authenticity of Lilly's evidence has been questioned.

9.   See below, §8.

10. The classic argument against immortality is David Hume's essay "Of the Immortality of the Soul," first published in 1777. A modern introduction to the topic can be found in T. Regan, *Understanding Philosophy* (Encino, Calif., Dickenson, 1974), ch. 6. See also B. Russell, *Why I Am Not a Christian* (New York, Simon & Schuster, 1957), and for a useful survey of the literature, Anthony Flew's article "Immortality" in *The Encyclopedia of Philosophy*, ed. Paul Edwards (New York, Macmillan, 1967).

11. See, for example, Joseph Butler, *The Analogy of Religion, Natural and Revealed* (Philadelphia, Lippincott, 1857), part I, ch. 1.

12. For Aristotle's position, see his *De Anima* II, 2, 3, 4; III, 12; for Aquinas, see *Summa Theologica* I, Q 76.3. See also C. W. Hume, *The Status of Animals in the Christian Religion* (London, Universities Federation for Animal Welfare, 1957), pp. 49–50.

13. At least one Christian *has* drawn the opposite conclusion. Cardinal Bellarmine is said to have allowed vermin to bite him, saying "We shall have heaven to reward us for our sufferings, but these poor creatures have nothing but the enjoyment of this present life." (Quoted from W. E. H. Lecky, *History of European Morals* [London, Longmans, 1892], vol. II, p. 172n.)

14. *Phaedo*, 62 6-c, in *The Dialogues of Plato*, 4th ed., tr. B. Jowett (Oxford, Clarendon Press, 1953), vol. 1, p. 412.

15. *Summa Theologica* II, ii, Q 64.5.

16. I. Kant, *Lectures on Ethics*, tr. L. Infield (New York, Harper & Row, 1963), pp. 153–154.

17. *Genesis* I, 29 and IX, 1–3.

18. *City of God* I, 20.

19. *Summa Theologica* II, ii Q64.1 and II, i Q102.6; the reference to "The Apostle" is to Paul, *Corinthians* IX, 9–10.

20. *Summa Contra Gentiles*, III, ii, ch. 112; reprinted in Regan and Singer, *op. cit.*, pp. 56–59.

21. See John Passmore, *Man's Responsibility for Nature* (London, Duckworth, 1974), ch. 2.

22. For a careful presentation and discussion of this argument, see H. J. McCloskey, *God and Evil* (The Hague, Nijhoff, 1974).

23. Kant, *op. cit.*, pp. 239–240.

24. Gregory Vlastos, "Justice and Equality," in *Social Justice*, ed. R. B. Brandt (Englewood Cliffs, N.J., Prentice-Hall, 1962), pp. 48–49.

25. William Frankena, "The Concept of Social Justice," in R. B. Brandt, *op. cit.*, p. 23.

26. H. A. Bedau, "Egalitarianism and the Idea of Equality," in *Nomos IX: Equality*, ed. J. R. Pennock and J. W. Chapman (New York, Atherton Press, 1967).

27. The term is not of my own inventing; I first came across it in a pamphlet written by Richard Ryder, the author of *Victims of Science* (London, Davis-Poynter, 1975). Several reviewers of *Animal Liberation* objected to the term on stylistic grounds, but no one suggested anything equally concise and more euphonious. Species chauvinism or human chauvinism would also be possible.

28. *The Hastings Center Report*, vol. 2, no. 5 (1972).

29. This account has an impeccable philosophical ancestry. John Locke, for example, defined a person as "A thinking intelligent being that has reason and reflection and can consider itself as itself, the same thinking thing, in different times and places." (*An Essay Concerning Human Understanding*, bk. II, ch. 29, par. 9.) Locke distinguished 'person' and

'man', holding that an intelligent animal—he instances a parrot—might be a person, though it could not be a man. Immanuel Kant, too, referred to the view that "that which is conscious of the numerical identity of itself at different times is in so far a *person.*" (*Critique of Pure Reason,* Paralogism 3.) For further references see "Persons," by Arthur Danto in *The Encyclopedia of Philosophy,* ed. Paul Edwards, vol. 6.

30. Michael Tooley, "A Defense of Abortion and Infanticide," in *The Problem of Abortion,* ed. Joel Feinberg (Belmont, Calif., Wadsworth, 1973), p. 60. An earlier version appeared in *Philosophy and Public Affairs,* vol. 2, no. 1 (1972).

31. Werner S. Pluhar, "Abortion and Simple Consciousness," *Journal of Philosophy,* vol. LXXIV, no. 3 (1977).

32. B. T. Gardner and R. A. Gardner, "Teaching Sign Language to a Chimpanzee," *Science,* vol. 165 (1969), pp. 664–672; see also W. H. Thorpe, *Animal Nature and Human Nature* (London, Methuen, 1974) pp. 283f.

33. Stuart Hampshire, *Thought and Action* (London, Chatto and Windus, 1960), pp. 98–99. Others who have espoused related views are Anthony Kenny, in A. J. P. Kenny, H. C. Longuet-Higgins, J. R. Lucas, and C. H. Waddington, *The Nature of Mind* (Edinburgh, Edinburgh University Press, 1972), p. 119, and in Anthony Kenny, *Will, Freedom and Power* (Oxford, Blackwell, 1925), pp. 18–21; Norman Malcolm, "Thoughtless Brutes," *Proceedings and Addresses of The American Philosophical Association* XLVI (1973), pp. 5–20 (but see the reply by Donald Weiss, "Professor Malcolm on Animal Intelligence," *Philosophical Review* LXXXIV [1975], pp. 88–95); and most recently, Donald Davidson, in "Thought and Talk," in *Mind and Language,* ed. S. Guttenplan (Oxford, Clarendon Press, 1975), and in an as yet unpublished paper entitled "Why Animals Can't Think."

34. Lilly, *op. cit.*

35. F. H. Rohles and J. U. Devine, "Chimpanzee Performance in a Problem Involving the Concept of Middleness," *Animal Behavior* 14, pp. 159–162. (Cited in Donald Griffin, *The Question of Animal Awareness* [New York, Rockefeller University Press, 1976], p. 43.)

36. Jane van Lawick-Goodall, *In the Shadow of Man* (New York, Dell, 1971), p. 107.

37. For an example involving playful rather than food-gathering behavior, see Gary Eaton, "Snowball Construction by a Feral Troop of Japanese Macaques Living under Semi-Natural Conditions," *Primate* 13 (1972), pp. 411–414. It is also appropriate in this context to refer to the many well-authenticated reports of apparently intentional behavior by whales and dolphins.

38. Tom Regan, "The Moral Basis of Vegetarianism," *Canadian Journal of Philosophy,* October 1975, and reprinted, in part, in T. Regan and P. Singer, *op. cit.,* pp. 197–204.

39. See the essay on euthanasia in this volume; and for a discussion of the value, if any, of life without consciousness, see the essay by William Blackstone.

40. Regan does make some suggestions about why the mentally incompetent should be granted a right to life in his article "Narveson on Egoism and the Rights of Animals," *Canadian Journal of Philosophy,* March 1977.

41. For a more detailed discussion of the principle of equal consideration, see *Animal Liberation,* ch. 1.

42. For an example, see Farley Mowat, "The Trapped Whale," in Joan MacIntyre, *Mind in the Waters* (New York, Scribners, 1974).

43. Farley Mowat, *Never Cry Wolf* (Boston, Atlantic Monthly Press, 1963).

44.   From *Social Rights and Duties,* quoted by Henry S. Salt, "The Logic of the Larder," in T. Regan and P. Singer, *op. cit.,* p. 186n.

45.   See *Animal Liberation,* ch. 3.

46.   Salt, *op. cit.,* p. 186.

47.   *Animal Liberation,* p. 254; for a similar view, see Mary Anne Warren, "Do Potential People Have Moral Rights?" *Canadian Journal of Philosophy* vol. 7 (1977), pp. 275–289.

48.   For my attempt to formulate a criterion for deciding upon an optimum population, see "A Utilitarian Population Principle," in *Ethics and Population,* ed. Michael Bayles (Cambridge, Mass., Schenkman, 1976); and for damaging criticisms of this attempt, see Derek Parfit's "On Doing the Best for Our Children" in the same volume.

SUGGESTIONS FOR FURTHER READING

The following works are relevant to the general topic of the morality of our treatment of animals.

Clark, Stephen R. L., *The Moral Status of Animals* (New York, Oxford University Press, 1977).

Godlovitch, Stanley and Roslind, and Harris, John (eds.), *Animals, Men and Morals* (London, Gollancz, 1972).

Linzey, Andrew, *Animal Rights* (London, SCM Press, 1976).

Paterson, D., and Ryder, R. (eds.), *Animal Rights: A Symposium* (London, Centaur Press, 1979).

Regan, Tom, and Singer, Peter (eds.), *Animal Rights and Human Obligations* (Englewood Cliffs, N. J., Prentice-Hall, 1976).

Singer, Peter, *Animal Liberation* (New York, The New York Review, 1975).

For further reading on the issues discussed in this essay, the reader is encouraged to consult the sources cited in the footnotes as well as those that follow.

§1. On the topics of how animals are raised as a food source and how they are used in research, see, respectively, Ruth Harrison, *Animal Machines* (London, Stuart, 1964), and Richard Ryder, *Victims of Science* (London, David-Poynter,1975). In this latter regard, see also John Vyvyan, *The Dark Face of Science* (London, Michael Joseph, 1971) and E. A. Westacott, *A Century of Vivisection and Anti-Vivisection* (London, Daniel, 1949).

§6. Two books that relate to the place of animals within the Christian view of the world are Ambrose Aquis, *God's Animals* (Catholic Study for Animal Welfare, 1970), and C. W. Hume, *The Status of Animals in the Christian Religion* (Universities Federation for Animal Welfare,1957). A strongly stated argument against vivisection by an influential twentieth-century Christian writer is C. S. Lewis's "Vivisection" (The National Anti-Vivisection Society Limited, 51 Harley Street, London, W1).

§7. A fuller account of Kant's position can be found in Alexander Broadie and Elizabeth Pybus, "Kant's Treatment of Animals," *Philosophy,* vol. 49 (1974). For a reply, see Tom Regan,"Broadie and Pybus on Kant," *Philosophy* (October 1976).

§8. The topic of speciesism is discussed in Bonnie Steinbock, "Speciesism and the Idea of Equality," *Philosophy* (July 1978). It is also touched upon by Michael Fox, "Animal Liberation: A Critique," *Ethics* (January 1978). For a reply, see Peter Singer, "The Parable of the Fox and the Unliberated Ani-

mals," *Ethics* (January 1978). See also Peter Singer, "All Animals Are Equal";
Kevin Donaghy, "Singer on Speciesism"; and Joseph Margolis, "Animals Have
No Rights and Are Not the Equal of Humans," *Philosophical Exchange* (Summer 1974).

§§12–14. For the debate over the idea of animal rights, the following
essays are relevant. Joel Feinberg, "What Sorts of Beings Can Have Rights?"
in *Philosophy and Environmental Crisis*, ed. William T. Blackstone (Athens,
Ga.: University of Georgia Press, 1974); R. G. Frey, "Animal Rights," *Analysis*
(October 1977); and "Interests and Animal Rights," *Philosophical Quarterly*
27 (1977); Dale Jamieson and Tom Regan, "Animal Rights: A Reply to Frey,"
Analysis (January 1978); H. J. McCloskey, "Rights," *Philosophical Quarterly*
vol. 15 (1965); Jan Narveson, "Animal Rights," *Canadian Journal of Philosophy* (March 1974); and Tom Regan: "Fox's Critique of Animal Liberation,"
Ethics (January 1978); "Frey on Interests and Animal Rights," *Philosophical
Quarterly* (Winter 1977); "Narveson on Egoism and the Rights of Animals,"
Canadian Journal of Philosophy (March 1977); "McCloskey on Why Animals
Cannot Have Rights," *Philosophical Quarterly* (Fall 1976); and "Utilitarianism, Vegetarianism, and Animal Rights," *Philosophy and Public Affairs* (Fall
1979). The October 1978 issue of *Philosophy* and the Summer 1979 issue of
Inquiry are devoted to essays relating to the nature and moral status of
animals. A more complete bibliography is included in the *Inquiry* volume.

8

The Moral Perplexities of Famine Relief

ONORA O'NEILL

§1 IS FAMINE A NEW MORAL PROBLEM?

It is unusual for there to be a wholly new moral problem. Most of the questions that give us pause or sleepless nights have been faced by others ever since (no doubt also before) the beginnings of systematic reflection about what to do. We know very well, for example, that we are not the first persons tempted to put career before everything else. If the temptation persists we may even want to consult our predecessors or other authorities. We may find ourselves thinking about Macbeth's vaulting ambition, perhaps comforted by the thought that unlike him we do not put career above everything—no murder for advancement, for example.

But when we wonder what we or others should do about global famine there don't seem to be familiar literary or religious traditions or philosophical discussions to which to turn. This is not because famine is new, but because there is today far more that we (or others) can do—or refrain from doing—that will affect the course of any famine there may be. Through history, millions have died of sheer starvation and of malnutrition or from illnesses that they might have survived with better nourishment. And whenever there were such deaths, nearby survivors may have realized that they might have helped prevent deaths and may either have done so or wondered whether they should. But nobody considered whether to prevent faraway deaths. Distance made an important difference, and with few exceptions there was nothing to be done for the victims of faraway famines.

In a global economy things are different. Corn from the North American prairies could be (and has been) distributed to the starving in Bangladesh or Somalia. Longer-term policies that affect economic development, fertility levels, and agricultural productivity may hasten or postpone far-off famines or make them more or less severe. Consequently, we now face moral questions about whether we ought to do some of these newly possible actions. Ought we (or others) to try to distribute food or aid or to introduce technical improvements? Who should foot the bill and suffer the other costs? To whom (if anyone) should aid be given and to whom should it be denied? How much hardship or sacrifice is demanded of those who have the means to help, if any?

In answering these questions, traditional moral theories are often not very useful. Consider, for example, the Christian injunction to love your neighbor as yourself. Christ explained who one's neighbor is in the Parable of the Good Samaritan.[1] The Samaritan, though an alien, helped the man who fell among thieves, so was neighbor to that man. Suppose the Samaritan had found on the road to Jericho a man who had not been mugged but who was starving. We have no doubt how to extend the Christian principle here: It is neighborly to feed the starving when we come upon them in distress. But what is neighborly when the starving are not lying on a lonely road where we are walking, but are hundreds or thousands of miles away where we can neither see nor name them? What should a Christian do then? Should the Christian send money? If so, to whom? To famine-relief charities? If so, to which? Or should Christians seek to influence the aid and trade policies of their own (or of other) countries to the advantage of starving persons or regions? If so, how is this to be done? How much aid should be sent and how much effort expended? May or ought Christians send so much that they (and their families) are reduced to hardship? Or are all these approaches futile? If all the world's distressed people are neighbors, even the wealthiest and most dedicated Christian can help very few of them. And how are these few to be selected? Are some people nearer neighbors than others, contrary to the apparent message of the Parable of the Good Samaritan? If so, who are the nearer? If charity begins at home, Christians should perhaps devote their efforts to nearby if less acute distresses. And should Christians take into account the likelihood that fortunate others will (or won't) contribute to the famine stricken?

The more we reflect on these questions the more we see how important it is in the Christian parable that the Good Samaritan directly encountered an isolated person in distress, for whose relief he had sufficient means. In saying this, we belittle neither the Samaritan's kindness nor his courage (he too might have been mugged). But we realize that famines in faraway places confront us with moral problems to which the Christian parable does not provide obvious answers. The parable leaves the answers to the above questions *undetermined,* and if we are looking for a moral theory that will help us work out what we may or ought to do, then we shall need one whose answers to these questions are *determinate*. Indeterminate answers to problems may rule out some solutions, but don't propose any solutions specific enough for us to act on them.

It is not only Christian ethics that leaves many problems about distant famines unanswered. Other moral theories also fail to answer these questions determinately. However, some moral theories are more adequate in dealing with some problems, while others do best at different problems. Few of these theories are applied to the allevia- tion of distant miseries, or show us how to work out who should help whom, to what extent, at what point, and at what cost to themselves or others. Because of this, I shall adopt an exploratory approach and tone in this essay. I shall try both to show something about how partic- ular moral theories can deal with some questions about famine (and not with others) and to use considerations about famine to show some of the strengths and limitations of these theories.

I. SOME CRITERIA FOR MORAL ARGUMENT

§2 MORAL THEORIES AND MORAL PROBLEMS

The project I've just described of simultaneously using and criticizing moral theories may strike you as about as likely to succeed as the proverbial task of pulling oneself up by one's own bootstraps. Once we've got a moral theory we can use it to solve (some) moral problems. We use the theory plus an account of certain facts or examples and try to work out what we ought to do. But having done so, it seems we cannot use those implications to criticize the theory from which they were (in part) derived.

For example, how can we use the Christian principle of love for one's neighbor to work out (some of) the things a Christian who finds another in distress ought to do, and then also use these findings to criticize the principle that led to them? Without the principle, we could not have worked out that helping the man in distress was the right thing to do. The Priest and the Levite, after all, acted on different principles (perhaps on the principle 'Don't get involved') and went past the Samaritan with averted eyes. It isn't enough to *come upon* a person in distress to know what one ought to do. One also needs a theory or principles or guidelines that will direct one what to do about that distress. How then can I propose to use a moral theory to work out the answers to some problems about famine, and then use the answers to criticize the theory? For it seems that if the criticism worked, it would undermine its own starting point. But this self- defeating circle can be avoided by using the criticism that we derive from a theory not so much to undermine as to revise and improve it. Just as scientists may use the inaccurate predictions their theories produce to work out better theories, so in ethics we can take hints from the implausible or inadequate result a theory implies in working out a better theory. To understand this process of building, checking, and improving moral theories we need to know a bit about such theories and some of the things that would show then to be inadequate.

§3 MORAL THEORIES AND MORALLY ACCEPTABLE THEORIES

Moral theories typically include a number of rather general principles that enjoin or forbid, commend or condemn some types of action. Examples of such general principles of action include the Good Samaritan principle and principles like 'Injure nobody' or 'Do whatever will produce the best results for everybody' or 'Do as you would be done by'. Many moral theories consist of more than one such principle, and when there is more than one, the theory usually explains their relationship. For example, a moral theory that includes the principle 'Always do what produces the best results for everybody' will probably explain what sorts of things count as good or bad results.

This view of moral theories accepts that there can be a large number of different moral theories. Some of these theories might be quite incompatible with others. For example, one moral theory might include the principle 'Always do the act likely to have the best results for everybody' and another might include the principle 'Do what appeals to you most, even when it will produce less good results for some people than you could achieve by suiting yourself less well'. In fact, on this minimal account of what a moral theory is, one could find some moral theory or another that would enjoin any imaginable act, however repellent or bizarre. For I have characterized a moral theory only as *a theory consisting of (one or more) principles that enjoin or forbid, commend or condemn some sorts of acts.*

If we want moral theories to help us decide about difficult moral problems, then we need to choose one of these theories. If we do not, we would be faced with theories that enjoin or forbid, commend or condemn incompatible actions, and so cannot give us guidance. In making this choice we want to pick not just any moral theory, but one that is *morally acceptable* or *morally desirable.*

Moral theories, as I have explained, enjoin or forbid, commend or condemn certain types of acts. Theories that are not moral theories may be of many different sorts. They might be geological theories or ecological theories or sociological theories. These theories are in all cases *nonmoral theories.* However, nonmoral theories are not generally morally unacceptable or immoral. (There may be some exceptions where a nonmoral theory, or the holding of such a theory, would be judged immoral. An example might be certain Nazi race theories. However, some people would say that these theories were bad science rather than immoral.)

The theories we want to avoid in working out solutions to moral problems are not these nonmoral theories, but moral theories that give morally unacceptable results. However, our moral perplexity over a matter like famine means that we are often unsure which results are morally acceptable. So we cannot simply sort out the theories by seeing whether they give us the answers we think acceptable. (If we were quite sure what was acceptable in all cases, we would probably not be looking at moral theories at all.) The best we can do is to examine the theories themselves and see how good they are as theories. In this way, although we may not discover a moral theory that is the only morally acceptable one, we may be able to show that some theories are inadequate in whole or in part, or that they are adequate for some purposes and not for others.

In §§ 4 and 5 I shall introduce two standards for assessing the adequacy of theories. These standards are of very general use and can be applied to nonmoral (e.g., scientific) theories as well as to moral theories. Initially, I shall use some scientific analogies to explain and show the appeal of these standards by which we can judge theories. In later sections I shall apply the standards to moral theories.

§4 THE SCOPE OF MORAL THEORIES

One way of showing that a moral theory is not morally adequate is by finding out whether it can deal with a considerable range of problems. If a moral theory can deal with only a very few problems, then its scope is small. It is, at best, a fragment of a morally acceptable theory. It is unacceptable as a complete theory for the fundamental reason that it fails to resolve enough problems. Consider, for example, a person who claims to live by a moral theory consisting of just the principle 'Never give or ask any help'. We may disagree about whether this principle is strange or odious or admirable. But there is no doubt that it is not going to be much help in lots of circumstances. Where no question arises of help being given or received, this principle is silent. A person who tried to get along with just this moral principle would be at a loss in many circumstances. The principle has too narrow a scope.

Moral theories are in *some* ways like scientific theories. Both moral and scientific theories can have greater or lesser *scope*. A theory has a greater scope than another theory if it can deal with more problems. A scientific theory is considered superior to another rival theory if it can account for more or more varied phenomena. For example, the seventeenth-century natural philosophers (physicists) who created a single science of motion created a theory whose scope included what had previously been handled in two separate theories, the theory of celestial dynamics and the theory of terrestrial dynamics. Previously, these two distinct theories had been used to explain respectively the movements of the heavenly bodies and those of "sublunar" (i.e., earthly) bodies. The heavenly bodies were thought to move in circles, while sublunar bodies fell down towards the solid earth. These earlier theories were very ingenious in explaining deviations from apparent circular and downward motion. Ptolemaic astronomers used an elaborate theory of epicycles—i.e., orbits on orbits—to explain why some heavenly bodies appear to move on noncircular orbits. The theory of the elements explained why some sublunar bodies—like fire—move upward, by attributing different weights to different sublunar bodies and theorizing that the heavier ones move down faster than the lighter ones. But the earlier theories never brought all sorts of motion under a single theory. Newton's theory did, and one of the reasons why it was a superior theory is that its scope was so much greater than the scope of either terrestrial or celestial dynamics. Similarly, we might expect any moral theory that is morally acceptable to have a relatively large scope—i.e., to give answers to an entire range of important problems. Of course, we may find that we can't come up with a moral theory that will deal with *all* moral problems. If so, we'll have to accept that limitation, just as we accept the fact that there is no scientific theory that covers all known natural phenomena.

§5 THE PRECISION OF MORAL THEORIES

However, not every theory of large scope is a good theory. There is little use for a moral (or for a scientific) theory that tells us very little about a great deal. A scientific "theory" that says merely that bodies move at varying speeds would have a large scope, but it would be useless because so vague. Similarly, we would not think much of a moral theory whose sole principle is 'Whatever the situation, do something'. In evaluating scientific theories, we look for theories that have a sufficient scope to cover an important range of cases *and* that are precise enough to give fairly detailed predictions. In looking for a moral theory that is morally acceptable, we will want one that has a sufficient scope to cover an important range of cases *and* that gives reasonably precise, determinate solutions to moral problems. Only such a theory could help us decide those problems. Of course, scope and precision alone won't be enough. Many moral theories, including no doubt some that are morally unacceptable, have considerable scope and precision. But many others lack one or the other. However, I shall not go on listing further necessary conditions that any morally acceptable theory must meet. At this point I shall take a major shortcut.

§6 LIMITING THE DISCUSSION

I shall consider only two potentially morally acceptable theories. I have chosen these two because they are leading contenders for being morally acceptable theories. One of these theories is utilitarianism; the other is a (simplified) version of Kantian ethics. Probably most serious writers on ethics in the English-speaking world today view some form of one of these two theories as likely to be a morally acceptable theory. I am going to present each of these theories and then see whether each has the scope and precision to answer some of the moral problems that famines raise. If I was right when I claimed in §1 that future famines may present moral problems that are different from those presented by past famines, then we may discover some new things about the scope and precision of these two moral theories by confronting them with these moral problems. For example, we may discover that one or both of these theories cannot cover some problems that future famines raise (the scope of the theories is too narrow) or that one or both of them cannot say anything usefully precise about some such problems. But we may also then be able to use these inadequacies to help us find a more acceptable moral theory.

Before I start this investigation of the adequacy of utilitarian and Kantian ethics in dealing with famine dilemmas, I shall consider whether there really is any likelihood that famines will occur. If famines are very unlikely, we don't need a moral theory that can handle famine problems. There is little point in strenuous thought about unlikely problems when there are so many problems that we know will arise and require decisions, if not of us, then of many of our contemporaries. The other problems discussed in this book—problems raised by war and abortion and penal systems and terminal illness—are problems we *know* will arise. Famine is one that we might after all escape. So I shall now try to show why I think we shall not escape future famines and the moral problems they raise, and why it is worth our time and effort to think about those problems.

II. THE FACTS OF FAMINE

There is an enormous amount of facts available about the numbers of people now living and about the resources they have to live on. There are also many careful and scrupulous studies of the likely rate of growth of population and resources in various regions and countries. One might then suppose that it would be quite easy to discover whether the world either is or will be overpopulated, whether there will be famines, and when and where they are most likely to occur. But it turns out that this is not easy, indeed that the experts disagree passionately about all these topics. They don't, on the whole, disagree about the particular figures (which all accept as being no more than careful estimates). But they disagree about the import of these figures. Because of this, I am going to try to sketch two quite different ways of looking at the known facts and figures. But first I shall discuss what famine looks like and provide a background of some of the most basic facts and figures.

§7 THE LOOK OF FAMINE

Famine is a hidden killer, a dark horse. In the Book of Revelation, other killers are symbolized by highly visible horses and horsemen: the White Horse of Conquest, the Red Horse of War, and the Pale Horse of Death itself.[2] But Famine is symbolized by a Black Horse and Horseman. And so it is in human experience. When famine strikes, relatively few people die "of hunger." They die for the most part of illnesses they would easily have survived if hunger had not weakened them. They die of flu and of intestinal troubles, and disproportionately many of those who die are very young or very old. When there is famine, the survivors too are affected in hidden ways. Children may suffer severe brain damage as a result of early malnutrition; whole populations may be listless and lethargic, unable to muster the energy needed for economic advance, still living but permanently weakened.

We have all seen pictures of starving, skeletal children in the appeals of famine-relief charities. But such emaciation is only the visible and publicizable fraction of the damage the Dark Horse can do. When we wonder whether famine is likely, we must remember that most of its impact is less dramatic. Wherever death rates are higher than they would be with adequate nutrition, famine is *already* taking its toll. Perhaps there will be future famines that are far more visible than most of today's famine, large-scale versions of the disastrous famines that have recently occurred in the southern Sahara and in Bangladesh. Perhaps there will be nothing so dramatic, but rather many lives of unrelenting hunger and premature deaths, without mass migration in search of food or any of the other horrors of extreme famine. If we remember that most of the impact of famine is of this sort, then we realize that famine is not some unknown evil that might strike human populations in the future, but an all-too-familiar evil for many people now living. The question that divides the experts is not so much whether or not there will be future, dramatic famines as whether the endemic hunger and malnutrition that millions now live with can be ended or will become more intense and severe as time goes on.

Famine does not have to be dramatic and catastrophic to inflict acute suffering. It is evident that premature deaths, especially the deaths of children, create great misery. And anyone who has gone hungry even for quite a short while knows how unpleasant, how distracting, and how enfeebling even a short fast (say thirty-six hours, while leading your normal life) can be. Hunger destroys lives in two senses: It literally kills—destroys—the biological basis of life; and it also destroys the lives persons lead, their biographical lives, even when it leaves the biological organism functioning. The survivors of famines suffer the biological deaths of persons they love; and their own biographical life is often shattered by the experience of hunger and the destruction of their way of life.

§8 THE EXTENT OF FAMINE

To get a feel for the extent of these miseries it helps to have a few figures. The population of the world today is around 4 billion—already rather more and rising very fast. Within thirty years it will double; and within another thirty redouble, and so on. But there is no point in projecting this sort of figure indefinitely and coming out with the fantasy of a world without resources but weighed down by or literally covered with living humans. In the end the expansion of resources sets the limit on the population which can remain alive.

The history of the last two centuries is one of rapid increases in resources, which have permitted a corresponding growth in human population. Two centuries ago there were only 800 million human beings alive. We do not know how many there will be alive in another two centuries. But however few or many there are, there will not be more alive than there are resources to sustain them. (There may be fewer, since some or all persons may live at a higher-than-subsistence standard.) Sustained overpopulation is impossible: as soon as there are more people than there are resources, some people will die. When populations expand beyond their resources, they are trimmed by famine. But we do not have to be at the mercy of famines. It is possible for populations to control their own rate of growth and to ensure that the number of additional persons does not exceed the rate of growth of resources available for those persons. A population that succeeded in this task (and some have) would not suffer famine. It would be free not only of the spectacular miseries of catastrophic famines but of the slower, hidden famine that shows itself in premature deaths, lack of resistance to illness, and lack of energy. On these matters the experts do not disagree.

§9 CAN FAMINE BE AVOIDED?

When, however, one turns to the question of how famine and malnutrition can best be ended and whether it is at all likely that they will be ended, the answers given vary widely. All agree that the task of avoiding famine is enormous and difficult. But some think it can be done only by curbing population growth, since economic growth cannot be adequately increased, while others think that the whole problem is to achieve economic growth and that population growth cannot be much affected while famine and poverty remain. I shall call these two outlooks on the problems posed by famine respectively the *neo-Malthusian outlook* and the *developmentalist outlook*. (I will explain the two terms shortly.) The difference between neo-Malthusians and developmentalists is as follows: Imagine a community you know (perhaps your home town) faced with a doubling of population in the next twenty years. If present living standards are to be maintained, then resources too will have to double in that twenty-year period. Now if one thinks of the additional people *just* as additional mouths to be fed and bodies to be clothed and sheltered and doctored—i.e., as consumers—then the task looks insuperable. That is how neo-Malthusians would look at the problems of this community. But if one thinks of the additional persons as additional hands—i.e., as producers—then the problem looks less daunting. Perhaps many hands will even make lighter work. If additional persons contribute as well as consume, then their arrival may solve any problem it creates. Developmentalists would see the imagined community in these terms.

§10 THE NEO-MALTHUSIANS

Neo-Malthusians take their name from Thomas Malthus (1766–1834), who argued as early as 1798, in his *Essay on the Principle of Population,* that it was necessary to seek voluntary curbs on the rate of population growth because unrestricted population growth would be faster than the growth in food supplies and so lead to famine. Since Malthus's time, more optimistic writers have thought him wrong, because in some countries the rate of economic growth has far outstripped the rate of growth of population. The average person in the developed countries today is far better off than his or her ancestors were in Malthus's day. Neo-Malthusians don't deny that this economic improvement has occurred. But they think it cannot be sustained, and correctly point out that it is in some part due to the smaller size of family now common in the developed world. Neo-Malthusians think Malthus was right, spectacularly right. They characterize population growth as an explosion or a bomb that economic growth cannot defuse.

Neo-Malthusians think economic growth faces technical and political obstacles. The main *technical* obstacles are that the most easily exploited natural resources (land, energy, minerals) have already been exploited; and further exploitation will run into increasing difficulties due to pollution and low yields. Further, the continued evasion of Malthus's predictions requires continued discovery and introduction of new technology, and we have no guarantee that innovation can continue indefinitely.

Other neo-Malthusians stress the *political* rather than the technical obstacles to sustained economic growth. It is apparent enough in the 1970s that there is nothing automatic about economic growth, and that long periods of history have seen no more fundamental changes than succeeding lean and fat years. It is apparent enough too that we have no science of economic growth: the management of economies is still a disputed art. The move from the invention of a new product or process to its effective introduction is far from routine. People often resist changes in their accustomed modes of life in spite of the lure of gain: in any case, they may often, sometimes rightly, suspect that it is not they who will gain. Those who most need to make economic changes may be least able to do so. They may lack know-how, capital, ambition, or traditions of sustained work and self-improvement. The regions where economic growth can be relatively easily achieved may be far from those whose poverty and rising populations make it most necessary. But it is hard and costly to transfer the products of prospering regions to distant and poorer areas.

All neo-Malthusians doubt the possibility of continued economic growth. Some of them—the optimists—believe that famine is not inevitable but can be reduced and averted by bringing the rate of growth of population below the rate of achievable economic growth. Such optimists think population growth can be directly controlled, whatever the economic context, and argue strongly for further fertility-control programs. Birth-control measures have affected population growth in developed countries for some generations, and efforts have been made (often funded by developed nations) to introduce birth-control programs to poorer countries.

Other neo-Malthusians—the true pessimists—do not believe that population-control programs can end or avert famine. Once more, as with the general Malthusian skepticism about sustained economic growth, the reasons are in part technical and in part political. The technical obstacles are perhaps less important here. There is no technical reason that contraception should become *more* difficult. Even so, there are technical problems. The only wholly safe and reliable contraceptive techniques are forms of sterilization that are not reliably reversible and so are unpopular. Reversible techniques (e.g., IUDs, rubber devices, chemical contraception, or early abortion) are either not entirely reliable or not entirely safe, especially for persons without access to medical care; nor are they generally cheap enough or easy enough for persons living in great poverty to use.

But the political and psychological obstacles to reduced fertility are more profound, as well as more poorly understood. Access to contraceptive technology in no way guarantees that persons will have smaller families. (Nor does lack of access always prevent reductions in family size.) In the now developed countries of Europe and North America, a *demographic transition* took place that so reduced family size that these countries now have, despite long-lived populations and little emigration, low rates of population growth. In most underdeveloped countries, no such demographic transition has taken place, even though death rates have fallen fast. Thus the net result is a rate of population growth that is now very fast indeed. In many places— e.g., in recent years, South Asia—it has been so fast that population growth has absorbed or more than absorbed the economic growth that might otherwise have made possible improved standards of life. At least some neo-Malthusians, contemplating the difficulties of economic growth and doubting that the rate of population growth can be curbed, have been led to the view that famines are inevitable, and that the curbing of the human population by lack of available food is unavoidable.

§11 THE DEVELOPMENTALISTS

Developmentalists take a different view of the facts of famine. Like neo-Malthusians, they hold diverse views, and I shall summarize only a representative sample.

Developmentalists join with pessimistic neo-Malthusians in their view of attempts to avert famine by controlling population growth. They note that where population growth rates fall this is often *after* a reasonable level of economic well-being has been reached. For the very poor, children are an asset as well as a liability. Only one's children can provide for old age or sickness or the other disabilities that in wealthier countries (and in planned economies) are covered by social or private insurance schemes. Further, the children of the very poor have a shorter period of dependence than those of the better off. They begin to earn their keep early in childhood, and their consumption is very low. Developmentalists tend to think that there will be no demographic transition in countries with rapidly growing populations until there has been at least some economic growth. Trying to achieve economic growth by limiting population growth is therefore going about the problem in the wrong way.

Nor are all developmentalists convinced that rapid population growth hampers economic growth. They point to countries like Brazil, where a high rate of economic growth in the last decade has been accompanied and perhaps helped by rapid population growth. They point to countries with low population density—e.g., Gabon—whose economic development appears to require more not fewer persons. They point above all to the disproportionate consumption of world resources by developed nations and argue that if population reduction is to make a difference it is there, and not among impoverished populations, that the most difference could be made. Many developmentalists are citizens or supporters of underdeveloped countries and view the control of population growth with some suspicion. It has generally been the case that population programs have been urged on poor countries by richer ones. Now experts from poorer countries often point out that poverty might also be alleviated by redistributing the excessive resources of the developed countries. Developmentalists are far from unanimous about the best strategy for economic growth and the part redistribution has to play in it. But they are convinced that attempts to sidestep the need for economic growth by seeking population control alone are at best futile and at worst a form of covert genocide practiced by the haves on the have-nots. In their view, the only route to avoiding famine is to use economic planning to overcome problems of economic production and distribution, which (though constrained by the problems neo-Malthusians emphasize) are nevertheless solvable.

I have given this rather long account of different views of population and resource problems as background for a discussion of what we ought or may do about these problems, and especially about the problem of avoiding famine. It is commonly said in writings on moral problems that 'ought' implies 'can'. This is taken to mean that we cannot have obligations to do things that are impossible for us to do. I may have an obligation to deliver a sack of potatoes to your house (perhaps I sold them to you); but I cannot have an obligation to deliver you the crock of gold that lies at the rainbow's end. Similarly, we cannot have obligations to do the impossible with respect to famine and population problems. If the neo-Malthusians are right that we cannot achieve indefinite economic growth, then nobody and no group of persons can have an obligation to do so, and it is in no way wrong to fail to do so. If the developmentalists are right in claiming that population growth cannot be curbed outside an overall strategy for economic growth, then nobody can have the obligation to restrict population growth in isolation. As we turn to utilitarian and Kantian arguments about the moral problems famine presents, we shall find repeatedly that uncertainty about what is possible makes the conclusions uncertain and indeterminate.

III. UTILITARIAN APPROACHES TO SOME FAMINE PROBLEMS

§12 BENTHAM AND UTILITARIANISM

The first person to call himself a "utilitarian" was an eighteenth-century polemicist and philosopher named Jeremy Bentham (1748–1832). Bentham is now best known for having written a work with the forbidding title *Introduction to the Principles of Morals and Legislation*. But his aim was anything but forbidding. What he wanted was to increase human happiness; and he hoped that legal and moral reform undertaken in a systematic and organized way would do so. His object, he wrote, was "to rear the fabric of felicity by the hands of reason and law." The first principle of this task he called the Principle of Utility, and he stated that he meant by this

> that principle which approves or disapproves of every action whatsoever, according to the tendency which it appears to have to augment or diminish the happiness of the party whose interest is in question.[3]

If faced with a decision, we should, according to Bentham's moral theory, ask ourselves which act is most likely to most increase the happiness of the person or persons affected. Legislators should ask which law would make most of those who have to live under it most happy. If we can discover the act or law that will do most for the happiness of the affected parties, then we have found the act that is right and required.

If we accept the Principle of Utility, we will solve problems by working out which of the many courses of action we might take will produce most happiness. That course of action is obligatory, and if more than one action is likely to yield maximal happiness, then it would be obligatory to do one or other of them, though perhaps it would not be morally important which was picked.

Bentham realized that his theory required decision makers to go through long calculations in order to work out which available action (or legislation) would produce the greatest happiness. He was undaunted. He thought we could list the available courses of action, and then work out how much happiness each would produce. He pointed out seven different aspects of happiness or pleasure that calculations should reckon with. If an act would affect only oneself, then one should consider the *intensity* of the pleasure or happiness; its *duration;* its *certainty* or *uncertainty* (counting unlikely pleasures like winning lotteries at a lower rate than sure things); its *propinquity* or *remoteness* (counting the pleasures we expect to enjoy soon at a higher rate); its *fecundity,* by which he meant its likelihood of being followed by more, similar pleasures; and its *purity,* which is the degree to which the pleasure is unmixed with pains. If an act would affect others as well as oneself, it becomes necessary to work out the pleasure's *extent* also, which is the number of persons who will be affected pleasurably or painfully by the proposed act. Bentham realized that using this 'felicific calculus' would be strenuous: he even provided a mnemonic poem to help us to remember what we should take into account:

> *Intense, long, certain, speedy, fruitful, pure—*
> Such marks in *pleasures* and in *pains* endure.
> Such pleasures seek if *private* be thy end:
> If it be *public,* wide let them *extend.*[4]

But this is really not enough. Bentham's calculus requires that we make calculations for which we *nearly always* lack the necessary information. We often are unsure how much happiness an act will produce, and how much unhappiness. In fact, we don't know how we are supposed to measure happiness. We often don't know who will be affected, to what extent, or for how long. Bentham apparently didn't find this sort of problem baffling. He was lifelong in the thick of political controversy taking determined stands in favor of one or another proposal for reform on the basis of utility calculations he felt able to make. He agitated tirelessly for reform of harsh or pointless laws, for the extension of the franchise, and for the abolition of slavery. When he died in 1832, some of the reforms he had advocated had already been enacted by the British Parliament; others were fought for and achieved in the following decades.

If we assess Bentham's system soberly and discount some of his enthusiasm, we might conclude that its scope is large but its precision spurious. For if we can't do the calculations, we won't get answers at all.

§13 MILL AND UTILITARIANISM

Bentham's successors, including some of his warmest admirers, were more skeptical about the felicific calculus. Even though they thought utilitarian moral theory right in principle, they doubted that moral decisions could be made a matter of calculation. The most famous of these successors was John Stuart Mill (1806–1873), whose main work in ethics has as its very title the word 'utilitarianism'. Like Bentham, John Stuart Mill took as the main principle of his moral theory the Greatest Happiness Principle. He formulated it as "actions are right in proportion as they tend to promote happiness, wrong as they tend to produce the reverse of happiness."

John Stuart Mill, even though he had grown up in Bentham's shadow and had been groomed as the heir to Bentham's reforming crusade, was not merely a disciple. He doubted that it was possible to make calculations of any precision about the amount of pleasure to be expected from each possible course of action. Pleasures, he thought, may vary in quality as well as in amount. And if some pleasures are of higher quality than others, then it is impossible to add them together, just as it is impossible to add together Bentham's height and John Stuart Mill's weight. To add things together they must be measured in the same units, or in units that (like inches and centimeters) can be reduced to one another. But on Mill's view, some pleasures are *irreducibly* superior to others. "It is better," he wrote, "to be a human being dissatisfied than a pig satisfied; better to be Socrates dissatisfied than a fool satisfied." However intense, fecund, long, or pure, the swinish or foolish pleasures are, they do not in Mill's view outweigh the pleasures of a nobler and more reflective life. This is shown, he claims, by the fact that all who have experience both of higher and of brutish pleasures prefer the former.

This division between Bentham and Mill did not end the influence of utilitarianism in moral thought. Utilitarianism of one form or another is advocated by many different thinkers. There are still some (mostly economists and decision theorists) who hope for Benthamite precision in handling problems. But there are more who regard utilitarianism in a humane rather than a scientific way. This majority does not claim that precise calculations of pleasure can be made to guide every decision, but only that we can bring informed judgment to bear on the question of which action is most likely to enhance human happiness, and that if we can identify such an action with reasonable certainty, we ought to embark on it, while if we can identify actions that seem likely to produce misery, we should avoid them. I shall now consider what such a humane version of utilitarianism would tell us about our moral duties towards those who do or may suffer famine.

§14 SOME UTILITARIAN ARGUMENTS ABOUT FAMINE

I shall now take the simplified utilitarian moral theory outlined in the last section and show how it can be and has been used to draw diametrically opposed conclusions about what affluent persons (ourselves, for example) ought to do about famines that they could help to relieve. I will try to use this embarrassing result as the basis for an assessment of utilitarianism, and then I will explore more intricate and, perhaps, more adequate versions of utilitarian moral theory.

To reach the opposing conclusions, I shall draw on the arguments of two well known recent articles about moral problems raised by the prospect of famine. The first of these articles is Garrett Hardin's "Lifeboat Ethics: The Case Against Helping the Poor," which argues that the affluent ought not to relieve famine. The second is Peter Singer's "Famine, Affluence and Morality," which argues that the affluent ought to relieve famine.[5]

Neither of these articles relies on an argument acceptable *only* to utilitarians. Both authors assume only a more general *consequentialist* position. Consequentialist moral theories regard acts as obligatory if they have better results than all other available acts. Some consequentialists are not utilitarians, since they think that there are other things besides human happiness and human suffering that are good and bad. For example, some consequentialists think that the existence of beauty, even when nobody is there to enjoy it, is a good thing, and that therefore we ought to try to make sure that there are beautiful things even if we believe that no human will survive to enjoy them. However, since all serious consequentialists have shared the utilitarian view that human happiness and misery are respectively good and bad, many of their conclusions can also be reached from utilitarian assumptions. The bad results to which both Hardin and Singer allude in their arguments about famine relief are results that *any* utilitarian thinks bad—namely the misery that famines cause. So Hardin's and Singer's conclusions can be reached by that special form of consequentialist argument that is utilitarian. Their conclusions do not depend on there being anything other than human happiness that is good, or anything other than human misery that is bad. Each argument can be framed as a straightforwardly utilitarian argument.

§15 A UTILITARIAN ARGUES AGAINST RELIEVING FAMINE

Hardin's argument can be summarized as follows. The citizens of affluent countries are like passengers in a lifeboat around which other, desperate, shipwrecked persons are swimming. The people in the lifeboat can help some of those in the water. But if the citizens of affluent countries help some of the starving, this will, unlike many lifeboat rescues, have bad effects. To begin with, according to Hardin, the affluent countries will then have less of a safety margin, like an overladen lifeboat. This alone might be outweighed by the added happiness of those who have been rescued. But the longer-run effects are bad for everyone. The rescued will assume that they are secure, will multiply their numbers and so make future rescues impossible. It is better, from a utilitarian point of view, to lose some lives now than to lose more lives later. So no rescue attempt should be made.

Hardin's (and others')[6] use of the lifeboat metaphor has been widely criticized. Persons in lifeboats have (often) some title to their seats. Rescue operations in lifeboats endanger the rescuers. There are few interests that those inside a boat share with the drowning. By contrast, it is not clear that affluent persons and nations are entitled to all they have. Some of it may have been acquired by exploiting poorer nations or persons; even if it has been acquired by standard market procedures, the terms of trade are often (and perhaps unfairly) weighted in favor of the powerful. Further, it is not clear that attempts at famine relief present any serious danger to the affluent. Some forms of famine relief may even benefit the donors—for example, if by sending more food relief, the prosperous give up diets that leave them fat and prone to heart attacks, then they too will be healthier. Finally, the interests of the rich and poor are often congruent, while those of the rescued and the drowning are diametrically opposed. Everybody has an interest in the preservation of peace and in the prevention of ecocatastrophes. But though the analogy between affluent nations and lifeboats has these limitations, Hardin's main point can be stated without depending on the metaphor.

His main claim is that famine relief *encourages* population growth to a level that cannot be indefinitely sustained. If we pool our resources with the poor of this world, soon nobody will have a safety margin and even local and temporary crop failures will have a drastic effect. If we pooled resources, we should all, aptly enough, be in the same boat; and the boat would not be stormworthy.

Hardin's view is that once population has been increased by the added children of those who would otherwise not have survived to have children at all, the total amount of suffering will be larger than the suffering from unrelieved famine of a smaller number of people. He writes:

> If poor countries received no food from outside, the rate of their population growth would be periodically checked by crop failures and famines. But if they can always draw on a world food bank in time of need, their population can continue to grow unchecked, and so will their "need" for aid. In the short run a world food bank may diminish that need, but in the long run it actually increases the need without limit.[7]

Hardin's view of famine is harsh, but reasoned. He thinks that feeding the hungry is merely likely to lead to population growth and greater suffering in the future. Feeding the hungry preserves lives and happiness now, but costs great loss of life and misery in the future. The prosperous not merely may but ought, if they are utilitarians, to leave the starving to themselves, to die or to survive as best they may.

§16 A UTILITARIAN ARGUES FOR RELIEVING FAMINE

Singer, however, thinks that the prosperous have an obligation to try to feed the hungry. He starts from the assumption that

> if it is in our power to prevent something bad from happening, without thereby sacrificing anything of comparable moral importance, we ought, morally, to do it.[8]

He then points out that contributing to famine relief, even contributing a large proportion of a prosperous income, say 50 percent, does not sacrifice anything of comparable importance. But it does help prevent the misery and loss of life that famines produce. So, he concludes, the prosperous ought to help feed the hungry and ought to do so up to that point at which they have indeed reduced their own standard of living so far that something of comparable moral importance would be sacrificed by further giving.

This conclusion too can be reached by a quite explicitly utilitarian route. For what makes famine bad, as Singer and all utilitarians agree, is that it causes acute human suffering; and what makes the sacrifices of the prosperous less bad is that they cause much less acute human suffering. (Compare what it would be like to have no car with what it would be like to go without half the food you now eat.) So if we think that we ought to do acts that will prevent or reduce suffering, or still better, produce happiness, then it seems that there is little doubt that we ought to relieve famine, even if it costs us a fair amount of minor unhappiness to do so.

§17 WHY DO HARDIN AND SINGER REACH INCOMPATIBLE CONCLUSIONS?

Reading Hardin and Singer presents any utilitarian and any consequentialist with a dilemma. For it seems that their starting points are not very different, but that they have come to incompatible conclusions. I believe this is due to their divergent views about the effects of attempts at famine relief and not to a difference over moral theory.

Hardin pays attention to the long-term effects of uncontrolled population growth. He is a pessimistic neo-Malthusian who thinks that there is no method to curtail population growth except by letting famines run their "natural" course. With luck, this experience may educate the survivors of "irresponsible" populations so that they then do curb the size of their families; but only the reality of famine can teach this lesson. If Hardin thought there was another less painful way in which population growth could be curbed, he would presumably have to modify his conclusion. For the suffering of those who would die of famine need not then be outweighed by the future suffering of those born as the result of unchecked population growth.

Singer is an optimistic neo-Malthusian who tends to underestimate the long-range effects of saving persons from famine without being able to prevent population growth that might later outstrip available resources. In a later appendix to his article, he modifies his view and claims that the obligation of the prosperous to the starving is an obligation to give aid that checks rather than promotes population growth. He is even prepared to think that countries that take no steps to reduce their population growth should not be given aid.[9] Here his conclusion is much closer to Hardin's. Unless we can resolve disputes about the facts and future of population growth, we cannot resolve the dispute between Singer and Hardin.

§18 THE UNCERTAINTY OF CONSEQUENCES

One of the many similarities between Hardin's and Singer's work is that both shift easily between talking about the obligations of nations and those of individuals. This ambidexterity has been a part of the utilitarian tradition of moral thought ever since Bentham wrote *Principles of Morals and Legislation.* It is one of the strengths of the utilitarian moral thought that it can be so generally applied; its scope is large. The actions of individuals, the policies of nations, and the activities of groups (ranging from multinational corporations to famine-relief charities to government departments) all affect human happiness. So the acts of all these agents and agencies can be morally assessed by the same arguments. But this enormous scope of utilitarian moral theory is no help unless we can know fairly precisely what effects proposed acts would have. A conscientious utilitarian, even one who does not credit Benthamite calculations, must try to work out the effects of his or her actions; and as we have seen in the case of Hardin and Singer, it is hard to work these out at all, let alone with precision, when we deliberate about famine relief.

This imprecision is reflected in the great diversity of (often incompatible) policies for which utilitarian arguments are offered. At the most general level, passionate utilitarian arguments have been made *both* for centralized economic planning *and* for reliance on free markets. At a less global level, utilitarians repeatedly disagree about policies and actions.

Consider, for example, the following policy for the distribution of famine relief that some utilitarians advocate. William and Paul Paddock in *Famine—1975!* suggest that famine relief should be allocated on a *triage* principle.[10] When resources are limited they should be given to those who can benefit most. The term 'triage' is taken from military medicine. In medical contexts it means that the worst injured should be left to die and the walking wounded left to hobble. All care should go to the third, in-between group. In the case of famine, this means that aid should be concentrated on those countries that have the best chance of survival if aided but won't survive otherwise. Triage is a policy that seeks to maximize the number of survivors. Lives are to be sacrificed, but only for the sake of preserving more lives by concentrating resources where they will do the most good.

Utilitarians would probably endorse the triage principle *if* they thought all lives tended on average to be equally happy. The preservation of life is necessary for the existence of happy lives, so that if other things were equal (which they seldom are) preserving as many lives as possible would produce the greatest total amount of happiness. Only if some of the lives to be preserved were likely to be on balance painful would utilitarians advocate that they not be preserved. By the same token, utilitarians would oppose 'heroic' medical measures to prolong painful lives; they do not value life itself but the happiness of lives. It does not bother utilitarians that triaging sacrifices some lives for the sake of others. For utilitarians, biological life is no end in itself, but a means to the enjoyment of living. And where a greater total of happiness or enjoyment would be achieved by triaging populations or countries, it is not merely permissible but a duty to adopt this policy. Happiness should be maximized even if doing so costs some lives.

However, it is far from clear that triaging would in fact maximize happiness. First, lives are *not* all equally happy, and if not all lives can be preserved, utilitarians would prefer policies that ensure that those whose prospects are happiest, rather than those whose survival is easiest to secure, are helped. Second, it is difficult to see how triaging can legitimately be applied beyond the medical context. For there are no clear standards to determine who is the "best risk." Any nation or region might be made more likely to survive if given the right sort of help. Some nations or regions seem to need more help, but since we lack a scientific account of the methods for achieving economic development (though theories are legion), we don't really know whom it will be hardest to save in the long run. In this century some seemingly desperate countries have achieved steady economic growth, and others that seemed as well placed have not. So it is not obvious whom the triagers should reject as hopeless cases, whom they should dismiss as walking wounded, and whom they should help. Thus it is unclear whether utilitarians would on reflection endorse a triaging policy.

Alternatively, consider some of the following dilemmas that individual utilitarians might meet while thinking about famine. In all of these examples, suppose that A is a moderately prosperous utilitarian who sincerely wants to use his extra money to help relieve famine and save lives, which he reasonably judges would greatly reduce human misery. A might wonder whether to try to send money to a poor family in a poor country. But how is he to be sure that they get the money, and that it doesn't fall into the hands of some nonneedy local official, who uses it to worsen the situation of others, perhaps by buying imported goods, leaving those who formerly sold to him without a customer? Might not the result of A's generosity also worsen the position of those needy families whom he cannot benefit, who find that the going price of goods has risen beyond their means because benefited families can afford to pay more and have driven up the price? Or suppose A thinks that the way to benefit the poor is to purchase the products of needy nations and areas. Might not this encourage production for fickle export markets, retard the development of local self-sufficiency, and make people more vulnerable in hard years? If A buys Brazilian coffee despite its high price, can he be sure whom he is benefiting? Might not he be encouraging the development of a one-crop economy with all its potential for disaster? Or suppose that in order to encourage development in the Arab world, A advocates (and, as a consumer, follows) policies that are heavily dependent on importing OPEC oil. May not this policy fuel nothing more productive of human happiness and life than the Middle East arms race? Or suppose A hopes to assist, through work in a multinational corporation, the introduction of more modern industrial processes in some under-developed economy. How can he be sure that this will not lead to a developed enclave within a traditional economy that, on the whole, causes friction for many, unemployment for some, and gain for a few who were not in the first place the most needy? Or suppose that A is an economic planner in a socialist country. Hoping to improve welfare by raising per capita meat consumption, he institutes heavy grain purchases (for animal fodder) on the world market, which prevent increased cereal production from benefiting the hungrier peoples and drive up world cereal prices.[11] Once more, the net effect of an act intended to increase happiness may be to increase rather than reduce human misery. The conundrums can be multiplied again and again. The point is that if we are to try to work out the consequences of our actions as utilitarian theory demands we should, we shall repeatedly find ourselves confronted with impossible calculations. Utilitarianism offers us spurious precision in moral argument.[12]

The reasons for these difficulties lie deep in the structure of utilitarian theory and are not likely to be remedied by further research. For utilitarians do not say that one should look *just* at the fairly local effects of one's own act. After all, if the aim is to maximize human happiness and to minimize human misery, then there is no point in basing one's calculations on the false assumption that the consequences of one's own act can be isolated. There is no point, for example, in aiding poor countries if the good effects of the aid are outweighed by bad effects, such as propping up a regime that opposes change and economic growth. There is no point, on utilitarian calculations, in spending all one's efforts in lobbying for reduced "defense" spending so that swords can be beaten into plowshares if the result is likely to be either that no reduction takes place but that one has no time to make more modest contributions to human happiness, or, on the other hand, that a reduction takes place but produces increased unemployment and no plowshares, while leading arms purchasers to turn to different sellers. For utilitarians, it is *results,* not *intentions,* that count, and the calculation of results must therefore be taken seriously. I can know my intentions fairly clearly, but I can never be sure about all the effects of my own acts or of an institution's policies.

The very comprehensive and systematic structure that makes utilitarian moral theory attractive to many people becomes on reflection one of its nightmares. We may often be fairly clear about the short-term effect on nearby people of what we propose to do. But we are seldom clear about the total effect or tendency of acts or policies in an economically interdependent world where we might affect the lives of persons thousands of miles or many generations away. We face in our own time decisions about energy policy that will deeply affect future lives. If we leave a world of nuclear radiation or terrorism, or of fossil-fuel famine, or of health- and crop-destroying pollution, we shall make future persons more miserable—or less happy—than they might have been had we made different decisions. Yet, which of us can be sure (including the disputing experts) which decision is likely to have the happiest results? Difficulties of calculations affect persons and agencies (from corner stores to nation states to the United Nations). They produce an uncomfortable feeling that we cannot make the most needed calculations, so can never say: "This is the way to minimize misery, so this ought to be done." Where there is no limit to the number of consequences, nearby or remote, that we ought to consider, conclusions seem to evaporate, not to crystallize. Utilitarians may start out wanting to be realists who soberly calculate the outcomes and the odds; but there seems to be no natural stopping point before they find themselves trying to be futurologists who seek to uncover the impact of their actions, or that of their institutions, in a vast and complex causal web that extends indefinitely into the future.

A serious utilitarian faces a morally strenuous life. Every decision is a moral decision, since any act affects human happiness or prevents another act that might affect human happiness. A utilitarian can never say: "I've done my duty." However great one's contribution has been, it is likely that there are further miseries one could in part reduce without causing oneself or others comparable misery. As each misery is vanquished there will be another waiting for one's ministrations. And so utilitarianism comes to seem not the most precise but at once the vaguest and the most demanding of moral theories. Utilitarian arguments founder, not just occasionally but systematically, on our uncertainty about calculating the effects of our own acts when combined with others'. Research might help a bit, but it would not resolve the indeterminacy in all cases. This is a standard difficulty of utilitarian moral theory, but it appears much graver in thinking about a problem like famine, where particularly long and intricate causal chains must *nearly always* be considered. Utilitarians can get nowhere unless they are reasonably sure about the effects acts they consider are likely to have. If utilitarians do not know this, then they have no way of telling whether a proposed act or policy is obligatory, forbidden, or neither. I shall turn now to a move that may help utilitarians overcome some of these difficulties. If this move fails, utilitarian thought about famine has achieved little. In spite of the theory's imposing scope, it cannot guide action unless reasonably precise calculations about happiness and misery can be made.

§19 UTILITARIANS ON JUSTICE AND BENEFICENCE

Many moral theories offer us a less ambitious view of what our duties are than does the simplified utilitarianism we have so far been considering. On that simplified theory, it seemed that however many good works one threw oneself into, more would be required of one. Duty would not be fulfilled until one was so exhausted in its pursuit that further striving would cause greater misery than any one could alleviate, or would make one less efficient in future relief of misery. Many moral theories, however, distinguish between a smaller core of duties that are stringently required and a larger number of acts that are meritorious but not so strictly required. This distinction is often thought to amount to a distinction between the demands of justice and those of beneficence.

John Stuart Mill claims that utilitarians can make this distinction. Obligations of justice are, he says, those to whose performance some other has a right. For example, justice requires that we not assault others without cause and that they have a right to our controlling ourselves and not doing so. Duties of justice can be contrasted with other duties to whose performance others have no right. As a utilitarian, one may have an obligation to share one's good fortune with needy others, since doing so would presumably increase the total happiness of humankind. But one cannot share with all others, since they are too many, and it is not possible to tell who has the best claim to beneficence. So none of the needy can be said to have a right to be helped. There are no rights to beneficent acts as there are rights to acts of justice. If a utilitarian gives no help to anyone needy, then he or she has done nothing unjust, though one who has some time to spare ought to do further acts that produce happiness.

Mill was not the first person to think justice more important than beneficence. This is a much older claim that he fitted into utilitarian thought. The problem is that borrowed clothes do not always fit. From the start there have been skeptics who claimed that there is no way in which utilitarian moral theory can show what we ordinarily think matters of justice—where others have rights—morally more important than other duties. But if Mill is right and the distinction between justice and beneficence can be made *within* utilitarian moral thought, then we may be able to make utilitarian calculations for the most important moral decisions. Precision may be possible in matters of justice even if it eludes us elsewhere; if this is so, utilitarianism is a plausible theory for thinking about many famine problems.

§20 JUSTICE AND RIGHTS

Duties of justice are duties we owe to others. If justice requires something of us, others have a legitimate claim to our performance. Sometimes all others have such a claim, as with the duty not to assault others. Sometimes, on the other hand, duties of justice are owed to particular others. If I have taken out a loan to buy a car, then I am obliged to repay the bank in accordance with the agreement made. But it won't help to pay anyone else. Only the bank that made the loan has a legitimate claim to be repaid. When a duty is owed to specific persons (and many duties can only be owed to specific persons), the corresponding right is a *claim right.* When a duty is owed equally to all others, it can be at most a duty not to harm or interfere, and the corollary right is a *liberty right.*

There is commonly thought to be a third sort of duty to which neither liberty rights nor claim rights correspond. Duties to help others, to do things that are kind or beneficent, are usually thought to lack corresponding rights of either sort. Utilitarians and others agree that, though we ought to be kind and helpful, if we are not, we violate nobody's rights.

If these distinctions can indeed be fitted into utilitarian theory, then utilitarians can say that there is a point at which we have done all that we are obliged to do. When we have filled the claims of justice —which may be hard enough—others have no further claim rights to our services. To be sure, it would be mean spirited never to help others. But if nothing unjust has been done, then nobody has been wronged and nothing further is stringently demanded. If utilitarians can reach this position, then they need not see the moral life as an unremitting quest to maximize happiness, but as a stringently required and fulfillable set of duties, to which should be added the embellishment of acts of kindness and helpfulness, no particular one of which is required or owed to anybody. They might conclude that famine requires of us stringent justice in trade and foreign relations, which can be precisely calculated, but that aid and assistance are not owed.

§21 UTILITARIAN QUANDARIES OVER CHOOSING A FAMINE-RELIEF POLICY

However, it is unclear how utilitarians are to distinguish duties of justice and those of beneficence, since they try to derive all duties from a single foundation—namely, their efficient contribution to human happiness. It is as though utilitarians characterized all duties as duties of beneficence but then held that some of them are owed more stringently than others, even though their contribution to human happiness is no more striking. The claim to distinguish justice from beneficence depends on showing that acts of justice *standardly* produce more happiness, and unjust acts, more misery. John Stuart Mill claims this in the final chapter of *Utilitarianism*:

> Justice is a name for certain moral requirements, which, regarded collectively, stand higher in the scale of social utility, and are therefore of more paramount obligation, than any others.[13]

Mill is no doubt right that some obligations are more important on utilitarian grounds than are others. It is not so clear that these more important obligations are obligations of justice.

Ever since utilitarianism was precisely formulated, there have been disputes over whether the utilitarian principle can really show that justice is more important for human happiness than beneficence. Can utilitarians really show that duties not to assault, steal, murder, breach faith, and the like are always more stringently required than duties to aid and assist? Mill himself allowed that there might be some occasions when a duty of justice should be breached for the sake of an act of kindness. Right after the passage just quoted he writes:

> Particular cases may occur in which some other social duty is so important, as to overrule any one of the general maxims of justice. Thus, to save a life, it may not only be allowable, but a duty, to steal, or take by force, the necessary food or medicine, or to kidnap and compel to officiate, the only medical practitioner.[14]

So it appears that Mill does not think that justice is always more important than benevolence. These are examples of cases where *unjust* acts may maximize happiness. But if there are such cases, how good is the distinction utilitarians try to draw between justice and benevolence? Perhaps there are no types of action that *standardly* maximize happiness.

This dilemma can be made quite sharp by considering its implications for famine. Suppose you are wondering whether to pay this month's mortgage or car payment or to give the money to famine relief. Let's also suppose that in this case you have no doubt that famine relief is really what the money will be used for. You are sure no corrupt officials will lay hands on this gift; the people to whom you send it really are desperately hungry and will use the gift well. With the amount of money you would send they will be well launched on the road to self-sufficiency. They will at any rate be able to sleep without pangs of hunger for months to come. Their children will soon be much healthier and may even start school and so have more chance of breaking out of the cycle of poverty. On the other hand, if you miss one mortgage or car payment, there is going to be considerable fuss. The bank will make it unpleasant for you. They probably will not foreclose, but they will write nasty letters and they may give you a bad credit rating. Still, nothing like so much unhappiness will be caused by your giving but not paying as by your paying and not giving. Surely then, any serious utilitarian ought to miss the mortgage payment for the sake of famine relief. Beneficence should here take precedence over justice.

If utilitarians cannot draw a firm distinction between the requirements of justice and those of beneficence, then we cannot hope for more precision in matters of justice than the theory as a whole offers us. There will be no area in which the theory can give reasonably precise results, and we may find the theory indeterminate even over the most urgent and perplexing questions. Utilitarianism is an appealing moral theory. Its scope is comprehensive and it seeks precise resolution of moral dilemmas. It aims to tell institutions and individuals which available act or policy is best, which next best, third best, and so on, *when the data are available.* But if it turns out that the comprehensive data that utilitarians need are *usually* not available, then the attraction fades. We are left with indecision rather than precision, even in matters of justice.

I shall now turn to a consideration of Kantian ethics—which does not have the same comprehensive aims, nor the same dependence on data being available—with the hope that it may provide a more usable theory for dealing with a causally intricate and little understood nexus of problems such as those posed by the prospect of "a time of famines."

IV. KANTIAN APPROACHES TO SOME FAMINE PROBLEMS

§22 A SIMPLIFIED ACCOUNT OF KANT'S ETHICS

Kant's moral theory has acquired the reputation of being forbiddingly difficult to understand and, once understood, excessively demanding in its requirements. I don't believe that this reputation has been wholly earned, and I am going to try to undermine it. In §§23–26 I shall try to reduce some of the difficulties, and in §§27–30 I shall try to show the implications of a Kantian moral theory for action toward those who do or may suffer famine. Finally, I shall compare Kantian and utilitarian approaches and assess their strengths and weaknesses.

The main method by which I propose to avoid some of the difficulties of Kant's moral theory is by explaining only one part of the theory. This does not seem to me to be an irresponsible approach in this case. One of the things that makes Kant's moral theory hard to understand is that he gives a number of different versions of the principle that he calls the Supreme Principle of Morality, and these different versions don't look at all like one another. They also don't look at all like the utilitarians' Greatest Happiness Principle. But the Kantian principle is supposed to play a similar role in arguments about what to do.

Kant calls his Supreme Principle the *Categorical Imperative;* its various versions also have sonorous names. One is called the Formula of Univeral Law; another is the Formula of the Kingdom of Ends. The one on which I shall concentrate is known as the *Formula of the End in Itself.* To understand why Kant thinks that these picturesquely named principles are equivalent to one another takes quite a lot of close and detailed analysis of Kant's philosophy. I shall avoid this and concentrate on showing the implications of this version of the Categorical Imperative.

§23 THE FORMULA OF THE END IN ITSELF

Kant states the Formula of the End in Itself as follows:

> Act in such a way that you always treat humanity, whether in your own person or in the person of any other, never simply as a means but always at the same time as an end.[15]

To understand this we need to know what it is to treat a person as a means or as an end. According to Kant, each of our acts reflects one or more *maxims.* The maxim of the act is the principle on which one sees oneself as acting. A maxim expresses a person's policy, or if he or she has no settled policy, the principle underlying the particular intention or decision on which he or she acts. Thus, a person who decides "This year I'll give 10 percent of my income to famine relief" has as a maxim the principle of tithing his or her income for famine relief. In practice, the difference between intentions and maxims is of little importance, for given any intention, we can formulate the corresponding maxim by deleting references to particular times, places, and persons. In what follows I shall take the terms 'maxim' and 'intention' as equivalent.

Whenever we act intentionally, we have at least one maxim and can, if we reflect, state what it is. (There is of course room for self-deception here—"I'm only keeping the wolf from the door" we may claim as we wolf down enough to keep ourselves overweight, or, more to the point, enough to feed someone else who hasn't enough food.)

When we want to work out whether an act we propose to do is right or wrong, according to Kant, we should look at our maxims and not at how much misery or happiness the act is likely to produce, and whether it does better at increasing happiness than other available acts. We just have to check that the act we have in mind will not use anyone as a mere means, and, if possible, that it will treat other persons as ends in themselves.

§24 USING PERSONS AS MERE MEANS

To use someone as a *mere means* is to involve them in a scheme of action *to which they could not in principle consent.* Kant does not say that there is anything wrong about using someone as a means. Evidently we have to do so in any cooperative scheme of action. If I cash a check I use the teller as a means, without whom I could not lay my hands on the cash; the teller in turn uses me as a means to earn his or her living. But in this case, each party consents to her or his part in the transaction. Kant would say that though they use one another as means, they do not use one another as *mere* means. Each person assumes that the other has maxims of his or her own and is not just a thing or a prop to be manipulated.

But there are other situations where one person uses another in a way to which the other could not in principle consent. For example, one person may make a promise to another with every intention of breaking it. If the promise is accepted, then the person to whom it was given must be ignorant of what the promisor's intention (maxim) really is. If one knew that the promisor did not intend to do what he or she was promising, one would, after all, not accept or rely on the promise. It would be as though there had been no promise made. Successful false promising depends on deceiving the person to whom the promise is made about what one's real maxim is. And since the person who is deceived doesn't know that real maxim, he or she can't in principle consent to his or her part in the proposed scheme of action. The person who is deceived is, as it were, a prop or a tool—a mere means—in the false promisor's scheme. A person who promises falsely treats the acceptor of the promise as a prop or a thing and not as a person. In Kant's view, it is this that makes false promising wrong.

One standard way of using others as mere means is by deceiving them. By getting someone involved in a business scheme or a criminal activity on false pretenses, or by giving a misleading account of what one is about, or by making a false promise or a fraudulent contract, one involves another in something to which he or she in principle cannot consent, since the scheme requires that he or she doesn't know what is going on. Another standard way of using others as mere means is by coercing them. If a rich or powerful person threatens a debtor with bankruptcy unless he or she joins in some scheme, then the creditor's intention is to coerce; and the debtor, if coerced, cannot consent to his or her part in the creditor's scheme. To make the example more specific: If a moneylender in an Indian village threatens not to renew a vital loan unless he is given the debtor's land, then he uses the debtor as a mere means. He coerces the debtor, who cannot truly consent to this "offer he can't refuse." (Of course the outward form of such transactions may look like ordinary commercial dealings, but we know very well that some offers and demands couched in that form are coercive.)

In Kant's view, acts that are done on maxims that require deception or coercion of others, and so cannot have the consent of those others (for consent precludes both deception and coercion), are wrong. When we act on such maxims, we treat others as mere means, as things rather than as ends in themselves. If we act on such maxims, our acts are not only wrong but unjust: such acts wrong the particular others who are deceived or coerced.

§25 TREATING PERSONS AS ENDS IN THEMSELVES

Duties of justice are, in Kant's view (as in many others'), the most important of our duties. When we fail in these duties, we have used some other or others as mere means. But there are also cases where, though we do not use others as mere means, still we fail to use them as ends in themselves in the fullest possible way. To treat someone as an end in him or herself requires in the first place that one not use him or her as mere means, that one respect each as a rational person with his or her own maxims. But beyond that, one may also seek to foster others' plans and maxims by sharing some of their ends. To act benefi-cently is to seek others' happiness, therefore to intend to achieve some of the things that those others aim at with their maxims. If I want to make others happy, I will adopt maxims that not merely do not manip-ulate them but that foster some of their plans and activities. Benefi-cent acts try to achieve what others want. However, we cannot seek everything that others want; their wants are too numerous and di-verse, and, of course, sometimes incompatible. It follows that benefi-cence has to be selective.

There is then quite a sharp distinction between the requirements of justice and of beneficence in Kantian ethics. Justice requires that we act on *no* maxims that use others as mere means. Beneficence requires that we act on *some* maxims that foster others' ends, though it is a matter for judgment and discretion which of their ends we foster. Some maxims no doubt ought not to be fostered because it would be unjust to do so. Kantians are not committed to working interminably through a list of happiness-producing and misery-reducing acts; but there are some acts whose obligatoriness utilitarians may need to debate as they try to compare total outcomes of different choices, to which Kantians are stringently bound. Kantians will claim that they have done nothing wrong if none of their acts is unjust, and that their duty is complete if in addition their life plans have in the circum-stances been reasonably beneficent.

In making sure that they meet all the demands of justice, Kantians do not try to compare all available acts and see which has the best effects. They consider only the proposals for action that occur to them and check that these proposals use no other as mere means. If they do not, the act is permissible; if omitting the act would use another as mere means, the act is obligatory. Kant's theory has less scope than utilitarianism. Kantians do not claim to discover whether acts whose maxims they don't know fully are just. They may be reluctant to judge others' acts or policies that cannot be regarded as the maxim of any person or institution. They cannot rank acts in order of merit. Yet, the theory offers more precision than utilitarianism when data are scarce. One can usually tell whether one's act would use others as mere means, even when its impact on human happiness is thoroughly ob-scure.

§26 KANTIAN DELIBERATIONS ON FAMINE PROBLEMS

The theory I have just sketched may seem to have little to say about famine problems. For it is a theory that forbids us to use others as mere means but does not require us to direct our benevolence first to those who suffer most. A conscientious Kantian, it seems, has only to avoid being unjust to those who suffer famine and can then be beneficent to those nearer home. He or she would not be obliged to help the starving, even if no others were equally distressed.

Kant's moral theory does make less massive demands on moral agents than utilitarian moral theory. On the other hand, it is somewhat clearer just what the more stringent demands are, and they are not negligible. We have here a contrast between a theory that makes massive but often indeterminate demands and a theory that makes fewer but less unambiguous demands and leaves other questions, in particular the allocation of beneficence, unresolved. We have also a contrast between a theory whose scope is comprehensive and one that is applicable only to persons acting intentionally and to those institutions that adopt policies, and so maxims. Kantian ethics is silent about the moral status of unintentional action; utilitarians seek to assess all consequences regardless of the intentions that led to them.

§27 KANTIAN DUTIES OF JUSTICE IN TIMES OF FAMINE

In famine situations, Kantian moral theory requires unambiguously that we do no injustice. We should not act on any maxim that uses another as mere means, so we should neither deceive nor coerce others. Such a requirement can become quite exacting when the means of life are scarce, when persons can more easily be coerced, and when the advantage of gaining more than what is justly due to one is great. I shall give a list of acts that on Kantian principles it would be unjust to do, but that one might be strongly tempted to do in famine conditions.

I will begin with a list of acts that one might be tempted to do as a member of a famine-stricken population. First, where there is a rationing scheme, one ought not to cheat and seek to get more than one's share—any scheme of cheating will use someone as mere means. Nor may one take advantage of others' desperation to profiteer or divert goods onto the black market or to accumulate a fortune out of others' misfortunes. Transactions that are outwardly sales and purchases can be coercive when one party is desperate. All the forms of corruption that deceive or put pressure on others are also wrong: hoarding unallocated food, diverting relief supplies for private use, corruptly using one's influence to others' disadvantage. Such requirements are far from trivial and frequently violated in hard times. In severe famines, refraining from coercing and deceiving may risk one's own life and require the greatest courage.

Second, justice requires that in famine situations one still try to fulfill one's duties to particular others. For example, even in times of famine, a person has duties to try to provide for dependents. These duties may, tragically, be unfulfillable. If they are, Kantian ethical theory would not judge wrong the acts of a person who had done her or his best. There have no doubt been times in human history where there was nothing to be done except abandon the weak and old or to leave children to fend for themselves as best they might. But providing the supporter of dependents acts on maxims of attempting to meet their claims, he or she uses no others as mere means to his or her own survival and is not unjust. A conscientious attempt to meet the particular obligations one has undertaken may also require of one many further maxims of self-restraint and of endeavor—for example, it may require a conscientious attempt to avoid having (further) children; it may require contributing one's time and effort to programs of economic development. Where there is no other means to fulfill particular obligations, Kantian principles may require a generation of sacrifice. They will not, however, require one to seek to maximize the happiness of later generations but only to establish the modest security and prosperity needed for meeting present obligations.

The obligations of those who live with or near famine are undoubtedly stringent and exacting; for those who live further off it is rather harder to see what a Kantian moral theory demands. Might it not, for example, be permissible to do nothing at all about those suffering famine? Might one not ensure that one does nothing unjust to the victims of famine by adopting no maxims whatsoever that mention them? To do so would, at the least, require one to refrain from certain deceptive and coercive practices frequently employed during the European exploration and economic penetration of the now under-developed world and still not unknown. For example, it would be unjust to "purchase" valuable lands and resources from persons who don't understand commercial transactions or exclusive property rights or mineral rights, so do not understand that their acceptance of trinkets destroys their traditional economic pattern and way of life. The old adage "trade follows the flag" reminds us to how great an extent the economic penetration of the less-developed countries involved elements of coercion and deception, so was on Kantian principles unjust (regardless of whether or not the net effect has benefited the citizens of those countries).

Few persons in the developed world today find themselves faced with the possibility of adopting on a grand scale maxims of deceiving or coercing persons living in poverty. But at least some people find that their jobs require them to make decisions about investment and aid policies that enormously affect the lives of those nearest to famine. What does a commitment to Kantian moral theory demand of such persons?

It has become common in writings in ethics and social policy to distinguish between one's *personal responsibilities* and one's *role responsibilities.* So a person may say, "As an individual I sympathize, but in my official capacity I can do nothing"; or we may excuse persons' acts of coercion because they are acting in some particular capacity—e.g., as a soldier or a jailer. On the other hand, this distinction isn't made or accepted by everyone. At the Nuremberg trials of war criminals, the defense "I was only doing my job" was disallowed, at least for those whose command position meant that they had some discretion in what they did. Kantians generally would play down any distinction between a person's own responsibilities and his or her role responsibilities. They would not deny that in any capacity one is accountable for certain things for which as a private person one is not accountable. For example, the treasurer of an organization is accountable to the board and has to present periodic reports and to keep specified records. But if she fails to do one of these things for which she is held accountable she will be held responsible for that failure—it will be imputable to her as an individual. When we take on positions, we *add* to our responsibilities those that the job requires; but we do not lose those that are already required of us. Our social role or job gives us, on Kant's view, no license to use others as mere means; even business executives and aid officials and social revolutionaries will act unjustly, so wrongly, if they deceive or coerce—however benevolent their motives.

If persons are responsible for all their acts, it follows that it would be unjust for aid officials to coerce persons into accepting sterilization, wrong for them to use coercive power to achieve political advantages (such as military bases) or commercial advantages (such as trade agreements that will harm the other country). It would be wrong for the executives of large corporations to extort too high a price for continued operation employment and normal trading. Where a less-developed country is pushed to exempt a multinational corporation from tax laws, or to construct out of its meager tax revenues the infrastructure of roads, harbors, or airports (not to mention executive mansions) that the corporation—but perhaps not the country—needs, then one suspects that some coercion has been involved.

The problem with such judgments—and it is an immense problem—is that it is hard to identify coercion and deception in complicated institutional settings. It is not hard to understand what is coercive about one person threatening another with serious injury if he won't comply with the first person's suggestion. But it is not at all easy to tell where the outward forms of political and commercial negotiation—which often involve an element of threat—have become coercive. I can't here explore this fascinating question. But I think it is at least fairly clear that the preservation of the outward forms of negotiation, bargaining, and voluntary consent do *not* demonstrate that there is no coercion, especially when one party is vastly more powerful or the other in dire need. Just as our judiciary has a long tradition of voiding contracts and agreements on grounds of duress or incompetence of one of the parties, so one can imagine a tribunal of an analogous sort rejecting at least some treaties and agreements as coercive, despite the fact that they were negotiated between "sovereign" powers or their representatives. In particular, where such agreements were negotiated with some of the cruder deceptions and coercion of the early days of European economic expansion or the subtler coercions and deceptions of contemporary superpowers, it seems doubtful that the justice of the agreement could be sustained.

Justice, of course, is not everything, even for Kantians. But its demands are ones that they can reasonably strive to fulfill. They may have some uncertain moments—for example, does advocating cheap raw materials mean advocating an international trade system in which the less developed will continue to suffer the pressures of the developed world—or is it a benevolent policy that will maximize world trade and benefit all parties, while doing no one an injustice? But for Kantians, the important moral choices are above all those in which one acts directly, not those in which one decides which patterns of actions to encourage in others or in those institutions that one can influence. And such moral decisions include decisions about the benevolent acts that one will or will not do.

§28 KANTIAN DUTIES OF BENEFICENCE IN TIMES OF FAMINE

The grounds of duties of beneficence are that such acts not merely don't use others as mere means but are acts that develop or promote others' ends and that, in particular, foster others' capacities to pursue ends, to be autonomous beings.

Clearly there are many opportunities for beneficence. But one area in which the *primary* task of developing others' capacity to pursue their own ends is particularly needed is in the parts of the world where extreme poverty and hunger leave people unable to pursue *any* of their other ends. Beneficence directed at putting people in a position to pursue whatever ends they may have has, for Kant, a stronger claim on us than beneficence directed at sharing ends with those who are already in a position to pursue varieties of ends. It would be nice if I bought a tennis racquet to play with my friend who is tennis mad and never has enough partners; but it is more important to make people able to plan their own lives to a minimal extent. It is nice to walk a second mile with someone who requests one's company; better to share a cloak with someone who may otherwise be too cold to make any journey. Though these suggestions are not a detailed set of instructions for the allocation of beneficence by Kantians, they show that relief of famine must stand very high among duties of beneficence.

§29 THE LIMITS OF KANTIAN ETHICS: INTENTIONS AND RESULTS

Kantian ethics differs from utilitarian ethics both in its scope and in the precision with which it guides action. Every action, whether of a person or of an agency, can be assessed by utilitarian methods, provided only that information is available about all the consequences of the act. The theory has unlimited scope, but, owing to lack of data, often lacks precision. Kantian ethics has a more restricted scope. Since it assesses actions by looking at the maxims of agents, it can only assess intentional acts. This means that it is most at home in assessing individuals' acts; but it can be extended to assess acts of agencies that (like corporations and governments and student unions) have decision-making procedures. It can do nothing to assess patterns of action that reflect no intention or policy, hence it cannot assess the acts of groups lacking decision-making procedures, such as the student movement, the women's movement, or the consumer movement.

It may seem a great limitation of Kantian ethics that it concentrates on intentions to the neglect of results. It might seem that all conscientious Kantians have to do is to make sure that they never intend to use others as mere means, and that they sometimes intend to foster others' ends. And, as we all know, good intentions sometimes lead to bad results, and correspondingly, bad intentions sometimes do no harm, or even produce good. If Hardin is right, the good intentions of those who feed the starving lead to dreadful results in the long run. If some traditional arguments in favor of capitalism are right, the greed and selfishness of the profit motive have produced unparalleled prosperity for many.

But such discrepancies between intentions and results are the exception and not the rule. For we cannot just *claim* that our intentions are good and do what we will. Our intentions reflect what we expect the immediate results of our action to be. Nobody credits the "intentions" of a couple who practice neither celibacy nor contraception but still insist "we never meant to have (more) children." Conception is likely (and known to be likely) in such cases. Where people's expressed intentions ignore the normal and predictable results of what they do, we infer that (if they are not amazingly ignorant) their words do not express their true intentions. The Formula of the End in Itself applies to the intentions on which one acts—not to some prettified version that one may avow. Provided this intention—the agent's real intention —uses no other as mere means, he or she does nothing unjust. If some of his or her intentions foster others' ends, then he or she is sometimes beneficent. It is therefore possible for people to test their proposals by Kantian arguments even when they lack the comprehensive causal knowledge that utilitarianism requires. Conscientious Kantians can work out whether they will be doing wrong by some act even though they know that their foresight is limited and that they may cause some harm or fail to cause some benefit. But they will not cause harms that they can foresee without this being reflected in their intentions.

V. RESPECT FOR LIFE: A COMPARISON OF KANTIAN AND UTILITARIAN VIEWS

§30 UTILITARIANISM AND RESPECT FOR LIFE

From the differing implications that Kantian and utilitarian moral theories have for our actions towards those who do or may suffer famine, we can discover two sharply contrasting views of the value of human life. Utilitarians value happiness and the absence or reduction of misery. As a utilitarian one ought (if conscientious) to devote one's life to achieving the best possible balance of happiness over misery. If one's life plan remains in doubt, this will be because the means to this end are often unclear. But whenever the causal tendency of acts is clear, utilitarians will be able to discern the acts they should successively do in order to improve the world's balance of happiness over unhappiness.

This task is not one for the faint-hearted. First, it is dauntingly long, indeed interminable. Second, it may at times require the sacrifice of happiness, and even of lives, for the sake of a greater happiness. Such sacrifice may be morally required not only when the person whose happiness or even whose life is at stake volunteers to make the sacrifice. It may be necessary to sacrifice some lives for the sake of others. As our control over the means of ending and preserving human life has increased, analogous dilemmas have arisen in many areas for utilitarians. Should life be preserved at the cost of pain when modern medicine makes this possible? Should life be preserved without hope of consciousness? Should triage policies, because they may maximize the number of survivors, be used to determine who should be left to starve? Should population growth be fostered wherever it will increase the total of human happiness—or on some views so long as average happiness is not reduced? All these questions can be fitted into utilitarian frameworks and answered *if* we have the relevant information. And sometimes the answer will be that human happiness demands the sacrifice of lives, including the sacrifice of unwilling lives. Further, for most utilitarians, it makes no difference if the unwilling sacrifices involve acts of injustice to those whose lives are to be lost. It might, for example, prove necessary for maximal happiness that some persons have their allotted rations, or their hard-earned income, diverted for others' benefit. Or it might turn out that some generations must sacrifice comforts or liberties and even lives to rear "the fabric of felicity" for their successors. Utilitarians do not deny these possibilities, though the imprecision of our knowledge of consequences often blurs the implications of the theory. If we peer through the blur, we see that the utilitarian view is that lives may indeed be sacrificed for the sake of a greater good even when the persons are not willing. There is nothing wrong with using another as a mere means provided that the end for which the person is so used is a happier result than could have been achieved any other way, taking into account the misery the means have caused. In utilitarian thought, persons are not ends in themselves. Their special moral status derives from their being means to the production of happiness. Human life has therefore a high though derivative value, and one life may be taken for the sake of greater happiness in other lives, or for ending of misery in that life. Nor is there any deep difference between ending a life for the sake of others' happiness by not helping (e.g., by triaging) and doing so by harming. Because the distinction between justice and beneficence is not sharply made within utilitarianism, it is not possible to say that triaging is a matter of not benefiting, while other interventions are a matter of injustice.

Utilitarian moral theory has then a rather paradoxical view of the value of human life. Living, conscious humans are (along with other sentient beings) necessary for the existence of everything utilitarians value. But it is not their being alive but the state of their consciousness that is of value. Hence, the best results may require certain lives to be lost—by whatever means—for the sake of the total happiness and absence of misery that can be produced.

§31 KANT AND RESPECT FOR PERSONS

Kantians reach different conclusions about human life. Human life is valuable because humans (and conceivably other beings, e.g., angels or apes) are the bearers of rational life. Humans are able to choose and to plan. This capacity and its exercise are of such value that they ought not to be sacrificed for anything of lesser value. Therefore, no one rational or autonomous creature should be treated as mere means for the enjoyment or even the happiness of another. We may in Kant's view justifiably—even nobly—risk or sacrifice our lives for others. For in doing so we follow our own maxim and nobody uses us as mere means. But no others may use either our lives or our bodies for a scheme that they have either coerced or deceived us into joining. For in doing so they would fail to treat us as rational beings; they would use us as mere means and not as ends in ourselves.

It is conceivable that a society of Kantians, all of whom took pains to use no other as mere means, would end up with less happiness or with fewer persons alive than would some societies of complying utilitarians. For since the Kantians would be strictly bound only to justice, they might without wrongdoing be quite selective in their beneficence and fail to maximize either survival rates or happiness, or even to achieve as much of either as a strenuous group of utilitarians, who somehow make the right calculations. On the other hand, nobody will have been made an instrument of others' survival or happiness in the society of complying Kantians.

§32 IS FAMINE A MORAL PROBLEM AFTER ALL?

Utilitarian and Kantian moral theories are not the only possible ones. There is no space here to examine further possibilities, but one basic criticism of our enterprise cannot be avoided. It is this: Many people would hold that no *moral* theory is appropriate for considering famine. These critics would assert that famine can be averted only by economic changes and that these can be produced only by political action, whether of a reforming or a revolutionary sort. They would point to China, where control over famine that was widespread and endemic has been achieved not by acting on a moral theory but by enormous social and political changes. They would hold that the theories relevant for controlling famine are political and social theories, and many would see Marxist theories of social change as particularly important.

Theories of political and social change and of economic development are vital in choosing *how* to lessen famine, and they may show us what is possible and what impossible in particular circumstances. Even so, these theories do not eliminate moral questions. We still have to decide (and the Chinese leaders had to decide) about any possible or proposed social or political change, whether the results it seeks and the means it uses are morally acceptable. Revolutions have costs as well as benefits, and some of these may be morally unacceptable. Some ways of ending famine may cost far more in human lives and misery than other ways. Choices between different policies are, of course, social and political choices; but they are also unavoidably moral choices. In making them we must rely on some moral theory or other, however vague or imprecise our understanding of the theory. So it is worth our while to make sure that the moral theory on which we do rely is not deficient in ways that can be avoided by care and reflection.

NOTES

1.   Luke, 10:5.
2.   Relevation, 6:5.
3.   J. Bentham, *Introduction to the Principles of Morals and Legislation,* Oxford, 1789, Ch. I.
4.   *Ibid.,* Ch. IV.
5.   G. Hardin, "Lifeboat Ethics: The Case Against Helping the Poor," *Psychology Today,* September, 1974; P. Singer, "Famine, Affluence and Morality," *Philosophy and Public Affairs,* vol. 7, no. 3, 1972; both are reprinted in W. Aiken and H. La Follette, *World Hunger and Moral Obligation,* Englewood Cliffs, N.J., Prentice-Hall, 1977.

6. Two anthologies in which the use of the lifeboat and similar analogies are debated are G. R. Lucas and T. W. Ogletree, eds., *Lifeboat Ethics*, New York, Harper & Row, 1976, and P. G. Brown and H. Shue, eds., *Food Policy: The Responsibility of the United States in Life and Death Decisions*, New York, Free Press, 1977.

7. G. Hardin, in W. Aiken and H. La Follette, *op. cit.*, p. 17.

8. P. Singer, in W. Aiken and H. La Follette, *op. cit.*, p. 24.

9. *Ibid.*, p. 34.

10. Triage is discussed in W. and P. Paddock, *Famine—1975!*, Boston, Little, Brown, 1967; it is criticized in D. Callahan, "Doing Well by Doing Good," *Hastings Center Report*, December 1974, in D. D. Gray, *Triage: Its Variants and Alternatives*, Cambridge, Mass., 1976, author's copyright, and in P. G. Brown, "Some Relationships Between Food, Population and International Economic Justice," *Occasional Population Paper*, New York, Hastings Center, 1977.

11. See L. P. Schertz, "World Needs: Shall the Hungry Be with Us Always?" in P. G. Brown and H. Shue, *op. cit.*

12. It is becoming increasingly clear that some of the difficulties of would-be utilitarian calculators in making decisions about population and resource policies and other matters that may affect future generations are not due *merely* to lack of data. Some of the distinctive problems faced by *any* account of obligations to future generations are discussed in articles by J. Narveson, especially in "Moral Problems of Population," in M. D. Bayles, ed., *Ethics and Population*, Cambridge, Mass., Shenkman, 1976, and by D. Parfitt, "Overpopulation," forthcoming in *Philosophy and Public Affairs*.

13. J. S. Mill, *Utilitarianism*, ed. M. Warnock, New York, New American Library, 1962.

14. *Ibid.*, p. 321.

15. I. Kant, *Groundwork of the Metaphysic of Morals*, tr. H. H. Paton, New York, Harper Torchbooks, 1964, p. 96.

SUGGESTIONS FOR FURTHER READING

Further readings are mentioned below in connection with the section (§) of the essay to which they are most pertinent.

§4 For a readable account of the seventeenth-century revolution in physics and astronomy, see T. Kuhn, *The Copernican Revolution: Planetary Astronomy in the Development of Western Thought*, Cambridge, Mass., Harvard University Press, 1957.

§7 The famine in Bangladesh (then Bengal) is the background of P. Singer, "Famine, Affluence and Morality," *Philosophy and Public Affairs*, vol. 7, no. 3, 1972. See also the article by L. R. Brown and E. P. Eckholm and the one by N. Borlaug and R. Ewell in *Ceres*, March–April 1974, and the items cited in §10 below.

Two books that portray famine vividly are Pearl S. Buck, *The Good Earth*, New York, J. Day Co., 1934, and Cecil Woodham-Smith, *The Great Hunger: Ireland 1845–9*, New York, Harper & Row, 1962.

§10 Two widely read neo-Malthusian books are P. R. Ehrlich, *The Population Bomb*, New York, Ballantine Books, 1968, and W. and P. Paddock, *Famine—1975!*, Boston, Little, Brown, 1967. For a general survey of neo-Malthusian views and a wide-ranging bibliography, see P. J. Henriot and M.

Daniel, "Population and Ecology: An Overview," *Occasional Population Paper,* New York, Hastings Center, 1976.

The political and technical obstacles to economic growth were dramatized by the first "Club of Rome" report, D. Meadows, *et al., The Limits of Growth: A Report for the Club of Rome's Project on the Predicament of Mankind,* New York, Universe Books, 1972. Another recent and readable discussion is R. L. Heilbroner, *An Enquiry into the Human Prospect,* New York, Norton, 1975, which particularly stresses the political implications of technical difficulties in sustaining economic growth. Some recent writers claim that economic growth is not merely difficult but impossible to sustain. See, for example, F. Hirsch, *Social Limits to Growth,* Cambridge, Mass., Harvard University Press, 1976.

The literature on population control and family planning is vast. Some short accounts of central issues are: G. Baraclough, "The Great World Crisis I," *New York Review of Books,* January 1975; H. Raulet "Family Planning and Population Control in Developing Countries," *Demography,* May 1970; D. P. Warwick, "Contraceptives in the Third World," *Hastings Center Report,* August 1975.

§11   The developmentalist position is to be found in numerous books and articles, many of them published in third-world countries. One accessible work is M. Mamdani, *The Myth of Population Control,* New York, Monthly Review Press, 1973. A lucid survey and extensive bibliography can be found in M. E. Conroy, K. Kelleher, and R. I. Villamizar, "The Role of Population Growth in Third World Theories of Underdevelopment," *Occasional Population Paper,* New York, Hastings Center, 1976.

9

The Search for an Environmental Ethic[1]

WILLIAM T. BLACKSTONE

Not so long ago, people tended to know little and care less about the environment. The environment was viewed as a given, something to be used as we humans happened to see fit. If it was coal we needed, then the land was there to be stripped of its hidden treasure. If industrial waste had to be moved, then nature had conveniently supplied us with rivers for this very purpose. Nature existed as a system of inexhaustible, renewable resources. If the supply of coal was depleted here, more could be found there. If freshwater fish could no longer survive in our rivers and lakes, nature would adapt and send forth new species that could survive in the muck. Besides, what were the lives of a few fish, or of whole species of fish, when compared to industrial prosperity?

Times are beginning to change. Today there is a steadily growing body of knowledge about the environment and its impact on the duration and quality of all forms of life. There is also steadily growing alarm. The more we learn, the more we realize that our misuse of the environment can come home to roost. Not only nonhuman life forms are endangered; human life itself is threatened. In Pogo's immortal words, "We have met the enemy, and it is us."

The case of aerosol sprays is a good example of the changing times. How accustomed we once were to their use! How convenient! What harm could they possibly be? An understanding of their harmful effects was slow to come, but recently the National Academy of Sciences has disclosed that the earth's ozone shield is damaged by the fluorocarbons in aerosol sprays. The possible harmful consequences of continued use of aerosol sprays are colossal. As the ozone layer is damaged, it loses its capacity to absorb ultraviolet rays. As this capacity is impaired, the life cycle itself may be threatened. For example, the inability to absorb ultraviolet light could cause the oceans to warm, and this in turn could cause the polar ice caps to melt. If that occurred, it would not be long before the entire world's coastal populations would be endangered. Such developments would be certain to have adverse consequences for all life forms, including humans. All this from a convenience item, the aerosol can.

The fact that the earth's resources are not inexhaustible is another lesson we have only recently begun to learn. There are limits to the supply of coal and copper, oil and tin, and the earth, with its limited resources, simply cannot support an unlimited human population. This means that curbs must be placed on both the rate at which we use the earth's resources and the rate at which we reproduce. Otherwise, widespread famine, poverty, and disease are predictable. Already there are those who maintain that such a future is unavoidable; it is too late to turn back. The food we eat (with its pesticide residue), the air we breathe (with its pollutants), the ever-expanding depletion of energy and mineral resources, the deforestation of our land, the exponential growth rate of the human population; all these factors (and more) combine to lead the more pessimistic among us to see little hope for progress. The dice have been loaded by the past and present. A global catastrophe is coming. It is only a matter of time. The question is not whether but when.

Not everyone regards the future so pessimistically. For some, hope remains. But even among the hopeful there is an emerging consensus that nothing short of a revolution in our thought and action is called for. It will not be enough to pick up litter and use returnable bottles. Profound changes are called for. Environmentalists tell us that this spaceship, earth, is a delicately balanced system of interdependent parts, an ecosystem, each part needing the other, each helping the other. To disturb one part is ultimately to disturb the whole. Though time is running out, we might yet begin to understand that all life forms are affected by how we treat some. Before it is too late, an environmental ethic might be developed; enlightened principles might still be discovered and take hold. Then the future that pessimists foresee can be avoided. But possibly only then.

What shape might such an environmental ethic take? In particular, will we be required to introduce totally new ethical principles, or might we be able to graft an environmental ethic onto long-established principles—for example, the Principle of Utility? This is one of the central questions we will be considering (see §§13–16 and §§18–20). But this question lies far down the road. A good many preliminary points must first be explored. The idea of the value of life calls for special attention. That life has value is an idea that figures prominently in the growing literature in environmental ethics; it is also an idea with a rich heritage in Eastern and Western thought.[2] We shall turn our attention to it in §1. From there we pass on to an examination (§§2–8) of the influential work of the German philosopher-theologian Albert Schweitzer (1875–1965). In §§9–12, the ideas of some other leading thinkers in environmental ethics are discussed. In §17, we summarize some of the main points of emphasis in environmental ethics, and then, in §18, we characterize two different models of how an environmental ethic might look. The remaining sections (§§19–20) consist of a critical examination of the merits of these two models.

This map of the essay that follows might suggest that it contains "the last word" on ecological ethics. That is far from the truth. Ecological ethics is so new, so unsettled, that we are now only beginning to get some sense of the *first* words. This essay aims principally at acquainting the reader with some of these initial mutterings. Its purpose is to provide a basis for further thought in a branch of moral philosophy that is as intellectually exciting as it is practically important.

I. VALUE AND REALITY

§1 THE PRINCIPLE OF THE VALUE OF LIFE

The Principle of the Value of Life is ambiguous. It has somewhat different meanings in different contexts of use. Generally speaking, the principle requires that one respect life, that one not unthinkingly destroy or alter forms of life. Living beings are to be regarded as having a special kind of value. They are not to be viewed as having instrumental value only—that is, they are not to be viewed as being valuable only if or so long as they are useful to some other being. Rather, living beings have a value of their own. Let us call this special kind of value *inherent value,* an expression that should remind us that this value is supposed to inhere in (or belong directly to) living beings themselves. With this terminology established, we can then go on to ask three different but related questions about the Principle of the Value of Life.

The first question we should ask concerns the *scope* of this principle. To ask about the principle's scope is to ask about what forms of life are thought to have inherent value. As we can expect, and as we shall shortly see, different answers might be given. The same is true of the two other questions we want to distinguish. The second question asks about *the degree of inherent value different life forms possess.* What this question brings out is the possibility that, while all living things might have some inherent value, some might be more inherently valuable than others. Inherent value might be a matter of degree rather than an all-or-nothing affair, and those beings that have inherent value might comprise a hierarchy, those with the most inherent value being at the top and those with the least occupying the bottom. Whether inherent value is a matter of degree or whether it is everywhere the same is what our second question asks. We can anticipate having to consider the merits of alternative answers.

Our third question asks not about inherent value itself but about a related matter—namely, *the stringency of the rule against killing* ("Thou shalt not kill" or "It is wrong to kill"). This is a related question because, arguably, what makes it wrong to kill some being, when and if it is wrong, is that something of inherent value is thereby destroyed. Now, when we ask about the stringency of this (or any other) moral rule, what we are interested in determining is what, if anything, could count as a *justified exception* to the rule. Consider the rule "Keep your promises." Most of us recognize that, in some cases, breaking a promise is not wrong; for example, suppose we have borrowed a pistol, promised to return it whenever the owner asks us to, and the owner now makes this request. Only suppose that he or she is in a mentally deranged state and has openly threatened to kill himself or herself or the next passerby. In such a case, we recognize a justified exception to the rule "Keep your promises." It is an exception because we most definitely do not have to return the gun; but it is a *justified* exception because stronger reasons can be given for keeping the gun than for keeping the promise.

Philosophers sometimes talk of "overriding" a moral rule. That is the sort of thing illustrated here. Because greater importance is placed on preventing someone from committing suicide or killing another than on keeping a promise, the fact that we can prevent a killing by not keeping a promise overrides our duty to keep it. So, another way of thinking about the matter of the stringency of a moral rule is to think of this in terms of whether the duty to observe the rule can ever be overridden. If not, then the rule can be said to be absolute, and the stringency of the rule will be absolute also: We are never, under any circumstances, to break the rule. If, on the other hand, justified exceptions to the rule are recognized—if, to put the point differently, it is allowed that the rule can be overridden—then neither the rule nor its stringency is absolute. Instead, the rule will be what philosophers sometimes call a rule of *prima facie* duty, a rule that declares what we ought to do unless we can rationally justify our not doing it by appealing to another, more stringent moral rule, as in the example we justified not keeping a promise by an appeal to the more stringent rule "Act so as to prevent killing."

So, again, we have three questions: (1) What is the *scope* of the principle that life has inherent value? (2) What is the *degree* to which different life forms have inherent value? (3) How *stringent* is the rule against killing? And what we can anticipate is that different thinkers might give different answers to one or all of these questions. We shall not be able to examine all the possible combinations of agreement-disagreement in what follows. Shortly, however, one combination will be examined with a view to dismissing it. Then we shall go on to examine how one thinker favored by environmental ethicists develops his position. This thinker is Albert Schweitzer, and his philosophy is that of "reverence for life." Before turning to these matters, however, something more needs to be said about the scope of the Principle of the Value of Life.

The Scope of the Principle of the Value of Life   Some of those who speak of "the value of life" hold that only *some* forms of *human* life are valuable inherently. According to this view, in other words, it is not the case that all humans are created equal, at least when it comes to inherent value; some human beings are more valuable inherently than are others. So, on this position, the scope of the Principle of the Value of Life is quite limited: It does not go beyond the borders of humanity, and, what is more, it does not even include all humans. Since not all humans are seen as equally valuable, this view presents us with an example of *moral inegalitarianism.* We will not be able to explore views of this type on this occasion.

A second view would have us widen the scope of the principle to include all humans, but it would stop short of including any other life forms within the principle's scope. On this second view, in other words, it is the life of *all and only* human beings that has inherent value. 'Human chauvinism' is a not inappropriate name for this view, though we shall normally refer to it as 'anthropocentrism' (literally 'human-centeredism'). We will discuss this view in considerable detail.

A third and fourth view of the scope of this principle differ in terms of how many forms of *nonhuman* life are thought to be covered by the principle. The third view, as we shall see more fully below, would increase the scope of the principle to include many nonhuman animals, while the fourth would have us go beyond this and include flora, fauna, and the environmental conditions required for sustaining plant and animal life. This fourth view, of course, gives the broadest possible scope to the Principle of the Value of Life, and it is the one that might seem to be required if a genuine environmental ethic is to be developed. We shall have occasion to say a good deal more about it as we proceed.

Rejecting the Extreme   The scope of the Principle of the Value of Life, therefore, has been understood differently by different thinkers. It is important to realize, however, that differences exist concerning the degree of value that different beings are thought to possess. The most extreme position here would be one that held *both* that all living beings have inherent value *and* that the inherent value of any one living being is equal to the inherent value of any other living being. For convenience let us call this position "radical biotic egalitarianism," and let us be certain that we understand what this position is. What it says is that, in terms of inherent value, any one living being (e.g., a carrot) is neither more nor less good than any other (e.g., a person). Thus, if we think that it is morally wrong to kill a person because people are inherently valuable, we would have to think that it is just as wrong, and wrong for the same reason, to kill a carrot.

It is difficult to see how this extreme view can secure any rational support. Life requires death. In the case of human beings, for example, we cannot survive unless we eat, and we cannot eat unless we (or someone else) kills what we consume, even if what we consume consists exclusively of vegetables and vegetable products. It is a bizarre view of morality indeed that would have us believe that, when we pick an apple, we have done something as wrong as killing a human being, or that, when we must choose what to eat, it is no less morally offensive to kill and eat people than it is to kill and eat turnips. Even for those who think that all forms of life have inherent value, therefore, it would be irrational also to think that all forms of life are equally valuable. Unless their position is to be dismissed out of hand, they must acknowledge that some forms of life are more valuable than others, a view that leaves open the possibility that while it is wrong to kill some beings for some reasons (for example, to kill people as a source of food), it may not be wrong, or at least not as wrong, to kill other beings for the same reason (for example, to kill carrots in order to eat them). In the search for a rational environmental ethic, the position of radical biotic egalitarianism must be avoided. As we now turn our attention to Schweitzer's thought we shall want to see whether his celebration of "reverence for life" avoids this.

§2 REVERENCE FOR LIFE

Much of Western ethical and philosophical thought has been anthropocentric. It has conceived of value basically in terms of what has value for us or our Creator. We will discuss this anthropocentrism in greater detail later (§§9–11). Unlike much of Eastern thought—Buddhism and Taoism, for example—where ethical theory attempted to delineate rules and principles not merely relating humans to humans but also humans to nature, Western ethical theory focused more exclusively on the formulation of rules relating humans to each other or humans to God, and God was often conceived as a Creator quite apart from nature. One Western thinker who constitutes an exception to this anthropocentrism is Albert Schweitzer, whose philosophy of reverence for life strongly emphasizes both the value of nonhuman forms of life (animals and plants) and the human obligation to protect and conserve these forms of life. It cannot be justifiably claimed that Schweitzer was aware of the complex ecological interdependence of the phenomena of nature and that that awareness was the key factor in his formulating a reverence-for-life philosophy. The complex causal and ecological knowledge of the intricate regulatory mechanisms of nature was nonexistent when Schweitzer wrote. Ecology is a relatively new science. Some say that it is only forty years old.[3] Schweitzer's ethical stance, rather, is rooted in what he calls "spirituality," the recognition that all living things spring from the same creative source, that all forms of life have certain similarities, and that there is a "spiritual reunion and harmony with the Creative Will which is in and throughout all."[4] Let us examine the major principles of the reverence-for-life ideal.

§3 THE EVOLUTION OF ETHICAL ATTITUDES

Schweitzer claims that ethical attitudes change and evolve over time, and that there is an "advancement of human consciousness." Primitive ethical stances are narrowly oriented. Family relationships, tribal relationships, even relationships of citizens within nations—the scope of ethical concern varies in these cases, but it is too narrow in all. Slavery, the caste system, racism, sexism, excessive nationalism, and other forms of discrimination narrow the scope of ethical concern. Other persons are not recognized as equals, as neighbors, even as fellow citizens within these narrow perspectives. But Schweitzer argues that "in the course of gradual evolution, man sees the circle of his responsibilities widening until he includes in it all human beings with whom he has any dealings."[5] The idea of the brotherhood of all people gains a stronger hold. Moreover, the idea that the world of nature is to be despised, the attitude of "negation of the world," which was taught by Indian thinkers (in the *Bhagavad-Gita,* in particular) and by Christianity (in which our real home is heaven, not the earth) is being overcome by thinkers who urge "affirmation of the world." Schweitzer includes under world-affirmers "the Chinese sages, the prophets of Israel, Zarathustra and the European thinkers of the Renaissance and of modern times."[6] Along with the expansion of the ideal of the brotherhood of all people and the evolution of world-affirmation, Schweitzer sees progress in ethics as including not only the attitude that we must refrain from evil but that we must act for good. "Only the kind of ethics that is linked with affirmation of the world can be natural and complete."[7] Christianity, he declares, is gradually entering into that spirit. It includes now "not only the ideal of self-perfection formulated by Jesus, but also the other ideal of creating new and better material and spiritual conditions for man's existence in this world."[8]

§4 THE WELFARE OF NONHUMAN CREATURES

Advanced ethical consciousness, however, requires not merely the three components mentioned above—the brotherhood of all people, the affirmation of the world, and the requirement that we not only refrain from evil but act for good. It also requires concern for the welfare of nonhuman creatures:

> ... ethics deals not only with people, but also with creatures. Even as we, they have the desire for well-being, the endurance of suffering, and the horror of annihilation. Those who have retained an un-

blunted moral sensibility find it natural to share concern with the fate of all living creatures. The thoughtful cannot help recognizing that kindly conduct toward nonhuman life is a natural requirement of ethics. That men hesitate to practice this law has its reasons. In fact, concern with the lot of all living creatures with which we have dealing plunges us into more variegated and more confusing conflicts than concern restricted to human beings. The novel and tragic element is that in this field we are continually facing the decision between killing or letting live. The farmer cannot raise all the animals that are born in his herd. He will keep only as many as he can feed and raise with assurance of profit. Moreover, in many cases we are compelled to sacrifice some living creature in order to save others threatened by it.[9]

§5 THE NECESSARY SACRIFICE OF LIFE

Schweitzer's reverence-for-life ethic recognizes that some forms of life must be sacrificed to assure the survival of other forms. "It recognizes as good only the preserving and benefitting of life: any injury to, and destruction of life, unless it is imposed upon us by fate, is regarded as evil."[10] If harming and destroying other forms of life are necessary, we must incur "the guilt of such actions." But killing other creatures from "sheer thoughtlessness" or for sport is the destruction of life for no good reason. Such action violates not only the commandment to love, which is contained in the principle of reverence for life. It also violates the principle itself, which "calls for compassion for all creatures of life."[11] Speaking specifically of the suffering of animals, Schweitzer says:

> When abuse of animals is widespread, when the bellowing of thirsty animals in cattle cars is heard and ignored, when cruelty still prevails in many slaughterhouses, when animals are clumsily and painfully butchered in our kitchens, when brutish people inflict unimaginable torments upon animals and when some animals are exposed to the cruel games of children, all of us share in the guilt.[12]

All life forms a continuum for Schweitzer, and "the ethic of reverence for life makes no sharp distinction between higher and lower, more precious and less precious lives."[13] If such gradations in value are made, they rest on a "wholly subjective standard." "How can we know what importance other living organisms have in themselves and in terms of the universe?"[14] Implicit here is a nonanthropocentric approach to value. It is beyond our capacity to estimate the value of other forms of life: ". . . the absolute ethics of the will-to-live must reverence every form of life, seeking so far as possible to refrain from destroying any life."[15]

This reverence applies not just to sentient life but to nonsentient life as well. One must not "decapitate some flower by the roadside," just by way of thoughtlessly passing the time. For then one sins against life without being under "the compulsion of necessity."[16]

Schweitzer has great respect for the ethic of Jesus Christ and for that of David Hume (1711–1776), the philosopher. But both, he believes, are inadequate for the same reason. The scope of their concern is too narrow. The ethic of Christ involves the principle of love, but it is confined basically to the relationships between persons and between persons and God. Hume's ethic of sympathy, the view that our ethical attitudes are the result of our ability to sympathize with other similar beings—"The capacity to understand and live other's lives in our own"—is "headed in the right direction . . ."[17] But it stops short because it is "dominated by the contemporary dogma that ethics is concerned only with the relationship of man to man. Therefore . . . Hume twisted sympathy to mean only a relationship between like kinds."[18] For Schweitzer "sympathy" must be expanded into reverence for life. We must break loose from purely anthropocentric ethical traditions: ". . . we find sympathy to be natural for any type of life, without any restrictions, so long as we are capable of imagining in such life the characteristics which we find in our own. That is, dread of extinction, fear of pain, and the desire for happiness. In short, the adequate explanation of sympathy is to be found rooted back in reverence for life."[19]

Much of this expanded sense of sympathy, this reverence for all of life rooted in our ability to see that all forms of life have some similarity to the life that is in each of us, reverberates in the writings of current ecological ethicists. The overall rationale of current theorists may emphasize the ecological interdependence of natural objects and processes more specifically—though Schweitzer himself explicitly states that "nature compels us to recognize the fact of mutual dependence, each life necessarily helping the other lives which are linked to it. In the very fibers of our being, we bear within ourselves the fact of the solidarity of life."[20] But the expanded sense of sympathy for all of life, the wider theory of value, and the expanded approach to moral and legal rights found in the writings of some current environmental ethicists reflect to a remarkable extent the components of Schweitzer's reverence-for-life ethic. The ecological threats to the existence and quality of life of man may have brought on these current ethical reflections. But the "spirituality" stressed by Schweitzer comes out loud and clear, as we shall see. It offers an ethical alternative that, in the language of Schweitzer, will liberate mankind from the "poverty-stricken pragmatism in which it has been limping along."[21]

§6 SOME PROBLEMS FOR SCHWEITZER'S POSITION

Schweitzer, then, as we have seen, gives us answers to the three questions we posed earlier. In response to our question about the *scope* of the Principle of the Value of Life, he replies that all life, not just all and only human life, has a value of its own. In response to our question about the *degree* to which different beings have inherent value, he replies, in effect, that there is no objective basis for making such a distinction: "the ethic of reverence for life makes no sharp distinction between higher and lower, more precious and less precious forms of life." And in response to our third question, the one that inquires about the *stringency of the prohibition against killing,* he answers that killing may sometimes be justified, which commits him to the view that this prohibition is not absolute but instead imposes a *prima facie* duty, one that can be overridden by an appeal to more stringent moral rules. This combination of answers to our three questions gives rise to serious problems for those who would accept Schweitzer's position. Our interest here will be to characterize what some of these problems are and to explain why they do pose serious threats to the adequacy of Schweitzer's position. We shall not here attempt a resolution of these problems ourselves.

The first question that must arise is what, according to Schweitzer, counts as a justified exception to the prohibition against killing? If someone tells us that it is wrong to kill anything "unless it is necessary," then we shall surely want to know how we are supposed to determine what is and what is not "necessary." Necessary for what and to whom? It is not unfair to Schweitzer to note that he gives us no clear direction on these matters. But clear direction is what is wanted. Otherwise we run the risk of having "what is necessary" determined by the interests of the stronger, especially by the interests of human beings. The use made of animals in scientific research, for example, often is defended on the grounds that this is "necessary." But those for whom this use of animals is "necessary" turn out to be human beings. It is because human beings have an interest in their health and in the acquisition of knowledge that animals are used as "necessary" research subjects. Take away these ends and we take away the "necessity" of using them in this way. So, what must be established, if the "necessity" of killing any being is to be justified, is what goals are morally worth pursuing. Unless or until we have established this, we will not be in any position to establish when killing is, and when it is not, necessary. It is not clear that Schweitzer has given us any workable basis for evaluating the worth of those ends we do or might pursue, and, to that extent, it is not clear that he has given us a workable basis for determining what makes killing necessary.

This problem of the necessity of killing is made all the more acute by Schweitzer's claim that there is no objective ground for judging to what degree various life forms are inherently valuable. If all forms of life are equally valuable, then it should be just as wrong to kill a daisy as it is to kill a person. This is a position that must strike us as incredible, and it is reasonably clear that Schweitzer himself did not have any such position in mind when he celebrated the ethic of reverence for life. Schweitzer is no radical biotic egalitarian! But the problem remains of how to account for the hierarchy of inherent value various kinds of life are supposed to possess, assuming, as Schweitzer evidently does, that some forms of life are inherently more valuable than others. Moreover, we must endeavor to do this without lapsing into the very kind of anthropocentrism that Schweitzer would have us abandon; that is, we cannot be content just with saying that human lives are inherently more valuable than other forms of life *because they are human*. If we are right, and Schweitzer does not give us the kind of theory required by the philosophy of reverence for life he extols, then, though it does not follow that reverence for life must be abandoned as a viable foundation for an environmental ethic, it does follow that those who would use Schweitzer's philosophy as a basis for their environmental ethic must strengthen this philosophy where it is weakest. Whether this can be done is something we shall explore later on (§§18–20). For the present, there are two further points about Schweitzer's position that should be noted, the first with direct ethical implications, the second with implications of a more indirect sort. Let us consider these points in order.

§7 THE VALUE OF LIFE AND COMPENSATION

Schweitzer states that

> No one has the right to take for granted his own advantages over others in health, in talents, in ability, in success, in a happy childhood or congenial home conditions. One must pay a price for all these boons. What one owes in return is a special responsibility for other lives.[22]

This aspect of Schweitzer's ethic is strongly emphasized in recent essays by Herbert Spiegelberg.[23] He interprets Schweitzer as maintaining that "fortune obligates." If one, through the luck of the natural draw, inherits certain natural abilities and opportunities, and others, through contingencies over which they have no control, do not, then those blessed by good fortune *owe* those who are not so blessed. The moral debt is rooted in the natural inequalities. Persons who enjoy unearned benefits from the luck of the draw, biological and social, must compensate those who are deprived because of a bad natural draw. "The more fortunate owe to those less fortunate a compensation in proportion to their handicaps."[24] Prior to any voluntary activity, nature itself creates a moral imbalance for which the fortunate *owe* compensation and for which the unfortunate are *due* compensation.

Now, it is vital that we understand what is and what is not being said here. We can gain some understanding if we make use of a distinction sometimes drawn in moral philosophy between (a) duties of benevolence and (b) duties of justice. Suppose we agree that we have a set of duties that include being kind, helpful, and generous. These we will call duties of benevolence. And suppose we also assume that we have another set of duties that include the duties to be fair, impartial, and honest. Let us call these duties of justice. Now, duties of benevolence seem to differ in important ways from duties of justice. Take the duty to be generous, for example. Even if I have such a duty, it does not follow that I owe it to be generous to any particular person or agency. A representative of the United Fund, for example, certainly cannot claim that, because I have a duty to be generous, I have a duty to be generous to the United Fund in particular. How I discharge my duty to be generous is a matter left up to my personal discretion. I can pick and choose between those to whom I wish to contribute, how much I wish to contribute, when I wish to contribute, etc., and no one can claim that I have failed to fulfill my duty if I have not shown him or her generosity in particular.

The situation with duties of justice seems different. If I have a duty to be fair, I have this duty to *everyone* I can treat fairly or unfairly. Unlike generosity, if I fail to treat some particular individual fairly, that individual can justly complain that I have failed to fulfill a duty I have to him or her; and also unlike my duty to be generous, it is not left up to my personal discretion to determine to whom to be fair, when, to what extent, etc. The point is, fairness is something I *owe* to each and every person, whereas generosity is not.

When, therefore, Spiegelberg, echoing Schweitzer, declares that "fortune obligates," what he evidently means is that those who have benefited from "the luck of the draw" have a *duty of justice* to those who have not been so fortunate. It is not a matter of generosity on the part of the lucky ones to help those who are less lucky; it is not a matter to be decided by personal discretion. It is a matter of fairness, which means that, to the extent that we who are lucky have failed to compensate any less fortunate person whom we can compensate, it follows that we have not fulfilled a duty we have to that person, and he or she, in turn, may justifiably maintain that justice has not been forthcoming.

The main thrust of the Schweitzer-Spiegelberg thesis is picked up by John Rawls in his famous *Theory of Justice.* Benefits, Rawls argues, should not be distributed by society simply on the basis of achievement or merit, because this gives an unfair advantage to those who have been given an arbitrary head start by nature, just as much as it gives an unfair disadvantage to those who have to bear nature's arbitrary handicaps. We would not think it fair to distribute the good things in life (the opportunities for an education, a job, or leisure time, say) on the basis of who can run the fastest; this would be certain to exclude many people from these benefits simply because of certain natural liabilities—for example, those who are born without the use of both legs. The just distribution of life's goods must take into account the fact that nature itself is not just in its distribution of natural capacities. Justice in the distribution of goods (distributive justice) requires what Rawls calls a "difference principle," which represents "an agreement to regard the distribution of natural talents as a common asset and to share in the benefits of this distribution whatever it turns out to be. Those who have been favored by nature, whoever they are, may gain from their good fortune only on terms that they improve the situation of those who have lost out."[25] In other words, those blessed by nature's advantages may use these blessings to their own advantage only so long as, by doing so, the situation of those who are less fortunate is also improved.

Rawls's difference principle has spawned a vast critical literature. We cannot explore that here. What we want to note is how this principle, the seeds of which we seem to find in Schweitzer and Spiegelberg, could play a role in the development of an environmental ethic. If sense can be given to the idea that whole nations and peoples are *ecologically handicapped,* then the implications of Rawls's difference principle would be monumental. What we would be faced with is the duty, not of benevolence but of justice, to compensate those who, because of the *natural disadvantages of their environment,* must endure the limitations of ecological handicaps. The implications of this approach to the problem of famine relief, for example, should be obvious. That *we* have enough food to eat because we have enough arable land to grow enough crops is part of the luck of the draw: We're lucky. That others are not so blessed with such natural advantages is their bad luck. But if the luck of the (natural) draw obligates, and then not because of beneficence but because of justice, then we who are affluent *owe* it to those who are less well-off that we begin to change our life style in order to bring about a more equitable state of affairs. Surprisingly, perhaps, plumbing the depths of an ecological ethic ends up having possibly profound implications concerning our obligations *to other human beings!* It is not just our moral relations to flora and fauna that are at stake. We will not be able to explore the topic of famine relief at any greater length, but we can at least come away from our brief exposure to it understanding that it must find its rightful place in a fully developed environmental ethic.

§8 METAPHYSICS AND VALUE THEORY

There is another thing that is at stake, and this concerns what philosophers call metaphysics. For our purposes, we can understand a metaphysical theory to be a *theory of the scheme of things,* a general account of what kinds of beings exist and how they are related. A move toward an environmental ethic can be seen as in part a search for a supporting metaphysic. The question that must be asked is how must we understand the world if we are to find a place in it for the inherent value of nonhuman life forms? Anyone seeking an answer must reckon with the influential metaphysical theory of René Descartes (1596–1650), especially as this relates to animals. Nonhuman animals, Descartes argued, have no souls; they are automata—that is, machines.

They lack—at least Descartes can be interpreted as maintaining that they lack—all semblance of consciousness. They are like clocks that act according to mechanical laws, the only difference being that where clocks have cogs and wheels, springs and gears, animals have nerves and tissues, organs and veins. Schweitzer, not surprisingly, has little sympathy with Descartes's metaphysic. He states:

> It would seem as if Descartes, with his theory that animals have no souls and are mere machines which only seem to feel pain, had bewitched all of modern philosophy. Philosophy has totally avoided the problem of man's conduct towards other organisms. We might say that philosophy has played a piano of which a whole series of keys were considered untouchable.[26]

The keys that were made untouchable by Descartes's metaphysic were the pleasures, pains, and welfare of animals and the good of nature in its own right. For to argue, as Descartes did, that the material world, including animals and plants, can be explained simply by the laws of physics, and that humans but not animals have consciousness, minds, or souls, led to, or was itself an expression of, a largely anthropocentric theory of value. Plants and animals have value only as instruments to the ends of conscious beings with souls. There is no room for an ecological ethic within the Cartesian metaphysic.

Schweitzer and others reject Descartes's sharply dichotomized view of nature and the theory of value that goes with it. Granted, the difference between man and other animals is enormous. But, in many cases, it is a matter of degree, not of kind. In fact, as many researchers have now documented, some animals can learn to use languages such as those devised by computers and the American Sign Language. The rejection of Descartes's metaphysic, even if this rejection itself does not erect a settled metaphysic in its place, at least leaves one with a piano with many more keys. If, in time, we find a metaphysic suitable as a companion to a genuine environmental ethic—and it may be that what we need to do is rediscover this in such thinkers as Aristotle (384–332 B.C.), Spinoza (1632–1677), or St. Thomas Aquinas (1224–1274)—one thing is certain: It will be far more complex than the one Descartes offered to us.

II. ANTHROPOCENTRISM AND MORALITY

§9 ANTHROPOCENTRISM

Albert Schweitzer thought that Christianity and the Church promulgated largely an anthropocentric theory of value and an ethic in which moral obligations are reduced fundamentally to those between people and between people and God. It is this narrow anthropocentric attitude that has caused much of the ruthless, exploitive attitude toward nature and other forms of life, and some current analysts of our environmental problems believe that the Christian religion must share a heavy burden of guilt for those problems. Lynn White, Jr., for example, claims that "both our present science and our present technology are so tinctured with orthodox Christian arrogance toward nature that no solution for our ecological crisis can be expected from them alone. Since the roots of our trouble are so largely religious, the remedy must also be largely religious."[27] Let us spell out in more detail the relationships of arrogance and exploitation that White believes have been fostered by Christianity.

White argues that Christianity paints this vivid picture of our relationship with the environment: The environment was created by God as an instrument of our well-being. It was intended for exploitation. As Genesis (I: 26–28) proclaims, "God created man in his own image, and blessed them and said to them, 'Be fruitful and multiply and fill the earth and subdue it; and have dominion over the fish of the sea, and over the birds of the air, and over the cattle, and over the whole earth.'" Humanity is declared as having the superior status in nature. Nature and other forms of life exist to fulfill our purposes and those of God. Humans themselves are largely supernatural creatures. They were created by God in God's image and are not simply evolutionary products of nature. The earth is our temporary home in a theological plan. Our real home is heaven.

White is convinced that "Christianity made it possible to exploit nature in a mood of indifference to the feelings of natural objects."[28] Contemporary science and technology have roots, he believes, in Christianity, a religion that emphasizes humanity's transcendence and ordained control over nature. "Despite Copernicus, all of the cosmos rotates around our little globe. Despite Darwin, we are not, in our hearts, part of the natural process."[29] We conceive of nature purely in pragmatic terms, a reality to which we must adjust but which we can justifiably rearrange and control for our ends. White is convinced not only that Christianity is a basic cause of our ecological ills. He is also convinced that until mainstream Christian attitudes toward nature are altered, until we adopt a religious attitude toward nature in which it is not seen as simply material clay in our hands, until we recapture in our religious perspectives the theme that nature and other forms of life have both value and rights of their own, we will not solve our burgeoning environmental problems. More science and more technology in the service of anthropocentrism and pragmatism will simply create more long-range problems. We must develop a new perspective toward nature, in which humans and all other forms of life are seen as one ecosystem and in which all existents are conceived as mutually dependent, each having its role and place.

White recognizes that Christianity is a complex religion and that it embraces many beliefs and traditions. Though the mainstream engenders environmentally destructive attitudes and actions, more radical traditions, such as those engendered by St. Francis of Assisi, do not. St. Francis spoke of a "democracy of God's creatures." Nature is not our instrument. Nor are we nature's monarchs. All life is the sacred creation of God, and we are not to be exploiters of nature but *stewards* of God's resources. White in fact proclaims St. Francis as the patron saint for ecologists.

The vision that St. Francis seems to propound is one in which life constitutes a spectrum, and its continued existence, and the quality of life itself, requires a cooperative venture among all members. Nature is our home, as it is that of all creatures. It is not simply our temporary stomping ground.

§10 RATIONAL ANTHROPOCENTRISM

Despite the appeal of the Franciscan vision, serious problems remain. To go as far as D. S. Jordan anticipates, to a time when "civilized man will feel that the rights of all living creatures are as sacred as his own," seems to lead us to the absurdities of radical biotic egalitarianism discussed earlier (§16). Granted, it is narrow indeed to deny value to all nonhuman elements of nature. The sheer exploitation of nature based on insensitivity to the ecological interrelatedness of life systems is mistaken. But this does not rule out the view that other things in nature are valuable, as W. H. Murdy states, "as instruments to man's survival or well-being."[30] In fact, "as knowledge of our dependent relationships with nature grows," he writes, "we place instrumental value on an ever greater variety of things."[31] We value the ozone shield more highly when we realize it protects us from excessive radiation. We value phytoplankton in the oceans when we recognize that those organisms provide much of the earth's free oxygen. And so on. Greater sensitivity to the causal chains in nature will make us acknowledge an enormous range of instrumental value that other parts of the biosphere possess. But for Murdy, that is all part and parcel of a sophisticated anthropocentrism. "A human being is both a hierarchical system (composed of subsystems such as organs, cells, and enzyme systems) and a component of super-individual, hierarchical systems (populations, species, ecosystems, cultural systems). Man is therefore a set within a hierarchical system of sets."[32] What is needed is not the denial of anthropocentrism, the placing of the highest value on humans and their ends and the conceiving of the rest of nature as an instrument for those ends. Rather, what is needed is the explicit recognition of those hierarchical systems and an ecological approach to science and the accumulation of scientific knowledge in which the myriad causal relationships between different hierarchical systems are recognized and put to the use of humanity. The freedom to use the environment must be restricted to rational use. If there is irrational use—widespread pollution, overpopulation, crowding, a growth in poverty, and so on—people may wipe out hierarchies of life related to their own survival and to the quality of their own lives.

This kind of anthropocentrism does not maintain that man is the measure of all things. "He is not the center of the universe, nor the source of all value, nor the culmination of terrestrial evolution."[33] But Murdy does believe that humans are the apex of the evolutionary crest at this time and the vehicle by which greater organizational complexity and higher values can be developed. Humans and their values ought to take priority over other systems of life and values in this world. This sort of anthropocentrism is essential even to human survival, and a radical biotic egalitarianism, where all forms of life are regarded as of equal intrinsic value, would undermine a condition for that survival. Rational anthropocentrism, one that recognizes that the value of human life "transcends our individual lives" and one in which we "form a collective bond of identity with future generations," is essential to the process of human evolution.[34]

§11 ANTHROPOCENTRISM AND SCHWEITZER

How far is the modern version of anthropocentrism just discussed from the reverence-for-life ethic of Schweitzer? Schweitzer's ethic is not spelled out in careful detail and, as noted, much of it rests on a kind of skepticism—on the fact that humans can know so little about the universe. But Schweitzer does recognize the necessity for killing other forms of life for survival. He recognizes human obligations to other forms of life—to animals that are often used medically to enhance human life. He recognizes the value of other forms of life. He recognizes that special duties and obligations are placed on those whom nature has generously endowed to assist those not so endowed. All of this is consistent with the modern version of anthropocentrism offered by Murdy. The gap between modern anthropocentrism and the reverence-for-life ethic becomes large only if the latter is seen as entailing a radical biotic egalitarianism—the view, again, that all forms of life have equal value and equal rights to survive. Not just all humans but all forms of life. If one subscribes to this, there is no moral basis for the human use of other forms of life. There is only a power basis. But there can be an extension of ethics to recognize the value of nonhuman forms of life and of obligations to animals and nature without involving such a radical egalitarianism.

On the issue of the *rights* of animals and the *rights* of nature we will have more to say later, when we discuss some positions in which such rights are pressed (§§13–16). Philosophical questions concerning the logical conditions required for the proper ascription of rights certainly arise. But before reaching that point in the development of an environmental ethic, let us take the preliminary step of recognizing the main points emphasized by the acknowledged seminal leader of the quest for an environmental ethic, Aldo Leopold.

§12 THE LAND ETHIC

Leopold, like Schweitzer, sees ethics and rules of proper conduct as evolutionary. The following quote indicates the "ethical sequence" through which we are evolving:

> When god-like Odysseus returned from the wars in Troy, he hanged all on one rope a dozen slave-girls of his household whom he suspected of misbehavior during his absence.
>
> This hanging involved no question of propriety. The girls were property. The disposal of property was then, as now, a matter of expediency, not of right and wrong.
>
> Concepts of right and wrong were not lacking from Odysseus' Greece: witness the fidelity of his wife through the long years before at last his black-prowed galleys clove the wine-dark seas for home. The ethical structure of that day covered wives, but had not yet been extended to human chattels. During the three thousand years which have since elapsed, ethical criteria have been extended to many fields of conduct, with corresponding shrinkages in those judged by expediency only.

The Ethical Sequence

This extension of ethics, so far studied only by philosophers, is actually a process in ecological evolution. Its sequences may be described in ecological as well as in philosophical terms. An ethic, ecologically, is a limitation on freedom of action in the struggle for existence. An ethic, philosophically, is a differentiation of social from anti-social conduct. These are two definitions of one thing. The thing has its origin in the tendency of interdependent individuals or groups to evolve modes of co-operation. The ecologist calls these symbioses. Politics and economics are advanced symbioses in which the original free-for-all competition has been replaced, in part, by co-operative mechanisms with an ethical content.

The complexity of co-operative mechanisms has increased with population density, and with the efficiency of tools. It was simpler, for example, to define the anti-social uses of sticks and stones in the days of the mastodons than of bullets and billboards in the age of motors.

The first ethics dealt with the relation between individuals; the Mosaic Decalogue is an example. Later accretions dealt with the relation between the individual and society. The Golden Rule tries to integrate the individual to society; democracy to integrate social organization to the individual.

There is as yet no ethic dealing with man's relation to land and to the animals and plants which grow upon it. Land, like Odysseus' slave-girls, is still property. The land-relation is still strictly economic, entailing privileges but not obligations.

The extension of ethics to this third element in human environment is, if I read the evidence correctly, an evolutionary possibility and an ecological necessity. It is the third step in a sequence. The first two have already been taken. Individual thinkers since the days of

Ezekiel and Isaiah have asserted that the despoliation of land is not only inexpedient but wrong. Society, however, has not yet affirmed their belief. I regard the present conservation movement as the embryo of such an affirmation.[35]

It is plain from what Leopold says that he regards a land ethic (in the broad sense, including any use of the environment), an ethic in which ethically relevant entities are not just humans but soils, waters, plants, and animals, as a *higher* form of ethics. One who assumes an ecological interpretation of history will recognize that man is "only a member of a biotic team . . ."[36] "Many historical events, hitherto explained solely in terms of human enterprise, were actually biotic interactions between people and land. The characteristics of the land determined the facts quite as potently as the characteristics of the men who lived on it."[37] Given those facts, ethics requires a state of harmony between humans and land. That harmony, or an adequate ethics of land use, cannot be "governed wholly by economic self-interest," for there are values at stake other than economic ones. Even if one's value perspective is narrowly economic, land-use practices require far better judgment than has been shown by humans. But, Leopold points out, "most members of the land-community have no economic value," at least not directly for man.[38] Yet, as members of the biotic community, they are "entitled to continuance," for the stability of that community depends upon them. Noneconomic creatures like birds "should continue as a matter of biotic right . . ."[39]

Leopold would have us recognize that all species, including the human species, are links in a complex causal chain, one in which each successive layer depends on another. We are only one of those layers in the pyramid of life, and our continued existence depends on the proper functioning of the entire chain. Only if we develop "love, respect and admiration for land," a perspective "far broader than mere economic value," can we have an adequate ethic for dealing with environmental problems. Extending the criterion of right conduct concerning the environment, Leopold declares: "A thing is right when it tends to preserve the integrity, stability, and beauty of the biotic community. It is wrong when it tends otherwise."[40] The concept of the ethical community and of ethical relevance is extended, not unlike Schweitzer, to include "The seeds of a new fellowship in land . . . , a realization of Whitman's dream to 'plant companionship as thick as trees along all of the rivers of America.' "[41]

How far the notion of "biotic rights" can be carried is a difficult question to which we will turn later (§§13–16). But quite clearly, the narrow perspective of economics vis-à-vis the environment is being challenged. Leopold points out that slavery is incompatible with any concept of human rights. He also points out that the concepts of "property rights" in most societies is incompatible with a land ethic, for it permits highly destructive environmental action. The question raised by the institution of property rights, given the data uncovered by the ecologist, is whether those rights should be more heavily restricted to prevent the destruction and pollution of our environmental resources upon which present and future generations of living creatures depend. The economist Nathaniel Wollman argues that the price system excludes value factors that ought to be included in environmental use assessments. "It does not account for benefits or costs that are enjoyed or suffered by people who were not parties to the transaction."[42] The concept of *human* welfare, certainly that of *environmental* welfare, requires more than just the interplay of market forces and more than the sovereignty of the consumer. It requires a broader value perspective. As I have pointed out elsewhere, stockholders do not ask of a company, "Have you polluted the environment and lowered the quality of the environment for the general public and for future generations?" Rather they ask, "How high is the annual dividend and how much higher than the year before?"[43]

The famous contemporary ecologist Eugene Odum strongly picks up Leopold's suggestions to develop a land ethic, in which economics functions as only one component. In fact, he suggests that the first two stages of ethics that Leopold describes cannot continue to exist unless the third stage, the land ethic, is put into operation.[44] In his books *Fundamentals of Ecology* and *Ecology,* Odum clarifies for the layperson what is embraced by the science of ecology by speaking of levels of organization and by asking us to think of the biological spectrum as including protoplasm, cells, tissues, organ systems, organisms, populations, communities, ecosystems, and the biosphere. Ecology as a science is concerned largely with the levels beyond the individual organism and with regulatory mechanisms that operate at the population, community, and ecosystem level. Those regulatory mechanisms are responsible for a state of stability or homeostasis in the community and ecosystem level, just as individual bodies have such mechanisms for preserving their states of homeostasis. What the ecologist tries to do is provide models for understanding the regulatory mechanisms in nature and what will likely happen if man injects himself into the causal chain in this way or that, say, by building an Aswan Dam or by using DDT in large quantities. Odum admits that his science is relatively new and that ecological knowledge is highly context-dependent; that is, ecology has not yet provided the broad scientific generalizations characteristic of physics and chemistry.[45] Still, the data ecologists have come by, though tenuous in some contexts, is essential in making assessments of environmental impact and in looking after not only our welfare but that of other life systems upon which our welfare depends.

Having made us aware of all this, Odum and other ecologists go on to point out that

> ... sooner or later transition from youth to maturity must be faced at all levels of life, whether they be cells, organs, teenagers, society, or the ecosystem as a whole. In the individual there is a built-in

governor in the form of a genetic code (a sort of computer) that first organizes growth, then slows it down, and then maintains optimum coordinated function in a state of maturity for a relatively long time. Viewing the United States as an ecosystem, we see that environmental constraints (depletion of resources, pollution, declining quality of living space, etc.) are beginning to provide negative feedback. As writers in the popular press are beginning to stress, this nation, whether we like it or not, is beginning to mature and stratify. Many of our current problems, both domestic and international, stem from our failure to face up to this fact. Thus, what was desirable in the youthful stage becomes undesirable in the mature stage. For example, high birth rates, rapid industrial growth and exploitation of unused resources are advantageous in a pioneer society. We can be justly proud of the fact that the United States has been able to grow and develop so well. However, as saturation levels are approached, all the "good" things become "bad" and the strategy of survival requires a shift to opposite poles, as for example, birth control, recycling of resources, regulation of land use, waste treatment, and so forth. Growth beyond the optimum becomes cancer ...[46]

Ecologists agree that stability or homeostasis is always context-dependent, that variables operating at the population, community, and ecosystem levels are constantly changing, and that there is no general agreement on what is to be meant by *optimum* levels of population, *adequate* economic growth, and so on. In particular, when we speak of a state of *stability* or *homeostasis* in a human ecosystem, we must be careful not to extrapolate from life systems with less complexity to human communities, without making all the additions and corrections. These concepts and, in particular, the concept of homeostasis, are normative as well as descriptive—that is, not only does homeostasis describe a stable state of the ecosystem, it also describes a state *worth pursuing,* a state that, within an environmental ethic, we *ought* to seek to achieve. The problem, of course, in formulating an environmental ethic, is to explain what principles and values are to guide us in the pursuit of this goal. It is not unreasonable to hope that some traditional ethical values and principles, including the principles of utility, justice, and equality, can play a decisive role here. To understand why this is so, let us begin by examining how some thinkers would extend some or all of these principles to animals.

§13 JUSTICE, UTILITY, AND ANIMALS

One aspect of an environmental ethic concerns the treatment of animals, and a good number of contemporary thinkers maintain that humans, for the most part, have been immoral in their treatment of animals. They hunt animals for sport. They experiment, medically and psychologically, on animals, ignoring the pain and suffering of animals. They adopt life styles in which the raising of animals and the eating of their flesh are a central part. They wipe out entire species of animals with little reflection on the impact. The utilitarian philosopher Jeremy Bentham (1748-1832) was especially sensitive to all this. Though he rejected any doctrine of natural, inalienable rights for humans or other creatures, he did see moral and legal rights as important devices to maximize the pleasure or happiness of *sentient* beings; and animals as well as men are such beings—that is, they can suffer pain and enjoy pleasure. The important question to ask when trying to decide on the scope of moral concern, he thought, is not "Can the creature reason or talk?" But "Can it suffer?"[47]

Speciesism   The contemporary Australian philosopher Peter Singer picks up the Benthamite stance on animals with force.[48] "A liberation movement," he declares, "demands an expansion of our moral horizons and an extension or reinterpretation of the basic moral principle of equality."[49] That principle must not only be extended to women, blacks, and other racial minorities—that is, to all members of our own species. It must also extend to nonhuman species. For they too have the capacity to suffer. Many of us are still immersed in racism or sexism; but another form of discrimination that is practiced nearly universally is *speciesism,* the refusal to extend equality of consideration to members of other species. If a being has interests, that is, is capable of suffering and of enjoying, then there is no reason for excluding it from consideration. "No matter what the nature of the being, the principle of equality requires that its suffering be counted equally with the like suffering—in so far as comparisons can be made—of any other being."[50] Just as it is irrational and wrong to discriminate in favor of one's own race or sex, since race and sex are not fundamentally morally relevant factors, so also it is irrational and wrong to exclude any sentient being from the scope of the principle of equal consideration. Neither the possession of intelligence (or reason) nor the capacity to make free choices is the ground for ascribing equality of consideration. The ground is the fact that a being can suffer or enjoy. When we exclude members of other species from equality of consideration of their interests, their pleasures, and their pains, we are guilty of speciesism. When we treat members of other species as objects whose lives are no more than instruments for human well-being, we are guilty of speciesism.

   Equality of consideration of other species, however, does not mean *identity* of treatment. Relevant differences among members of *Homo sapiens* justify differential treatment of those members. Special educational opportunities, for example, are provided for the blind, which are unnecessary for the sighted. In the same way, relevant differences among dogs, horses, and humans justify differential treatment of the members of these species. For example, we do no wrong to a pig by declining it the opportunity to vote, since a pig *cannot* vote. But the fact that pigs can enjoy and suffer, the fact that their lives and their experiences have value independently of their relationship to members of the human species, means that they cannot be treated *merely* as objects and *simply* exploited for human use. Given a certain hierarchy of values in which the pleasures and pains of humans have priority status over those of other animals, the use of other animals for human survival and health may be justified. But the decision so to use animals under these circumstances must at least take into consideration the pleasures and pains of the animals. Albert Schweitzer recognized, for example, that animals must sometimes be used in medical experimentation to ensure human health. He insisted, however, that the cost in terms of animal suffering be explicitly recognized and that no such suffering be inflicted without very good reason.

Peter Singer holds a similar position. For justified purposes, the lives of animals may be used, but those purposes must at least acknowledge the cost of the suffering of the animals. Animals cannot be used for trivial purposes of life style—the having of leather gloves, fur coats, or the satisfaction of palates. Animals should not be raised and their flesh consumed simply as a matter of taste. If such consumption were required for human survival, then it would be justified. But such consumption is simply a matter of taste and life style, for it has been shown, Singer argues, that humans can survive in excellent health without meat, consuming vegetable protein alone. In fact, more humans could survive on a vegetable-protein diet, since the conversion ratio of vegetable protein is roughly five to one. Therefore, the moral principle of equality and the empirical fact that humans can survive, perhaps in greater numbers, and in better health, without consuming meat, combine to require *vegetarianism.* Animals must not be treated "like machines that convert fodder into flesh . . ."[51]

Is Singer saying that sentient creatures have a *right* to equal consideration of their interests? It must be noted that sometimes[52] he writes as though he is ascribing such a right to animals. More recently, he has stated that it is not his intention to ascribe rights to animals.[53] However, this should not be construed as an admission on his part that animals have an insecure moral standing. Rather, Singer's refusal to grant rights to animals is based on his considered belief that the concept of a right is inessential in moral theory and tends instead to be a device of rhetoricians. When he says that animals do not have rights, he is not saying anything that he would not say about humans: we too fail to have rights, in the sense of having basic *natural* rights. As a utilitarian, Singer denies that there are such rights possessed by anybody. Everything we need or want to say about what is morally right or wrong, he thinks, can be expressed without having recourse to the concept of a natural right. (For a fuller discussion of this matter, and for Singer's views on what beings would have to be like to have rights [*assuming that some do*], the reader is referred to his essay in this anthology.)

Now, whether talk of rights is inessential in moral theory is without doubt one of the most basic questions for moral philosophers, and it is one that, understandably, we cannot enter into in sufficient detail here. Short of trying to settle this question, however, what we can begin to appreciate is that even self-professed utilitarians like Singer and Bentham can (and have) extended the scope of the principles of utility and equality to include sentient nonhuman animals. The experiences of these creatures, their suffering and pleasure, are morally relevant factors that must be taken into account in determining what we ought or ought not to do, not just with a view to how we humans will be affected, but with a view to how all sentient creatures shall fare. In the case of beings lacking sentience, however—for example, flora and fauna—Singer believes that there are no interests of the flora and fauna themselves to take into account; nonsentient beings have no inherent value in their own right but have merely an instrumental value, according to Singer. Thus, Singer would have us extend the scope of the Principle of the Value of Life in a way that avoids human chauvinism (or anthropocentrism) but that stops far short of a radical biotic egalitarianism.

Interests and Rights   Like Singer, Joel Feinberg[54] agrees that it is not the capacity for making free choices or for rationality that is morally crucial; it is the fact that animals have interests and "a good of their own" that matters. Animals themselves can be directly benefited or harmed by what we do, and it is only such beings—those who can be directly benefited or harmed by our actions or inactions—who can have rights. Thus, "in general, animals are among the sorts of beings of whom rights can be meaningfully predicated and denied,"[55] Feinberg argues. For most animals, "especially those of the lower orders, we have little choice" but to treat them as "mere pests and deny that they have any rights."[56] But the higher animals have appetites and rudimentary purposes and they, at least, have rights. The fact that animals cannot have duties does not make it meaningless to say that they have rights; wee babies, for example, do not have duties, but it does not follow from this that they do not or cannot have rights. The fact, moreover, that animals cannot enter into contracts and that they themselves cannot claim their rights are similarly irrelevant, and are so for the same kind of reason; human infants or retardates can have rights despite their inability to do these things. There is no logical reason to regard animals any differently.

Suppose Feinberg is correct that animals, or at least the higher ones, do have rights. What would follow from this? Morally, what would follow is that treating animals in certain ways is not something that is left to our discretion; rather, such treatment will be *required* of us. To put the point differently, our duties to treat animals in certain ways will be what we earlier (§7) called *duties of justice, not* duties of benevolence. Treatment that recognizes the good of the animal will be something we *owe* the animal, not something it would be "nice" for us to do. At the heart of the ascription of rights to animals, therefore, we find the extension of the Principle of the Value of Life: It is because animals have a good of their own, independent of human purposes and interests, that they qualify as possessors of rights and thus ought to be protected by an enlightened principle of justice.

§14 THE VALUE OF LIFE, EQUALITY, AND THE BURDEN OF JUSTIFICATION

It must be noted that the extension of the Principle of the Value of Life to animals; the extension of the doctrine of rights, moral and legal; the extension, in particular, of a right to life to animals—all this is consistent with the morality of killing animals. Just as, in the human case, we recognize that a violent assailant (for example, a terrorist) might justifiably be killed because of other, stronger, moral considerations, so also an animal's right to life, assuming that it has one, may be justifiably overridden by stronger moral considerations. But the extension of the Principle of the Value of Life and the right to life to animals does put the burden of moral justification of overriding that principle or right on the person who would violate it. If we have a *prima facie* duty not to kill animals, and if they, in turn, have a *prima facie* right not to be killed, then anyone who would kill them must have *very* strong reasons for doing so, if their action is to be morally justified. When a moral commodity as strong as a right is overridden, the moral grounds for doing so must be proportionately stronger. Indeed, Tom Regan has argued[57] that the onus of justification is always on one who kills an animal or makes one suffer and that, unless or until we are shown how such treatment is justified, we are rationally entitled to believe and morally required to act in such a way that we do not support such treatment. A vegetarian way of life, once again, is thought to follow for all of us who have a choice regarding what we eat.

§15 THE VALUE OF LIFE, EQUALITY, AND FLORA

If Feinberg is correct, it is not merely the possession of sentience but the possession of "interests" and "a good of one's own" that is necessary for the possession of rights. What these crucial concepts mean— 'interests' and 'having a good of one's own'—needs careful examination, and it is plain that a number of thinkers who would extend rights to flora, for example, have a very extended concept of "interests" and "a good of one's own." Feinberg would have us restrict these concepts to *conscious* beings, or at least to those beings who have the potential for consciousness; thus, assuming, as seems reasonable, that flora are not conscious and lack the potential for becoming so, Feinberg's position is that these living beings have no rights of their own, and the value they have is instrumental not inherent.

Other thinkers would disagree. Schweitzer, in particular. Natural objects may have *a good of their own,* Schweitzer believes, even if they have no interests, even if no interest-possessing being takes an interest in them, and even if an interest-possessing being has an interest in destroying them. Schweitzer does not spell this out in detail, but he seems to ascribe not only instrumental value to flowers, trees, and plants generally but also a kind of good of their own rooted in their biological capacities. When some action impairs these capacities, then the good of the plant or tree, for example, is lessened; and the lessening of the good occurs even if no interest-possessing being is aware of it and even if the plant or tree does not consciously suffer pain.

Aldo Leopold far more explicitly extends rights to natural, nonsentient objects. Recall his principal thesis that "a thing is right when it tends to preserve the integrity, stability and beauty of the biotic community. It is wrong when it tends otherwise."[58] This is a general definition of moral rightness. But, in speaking of soils, waters, plants, and animals, he claims more specifically that a land ethic "affirms their right to continued existence, and , at least in spots, their continued existence in a natural state."[59] Here Leopold specifically ascribes rights to nonsentient entities and processes. The "right to continued existence" of plants, trees, soils, and rivers may be justifiably overridden by the rights of man. This seems consistent with Leopold's land ethic. But the rights of plants and soils exist nonetheless.

Some recent work of Tom Regan's is relevant to the dispute over the rights of plants, etc.[60] In a direct response to Feinberg's position, in which Feinberg claims that it is "inconceivable" that beings lacking consciousness or the potential for consciousness can have rights, Regan argues that this is not inconceivable. Plants, themselves, can be directly benefited or harmed by what we do (or fail to do) to them, and, if this is so, then they can be conceived to have a good of their own. If a plant is denied water, for example, it will eventually wither and die, hardly conditions that could benefit it; if, on the other hand, it receives its proper nutrients, it will flourish and realize the sort of good of which it is capable—for example, it will become *a good gardenia.* Thus, if Feinberg is correct in thinking that only beings having a good of their own (an inherent good) can have rights, then, Regan argues, plants can have rights also, and this despite the fact that they lack consciousness or the potential for consciousness.

However, to argue that plants, etc., can have rights because they can have a good of their own leaves us with a great many unanswered questions. How, precisely, are we to understand the inherent good of nonconscious beings? Are there any general truths about the varieties of goodness that can be realized by different kinds of plants, say? Regan explicitly disavows having answered any of these pressing questions, but he, along with John Rawls, indicates the direction in which he thinks our thought ought to go in search of an answer. It is to Aristotle and St. Thomas that we should turn, especially to a reinvestigation of their metaphysics in the light of our growing understanding of ecology.

The point seems clear: In order to understand man's place in the scheme of things—and that of animals, plants, soils, and rivers—we require some *theory of the scheme of things,* an enlightened metaphysic. One philosopher has proclaimed that "ethics without metaphysics is nonsense." This may be a bit strong, but there appears to be no way of answering some of the environmentalists' questions about value, right conduct, and rights without some such metaphysical scheme. In the end, it may not resemble that scheme found in, say, St. Thomas. But at the very least it would take one beyond a purely anthropocentric theory of value. Whether a theory of rights that included rights for nonsentient natural entities or processes would emerge from such a scheme is an open question.

§16 LEGAL RIGHTS

Without invoking a full-fledged metaphysic, some environmental thinkers have sought to extend rights to natural objects by emphasizing that humans and nature *are alike* in relevant respects and thus are entitled to similar treatment. For example, referring to our growing sensitivity to the chain of causes responsible for balances in nature, Christopher Stone remarks: "This heightened awareness enlarges our sense of the dangers to us. But it also enlarges our empathy. We are not only developing the scientific capacity, but we are cultivating the personal capacities *within us* to recognize more and more the ways in which nature—like the woman, the black, the Indian and the alien —is like us ..."[61] Just as women and racial minorities are similar to middle-class white males in nearly all relevant respects bearing on the ascription of rights, so also natural entities and processes are similar in significant ways to humans. Lawrence Tribe puts it this way: "Humans share fundamental needs with plants. Humans and plants both require water, oxygen and nutrition; both grow and reproduce; both die. A set of basic reference points for analogizing plant requirements to human needs thus exists. Some research even suggests that plants exhibit electrical and chemical reactions which are functionally analogous to pain."[62] Stone adds: "It is not easy to dismiss the idea of 'lower' life having consciousness and feeling pain, especially since it is so difficult to know what these terms mean even as applied to humans."[63] Both Stone and Tribe are concerned with expanding the basis for environmental law. Traditional property law, "public nuisance" law, and so on are inadequate grounds for legal environmental conservation and preservation. Stone, in fact, argues that natural objects should have a legal standing in their own right. Though natural objects cannot initiate court action on their own behalf, the courts can appoint guardians on their behalf in the same way that they do for idiots, human "vegetables," fetuses, and the like. Such standing would mean "first, that the thing can institute legal actions *at its behest;* second, that in determining the granting of legal relief, the court must take *injury to it* into account; and, third, that relief must run to the *benefit of it.*"[64] Legal standing for natural objects would be an enormous improvement in protecting the environment. But Stone and Tribe also seem to endorse the view that such entities and processes have moral rights, and that ultimately those moral rights are the basis of instituting the legal rights. As Tribe says, "we might plausibly hope for more" than the recognition of the rights of natural objects as legal constructs for fictitious legal entities, such as corporations and trusts. A purely anthropocentric rationale for the rights-status of natural objects will not do. "At least as long as we remain within empathizing distance of the objects whose rights we seek to recognize, it seems reasonable to expect the acknowledgement of such rights to be regarded as more than fictitious."[65]

III. LOOKING BACK AND AHEAD

§17 THE MAIN POINTS OF EMPHASIS IN ENVIRONMENTAL ETHICS

We have surveyed only a small portion of those philosophical writings that bear on the attempt to develop an environmental ethic. Let us now note some of the main points stressed, but it must be kept in mind that not all of these points are accepted by each of these thinkers. In fact, as we have seen there are widely divergent views represented in the literature on environmental ethics.

Some of the points of emphasis are the following:

1. We must expand the principle of the brotherhood of all people to exclude racism and sexism.
2. We must reject the ideal of the "negation of the world" and become world-affirmers, recognizing that ethics requires the solution of our problems in the here and now.
3. We must expand our ethical attitudes beyond mere refraining from doing evil to acting for good.
4. Ethics requires that the Principle of the Value of Life be expanded to include nonhuman creatures (not unlike the extension of the principle of the brotherhood of all people in 1).
5. The purely pragmatic or purely economic approach to killing must be abandoned.
6. Those who derive unearned benefits from the luck of the draw, biologically and socially, *owe* some form of compensation to those who drew poorly.
7. A "rational" anthropocentrism is a radical improvement over the traditional unsophisticated type. The former recognizes the inherent value of nonhuman forms of life but sees it as

secondary to the development of human values. Some think that the ecological interdependence emphasized by "rational" anthropocentrism is adequate to resolve environmental problems. Others do not.

8. An adequate environmental ethic must adopt a "land ethic" in which *rights* are extended not only to animals but also to nonsentient entities and processes. A purely property-oriented attitude toward land will result in the destruction of the environment, because humans, if everything is reduced in some way or another to *human* interests, will find multiple rationalizations to ruin the very environment on which their lives and those of future generations depend.

9. An adequate environmental ethic must also recognize the obligation to future generations, perhaps even their *rights* against us now.

10. An adequate environmental ethic must adopt an ecological interpretation of history, in which humans are recognized as members of a biotic team.

11. Strategies for both survival and a quality of life must be recognized as highly context-dependent. At different times in the life of a community, population, or ecosystem, quite different strategies or policies may be required for survival. The meaning of 'stability' or 'homeostasis' depends on the context. In some cases, growth and radical change in the environment may be defensible; in others, not.

12. Principles and ideas central to traditional moral philosophy—for example, utility and rights—can play a role in developing an environmental ethic.

13. The extension of the Principle of the Value of Life, which some see as an extension of the principle of equality of consideration not only to animals but to flora and natural processes as well, does not require identity of treatment of all humans, all animals, and all flora. The extension permits differential treatment.

14. Some environmentalists insist that there is no justification of the routine killing of animals and the eating of their flesh.

15. Only some animals can possess rights, some philosophers argue, because not all animals fulfill the logical requirements for the possession of rights (having interests, a good of one's own, and the like). (There is disagreement, we saw, over what those conditions must be.)

16. The extension of the Principle of the Value of Life, the Principle of Utility, and the principle of equality to animal and plant life and natural processes, in spite of the fact that the extension allows for differential treatment among species and that it allows for some kind of priority for the values of humans, does place a *higher burden of moral justification* on the per-

son who would kill or alter animals or plant life or natural
processes.

17. A full-fledged environmental ethic may require some metaphysical theory, some theory about nature and the place of
humans, animals, and plants within nature. Such a theory may
be required to resolve the extension of the concepts of value,
obligation, utility, and rights; for as long as a Cartesian metaphysics holds sway, the role and scope of these normative
concepts is much narrower than some environmentalists
would have.

18. An environmental ethic in which expanded and extended
normative concepts are at work is not enough. Those concepts
must be seen as grounds of justification for new legal frameworks for the resolution of environmental questions.

§18 TWO MODELS

By no means is it being claimed that any one of the environmentalists
examined subscribes fully to each and every point summarized above.
It is plain indeed that widely divergent environmental ethics would
emerge by the adoption of some of these points and the rejection of
others, and it would be futile to spell out here the different ethical
frameworks that might be developed from this list. But I do want to
emphasize two quite different frameworks found in the literature, so
that these two frameworks at least are reasonably clear.

1. Roughly, the first position would be held by Joel Feinberg, Tom
Regan, Stanley Benn,[66] and William Blackstone. It maintains that the
past freedom to use the environment must be carefully restricted, that
enormous damage can be done without those restrictions, that those
restrictions must be formulated in the interest and rights of all humanity, present and future, the interests and rights of some animals, and
to preserve the value of nonsentient natural entities and processes.
Here we have an extension of the concept of value beyond narrow
anthropocentrism, the explicit recognition that *some* animals have
interests and rights, that there are obligations to care for the welfare
of nonsentient existents, and obligations to and rights of future humans. This position thus rejects a pure anthropocentrism and embraces an expanded concept of value, obligations, and rights, while
stopping far short of radical biotic egalitarianism. Given our new ecological knowledge, moreover, advocates of this type of position argue
that traditional freedoms and property rights must be restricted, and
there must be certain concomitant changes in our life styles. Without
these restrictions, the material base required for the realization of all
of our traditional rights—equality, liberty, security, welfare, and so on
—is threatened. Unrestricted use of the environment is a threat to the
fulfillment of all of these traditional rights. Therefore, a case may be
argued that we must recognize both a moral and legal right to a decent

environment.[67] But an effective environmental ethic need not extend rights to everything in the biosphere, for some members of the biosphere cannot meet the logical requirements for the ascription of rights.

Those who fall into (1) believe that an adequate environmental ethic—in which humans understand and appreciate the intricate regulatory mechanisms of the biosphere, in which the value and rights of nonhuman forms of life are respected, in which future generations of humans or humanlike beings are properly considered, in which styles of life that injure the environment are forbidden, and so on—can be formulated without the massive conceptual and metaphysical changes suggested by (2).

2. Subscribers to this second position agree with much of (1) but maintain that (1) does not go far enough. As long as most of nature and most animals cannot be the possessors of rights, then restrictions on human freedom to use the environment as they please will not go very far. For humans are excellent rationalizers in terms of what is in their own interest. Conceptually, we must extend rights to *all* animals and, some members of (2) hold, to nonsentient nature. Metaphysically, we must see all of life as a continuum in which there are different degrees of consciousness. Without this conceptual and metaphysical extension, we do not have a strong ethic for dealing with environmental problems. We are left with a mere superficial type of utilitarianism and anthropocentrism that permits the technological exploitation and manipulation of nature to satiate every desire of man, an ethic that now threatens the biosphere itself.

Not all environmental thinkers whom I would classify roughly under (2) hold exactly the same thing. Schweitzer, we saw, was difficult to classify. But Leopold, Stone, and Tribe fit *roughly* under (2). Stone, Tribe, Leopold, and Holmes Rolston would go even further and insist upon an attitude not just of respect but of *love* for all of nature.[68] In the next two sections I shall indicate my reasons for rejecting theories of type (2).

§19 ECOLOGY AND ETHICS

It is obvious from what has been said that there can be enormous differences of principles among environmental ethicists. In fleshing out a complete environmental ethic and contrasting it with other possible types of environmental ethics, all major differences would have to be explored in great detail, perhaps also within the contexts of great environmental issues like world hunger, world population problems, and the need to perceive events of the world in ecological and interdependent style, not as isolated occurrences. As the ecologist Eugene Odum has said, when we decide to alter the environment in this way or that, we are not doing *one* thing but *many* things. An ecological ethic requires that we take all of those things into consideration in making environmental decisions.

Our earlier discussion of some problems for Schweitzer's position (§6) shows that much hangs on how far the scope of value, obligation, and rights is pressed; also, on the methods and criteria for the resolution of conflicts of obligation and rights among "citizens" of the biosphere. But ecologically concerned ethicists *in some sense* want to return us to the concept of *nature* as the proper home for concepts of value, obligation, and rights. *In what sense?* In the Aquinian sense in which norms for human behavior, ecological or not, can be read out of nature? Neither Schweitzer nor many of the environmental theorists would reject the possibility of reading norms out of nature; in some cases by reason, in others by revelation. But they seem to have a different idea in mind. Let us try to spell it out a little further.

§20 NORMS AND NATURE

We noted earlier that ecology is a young science. The effort to see the intricate regulatory mechanisms operative at different hierarchies or levels of life and the way in which those levels impact upon one another is relatively new. Humans and populations generally are not to be seen as *created* objects existing apart from nature but as part of a total package of life, which has evolved over time. It is not simply our will and our purposes around which reason must calculate; nor, simply, is it around that of all animal life. Rather, it is around all of life. The ecologist-environmentalist would have us become keenly aware of the regulatory mechanisms in nature claiming that we must achieve some form of homeostasis or balance in the utilization of natural resources. This does not tell one very much, but it is far from being vacuous. Intelligent resource use at one stage of history may *permit* a great deal of play and freedom, which must be *denied* at another stage. *The existence of homeostasis or stability in nature is the general norm at which the ecologist drives.* But this general norm does not give one a definite answer to every problem of resource use. It lets one know what is at stake. It does not always answer the questions: Are the building of this dam and the creation of greater electrical power worth wiping out this species of fish? Is the widespread use of DDT worth the results in terms of its impact on other ecosystems and on human life? The general norm does not answer such questions, but it does let us know that if we go too far in one direction, there will be costs to pay. *Perhaps* what we need is a kind of *ecological utilitarianism* in which the welfare of every form of life that can suffer is taken into consideration in our calculus. Then one decides on environmental policy on the basis of what act or kinds of act will maximize the welfare of every form of life.

But how does one accomplish this? If Mark Sagoff is correct, this form of utilitarianism "permits us not only to justify any policy we want, but also in doing so, to adopt a lofty moral tone."[69] When a policy is expanded to include the impact on a larger, stronger population, then the smaller, weaker population group simply loses. An expanded, ecological utilitarianism will not give us an adequate environmental ethic. The theory of Rawls—that we must discover the right place for ourselves within the nature of things (endorsed as we saw also by Tribe and Stone), a theory of *social justice* and *rights* for all creatures, not just a theory of what might maximize the satisfaction of interests—requires even more information, it seems, than an ecologized utilitarianism. It may be information beyond the scope of human ability. Sagoff would reject *both* of these possible bases for an ecological ethic. He suggests that value concepts and norms, like liberty, equality, security, justice, and so on, are the result of the obligations toward these qualities themselves: "The obligation toward nature is an obligation toward them."[70] "Our rivers, forests, and wildlife do serve our society as paradigms of concepts we cherish . . ."[71] Our obligation to preserve and conserve nature is in fact our obligation to the values of our cultural and national tradition.[72] This is a nonutilitarian rationale, rooted in the desire "to preserve [our values] for [their] own sake."[73]

I remain unconvinced by Sagoff's argument. Our attitude toward the properties or values that we interpret nature as *expressing* and that we want to preserve seem to change as humanity and nature themselves evolve. Quite different philosophies of protection of the national environment would emerge from different nations at different stages of their historical development. That is all right too! But the sort of ethical base Sagoff has in mind will not produce one general kind of base for an environmental ethic. There would be as many different environmental ethics as there are different cultures, historical epochs, etc. For that reason, I set his theory on the shelf alongside the theory implicit in Rawls and explicit in Tribe and Stone; and alongside the general utilitarian theories that appear to be unworkable. What is left? Given what has been said above about the two general models, some form of model (1) remains. It would include (a) an expanded theory of value that goes well beyond anthropocentrism; (b) an expanded concept of the value of life; (c) a new theory of both compensatory and distributive justice in which the "citizenship" of the biosphere is expanded, but not one in which every creature that lives has a right to life; (d) the explicit recognition of our obligation to, and the rights of, future generations of humans; (e) the recognition that strategies for survival and for a certain quality of life require highly context-dependent information; (f) the recognition that equality of consideration for forms of life other than human is consistent with highly differential modes of treatment for those forms of life; (g) the adoption of new legal rationales for environmental protection, and so on. These various points of emphasis would provide a complex ethical base (including deontological and utilitarian components) concerning the decision to use resources in one way or another. In the process of putting these norms for environmental use into effect, we would have to apply them contextually and in ways in which *conflicts* among values, obligations, and rights might be clarified and value priorities displayed. Some kinds of traditional freedom might be justifiably reduced to preserve other important values and to protect the long-range interests of rights-possessing beings. In some contexts, certain traditional rights might best be preserved even in the face of apparently bad results; in others, utilitarian benefits might justifiably restrict traditional rights—property rights, for example—that have been generally honored. Decisions must be made within the framework of value principles that we accept, and that, under sufficient use, might result in a significantly different code for both the preservation and the protection of our environmental resources.

Environmentalists have been waylaying us with an incredible amount of information about highly context-dependent variables in nature. If they are correct in many of those cases, they inject new information into contexts of decisions on environmental use. Their basic thought is that we take that information seriously. Some of it may turn out to be false. But if most of it is true, if a great deal of it is true, they are asking that we take very seriously the ecological perspective about the complexity of the regulatory mechanisms in nature impacting upon different levels or forms of life. If we do take that seriously, then the value of homeostasis or stability—the demand that systems of resource use be compatible with the ecosystems of nature—becomes *one* of the fundamental norms, which along with other norms, constitutes a framework of value principles within which rational decisions or policies on environmental use can be made. *In that sense* at least, environmentalists have reestablished a crucial sense of the relationship between norms and nature, and they have given us new applications of principles like utility and equality; but not new principles.

NOTES

1. At the time of his death Professor Blackstone had completed a first draft of his essay and was at work on revisions. I have completed this task. Though I have introduced some changes, most of the actual wording is Professor Blackstone's, and, to the best of my knowledge, the ideas presented always accord with his own considered beliefs.—ED.
2. See, for example, Glanville L. Williams, *The Sanctity of Life and The Criminal Law,* Faber and Faber, London (1958); Diana Crane, *The Sanctity of Social Life,* Russell Sage Foundation, New York (1975); and Abraham Kaplan, ed., *The Sanctity of Life,* University of Washington Press, Seattle (1970).
3. William Murdock and Joseph Connell, "All About Ecology," *Center Magazine,* vol. 3, no. 1 (Jan.–Feb., 1970), p. 59.
4. See the concluding page of Albert Schweitzer's "The Ethics of Reverence for Life," *Christendom,* I, no. 2 (Winter, 1936), 225–239.

5. Albert Schweitzer, *The Teaching of Reverence for Life,* trans. Richard and Clara Winston, Holt, Rinehart and Winston, New York (1965), p. 9.
6. *Ibid.,* p. 12.
7. *Ibid.,* p. 13.
8. *Ibid.,* p. 16.
9. *Ibid.,* p. 22.
10. *Ibid.,* p. 31.
11. *Ibid.,* p. 26.
12. *Ibid.,* p. 49.
13. *Ibid.,* p. 49.
14. *Ibid.,* p. 47.
15. Schweitzer, "The Ethics of Reverence for Life," *op. cit.*
16. Schweitzer, *The Teaching of Reverence for Life, op. cit.,* p. 48.
17. Schweitzer, "The Ethics of Reverence for Life," *op. cit.*
18. *Ibid.*
19. *Ibid.,* p. 192.
20. *Ibid.,* p. 192.
21. Schweitzer, *The Teaching of Reverence for Life, op. cit.,* p. 35.
22. *Ibid.,* p. 40
23. Herbert Spiegelberg, "Albert Schweitzer's 'Other Thought', Fortune Obligates," *Africa: Thought and Praxis,* vol. 1 (1974), and "Ethics for Fellows in the Fate of Existence," in Peter Bertocci, ed., *Mid-Twentieth-Century American Philosophy,* Humanities Press, New York (1974).
24. *Ibid.,* p. 15.
25. John Rawls, *A Theory of Justice,* Harvard University Press, Cambridge, Mass. (1971), p. 100.
26. Schweitzer, *The Teaching of Reverence for Life, op. cit.,* pp. 49–50.
27. Lynn White, Jr., "The Historical Roots of Our Ecologic Crisis," *Science,* vol. 55 (1967).
28. *Ibid.,* p. 1205.
29. *Ibid.,* p. 1206.
30. W. H. Murdy, "Anthropocentrism: A Modern Version," *Science,* vol. 187 (March, 1975), p. 1169
31. *Ibid.*
32. *Ibid.* See also E. Laszlo, *The Systems View of the World,* Braziller, New York (1972).
33. *Ibid.,* p. 1171
34. *Ibid.,* p. 1172.
35. Aldo Leopold, *A Sand County Almanac,* Oxford University Press, New York (1949), pp. 201–203.
36. *Ibid.,* p. 209.
37. *Ibid.*
38. *Ibid.,* p. 210.
39. *Ibid.*
40. *Ibid.,* p. 217.
41. Aldo Leopold, "The Conservation Ethics," *Journal of Forestry,* vol. 3, (1933), p. 642.
42. Nathaniel Wollman, "The New Economics of Resources," *Daedalus* 96, pt. 2 (Fall, 1967), p. 1100.
43. William T. Blackstone, "Ethics and Ecology," in *Philosophy and Environmental Crisis,* ed. William T. Blackstone, University of Georgia Press, Athens, Georgia (1974), p. 37.
44. See Eugene Odum, "Environmental Ethic and the Attitude Revolution," in Blackstone, ed., *op. cit.,* p. 12.
45. See Murdock and Connell, *op. cit.*

46. Odum, *op. cit.,* p. 14.
47. Jeremy Bentham, *Introduction to the Principles of Morals and Legislation,* ch. XVII.
48. See Peter Singer, "All Animals Are Equal," *Philosophic Exchange,* vol. 2, no. 1 (1974), and his book *Animal Liberation,* Random House, New York (1975).
49. Singer, "All Animals Are Equal," *op. cit.,* p. 284.
50. *Ibid.,* p. 288.
51. *Ibid.,* p. 289.
52. See, for example, *Animal Liberation, op. cit.,* p. 8, and "All Animals Are Equal," *op. cit.,* p. 284.
53. See his "The Fable of the Fox and the Unliberated Animal," *Ethics,* vol. 88 (January 1978), pp. 119–125.
54. Joel Feinberg, "The Rights of Animals and Unborn Generations," in Blackstone, ed., *op. cit.*
55. *Ibid.,* p. 50.
56. *Ibid.*
57. Tom Regan, "The Moral Basis of Vegetarianism," *The Canadian Journal of Philosophy* (October 1975).
58. Leopold, *A Sand County Almanac, op. cit.,* p. 217.
59. *Ibid.*
60. Tom Regan, "Feinberg on What Sorts of Beings Can Have Rights," *The Southern Journal of Philosophy* (Winter 1976).
61. Christopher Stone, "Should Trees Have Standing?—Toward Legal Rights for Natural Objects," *The Southern California Law Review,* vol. 45 (1972), p. 498.
62. Lawrence Tribe, "Ways Not to Think About Plastic Trees: New Foundations for Environmental Law," *The Yale Law Journal,* vol. 83, no. 7 (June 1974), p. 1344.
63. Stone, *op. cit.,* p. 479, note.
64. *Ibid.,* p. 458.
65. Tribe, *op. cit.,* p. 1343.
66. Stanley Benn, "Personal Freedom and Environmental Ethics: The Moral Inequality of Species," in *Equality and Freedom: International and Comparative Jurisprudence,* ed. Gray Dorsey, Oceana Publications, Inc., and A. W. Sijthoff, the Netherlands (1977).
67. See William T. Blackstone, "Ethics and Ecology," in Blackstone, ed., *op. cit.*
68. See the Stone, Tribe, and Leopold references above; also Rolston's "Is There an Ecological Ethic?" *Ethics,* vol. 85 (January 1975).
69. Mark Sagoff, "On Preserving the Natural Environment," *The Yale Law Journal,* vol. 84 (1974), p. 223.
70. Sagoff, *op. cit.,* p. 245.
71. *Ibid.,* p. 229.
72. *Ibid.,* pp. 265–267.
73. *Ibid.,* p. 264.

SUGGESTIONS FOR FURTHER READING

Students wishing to gain a closer understanding of Schweitzer's thought, which is at the heart of §§2–8, are advised to read his *The Teaching of Reverence for Life,* trans. Richard and Clara Winston, Holt, Rinehart and Winston,

New York (1965). Those desiring a fuller explanation of the idea that "fortune obligates" (§7) might examine John Rawls's challenging *A Theory of Justice,* Harvard University Press, Cambridge, Massachusetts (1971), especially chapters 11 and 17.

On the theme of anthropocentrism, "must" readings include Lynn White, Jr., "The Historical Roots of Our Ecological Crisis," *Science,* vol. 55 (1967), and W. H. Murdy, "Anthropocentrism: A Modern Version," *Science,* vol. 187 (March 1975). Aldo Leopold's *A Sand County Almanac,* Oxford University Press, New York (1949), is a pertinent resource in all corners of the search for an ethic of the environment. Also meriting close reading are two works by Eugene Odum, *Fundamentals of Ecology,* W. B. Saunders Company, Philadelphia and London (1959), and *Ecology,* Holt and Rinehart, Inc., New York (1963).

Suggestions for further reading in regard to the moral status of animals are given at the end of Professor Singer's essay in the present anthology. A collection of essays dealing with a variety of topics central to environmental ethics is *Philosophy and Environmental Crisis,* ed. William T. Blackstone, University of Georgia Press, Athens, Georgia (1974).

INDEX

ABOUT THE AUTHORS

TOM L. BEAUCHAMP was born in Austin, Texas, in 1939. He received an undergraduate degree from Southern Methodist University and graduate degrees from Yale University and The Johns Hopkins University. He is currently a member of the Department of Philosophy at Georgetown University and Senior Research Scholar at the Kennedy Institute of Ethics, Georgetown University. He is coauthor of *Principles of Biomedical Ethics* and has edited or coedited seven other books, including *Ethical Issues in Death and Dying.* His main interests in philosophy are ethical theory, the philosophy of David Hume, and contemporary issues in causation. He has written extensively on each of these subjects in philosophical journals.

HUGO ADAM BEDAU was born in Portland, Oregon, in 1926. He entered the Navy Officer Procurement Program at the University of Southern California in 1944, served two years in the Naval Reserve, and graduated *summa cum laude* from the University of Redlands in 1949. He received his Ph.D. from Harvard University in 1961 and has taught at Dartmouth College, Princeton University, Reed College, and, since 1966, at Tufts University, where he is now Austin Fletcher Professor of Philosophy. He is the author of *The Courts, The Constitution, and Capital Punishment,* editor of *The Death Penalty in America, Justice and Equality,* and *Civil Disobedience,* and coauthor, with Edwin Schur, of *Victimless Crimes.* He has written widely on topics in political, legal, and social philosophy.

WILLIAM T. BLACKSTONE was born in Augusta, Georgia, in 1931. He graduated from Elon College and received his Ph.D. from Duke University. He taught at Elon College and the University of Florida before joining the faculty at the University of Georgia, where, from 1964 until 1972, he served as Head of the Department of Philosophy and Religion. He was serving there as Chairman of the Division of Social Sciences and as Research Professor of Philosophy at the time of his death in 1977. He wrote extensively on ethics, the philosophy of religion, political philosophy, and the philosophy of law. Among his books are *Problems of Religious Knowledge, Francis Hutcheson and Contemporary Ethical Theory, The Concept of Equality,* and *Philosophy and Environmental Crisis.* He served as president of both the Southern Society for Philosophy and Psychology and the American Society for Value Inquiry.

JOEL FEINBERG was born in Detroit, Michigan, in 1926. He graduated from the University of Michigan, where he was also awarded a Ph.D. in philosophy in 1957. He has held regular teaching positions at Brown University, Princeton University, the University of California at Los Angeles, and Rockefeller University. At present, he is Professor of Philosophy at the University of Arizona, where he has taught since 1977. He is the author of *Doing and Deserving, Social Philosophy,* and numerous articles on moral, social, and legal philosophy.

JAN NARVESON is a native of Minnesota. He received his undergraduate degrees at the University of Chicago and Harvard University, where he also received his Ph.D. in 1961. He has taught at the University of New Hampshire and, since 1963, at the University of Waterloo in Ontario, Canada, where he is now Professor of Philosophy. He has also served as Visiting Professor at The Johns Hopkins University, Stanford University, and the University of Calgary. His publications include *Morality and Utility* and numerous articles in professional journals and anthologies on ethics, political philosophy, and other subjects. His main nonprofessional interest is music, and he is founder and president of the Kitchener-Waterloo Chamber Music Society.

ONORA O'NEILL was born in Aughafatten, Northern Ireland, in 1941 and educated at Oxford and Harvard universities. She has taught at Barnard College (Columbia University) and is now at the University of Essex in Colchester, England. She is the author of *Acting on Principle,* and she has written on a variety of topics in ethics, social and political philosophy, and Kantian studies.

JAMES RACHELS was born in Columbus, Georgia, in 1941. He graduated in philosophy from Mercer University and received his Ph.D. from the University of North Carolina at Chapel Hill. He has held teaching positions at the University of Richmond, New York University, the University of Miami, and Duke University. At present he is Professor of Philosophy at the University of Alabama in Birmingham, where he has taught since 1977. His writings on moral philosophy have appeared in numerous books and journals.

TOM REGAN was born and raised in Pittsburgh, Pennsylvania. He received his A.B. degree at Thiel College and his M.A. and Ph.D. at the University of Virginia. Since joining the faculty of North Carolina State University in 1967, he has been twice recognized as Outstanding Teacher and was named Alumni Distinguished Professor in 1977. The author of *Understanding Philosophy* and coeditor, with Peter Singer, of *Animal Rights and Human Obligations,* he has published essays on a wide range of topics in moral philosophy. At forty-one, he is a sometime potter and poet and a committed vegetarian and long-distance runner.

PETER SINGER was born in Melbourne, Australia, in 1946 and educated at the University of Melbourne and Oxford University. He has taught at University College (Oxford), New York University, La Trobe University, and Monash University in Victoria, Australia. He is the author of *Democracy and Disobedience, Animal Liberation,* and, most recently, *Practical Ethics.* He has also published in philosophical journals and popular publications such as *The New York Review of Books, The New York Times,* and *Nation.*